GOD IN THE OBAMA ERA

PRESIDENTS' RELIGION AND ETHICS FROM GEORGE WASHINGTON TO BARACK OBAMA

NIELS C. NIELSEN

New York

God In The Obama Era
Presidents' Religion and Ethics from George Washington to Barack Obama

ISBN 978-1-60037-646-7

Library of Congress Control Number: 2009928323

MORGAN · JAMES
THE ENTREPRENEURIAL PUBLISHER

Morgan James Publishing, LLC
1225 Franklin Ave., STE 325
Garden City, NY 11530-1693
Toll Free 800-485-4943
www.MorganJamesPublishing.com

In an effort to support local communities, raise awareness and funds, Morgan James Publishing donates one percent of all book sales for the life of each book to Habitat for Humanity. Get involved today, visit **www.HelpHabitatForHumanity.org.**

Contents

POPULAR HISTORICAL QUESTIONS BEARING ON THE UNITED STATES PRESIDENCY

What would have been the result ...

- if King George III of England had been a more benevolent sovereign and the American colonies had not revolted?

- if George Washington had sought political power rather than returning to his home at Mount Vernon after victory in the Revolutionary War against England?

- if Thomas Jefferson had not championed religious tolerance and freedom of worship?

- if Alexander Hamilton had refused to duel with Aaron Burr?

- if the North and South had reconciled and slavery had been abolished without civil war?

- if Abraham Lincoln—the most religiously discerning of American presidents—had not been assassinated and had lived on to direct Reconstruction?

- if Lincoln's successor, President Andrew Johnson, had been a wiser and more competent religionist, less ideological in his oratory?

- if Woodrow Wilson had thought in less absolutist religious terms as he sought to lead the United States into membership in the League of Nations and "make the world safe for democracy"?

- if Wilson's plans for lasting international peace had been accepted by the United States Senate?

- if Franklin Roosevelt had been assassinated (as he nearly was in Miami) before he took office?

- if Franklin Roosevelt had not initiated the New Deal and championed religious freedom worldwide?

- if Henry Wallace, rather than Harry Truman, had been Franklin Roosevelt's successor?

- if John F. Kennedy had not been assassinated? Could he have brought positive social and religious insights from Catholicism to the national ethos in the era of the Second Vatican Council?

- if Richard Nixon (truly affirming his Quaker heritage) had not collapsed morally in Watergate?

- if Ronald Reagan (inspired by his belief that God stands on the side of freedom) had failed to seize the opportunity to negotiate with Gorbachev and end the cold war?

- if George H. W. Bush had ordered American troops to go on to Baghdad during the first invasion of Iraq?

- if Bill Clinton had been more faithful to the teachings of his own Southern Baptist Church and not committed perjury in Monicagate? Or if he had resigned in repentance?

- if Hillary Clinton had divorced her husband because of his infidelities? If she had more successfully organized her political campaign for the presidency in 2008?

- if George W. Bush had followed the advice of both the pope and the bishops of his own denomination (Methodist) and had not ordered the invasion of Iran?

- if Barack Obama had not converted to Christianity?

PREFACE

Barack Obama has brought historic changes to the ethics and religion of the presidential office. This is the case in part because he is the first African American to occupy the White House. This book attempts to avoid the extremes of both the left and the right—to see the Obama phenomenon with greater objectivity and perspective through a historical approach. Religion is a cultural and not just a sectarian matter. It continues to be powerful politically and culturally in the United States—for good and evil. Obama's story is incomplete without it. If one seeks to secularize his presidency radically, the view is incomplete and truncated.

My book is written for persons who wish to evaluate what an ambitious new leader has done and may do in the larger and longer setting of the history of his office. At the beginning of each chapter, I comment on the similarities and differences between the forty-fourth president and one of his predecessors. My approach is narrative and chronological, not dogmatic. My own field is the history and philosophy of religion. I am interested in the long-term moral values and religious symbols that motivate both voters and public officials. Of course, I am not so naïve as to suppose that truth is always on one side of the election divide. Clearly, the U.S. Constitution guarantees both freedom of worship and the non-establishment of religion. But faith convictions remain a powerful ideological force in American politics.

The English weekly magazine, *The Economist,* described the 2008 presidential race as "religion soaked." Yale Law School professor Stephen Carter has remarked that it is virtually impossible to envisage the American political scene today without faith questions. I seek to go beyond the rhetoric and polemics of current politics by appealing to history. It is crucial to the interpretation of this book that its narrative periodicizes. Internationally, the largest North American nation faced a much more complicated set of problems at in the post-modern world than before.

The presidency gives an opportunity for chief executives' faith to be exercised positively or negatively. It was Reinhold Niebuhr who argued that man's capacity for justice makes democracy possible, but man's inclination to injustice makes democracy necessary. Niebuhr's distinction between moral man and immoral society is still relevant. The perennial problem is not just one of individual virtue—important as that is—but of the responsible use of power.

A friend of mine who taught church history at Berkeley from time to time engaged his students dramatically by dressing up colleagues in the costume of a variety of religious figures—Aquinas, Luther, Wesley, among others—and conducting an imagined conversation between them. My question is what the forty-fourth president would say to Jefferson, Lincoln, and Wilson about faith questions, were such a dialogue possible today. Of course, the initial question before any such imagined conversation must be what presidents Washington, Jefferson, Lincoln, Wilson, Carter, and Reagan, among others, believed and practiced. How their ethics related to their philosophies of life must be considered before there can be authentic exchange with a living contemporary. For his part, Obama has introduced us to his religious background in *Dreams of My Father* and *The Audacity of Hope.*

My interest in the subject matter of this book needs to be explained further in this preface. During Jimmy Carter's presidency, his pastor lectured about past presidents' religion at the campus where I was teaching the history and philosophy of religion, and I began collecting historical materials for this volume. In fact, I had written my own short survey of Carter's born-again faith at the beginning of his time in the White House, and the book was translated into both German and Dutch. My school, Rice University, is a secular institution without either church or state sponsorship, and my approach was not denominational. I thought earlier, and I still believe, that justice cannot be done to the beliefs and thoughts of a particular leader in the White House simply by reference to his own time span.

There is further side to the motivation. My wife is an Austrian citizen who holds the Presidential Medal of Honor from her native country. For nearly three decades, she taught at the University of Houston, and we have spent virtually all of our summers since our marriage in her home country. My daughter teaches at the University of Vienna and is the only non-native faculty member in her department. She has become intensely involved in explaining the Obama phenomenon to her students. Some of them have come for short periods of study to the United States. North American religion, in particular, seems strange to most of them. Still, they have been very interested in the transition from Bush II to a very different sort of presidency. How is one to explain to Europeans what is going on in a regime change in the United States? Most of the intercontinental cultural exchange that they know about actually comes by means of television and computers.

I am grateful to my readers, Blake Ellis (history) of Rice University, Professor Ron Highfield (religion) of Pepperdine University, Professor Stanley Siegel (history) of the University of Houston and Reverend George Atkinson (theology) of Southern Methodist University, Perkins School of Theology South. Their comments and criticisms have enriched my understanding; they are not responsible for what I have written—its judgments are entirely my own. I also express thanks to my daughter, Camilla Regina Nielsen of the University of Vienna, for conversations about what I have written.

PRESIDENTS' RELIGION

PRAISE FOR OBAMA FROM HIS ADMIRERS

Barack Obama is distinguished from all of his predecessors by the fact that his faith was nourished from below by the black church, not received from above from white teachers. In a number of respects, his message of the audacity of hope echoes the biblical call for courage and faith amid oppression. He is realistic and tolerant without being weak or compromising about right and wrong or belief in God's power and presence. Professionally, he has showed himself to be a discerning, calculating Harvard and Chicago lawyer who understands the complex problems and responsibilities of presidential leadership. This book is written on the premise that description of his life and the office that he came to remains incomplete without consideration of the religious factors in his world view and career. These were more complex than his campaign rhetoric had revealed.

Bono, the lead singer of U2 and co-founder of The ONE Campaign, was effusive in his praise of the forty-fourth president. He found it rare to meet a person in whom intellect and intuition make such a perfect rhyme. He said, "I know your intellect—fashioned in the halls of Harvard and on the floor of the United States Senate ... has taken in the data and seen the analysis on the transformative power of effective aid in places where the U.S. flag is currently not smiled at." Bono was sure that it is much cheaper to make friends of potential enemies than to defend against them at a later date. Bono said that his prayer was that Obama's instinct and intellect would stay in harmony as he carried out the difficult responsibilities of the presidency throughout his term.[1]

John J. Dilulio, Jr., the first director of the Office of Faith-Based and Community Initiatives in George W. Bush's administration, and later professor of policy and public affairs at Princeton University, spoke from his own hard experience as White House liaison to religious communities. He judged that the hardest single thing for any modern president is to remain calm and controlled amid the daily storms, both real and media-manufactured, that pound in upon his office. The media makes short shrift of complex answers to complex questions. It is imperative that a president's instinct and intellect stay in harmony. "But come what may, you will be a great president if and only if, you retain ... the intellectual rigor and vigor that, more than any other single trait, got you into the Oval Office and into the history books forever."[2]

A significant change of outlook is apparent in Obama's approach since he has entered the White House. He is less optimistic than before as he points the way ahead, fighting for the programs on which he ran for office. Clearly, he had not anticipated the full dangers of the financial crisis as he faced admirers cheering him on, "Yes we can." In the Oval Office every morning, he receives confidential briefings from his staff about both world affairs and economics. But he has not retreated; he has remained confident and daring, speaking courageously and openly of difficulties and hope: The economy will be turned around; prosperity will return. Health care will be extended and reformed. Terrorists will be defeated! On February 25, three weeks after his inauguration, he spoke before a joint session of Congress, defending his administration's program. He is a leader who believes in himself and in God!

How will future historians appraise the religious ethos of the Obama era as compared with other times in the succession of United States presidents? How are we to understand his convictions about ultimate reality in relation to the beliefs of his predecessors? Some presidents have professed faith in God more fervently than others. It is hard to deny that from time to time, a number of them have invoked religion as a means of gaining political power. Some presidents have been more orthodox than others—Woodrow Wilson and Ronald Reagan, for example. Others have been more questioning—Jefferson and Lincoln, to mention two cases. Religion served as a defense of slavery in the minds of some pre-Civil War occupants of the White House. It has been a motivator of reform for others—Franklin Roosevelt and Jimmy Carter, for example. Faith has made for confidence and progress in many eras. In others, it has been a sop to the status quo. Frequently, it has bred tolerance in the American setting, but it has discouraged innovation in a number of situations. What will the Obama era be like?

Religion can be construed narrowly as adherence to a particular tradition and community, or inclusively as a more universal human phenomenon. No doubt, in a secular age, many critics deny its relevance and ultimate meaning. A variety of world faiths compete with each other around the globe, and they will continue to do so throughout the foreseeable future. In democratic traditions, church and state are separated from each other in greater or lesser measure; in theocracy, religious belief is politically controlling. Culturally, religion finds expression in music, literature, architecture, law, war, and peace.

Our narrative of presidents' religion and ethics seeks to avoid both dogmatism and agnosticism. Its premise is that the history of the world is the judgment of the world; the history of the presidency is the judgment of presidents. Before evaluation, there needs to come understanding. Statesmen ignore religious faith at their peril. We attempt to understand historically what presidents have said and done—what has gone on and is going on. Technically, we seek to avoid a reductionistic approach, instead using a phenomenological one. Religion is identified by sociology in terms of cult, creed, community, and conduct; it is not just ecclesiology! Religions are plural, many, and not just one within their own borders and without.

REALLY, WHAT CAN OBAMA ACHIEVE AS PRESIDENT?

It was clear at the outset of the Obama administration that there were broken pieces that the new leader in the White House would need to pick up and put together after his predecessor left office. As a candidate, Barack Obama had introduced his convictions and purposes to the public through his two bestsellers and their personal narratives, *Dreams of My Father* and *The Audacity of Hope*. He presented himself as a bridge figure, having an African black father from Kenya and a white mother from Kansas and Hawaii. His character was shaped by his existential struggle for personal identity. Eventually, personal faith in God became an important factor in his development. It was through the black church that he established social solidarity and found religious life meaning. At the same time, as a political leader, he is very explicit about the necessity for the separation of church and state. Even as he embodies a low-church evangelical piety, he is very shrewd and decisive. Running for the White House, he spoke often of the American Dream, though he was aware that throughout most of the nation's history, it was not available to blacks in the United States.

All criticism and derogation not withstanding, Obama's profession of Christian religious faith has been unambiguous and needs to be identified specifically, as in popular rumors it has been widely alleged that he is a Muslim. He has been explicit that he looks to Jesus Christ for the forgiveness of his sins and his eternal salvation. The term "religious" often serves as a general classification; more definite identification is necessary. Obama shares more specifically in the biblical tradition of monotheism—belief in the one God. Having held membership in an Afro-American church, he is not just Christian but comes from a particular milieu. Black spirituals and preaching express a distinctive piety, which is not the same as in white traditions in North America. Recent memories of discrimination and long centuries of slavery are still alive. Martin Luther King, Jr. is the national hero. This particular setting has shaped and conditioned Obama's ethics. Our argument is that description of his life and the office that he came to remains incomplete without consideration of the religious bases underlying his world view and morals.

Two international crises immediately confronted the forty-fourth president of the United States when he took the oath of office on January 20, 2009, at the beginning of his time in the White House. One was financial, the other military. Francis Fukuyama, professor of international political economy at Johns Hopkins University summed up the dismal prospects: More than a trillion dollars in stock-market wealth vanished in a day amid the implosion of the leading banks. U.S. taxpayers were left with a $700 billion tab. The Wall Street crackup could hardly have been more gargantuan. The more intangible danger of the financial meltdown was that it was imperiling America's "brand," Fukuyama concluded.[3]

Fukuyama seemed to use "brand" to refer to world view and faith. There were indeed political and financial issues that were debated intensely as government and the populace came to terms with the crisis. At the same time, in the background were ethical and religious questions, many of which are perennial. There had been depressions throughout the nation's history before. This one, however, was worldwide. Its coming had determined the outcome of the 2008 presidential election in the United States.

People from all over the world watched with bated breath as voters in America elected an African American for the first time to be their national leader. Having won office, in a number of respects Barack Obama held more power than any other person on the globe. Before Robert Kennedy's assassination, John Kennedy's brother had predicted that in forty years, the United States could have an African-American president; the time span to 2008 was forty-four years.[4] Old taboos were broken on every side. Women and blacks played a new revolutionary role in a watershed election, unequaled in United States history for its power in terms of candidates' gender and race.

Running on the Democratic ticket, the African American was pitted against the Republican candidate, Senator John McCain of Arizona, a decorated Vietnam war hero who had been held as a prisoner of war for more than six years and tortured in Hanoi. Earlier in the primary race, Obama, the junior senator from Illinois, had defeated Senator Hillary Clinton for his own party's nomination; she was the first woman ever to come so close to taking over the White House. Obama later chose her as his secretary of state. During the presidential campaign, a number of issues had dominated the debates: the option of pre-emptive attacks on potential enemies, global warming, border immigration control, the reform of social security, and state-sponsored universal health insurance.

Then suddenly, in the last part of September, little more than a month and a half before the November election, a new storm broke that changed the direction of the contest for the White House. The national economy was collapsing, the still-ruling incumbent president proclaimed, and both major candidates were summoned to Washington, D.C. to help craft legislation aimed at preventing the collapse of financial institutions. The world's only superpower was imperiling world business structures by its own self-caused implosion. Commentator George Will compared the economic situation to being on a life-threatening cliff; the national economy was about to plunge into the abyss below.[5]

Together the United States secretary of the treasury and the head of the Federal Reserve system demanded immediate preventive action, in a matter of days, not weeks or months, as the money flow of American capitalism was about to cease. They asked for a slush fund of 700 billion dollars to counter not only recession but a threatening world depression. The dominant issue in the national election campaign suddenly became economics. It was impossible to avoid questions of morality and world view, in fact, of religion.

How did it happen, apparently so suddenly? Server and Sloan reply: "Think of it as payback."[6] There was no need to worry about regulation; it was in disrepute. Derivatives such as credit default swaps seemed to have minimized all risks. Greed and ignorance were the order of the day on both Wall Street and Main Street. The commentators conclude: "When greed exceeds fear, trouble follows …. Great new fortunes were made and with them came great new hubris."[7]

"Hubris" is often used in religion to signify overreaching and arrogance, an attempt to "play God." Christian as well as Muslim theologians had condemned usury for centuries. In the United States, the assumption of hundreds of billion dollars of bad debts by the federal government was not enough to solve continuing structural problems. The burden thus taken on would limit the options of a new incumbent in the White House. Actually, what was taking place was a radical deprivatization of banks and the investment industry. Ever since the Reagan presidency, public opinion had opposed state regulation. Now banks and other the financial institutions literally collapsed into the federal government's arms. A new president would be compelled to ask not only about right and wrong at home but the direction of civilization internationally. The time was long since past when the Americans could live in isolation.

WAR

The continuing war in Iraq and Afghanistan was the other dominant crisis. Obama, the new leader in the White House, had taken a stand against the invasion of Iraq from the beginning of his political career. President George W. Bush's mistaken allegation of the presence of weapons of mass destruction—made in an address at the United Nations—remained unsubstantiated. The war in Iraq was dumb and unjustified, Obama was sure. It was not just common sense but ethically right to withdraw United States armed forces in an orderly way. He promised to do so as soon as possible if elected president.

In spite of all efforts to pacify the occupied country, religious strife between Sunnis and Shi'a Muslims had not ended. While a candidate, the Democrat had promised to strengthen American armed forces in Afghanistan. The situation was complicated by the problem of terrorism in Pakistan, amid whose mountains the terrorist leader, Osama bin Laden, was believed to be hiding. What could be done about threats against Israel from Iran, a Shi'ite nation that sought nuclear weapons? Here too, as in the national economy, the new president's options would be limited by his predecessor's destructive legacy. Moral and religious issues, international in scope, could not be avoided.

The initial crisis of the Bush II administration began dramatically with an unprecedented terrorist assault on New York and Washington, D.C. Nothing like it had happened in North America since the War of 1812. Early into his time in the White House, on September 11, 2001, the new Republican president of the United States and the nation he ruled were confronted with a sudden, unprecedented attack upon the American mainland. It joined violence with religious fanaticism in the suicide airplane bombings of New York and Washington, D.C. Two hijacked American airplanes rammed into the Twin Towers of New York City's World Trade Center in lower Manhattan, engulfing them in balls of fire. Dramatically, one after the other, the two buildings—which stood high above all others on the city's skyline, symbols of its prosperity and wealth—crumbled to earth. Nearly three thousand persons lost their lives.

"Who is the enemy?" Americans asked. The attack was the work of Muslim fundamentalists—not the world Islamic community at large. On the one hand stand Muslims who are confident enough to learn from outsiders, accepting democracy and willing to integrate into the modern world; on the other hand are fearful believers who seek to find security under strong rulers from the ambiguities of world civilization. The battle between tolerant and fundamentalist Muslims is likely to be long and difficult.[8] The situation has become even more intense in the post-9/11 situation in which the United States has been involved in a prolonged war in Afghanistan and Iraq.

Symbolically, what happened on September 11, 2001 could be compared to other watershed assaults; for example, the invasion and plundering of the city of Rome by Vandals in AD 410. The imperial city had long been seen as the impregnable center of civilization. Even more devastating, the Mongol conquest of Baghdad in 1258 ended a worldwide Muslim empire of still vaster geographical outreach than the Roman one. Of such historical watersheds it could be said: "civilization would never be the same again!" Still, a noteworthy difference stood out for one decisive reason, identifying the attack on the New York World Trade Center Twin Towers as not only modern but post-modern: it was seen—on the same day—worldwide on television.

In historical perspective, it was clear that not just the United States but humankind—including the former communist empire in Eastern Europe—had entered a different age. Throughout the Muslim world, there was widespread underdevelopment and poverty, as well as fabulous petroleum riches. Armed only with small knives and box cutters, the terrorists challenged the dominant superpower that was stronger than any other in the world. The modern technological revolution—what the University of Chicago historian of Islam, Marshall Hodgson, designated as "the Great Western Transmutation"—was now overwhelmingly global.[9] It was visible not just in automobiles and airplanes, but television, computers, Internet, atomic and hydrogen bombs, medicine based on genetics, and the possibility of biological warfare. Even as Russia and the United States held nuclear weapon superiority, the whole of humankind now was linked together by the fruits of scientific research and discovery.

The analogy of the elephant and the flea seemed applicable to the New York Twin Towers' destruction. A majority democratic way of life and its personal freedom was threatened by a handful of fanatics. The new-style combatants were extra-national. Al-Qaeda had cells in many different places, reaching out over national boundaries. Religious motivation was at the center of events on both sides—and President Bush's response was not just political but set forth in moral and religious terms along with military ones. He spoke of destiny and faith in God. Soon the forty-third president made the crucial decision to lead the nation into hostilities in the Middle East and the "War on Terrorism," extending the battle lines. Eventually, invading American soldiers became bogged down in Iraq's religious civil war.

Obama won the election as the forty-fourth president of the United States of America—the first African American to hold the office—on the promise of national renewal. His charisma often evoked near-Messianic response from massive audiences. There will be a new age of hope, he promised; citizens of the country will face their common problems together, no longer rationalizing in denial or seeking selfish party victory alone. Internationally, under his leadership he would promote peace throughout the world. The war in Iraq will be brought to an end; political prisoners will no longer be tortured but judged fairly with respect for their human rights. A new economic policy will, in time, restore prosperity. Health insurance is to be extended to the poor, its benefits not limited just to the more prosperous in the land. The problem of global warming will be tackled internationally.

Promises of hope! In short, Obama's presidency would be a transforming and not just a transitional one. Realistically, how much could these goals be realized after he came to office? It remained to be seen. New international leadership, a renewed economy, came with the audacity of promise. At this point, hope was a primary theme—an even semi-religious mythological expectation supporting the goal of a new era. It would not be the kingdom of God, but things would be better, much better! Elected to the White House, the new leader was confronted with the reality of partisan politics; it would not be easy to bring competing parties together.

OBAMA'S PERSONAL RELIGIOUS JOURNEY AS A PREFACE

In offering hope for a new less-partisan era, the forty-fourth president cited the narrative of his own past life. Who was he? He turned to his own personal history, an external history of places and events, and an existential internal history, "the life of the soul." It was autobiography. Lisa Miller and Richard Wolffe reflect: "Barack Obama, twenty years old and a student at Columbia University student in New York" was torn a million different ways: between youth and maturity, black and white, coasts and continents, wonder and tragedy.[10]

Later in life, Obama explained that in these circumstances he had lived an ascetic existence. In the midst of his spiritual exploration he deliberately withdrew from the world. In short, he was not a casual visitor to religion! He even fasted, sometimes going for days without speaking to anyone. It was at this stage of his life that he read Augustine, the English Roman Catholic novelist Graham Greene, and the German philosopher Friedrich Nietzsche. From time to time on Sunday he would visit the Abyssinian Baptist Church in Harlem. Sitting in the back he would listen to the choir and then to the sermon. Sometimes he would even start tearing as he heard the music and found a sense of release.

Miller and Wolffe argue that the story of Obama's religious journey is a uniquely American tale. They identify it as one of a seeker, an intellectually curious young man trying to cobble together a religious identity out of myriad influences. Always drawn to life's big questions, Obama embarked on a spiritual quest in which he tried to reconcile his rational side with his yearning for transcendence. Finally, he found Christ—but that hasn't stopped him from asking questions. "I'm on my own faith journey and I'm searching," he says. "I leave open the possibility that I'm entirely wrong."

The president-to-be had been brought up by his grandparents, two lapsed Christians, Methodist and Baptist. Their indifference was not enough to satisfy his religious needs, as much as he loved them. His mother Ann was often away, in Indonesia, for example, doing anthropological research. In her own intellectual life journey, she had been impressed by a variety of world religions but refused to join any of them. She had found the writings of Joseph Campbell, the liberal American historian of religion, most illuminating: she lived and traveled the world with appreciation for all religions but confessing no one of them.

Occasionally, Ann would take Obama and his half-sister to Catholic Mass or to the Christmas service at the Protestant Congregational Christian Church in Honolulu. While living with her second husband in Indonesia, she took Barack and his half-sister, Maya Soetoro-Ng, to visit the world-famous Buddhist temple at Borobudur. Such experiences were a regular part of their childhood upbringing, and were important to her because they involved ritual, Maya reports. In this pattern she gave her son a lasting sense of inclusiveness and tolerance.

The forty-fourth president has described his mother as an agnostic. "I think she believed in a higher power," he says. "She believed in the fundamental order and goodness of the universe." At least she would have been comfortable with Einstein's belief that God doesn't play dice. At the same time, she was suspicious of any claim by a particular organized religion that it offered the final truth about human life and destiny. Obama portrays his Kenyan Muslim father as "a confirmed atheist" who viewed religion as "mumbo jumbo." (The father left the family when Obama was two years old.)

During his years in Indonesia, the son first attended a Catholic school and then went to a public elementary school that had a weekly class of religious education that was about Islam. His mother had remarried, and his stepfather, a man named Lolo, "like many Indonesians … followed a brand of Islam that could make room for the remnants of more ancient animist and Hindu faiths," Obama writes in *Dreams of My Father*. Lolo "explained that a man took on the powers of whatever he ate." He introduced the boy to the taste of dog meat, snake meat, and roasted grasshopper. While living with Muslim neighbors in Indonesia, the boy witnessed women with and without Islamic head coverings living comfortably next to Christians. For him, the recollection of that time has led him to conclude that "Islam can be compatible with the modern world."

Miller and Wolffe identify young Obama's quest for life meaning as driven by two main impulses. He needed a place, a community he could call his spiritual home. His biracial, peripatetic childhood had left him with a sense of rootlessness. In the course of time, visits to black churches suggested an answer to this vacuum. "There's a side very particular to the African-American church tradition that was powerful to me," he reflects. Miller and Wolffe conclude: "The exuberant worship, the family atmosphere and the prophetic preaching at a church such as Abyssinian would have appealed to a young man who lived so in his head."[11] His major political interest was the civil rights movement. He had become convinced, through his reading, of the transforming power of social activism, especially when paired with religion. Ethics and religion were joined in a figure like Martin Luther King, Jr. He read with intense interest Taylor Branch's *Parting the Waters,* with its story of the civil rights movement, along with King's autobiography.

After he graduated from Columbia University in New York City, the young African American was on his own when he moved to Chicago. He had been recruited by Gerald Kellman to work as a community organizer. There he came in touch with serious Christians who were studying the books of Reinhold Niebuhr and Paul Tillich. From the Roman Catholic side, they were also reading Augustine, even as they also attempted to practice Liberation theology. Some of Obama's activities eventually won support from Roman Catholic sources.

In this setting, Christianity was understood as communal in character, not just the hopes and convictions of individuals in isolation. The religion came with a consciousness of human imperfection and original sin. In a sinful world, faith requires deeds. Jesus's call to perfection would be fully realized only at the end of time. In the present world, humanity is in quest of salvation. Matthew 25: "Whatever you neglected to do unto the least of these, you neglected to do unto me." Obama reflects: "It's hard for me to imagine being true to my faith— and not thinking beyond myself, and not thinking about what's good for other people, and not acting in a moral and ethical way."

Eventually, thought and emotion joined, and the seeker accepted Christianity and was baptized. "I felt God's spirit beckoning me. I submitted myself to His will, and dedicated myself to discovering His truth." Obama later explained that there was no epiphany. No bolt of lightning struck him from out of the sky. There was no "Aha" experience. "It was a more gradual process I found in my life, the values that were most important to me, the sense of wonder that I had, the sense of tragedy that I had—all these things were captured in the Christian story." Being part of a community and affirming his faith in a public had become important. After Obama was baptized, he says he studied the Bible with gifted teachers who would "gently poke me about my faith."

Obama was certainly no ordinary convert! Later, after he had risen to political fame, Franklin Graham, Billy Graham's son, asked the charismatic political leader how, as a Christian, he could reconcile New Testament claims that salvation was attainable only through Christ with a campaign that embraced pluralism and diversity. The future president acknowledges that it is a precept of his Christian faith that redemption comes through Christ. But he is also "a big believer" in the Golden Rule, which he views as an essential pillar not alone of his own faith and values—his ideals and experience here on Earth. "I've said this before, and I know this raises questions in the minds of some evangelicals. I do not believe that my mother, who never formally embraced Christianity as far as I know … I do not believe she went to hell."

While on the campaign trail, the candidate reported that he prayed every day, typically for "forgiveness for my sins and flaws, which are many, the protection of my family, and that I'm carrying out God's will, not in a grandiose way, but simply that there is an alignment between my actions and what he would want." On occasion, he read his Bible in the evening, a ritual that "takes me out of the immediacy of my day and gives me a point of reflection." As a candidate, he has had an army of clerics and friends praying for him and e-mailing him snippets of Scripture or Midrash to think about during the day. He has carried in his pocket a small statue of the Virgin Mary and Joseph, and the Hindu monkey god Hanuman.

How can one assess Obama in public life? Clearly, he affirms freedom and democracy in the tradition of the Founding Fathers and Lincoln, as well as Martin Luther King, Jr. He is pragmatic but not a relativist. The black church, for centuries living under slavery and later segregation, has not been caught up in contemporary secularism as much as mainline religion. Obama, for his part, has espoused a more traditional middle position, not simply liberal or fundamentalist, neither left wing nor right wing in contemporary terms. Instead, it is one of living realistically in the world, but with hope. There is evidently strong religious influence and motivation in his effort to renew culture and bring harmony to politics. He is not cynical, but a realist.

THE SUCCESS AND FAILURE OF PAST PRESIDENTS

What is to be said in historical comparison with earlier presidents' successes and failures in different situations—their ambitions and hopes in the American cultural and political setting? Max Lerner, a political scientist and careful observer of the White House from the time of Franklin Roosevelt to the beginning of the Clinton era, was thinking of the issues when he wrote his careful study on the perils of presidential power.[12] Lerner—who died in 1992, just as Clinton was coming to office in Washington, D.C.—proposed a number of standards for the evaluation of chief executives' characters and achievements in what can be identified as his "Ethical Realism." Reflecting on biographies and the history of recent presidents, he labeled a number of them as "fallen titans."

As a social scientist, Lerner looked first of all for a willingness to face the reality principle in the life of a great power—tough-mindedness enough to meet and offer challenge. Expanding his first cluster of traits, Lerner included the capacity for command—to be in control in times of crisis and to present an image of decisiveness and judgment! Here the examples of both Roosevelts, Truman—and to his admirers, Ronald Reagan—seemed relevant. In a second modern triad, Lerner began with character itself, "not in the sense of virtue but of the values a man or woman has settled upon during a turbulent life." His analysis went on to include credibility, "the presentation of a leader's selfhood in such a way as to win assent and form the consensus necessary for governing." And finally in this group of traits, a capacity for interacting with the people, "communication skills." Eisenhower and the early Jimmy Carter may be cited as examples.

A last triad in Lerner's analysis remained relevant at the end of the millennium. He pointed to perspective—the capacity for thinking in time and seeing both the nation and oneself in history. A mature president will be sure enough of himself that he can keep the nation in equilibrium. Finally, Lerner listed ripeness—the fruit that grows out of the bud. When he retires, will a president leave his country with a sense of confidence and hope, appreciably better than he found it? Actually, very few recent chief executives have come to the end of their tenure in the White House without suffering a loss of reputation—Lyndon Johnson in the Vietnam War, Nixon in Watergate, Reagan in Irangate, and Clinton in Monicagate—or defeat in re-election, as with Carter and Bush Sr.

Of course, Lerner's identified traits do not belong just to the twentieth century; they have been ascribed positively to Washington, Jefferson, and Lincoln. Lerner's historical conclusion, however, was that most recent presidents have left the White House as "wounded titans." Few indeed have retired with a sense of triumph. Instead, they have been worn out by the pressures and tensions of office. Lerner did not live to see the terrorist attack on the American homeland and the Bush II era which followed, or the Obama phenomenon.

In Obama's case, it is important to identify the ethical and religious traditions that he calls on to define and support the United States presidency. What is distinctive about the nation's values and ideological conviction? It is not just a truism to assert that the forty-fourth president believes in human rights and democracy. Alexis de Tocqueville, the French nobleman who traveled in the new nation in the 1830s, wrote home the following:

Upon my arrival in the United States, the religious aspect of the country was the first thing that struck my attention, and the longer I stayed there the more did I perceive the great political consequences resulting from this state of things, to which I was unaccustomed. In France I had almost always seen the spirit of religion and the spirit of freedom pursuing courses diametrically opposed to each other; but in America I found that they were intimately united and that they reigned in common over the same country.

Religion in America takes no direct part in the government of society, but nevertheless it must be regarded as the foremost of the political institutions of that country; for if it does not impart a taste for freedom, it facilitates the use of free institutions …. I do not know whether all the Americans have a sincere faith in their religion, for who can search the human heart? But I am certain that they hold it to be indispensable in the maintenance of republican institutions.[13]

De Tocqueville's commentary makes clear that the new country had already developed its own distinctive ethos of religious freedom. Christendom's millennium-long union of throne and altar had been abandoned and "demythologized" in the new land; it was no longer binding after the overthrow of monarchy in the American revolt against the British Empire. The change was radical, not the least with official sanction of pluralism at the time of the nation's founding. Especially in religion, the change was revolutionary! Full separation of church and state on the pattern of the First Amendment to the United States Constitution was, in many respects, more far-reaching than the institutional rejection of King George III's authority and the English Crown.

Religion, like ethics, is a complex and many-sided phenomenon, and interacts with individuals and society at many different levels. To exempt it from state control is not to end debate about faith questions; on the contrary, such a strategy may end in inviting it. This much can be said definitively politically: religion (joined to morality) has not faded away amid continuing life in the North American republic. In terms of practice, the United States is one of the most religious countries in the world—although what this means specifically is widely debated. No candidate who attacks piety can win the White House.

Religious conservatives are popularly identified as standing at the opposite extreme from secularism—on the right rather than on the left. "In God we trust," they proclaim. "Religion equals intolerance and persecution," iconoclasts reply. Some political pollsters go so far as to allege that no party nominee can win without professing personal faith in God. Religion has played a crucial part in the election of a series of recent presidents— Carter, Reagan, Clinton, and the Bushes. In explanation, a longer historical view of the orientation of past presidents is called for. No doubt, the Founding Fathers' separation of church and state was revolutionary. But few if any of them advocated a naked public square devoid of religious symbolism and heritage as developed in the French Revolution.

SYMBOLS OF ORIGIN

Anthony D. Smith, writing about the origins of nations, reflects on the power of story and symbolism—what some sociologists have designated as "civil religion," as distinguished from particular world faiths: "Successful nations require an overarching common culture, a language, and a certain degree of uniformity in customs, religion, and so forth."[14] He explains what he means by identifying similarities and dissimilarities in various countries' accounts of their own origin and descent. In spite of all differences, he finds a pool of potential materials upon which they draw in the narratives they honor—the events they commemorate and the foundational stories that they tell. When Smith identifies the latter as "myth," he is speaking as a social scientist, using the term to distinguish cultural traditions from legend or untrue narrative. Instead, it is a symbolic way of telling and retelling the life meanings of the nation's inclusive history, for example, in the figures of George Washington and Abraham Lincoln. The American Founding Fathers drew their symbolism from Greek and Roman statecraft as well as from the Bible and the Enlightenment. Smith's list of topics includes the following:

1. a myth of origins in time, i.e., when the community was "born";

2. a myth of the origins in space, i.e., where the community was "born";

3. a myth of ancestry, i.e., who bore us, and how we are descended from him or her;

4. a myth of migration, i.e., whither we wandered;

5. a myth of liberation, i.e., how we were freed;

6. a myth of a golden age, i.e., how we became great and heroic;

7. a myth of decline, i.e., how we decayed and were conquered/ exiled;

8. a myth of rebirth, i.e., how we shall be restored to our former glory;

Throughout United States history, these stories (of a particular "civil religion") have been confirmed as authentic by the sacrifice of patriots in war and peace. Communication about the past or the future—their significance and values—remains empty and incomplete without such narrative reference points.

The public response to presidents' judgments about good versus evil and human destiny are conditioned by a host of emotional feelings and symbolism that center on the president's person. "What he [a president] does affects the daily life of each of us in ways which doctors can scarcely ever dream. His actions sweep irrepressibly into the hearts of his admirers. He dwells in us. We cannot keep him out. That is why we wrestle against him, rise up in hatred often … or, alternatively, feel … as though his achievements were ours …."[15] Honor and dishonor are in his hands. Ideally, a president should have internalized the most deeply felt moral beliefs of the nation—its best conscience. Pictures from Moscow are seen on the television screen simultaneously with others from Washington, Cairo, and Beijing, at times with presidential explanation of United States policy. All are vivid reminders that the world has grown dangerously small. The leader's influence on events abroad may be as great or even greater than in his own country.

As we have already suggested, different presidents have had diverse ethical and religious symbolic models; some have been more farsighted and prophetic than others. Consider the crucial differences as between Buchanan and Lincoln, Wilson and Harding, Nixon and Carter, to mention only a few cases. Historically, the introduction of religion into the public square has carried good news or bad news, depending on what it has brought in moral standards. It has been used to support serfdom and slavery in the past. Yet it has also been prophetic and revolutionary—Martin Luther King, Jr. being an outstanding example as a statesman-martyr. The authors of the Constitution intended that questions of right and wrong should be debated openly in a pluralistic democracy committed to human rights. Their premise was that conscience cannot be compelled and it ought not to be silenced.

Obama looked for inspiration not only to Jefferson and Lincoln, but even more to Martin Luther King, Jr., a public figure who was not a politician but a preacher—and like Jimmy Carter, a Baptist. King understood how deeply communal evil is rooted in human life. A Southerner educated in the North at Boston University, King appeared at a crucial time during which the demand for social justice was bursting earlier bounds. He understood all too well that the legal abolishment of slavery did not bring the end of the oppression of blacks in the United States. That he was martyred extended his influence worldwide, giving him a lasting place as an ethical and religious model. King's way of change was Christian, based on Jesus's teachings about the Kingdom of God, and to be sure, he supplemented it by Mahatma Gandhi's insights about non-violence. His moral model was not a strategy of hate but of forgiveness and strength through the refusal of violence.

King, through preaching and organization as well as his own commitment and example, raised the ethical questions too often ignored by most American Christians ever since the end of slavery and the Civil War. The evils of racial discrimination were established in social custom and even had religious sanction throughout the United States, especially in the South. The issue was not just one of individual rapport and good will but of social patterns, supported by law; King called for implementation of Christian morality through structures of government. He sensed the right moment of kairos—the opportune time to do the right thing—in the social psychology of the time, and prophetically faced the reality of wickedness and evil. It was religion in politics at its best. King's appeal reached to the conscience of the North; white religious leaders, Jewish as well as Christian, joined in King's marches. He offered a powerful moral corrective against a mistaken image of Christianity as being only a defense of the status quo or otherworldly personal salvation. In short, King worked for the conversion of the culture, its politics and culture, and not just individuals. Of course, he had a vital black piety on which to build, with its songs and preaching.

THE PRESIDENCY AND THE AWE OF THE SACRED

Obama, for his part, has a unique charisma. He has enlisted the enthusiastic support of young voters on a level only rivaled by John F. Kennedy before him. An advisor to Richard Nixon, Ray Price—at the time that the vice president was first considering running for the highest office in the land—sent the Republican hopeful the following memorandum. "Selection of a President has to be an act of faith. That faith isn't achieved by reason; it's achieved by charisma, by a feeling of trust that can't be argued or reasoned, but that comes across in those silences that surround words."[16]

Millions of Americans shared faith and hope with the senator, elevating him to the White House.

The advisor was sure that citizens identify with a president as with no other public figure. Candidates for the highest office in the land are measured against an ideal that combines the symbolism of a "leading man, God, father, hero, pope, king, with maybe just a touch of the avenging Furies thrown in. They want him to be larger than life, a living legend, yet quintessentially human." The office and the office holder—a succession of some forty men—in their own person and belief, thus reflected and symbolized the ethos of their respective eras—Washington, Jefferson, Jackson, Lincoln, Wilson, and Franklin Roosevelt.

In short, from the outset, the United States presidency has carried heavy symbolic baggage and religious significance, and this continues to the present. George Washington understood this reality when he added to his inaugural oath of office, after swearing on the Bible, "so help me God." In times of crisis—as well as amid defeat and tragedy—the American people identify uniquely with their president, blaming or praising him. He becomes an icon of their deepest hopes and fears.

When presidents succeed, the pious imagination imposes a whole series of positive symbols and stories on their person. In Washington's case, it included the cherry tree incident—"I cannot tell a lie!—which was spread by Parson Weems's eulogy. That the general prayed in the snow at Valley Forge seems not to have been the case, academic researchers claim.

Lincoln was eulogized as a rail splitter and probably portrayed as more pious than he was in real life—at least so his law partner, William Herndon, believed. It is in violent death by assassination that presidents have been judged to be martyr-heroes of sacred and eternal significance, most notably father Abraham Lincoln and John F. Kennedy. Ronald Reagan's stature increased geometrically when he survived an assassination attempt in good spirits.

So again, what enables a president to succeed? Simply put, what are Obama's chances in the face of enormous obstacles and dangers? Roman Catholic theologian Michael Novak identifies eight presidential qualities that mark the difference between success and failure: action, honesty, goodness, self-control, genuine emotion, administrative control, decisiveness, and instinct for ends and means that is characteristically American—what Clinton Rossiter called "A grand and durable pattern of private liberty and public morality." In the modern setting, citizens value them not just as belonging to the secular state but as semi-religious virtues.

Woodrow Wilson understood correctly that chief executives succeed best when they manage to connect with the mainstream of belief in the country. Should an occupant of the White House fail to do so, an immense power vacuum is created into which a host of forces—both from the opposition as well his own party—are prepared to rush. The public imagination fantasizes negatively about his faults and sexual mores, as in the case of Bill Clinton.

It is important to recognize the diversity of the different settings and versions of ethics and religion that have been dominant in various eras of the nation's history. A presidency's geographical, political, and social model (for example, pro- or anti-slavery) interacts with the moral and religious ethos and convictions of its time—war and peace, technology, social practices. Neither ethics nor religion is simply static; together, both are dynamic. The interrelation between politics and religion in various presidencies can be seen from the different paradigms of successive periods of the office. Americans' faith has not been the same at all times and in all places.

In the longer historical view, it is commonly said that in the United States, religion (and its bearing on morality) has undergone a threefold disestablishment. Initially, this took place with the First Amendment of the Constitution, as the idea of a national church was rejected. The second occurred less officially following the First World War, when evolution and higher criticism destroyed the reigning "non-sectarian Protestantism" premised on dual revelations of God in nature and scripture. In short, the harmony between the two books—revelation and science—which had reigned ever since Sir Isaac Newton, disintegrated. Nature was no longer seen as ordered on an Enlightenment rational pattern; cultural Protestantism lost its apologetic power. The third disestablishment followed the Second World War, as the Supreme

Court insisted on the full separation of church and state, for example, abolishing prayer in public schools.

The University of Chicago church historian, Martin Marty, distinguishes between an "ordering faith" and a "saving faith." The work of the latter is to "save souls, make hearts glad, give people wholeness, [and] provide them with the kind of identity and sense of belonging they crave ...."[17] It is not the president's chief responsibility, as de Tocqueville recognized. Rather, as the French visitor judged, his task is rather a non-sectarian, ordering, non-ecclesiastical faith (civil religion), which functions culturally as the bridge between various confessions with their distinctive doctrines. Marty writes: "The two-sided equation of the founding fathers is still at the heart of the American proposition: institutional separation of church and state in a multifaith society, but cultural ... religion and society to produce a workable consensus undergirding 'public virtue.'"

"God bless America" is a phrase widely used by politicians of both major political parties. It is expressed in the federal tradition that United States money bears the motto, "In God We Trust." When President Theodore Roosevelt in 1905—allegedly for purely aesthetic reasons—approved the design of a new penny as well as ten- and twenty-dollar gold pieces without these long-accepted words, "a violent storm broke out"—against the godless coinage! Congress soon passed a bill restoring the motto—probably to Roosevelt's relief. Unhappily, the controversy about the Supreme Court's ban against prayer and Bible-reading in the public schools has not been so easily resolved.

Summing up the position of the Founding Fathers, University of California sociologist Robert Bellah argues: "Beyond the Constitution, then, the president's obligation extends not only to the people but to God .... The will of the people is not itself the criterion of right and wrong." Instead a higher criterion is recognized from which it can be judged. In short, the people may be wrong! A president's obligation is to the higher criterion.[18] Writing as a social scientist, Bellah identifies it as "a collection of beliefs, symbols and rituals with respect to sacred things" that "while not antithetical to, and indeed sharing much in common with Christianity, was neither sectarian or in any specific sense Christian." The beliefs of the Founding Fathers were primarily Protestant Christian and Enlightenment. Belief in a personal God who is both transcendent and immanent is explicit in George Washington's Farewell Address, Abraham Lincoln's Gettysburg Address, and John F. Kennedy's first inaugural speech. This is not ecclesiastical but "civil religion."

Over more than two centuries in the United States, Bellah finds that there has been a religious and patriotic "habit of the heart that the Founding Fathers would have commended." Obama shares in such "civil religion"; his version of the American dream embodies it.

PREDECESSORS AND THE OBAMA ERA: CHRONOLOGY

1. Federalism. Reason and not special revelation dominated the Enlightenment thought of the Founding Fathers. Still, religion was believed to be indispensable in the support of civic virtue.

2. Jeffersonian Disestablishment: A wall of separation between church and state was called for by the third president. Jefferson, a liberal, expected Unitarianism to win out as the nation grew and expanded. Instead, frontier revival-style awakenings grew and predominated.

3. The Age of Jackson. Jacksonian populist democracy dominated in the national ethos. The frontier president, hero of the Battle of New Orleans, himself a slaveholder and personally pious, championed Western expansion in the name of American Manifest Destiny.

4. The Civil War. The controversy about slavery overshadowed the immediate period before Lincoln. The issues, unresolved in compromise, were both ethical and religious. The outcome of the war was a moral watershed without parallel to date in the nation's history.

5. Post-Civil War. In the Gilded Age after the war, there was a significant shift in cultural model. The South, having lost leadership in the presidency, became defensively religious. In the North, belief in evolution and an accompanying secularism were on the rise. Immigration brought growing religious pluralism. Negroes would have to wait a century for the civil rights they had been promised!

6. The Era of Reform. It was against a background of new wealth and presidential weakness that Theodore Roosevelt and Woodrow Wilson (both "culture Protestants") took leadership. Populism, a major factor promoting reform, had strong religious roots in leaders like William Jennings Bryan.

7. The First World War. International involvement brought a watershed change of religious and moral ethos. Wilson interpreted the armed struggle as a crusade to make the world safe for democracy—in the name of God!

8. The Franklin Roosevelt Era of the New Deal and the Second World War. The president borrowed moral idealism from the Christian social gospel, even as he included Roman Catholics and Jews among his advisors. He did not prosecute the war as much in theological terms as did Wilson; he was, in fact, a religious liberal.

9. The cold war against communism. Soon after Roosevelt's death, the course of events made evident the intensity of the struggle still to come against totalitarianism. Civil religion joined Americans—Roman Catholic, Protestant, and Jewish—in a common faith. United States ideology—reflected in the presidency—was both morally and religiously inspired. The fact was that communists did carry on atheistic campaigns of persecution, denying basic human rights.

10. The end of the Russian-American great power confrontation and the fall of the iron curtain. Moral as well as religious issues, human rights as well as peace, remained at stake in the Middle East, the former Yugoslavia, and the former USSR, as well as in Asia and Africa. The struggle against militant Islamism predominated in the defense against terrorism in the Middle East.

THE LONGER HISTORICAL VIEW

The roots of the North American quest for religious liberty reach back to early Colonial history, long before the Revolution, and even to confessional warfare and persecution in England. Throughout New

England, the Puritan colonists believed that they were following the model of the Chosen People of Israel in the time of the Judges. God Himself was their sovereign. Earthly kingship—a concession to human weakness and sinfulness—had in the end proved unsuccessful in Israel, as the Babylonian captivity followed. A new Israel would heed and fulfill the message of the prophets—Amos, Hosea, Isaiah, and Jeremiah. Christians, in their later-founded religion, claimed fidelity to the divine will in their own way.

During the long centuries in which Christianity was the established state religion—Jefferson and Madison were sure—rivers of blood had flowed in persecution. It was this fruit of intolerance that they were determined to end in the New World. Already in the English colonies before the break with Great Britain, denominational pluralism had developed in power—encouraged by the open land of the frontier. Jefferson and Madison joined with Presbyterian laity, Baptists, and Quakers to end establishment in Virginia and subsequently in the new United States. In the newly founded republican country, religious allegiance was to be determined from below. For decades, the diversity had been too great to allow for any other arrangement in the new nation; an established church might even have brought civil war.

This much can be said historically: the American republican form of life and government is the antithesis of the longstanding union of throne and altar, church and state, which led to a polity of religious warfare and persecution in Christendom. After the Roman emperor Constantine had converted to Christianity in 313 CE, he decided to continue the imperial Roman tradition of state religion. Freedom of conscience soon was restricted and the creed of the emperor was imposed on his realm. Personal faith was largely displaced by dogma.

Constantine first tolerated and then officially established Catholic Christianity. Having seen a vision of the cross in the sky before his decisive military victory in 313 CE, he took as a divine command the words that accompanied it, "in this sign conquer." Direction and establishment of religion from above—the Constantinian solution— (continuing in force even during the first centuries of the Protestant Reformation) was first challenged effectively more than a millennium later in the Enlightenment. The ruling belief had been that without state support of religious establishment, morality and the common life would disintegrate. Widespread fear of Muslim invasion was perennial in post-Reformation Europe. The Turkish army was at the gates of Vienna for the last time in 1683. There was no such Islamic threat in the New World.

In 1797, when President John Adams signed a treaty making peace with the Muslim state of Tripoli, he issued the following statement:

> As the government of the United States of America is not in any sense founded on the Christian religion as it has in itself no character of enmity [hatred] against the laws, religion or tranquility of Musselmen [Muslims] and as said States [America] have never entered into any war or act of hostility against any Mahometan nation, it is declared by the parties that no pretext arising from religious opinions shall ever produce an interruption of the harmony existing between the two countries.[19]

Eboo Patel, author of *Acts of Faith, The Story of an American Muslim, the Struggle for the Soul of a Generation,* argues that religious conflict is the dominant global challenge of the twenty-first century. "America is the most religiously diverse country in the world and the most religiously devout nation in the West." Patel believes that Barack Obama has an opportunity to translate this religious diversity into a pluralism that strengthens American civil society, transforming American diplomacy, and contributing to global stability. "The next administration must bridge America's religious communities by supporting and increasing interfaith service initiatives."[20]

President George W. Bush was faithful to Adams's historic precedent when he proclaimed, following the 9/11/01 attack on the United States that this nation was not at war with Islam. The suicide bomber terrorists betrayed the morality of their own professed religion and did not authentically represent it. Of course, suicide bombers (although they come from a very different religious background than North American democracy) have been condemned by major leaders in their own tradition. Muslim history (much richer) long predates the discovery of America. Historically, Muslim rulers—until 1258 CE—presided over a world empire stretching from Africa to India, the greatest to date. After their capital city, Baghdad, was captured and destroyed by Mongol hordes, Muslim rule was divided among the Turks (who in 1453 captured Constantinople), the Persians, and Indian Moguls. In the modern period, especially following Napoleon's invasion of Egypt, much of the Islamic world fell victim to colonialism. Historically, Islam has not separated church and state as in the European Enlightenment. Its model is being debated among its adherents to the present.

Obama's coming to power offers a new opportunity to re-appraise interfaith relations internationally. The promise he offers has been set down by Soon-Chan Rah, who teaches at North Park Theological Seminary in Chicago. He writes of "The Face of America": "I too am a child of immigrants. I too have a funny-sounding name. I became a Christian in a church that would be considered outside the boundaries of a typical white evangelical church." Rah reports that he was stunned when he was not accepted as someone worthy of trust in the white evangelical church he visited. He believed himself to be a Christian whose testimony of conversion was about as evangelical as one could be. He has concluded, however, that the nation is changing. There is not only a multiethnic future, but a multiethnic present. As an atypical American, a non-white evangelical Christian, he looks to a political leader who symbolizes in his own person the ethnic and cultural diversity of the United States of America. "Now I believe that there is a seat at the table for those with funny-sounding names and of a different ethnic origin."[21]

PRESIDENTS' ETHICS

"[I]f we truly hope to speak to people where they're at—to communicate our hopes and values in a way that's relevant to their own—then as progressives, we cannot abandon the field of religious discourse ... Because when we ignore the debate about what it means to be a good Christian or Muslim or Jew; when we discuss religion only in the negative sense of where or how it should not be practiced, rather than in the positive sense of what it tells us about our obligations towards one another ... others will fill the vacuum, those with the most insular views of faith, or those who cynically use religion to justify partisan ends."[1] Barack Obama-- Call to Renewal Addresses

COURAGE IN THE PRE-OBAMA ERA— FANNIE LOU HAMER

The compelling political presence of mature faith and character can be seen from the following incident from the earlier Martin Luther King, Jr. struggle against racial segregation. Fannie Lou Hamer, a devout black evangelical Christian and founder of the Mississippi Freedom Democratic Party (MFDP), suddenly discovered that she had come to a position of national power. When Lyndon Johnson ran for the first time on his own for the presidency in 1964, he deemed it necessary to enlist her support for his courageous campaign against segregation.

President Johnson's immediate problem was that he wished to avoid any division at the Democratic Party Nominating Convention. His dilemma arose because Mrs. Hamer's MFDP had challenged the credentials of the exclusively white slate of Mississippi delegates who had been selected for the Democratic National Convention. Could a compromise be reached that would enable her to withdraw the protest? Mrs. Hamer herself had once tried to register as a voter and in consequence suffered beating and torture in Mississippi jails. President Johnson, wishing no party conflict, sent Hubert Humphrey to the South to negotiate. He gave Humphrey the assignment of winning the African-American woman's support for a pragmatic compromise that would bring great benefit to her people—at least according to the politicians.

When Humphrey arrived on the scene in Mississippi, he asked Mrs. Hamer what she really wanted, and she replied to Humphrey in New Testament terms: "[T]he beginning of a New Kingdom right here on earth .... Senator Humphrey, I know lots of people who have lost their jobs for trying to register to vote. I had to leave the plantation where I worked in Sunflower County. Now if you lose this job of vice president because you do what is right, because you help MFDP, everything will be all right. God will take care of you .... But if you take [the vice presidential nomination] this way, why, you will never be able to do any good for civil rights, for poor people, for peace or any of those things you talk about. Senator Humphrey, I'm gonna pray to Jesus for you."[2]

For Mrs. Hamer, faith in God was not an aspect of life to be separated from other parts, but relevant for all of it. In short, she wanted the Kingdom of God, not just liberal social change. It was the ultimate that concerned her, not expediency. Professor Stephen L. Carter of the Yale Law School, who relates her story, comments that "in fact, there is nothing un-American, undemocratic or even strange about religious activism and religious language in politics." Mrs. Hamer, in her own way, was giving her personal commentary on the question of separation of church and state. Like millions of other citizens, she did not want to live in an exclusively secular realm—with a naked public square devoid of religion. For her, the world of the sacred was alive and powerful. And in her case—like that of millions of her fellow citizens—whoever wanted her vote would have to speak to her religious convictions. She was not only idealistic but realistic about national politics.

In this case, we are dealing not just with a rationalist philosophy (as in the Enlightenment) but with a specific confessional witness. Indeed, a whole series of issues was implicit in Mrs. Hamer's response to Senator Humphrey: What is meant by the New Testament proclamation of the Kingdom of God? What is the responsibility of a convinced Christian believer to the political regime (embodied concretely in the presidency)? How can one confront evil? How much compromise should be made for expediency's sake? When, if ever, does the end justify the means? In short, what is right and wrong in religious and not just secular terms—although the two approaches may overlap?

For Mrs. Hamer, the need for ethical realism—distinguishing positive conviction about morality and the presence of good and evil from the simplicities and prejudices of campaign rhetoric—came with belief in the Kingdom of God. "The triumph of theatricality over truth, of sentiment over justice, of cant, cliché, and bromide over conviction" has been all too evident in party conventions and subsequent electioneering—Mrs. Hamer knew quite well. So Mrs. Hamer refused the request of Johnson and his vice president, Hubert Humphrey! In terms of Fowler's scale, she had a mature faith.

In his study, *God's Name in Vain, The Wrongs and Rights of Religion in Politics*, Stephen L. Carter, the Yale Law School African-American Episcopalian who publicized the story of Mrs. Hamer, comes to the point: "Religion has been inseparable from American politics for as long as America has had politics, and will as long as Americans remain religious." Yet in every generation, he finds, there have been commentators who are surprised at its relevance and power in national life. "If they had done a little digging, if they had gone back further historically, they would have understand what goes on to the present better! In the 1950s Dwight Eisenhower argued before the world that belief in God was the first principle of Americanism .... If reporters ... had checked out Thomas Jefferson's campaign for the White House two hundred years earlier they could hardly have escaped the fact that he spent a large part of his rhetoric denying that he was an atheist!"[3] Of course, Jefferson recognized that religion has been misused ethically.

NATURAL LAW ETHICS

C. S. Lewis gave the concept of natural law a popular definition. To indicate its universality, he pointed to what he called the Tao of morality; the Chinese term, "Tao," means simply "the way." Lewis argued that there are ethical norms that transcend individuals and cultures.[4] He noted that they recur in the writings of the ancient Egyptians, Babylonians, Hebrews, Chinese, Norse, Indians, and Greeks, along with Anglo-Saxon and American writings. In sum, they are:

1. **The Law of Beneficence.** This rule recognizes the importance of kindness, shared generosity for the sake of society. For example, do not murder, oppress, bear false witness, hate.

2. **Duty to Family.**

3. **The Law of Justice.** It encourages impartiality and fair-mindedness before the law. "Regard him whom thou knowest like him whom thou knowest not."

4. **The Law of Good Faith and Veracity.**

5. **The Law of Mercy.**

6. **The Law of Magnanimity.** For many ancients, there were some things worse than death, such as treachery, murder, betrayal, and torturing another person.[5] Together, these six laws make up a kind of common-sense realism. Their reality is not just imagined; they have a kind of objective reality

In traditional morality, these imperatives have been attributed to conscience; in major theologies, they have been associated with the image of God in humans. Historically, laws and taboos were established by priestly and prophetic leaders and enforced by state functionaries. They were not abandoned later (as in the French Revolution) when the new North American republic was established. University of California sociologist Robert Bellah describes ethics and religion in the United States in terms of "habits of the heart."[6] Such habits have been nurtured traditionally in community, in the family, the town and country, he points out. Now earlier socialization often has been replaced by an isolated individualism and relativism. In the midst of war and rapid social change, its longstanding power has been weakened; many citizens have become alienated from their past and have lost confidence in the future.

Bellah emphasizes that ethical customs (or mores) in the United States have been conditioned historically by biblical and republican legacies. Today these legacies are often suppressed in secularization, but no abiding substitute has been developed to take their place as bearer of moral authority. Throughout much of the history of North America, there was an optimistic, frontier-inspired morality, sustained by faith in Manifest Destiny and deity. Now in the post-communist era, there is a defensive reaction against a cynical view that is judged to lack moral basis in a philosophical and religious vacuum.

Positively, Bellah's claim, made from a sociological perspective, is that citizens live from historical cultural and value traditions. These are now more in flux than before. Longstanding norms remain powerful even when retained only in the background of national life. Today, they are threatened by an "ontological individualism," one in which there are no borders. This phenomenon appears even in the presidency. Certainly it was exemplified by Nixon in the latter part of his tenure in office. Many Americans, like Nixon, concerned only with power and "what works," Bellah argues, no longer try to answer the question, "works for what?" But practicality and usefulness, pragmatism and utilitarianism, by themselves no longer bring either community or long-term satisfaction. They do not tell citizens who they are or what they ought to be.

THE MORALITY OF TRADITIONAL RULERS

Still visible on the walls of the old City Hall in Siena, Italy, are two murals painted by the artist Lorenzo in the fourteenth century. Good government is depicted on one side, bad government on the other, both with their accompanying effects.[7]

The magisterial figure of a ruler—calm, austere, and white-bearded—symbolizes good government. Beside him are to be seen the six civic virtues: justice, temperance, magnanimity, prudence, fortitude, and peace. The benefits that flow from the practice of these virtues are identified in handsome public buildings (including Siena's cathedral) that appear in the background. The mural also depicts comfortable private homes, well-tended olive groves, vineyards, and wheat fields, and citizens dancing in the streets. The whole scene is full of activity and supported by Security, a winged figure that floats in the sky. Invisible to travelers on the road below, Security safeguards their interests.

Bad government is depicted on the opposite wall of City Hall, represented by a figure with horns and fanglike teeth. This figure holds a sword and sits clad in chain mail, enthroned among cruelty, perfidy, fraud, anger, discord, and war, while vainglory, avarice, and tyranny hover above.

Justice cowers in chains below. The consequences of bad government are depicted all around. Once-grand palaces stand in ruins. Violence, murder, and rape are at hand. A sinister band of armed men moves on horseback and foot toward a new victim as the desolate countryside is ruled over not by Security but by Terror.

The painter Lorenzo, like the citizens of Siena, believed that the outcome of good government was different from that of bad government. Good government means well-tended fields and plentiful harvests; bad government means civil disorder and physical desolation. Public virtue and morality have inevitable consequences.

Of course, traditionally the term "virtue" has not been limited to family morality. Simply defined, virtue is a quality of life by which persons habitually recognize and do the right thing. For the Greeks, the desired qualities (the classical virtues) were fortitude—the strength of mind and courage to persevere in the face of adversity; temperance—self-discipline, the control of all unruly human passions and appetites; prudence—practical wisdom and the ability to make the right choice in specific situations; and justice—fairness, honesty, lawfulness, and the ability to keep one's promises.

To the Greeks' list of fortitude, temperance, prudence, and justice, the Christian Church added the religious virtues of faith, hope, and love.

In what ways does the morality of United States presidents today differ from that of earlier monarchs? Of course, there are radical differences, but they need not be overstated to the point of moral indifferentism. To the present, the question of standards—what is right and wrong?—probes the ethics and norms of the American republic in depth. A president as commander-in-chief stands near "the gate to hell." For example, throughout the war in Vietnam, President Lyndon Johnson was haunted by deep fear of expanded hostilities using atomic or hydrogen bombs in warfare, with Russia or China as belligerents. He pursued one strategy and then another. In spite of mistaken policy calls, judged retrospectively, it is clear that he was right in seeing a significant difference between Americans and the communists during the cold war. Marxists judged both morality and religion as epiphenomena that could be explained fully in terms of other factors such as economics and politics. Democracies that did not persecute religion viewed them more positively as having authentic truth claims of their own. Actually, the end of the cold war has not relaxed the demand for moral principles in support of democracy and human rights throughout the world.

Do we still have perennial virtues and vices, good and evil with accompanying consequences? In short, is there still character with real "objective values"? Or does anything go in a world in which all is only relative and subjective? Intellectually, the distinction between facts and values is crucial to our answer. Philosophical reductionism more often than not equates the two in what its critics identify as the naturalistic fallacy. Theists generally deny its first premise, insisting intellectually and in practice that the *ought* cannot be reduced to the *is!* Serious morality requires a perennial tension between the two. Traditional philosophers like Aristotle and Kant, who were not Christians—along with church theologians like Augustine, Luther, and Bonhoeffer—have based their ethics on this claim, affirming objective values supported by deity.

Historically, the introduction of religiously sanctioned ethics into the public square has been good news or bad news, depending on whether or not it has respected human rights. The result has not always been positive. Belief in God has been used to buttress serfdom and slavery at times. Yet it has also been prophetic and revolutionary—Martin Luther King, Jr. being an outstanding example as a statesman martyr. Of course, even a moment's reflection makes evident that peace and prosperity cannot be established in the modern world simply by the fiat of a ruler dispensed from above. The framers of the American Constitution intended that questions of right and wrong be debated openly in a pluralistic republic committed to religious tolerance. Their premise was that conscience cannot be compromised and it should not be silenced.

LEARNING FROM A NEGATIVE MORAL MODEL IN THE PRESIDENCY

A moral crisis in foreign affairs could serve as an example. Readers of former secretary of defense Robert McNamara's book, *The Tragedy and Lessons of Vietnam,* have noted how much it reveals a vacuum of moral common sense during the Vietnam War. McNamara summarizes:

> We thus failed to analyze and debate our actions in Southeast Asia, our objectives, the risks and costs of alternative ways of dealing with them, and the necessity of changing course when failure was clear .... We did not recognize that neither our people nor our leaders are omniscient .... We do not have the God-given right to shape every nation in our own image or as we choose.[8]

Theodore H. White, observing all of the campaigns for the presidency from the election of Eisenhower in 1956 to that of Reagan in 1980, reflected that "All civilizations rest on myths." One could also say "models" or "moral paradigms." White argues that in their American versions, they have special meaning. He describes them as a way of pulling together "the raw and contradictory evidence of life as it is known in any age." As living symbols, they join the presidency to religion and not just in a sectarian way.

> *The myth [or model] that binds America together ... [is] that somewhere in American life there is at least one man who stands for law, the President. That faith surmounts all daily cynicism, all evidence or suspicion of wrongdoing by lesser leaders, all corruptions, all vulgarities, all the ugly compromises of daily striving and ambition. That faith holds that all men are equal before the law and protected by it; and that no matter how the faith may be betrayed elsewhere, at one particular point, the Presidency, justice*

will be done beyond prejudice, beyond rancor, beyond the possibility of a fix.[9]

As we have already noted, such invocation of the term "myth" can be confusing, as it contrasts with the popular usage. Many political scientists would prefer to speak of national "faith symbols" and traditions. The term is used by psychologists and sociologists in a more technical way as models or paradigms for structuring thinking. To the extent that myths sum up common experience in story, their meanings are not arbitrary or just invented but grow up out of the experience of conscience and piety. Such symbols let "people make sense of their own lives within the larger pattern" in this case, the meaning of the presidency, White explains. Their models are moral but also religious in the sense of the Founding Fathers' or Lincoln's "civil religion."

Take away America's guiding myths (what has sometimes been called its common faith) and there would be only a sad geographical expression of a multitude of conflicts—racial, religious, and economic—White argues. Equal justice was promised under the law in the Declaration of Independence and the Constitution at the time of the nation's founding. The derivative myth was that the presidency would make noble any man who held this office; it would burn the dross from his character, White argues:

> *That myth held for almost two centuries. A man of limited experience like George Washington was transformed, almost magically, into one of the great creative architects of politics .... An ambitious politician like Abraham Lincoln of Illinois could in the crucible of the Presidency, be refined to a nobility of purpose and a compassion that hallow his name. A snob like Franklin D. Roosevelt and his missionary wife, Eleanor, could find in themselves and give to their country a warmth, a humanity, a charity that makes them universal symbols of mercy and strength.[10]*

The myth was broken decisively in the Watergate scandal, White argues, and the country still suffers from the suspicion and nihilism that were generated. But Nixon would not be the only president who would not live up to public expectations of morality, he himself seeing the Watergate break-in simply as a continuation of "normal politics."

What can religion contribute to presidential vision and ethics in a representative democracy? Certainly, a sense of the absolute as opposed to nihilism. Belief in God brings a kind of realization of finitude and relativity. History and the visible world are not the totality of reality. The generations come and go as a watch in the night before God's eternity. Morality becomes less elusive and richer in content when it is understood not simply in static, perfectionistic terms, but as dynamic in relation to the providence and judgment of God. Too often, religious persons mistakenly suppose that only motive and intention, apart from consequences, are all that matter. "The road to hell is paved with good intentions." The church father, Augustine, argued by contrast for a directional model of morality; character and virtue depend on whether intention and action are directed toward the highest good or away from it. Much of the time, it is impossible to foresee fully the consequences and effects of particular policies and actions. Nations and their rulers like individuals must take risks based on principle—the faith ("ultimate concern") they believe to be just and right.

The Enlightenment belief in God, freedom, and immortality was crucial to the ideology of the Founding Fathers—Washington, Jefferson, and Madison. This basic premise was summed up most succinctly by the German philosopher Immanuel Kant in his *What Is Enlightenment?*[11] Throughout most of history, citizens have been ruled hierarchically from above, Kant observed. Truth has been handed down from authorities in both church and state, from clergy and kings. Enlightenment means that human beings now must make their judgments from their own conscience, deciding for themselves. Kant believed this is possible in principle because each individual is a bearer of the moral law in his own person. Whatever can be said about religious dogmas—and Kant was skeptical about them—the truth of morality was self-evident, in his judgment. Moral conscience was not to be limited to rulers or the educated. As an Enlightenment philosopher, Kant called for a new democratic understanding based on conscience "from below." At the same time, he concluded that no lasting ethic can be justified only pragmatically and premised God, freedom, and immortality.

A PARABLE: "AFTER VIRTUE"

In his book, *After Virtue,* the moral philosopher, Alasdair McIntrye, presents a parable: suppose, he says, that an attempt suddenly was made to destroy all science in the modern world. Scientists would be arrested and imprisoned, their works destroyed, and their theories banished. Their mode of knowledge was to be forgotten forever. Of course, there would be remnants of science; for example, parts of machines used as apparatus would be discovered, and science's cultural heritage could not be completely eradicated immediately. But in its full outlook and methods, it would not be known.[12]

McIntyre now applies his parable about science to morality. It is ethics and not science that suffers in today's world, he urges, and the traditional moral virtues of the past have become inoperative. Unfortunately, classical ethical virtues as expounded by the Greek philosophers Socrates, Plato, and Aristotle are viewed with suspicion and disbelief. McIntyre is not optimistic about progress in the future, and he believes that it is impossible for national life to continue positively within a moral vacuum. His parable bears directly on the life convictions of the person who leads government, be he king, prime minister, or president. Very often, it is simpler to rule solely on the basis of power and rhetoric, disregarding ethics. Our question is how ethical standards have or have not impinged upon the United States presidency throughout the history of the office.

"The reverence people pay to the President, the awe his visitors experience in his presence all that is in their heads and his .... The President exists solely in the minds of men .... This 'institution' is nothing more than images, habits, and intentions shared by the humans who make them up and by those who react to them."[13] So argues John David Barber, the political scientist who devoted his career to researching presidential character. But Barber does not believe that this is the end of the matter or agree that there are no abiding moral constants.

A RELIGIOUSLY SUPPORTED
PRESIDENTIAL MORALITY

The state is not an end in itself (as in totalitarianism). Government is by, for, and of the people. Might does not make right. Don't lie; tell the truth. Don't demonize opponents. The end does not justify the means. Absolutes—everything is not relative; but neither is everything absolute. In a democracy, politics is complex.

GOALS: Liberty of conscience and worship; freedom *for* and not freedom *from* religion.

Racial tolerance; no discrimination by race or creed.

A free, creative, civil society based on voluntary participation of citizens.

Justice in an imperfect world.

Responsible use of power; power is not wrong in itself, only in its misuse.

VALUES: Morality requires concern about consequences, not just good intentions.

The "road to hell" is paved with the latter.

Freedom once discovered will not be given up without struggle.

Community and democracy require more than solitary individuals.

Restraint of crime and violence.

Recognition of moral purpose in history; suspicion of cynicism.

VIRTUES: Concern for family and children.

Compassion and care for the weak and helpless.

Peace.

Prudence, courage, avoidance of enchantment with power and the hubris of attempting to "play God."

GEORGE WASHINGTON

MORALS AND ETHICS

Professing Christianity but not a frontier revivalist, the first president of the United States and "Father of his Country" would have been dismayed with contemporary controversies—religious and secular. The threat of atomic weapons and their use against civilians would have been beyond his wildest imagination. As commander-in-chief of the Continental Army, he achieved his initial laurels as a military leader whose tenacity and sense of situation led to victory. Washington lost many battles but won the Revolutionary War! At home at Mount Vernon, General Washington owned slaves and lived the life of a gentleman aristocrat, a characterization that hardly befits Obama. The forty-fourth president's world is much more complex than that of this Founding Father. His African-American tradition of piety places higher priority on emotion than did Washington's Anglicanism. Still, Obama's concern, expressed in his first Democratic Convention address—to "bring the country together"—is in the first president's tradition. While Washington in his time warned against entangling foreign alliances, Obama must live in the midst of them every day.

"George Washington was one of the few in the whole history of the world who was not carried away by power."[1] Thomas Jefferson summed up Washington's character and achievement:

His mind was great and powerful, without being of the very first order; his penetrations strong though not as acute as that of a Newton, Bacon, or Locke, and as far as he saw, no judgment was ever sounder. It was slow in operation being little aided by invention or imagination, but sure in conclusion....He was incapable of fear, meeting personal dangers with the calmest unconcern. His integrity was most pure, his justice the most inflexible I have ever known. ... He was indeed, in every sense of the words, a wise, a good, and a great man.[2]

Already during his lifetime, Washington had become a figure of patriotic reverence and pious eulogy. Hortatory accounts and legends multiplied geometrically about his stature as a general and president, following his death. Who was the Washington of history? Can he be rediscovered behind the tales of Parson Mason Locke Weems, inventor of the cherry tree story along with other such moralistic fables? For historians, thousands of letters remain from his correspondence as they research his lifetime to the present, comparing him with his successors as leader of the nation.

The presidential historian, Forrest McDonald, compares the last decade of the eighteenth century—while Washington was in office—to the age of Romulus and Remus in Rome. It was a seminal period that set paradigms for the future. In short, it was a myth-making time. McDonald formulates his own critical appraisal of Washington: "Here we are dealing with a myth that happens also to have been true."[3]

For the majority of citizens, more than any other figure, the wartime general who had accepted the new office of the presidency guaranteed the moral integrity of the new nation. Other generals from Caesar to Cromwell, gaining power, had refused to hand over their command following victory. By comparison, Washington did so promptly, and returned home to Mount Vernon. Elected the first president, he embodied a commitment to national unity as well as continuity with the revolution. In short, his person legitimated the regime in power.

Washington had already made his name as a general. He knew that he had nowhere to go but down when he entered the presidency, yet it remains a monumental part of his achievement. Self-conscious of his role and one who did not fall into office casually, "he was both proud and modest, simple and canny, aristocratic by nature and republican by choice.

"Like Franklin Roosevelt one and a half centuries later, Washington was a patrician idolized by the man in the street and opposed by entrenched forces to whom his—and Hamilton's—economic policies promised social upheaval."[4]

"He was no Rooseveltian swashbuckler, wielding the personal pronoun like a deadly weapon while placing his personal stamp upon every program of his age. He did not martyr himself for a great cause, like Lincoln, or thrill the multitudes with Wilsonian eloquence; indeed, by all contemporary evidence he was something less than a Great Communicator."[5] So observes one of his late-twentieth-century biographers. The following sums up Washington's ethics in contemporary relevance:

> *One day in the 1790s word spread through the capital that George Washington was sick and tired of Thomas Jefferson's constant bickering with Alexander Hamilton. That afternoon a man named J. Edgar Hoover was admitted to George Washington's office. "I have been keeping an eye on this Jefferson," said the visitor, "and have here ye goods to justify giving him ye heave ho from ye Cabinet." Hoover offered George Washington a dossier. George Washington recoiled and asked what was in it. "Ye transcripts of Jefferson's activities while wenching," said Hoover, "as well as his dinner table criticism of ye Government." George Washington took the dossier and deposited it in his fireplace where it burned to ashes while he was having Hoover thrown into the street. "It would have been unworthy of my office," he told Martha Washington afterwards, "to do ye throwing myself."[6]*

This imaginary incident was composed by columnist Russell Baker as an attempt to say how Washington would and would not act today; in short, what he would not do!

A historical incident, at the end of his military career, after the war had been won, in fact showed the power of the general's person. The Continental Army was encamped at Newburg, New York, early in 1783, waiting for the official end of hostilities and a peace treaty. Soldiers had received very little pay in hard currency, and many feared that when they returned home, they would not have immunity from payment of personal private obligations. Not only did they demand mustering out bonuses, but there was talk of insurrection. Should peace come, some dissidents urged, they ought to abandon the nation and head out for the wilderness. *"Do not sheath the sword until you have received full justice."*

In this situation of possible mutiny, General Washington presided over a meeting of officers whose tempers were out of control. He spoke out: "The dreadful alternative, of either deserting our Country in the extremest hour of her distress, or turning our arms against it ... has something so shocking in it, that humanity revolts at the idea .... I spurn it as must every man who regards that liberty and reveres that justice for which we contend." Subordinate officers even wept as he spoke, and the mutiny never took place.

Jefferson reflected later: "The moderation and virtue of one man probably prevented this Revolution from being closed by a subversion of the liberty it was intended to establish."

WHIG VIRTUE

Washington's leadership and character evidenced firm ethical conviction in a particular tradition—that of the moderate Enlightenment. This intellectual movement had a given context and meaning that its adherents (rightly or wrongly) viewed as universal, established by reason and nature's God. Americans committed to the revolution drew heavily on the ideas of British dissidents a century before, at the time of England's Glorious Revolution of 1688. Political pamphlets sent throughout the colonies reflected the influence of the "Real Whigs" who had been a major party in bringing about change at home in the mother country.[7] In short, convictions and ideology from this time—Real Whig themes—were used to legitimate the American colonists' own assertion of liberty and self-rule. Jefferson summed it up: "Before the Revolution, we were all good Whigs, cordial in free principles ... jealous of the executive Magistrate."[8]

In time, as the revolutionary cause grew and developed, the term

Whig became synonymous with *Republican*. Envisaging a continual struggle between power and liberty, persons of this outlook did not hold a high judgment of human nature. "Such is the depravity of mankind that the ambition and lust of power above the law are predominant passions in the breasts of most men." [9] In short, insatiable power, grasping and tenacious—its jaws always open to devour—creeps by degrees until it subdues the whole. Across a wide spectrum of opinion, from free thinkers to Orthodox Christians, there was major agreement about such realism, Samuel Adams of Massachusetts noted.

Against this pessimistic picture of human nature, a variety of virtues were believed to be salutatory: justice, temperance, courage, honesty, sincerity, modesty, integrity, calmness, benevolence, sobriety, piety, and nationality—all the antithesis of brute power. Simply put, might does not make right. The virtues were justified as both Roman and Christian in precedent, and they were formulated not just abstractly but in heroic images. Not surprisingly, these images were projected onto Washington's person. Laudable and exemplary character came from principles and motives; it was not simply subjective, but arose from ultimate grounds or reasons. Examples included Moses from the Old Testament and Cincinnatus from Roman history.

The patriotic Whig view of virtue called for renunciation of self-interest for the public good. According to this moral realism, human beings are born not to serve themselves but their country and to thwart tyrannical designs. Public virtue requires that the state be kept beyond the grasp of ambitious power-seekers and remain under control of its citizens. [10] Such was the ideological background of the formal address tendered to George Washington by the Massachusetts Congress when he arrived in Cambridge in July 1775.

"We applaud that attention to the public good, manifested in your appointment, we equally admire that disinterested virtue and distinguished patriotism, which alone could call you from those enjoyments of domestic life, which a sublime and manly taste, joined with a most affluent fortune, can afford, to hazard your life, and to endure the fatigues of war, in defense of the rights of mankind, and the good of your country."

"If the American Revolution is viewed as an essentially conservative uprising—a struggle not to create a new order but to restore and maintain ancient liberties and rights—then it found its perfect symbolic expression in the image of Washington."[11] A military leader of solid judgment and courage on the battlefield, he appeared in his time to be a perfectly balanced model of the sound character and virtue that reason required.[12] In sum, the general exemplified the virtues Americans wished to maintain as against the vices they condemned:

Self-sacrifice — Self-indulgence
Disinterest — Ambition
Moderation — Excess
Resoluteness and Self-control
Licentiousness
Piety — Religious Indifference [13]

A number of American generals have received overwhelming popular adulation for their military leadership and have been elected president; Washington, Jackson, Grant, and Eisenhower among the most prominent. Washington rightly stands at the head of the list. For the European romantic tradition, a leader's greatness is revealed through his stunning use of power; so Thomas Carlyle argued. Followers were expected to submit to the hero's commands because he had unusual traits of body and mind. Not so with Washington. By contrast, Napoleon Bonaparte, on his deathbed at St. Helena, sighed, "They wanted me to be another Washington."[14] In short, Napoleon lost as an emperor; Washington chose not to be one, Bonaparte thought ingloriously!

CHARACTER AND BEARING

Tall, broad-shouldered, and narrow-hipped, Washington's towering person was impressive, even as he often seemed severe and unapproachable. During the French and Indian War in which he fought as a young man alongside British troops, he was at times more courageous than wise. Still, his service under the mother country explains much about his later loyalties. It was in this war that he came to mistrust the English crown and parliament, and he saw English policies as a conspiracy to deprive Americans in the colonies of life, liberty, and property.

More than the English generals who opposed him, Washington

understood that the kind of resistance his fellow countrymen were engaged in was very different in pattern and style than that of European continental armies. When he came to command as a military leader, he refused to go into battle decisively and waited for the British to make their fatal mistake; the odds turned in his favor. The Battle of Yorktown was the only major military engagement he ever won; his American strategy had proved insightful and correct. In this situation, the qualities his countrymen admired became clear. He possessed steadfastness, judgment, and self-control.

What of his relations with women? Washington, as a young man, had been in love with Sally Fairfax, who served as his social tutor. More than a quarter century later, he wrote to her of "the recollection of those happy moments, the happiest in my life, which I have enjoyed with you."[15] But there was no sexual affair with Sally, who was already married when Washington knew her. Instead he courted and won the wealthy widow, Martha Custis. They were married on a snowy afternoon in January of 1759.[16] He was six feet three inches tall, a natural athlete, red-haired, and graceful in his movements. She was diminutive and barely reached to her husband's shoulder, had hazel eyes, and was round! She described herself as an "old-fashioned housekeeper, steady as a clock, busy as a bee, and cheerful as a cricket."[17]

RELIGION

Washington was a Republican, but not a Democrat of the Jefferson or Jackson populist type. He did not have the philosophical curiosity of a Jefferson. Nonetheless, during his presidency, he encouraged the intellectual and religious pluralism that leaders like Jefferson and Madison championed. As president, he attended worship and was friendly in his attitude toward Christian values.

David I. Holmes, writing in *The Faiths of the Founding Fathers*, argues that Washington was a Deist. "With only a few exceptions (which may or may not have stemmed from the work of pious assistants), Washington's speeches, orders, official letters, and other public communications on religion give a more or less uniform picture." Holmes concludes that Washington was a Deist; he did not apply such titles as Father, Lord, Redeemer, and Savior to God. Instead, he spoke in Deistic fashion of Providence, heaven, the Deity, the Supreme Being, the Divine Architect, the Author of all Good, and the Great Ruler of Events. Holmes also notes that the first president only infrequently referred to Christianity, and rarely to Jesus.[18]

Gary Scott Smith more discerningly describes Washington's position as one of Theistic Rationalism. "This 'hybrid belief system' mixes 'elements of natural religion, Christianity, and rationalism,' with rationalism serving as 'the predominant element.'"[19] Any conflict between the elements was to be resolved by reason. Washington believed that God was active in human affairs and that prayer was effectual. Smith points out that the first president held a higher view of the person of Jesus than deists and judged that revelation was designed to complement reason—a typically Anglican position. There was a good reason why Washington was never confirmed in the Church of England: there was no bishop of his communion in the colonies.

The first president premised an Enlightenment moral common sense deeper than any particular sectarian religious conviction—as well as what has since been called "civil religion." Still, as a Freemason, he did believe in deity and divine providence, and he linked morality and religion. As the French Revolution grew in violence, he clearly disassociated his new nation from its militant anti-religious stance. Not a Biblicist or daily Bible reader like many of his successors, he gave priority to conduct over belief and did not speak of Christ's resurrection or atonement in his general pronouncements. In his anthropology, the Virginia planter judged that all persons are motivated by selfish interests and love of power, and are prone to abuse. Toward the time of his death, he showed a stoic attitude at the same time that he resisted doctrines of personal annihilation. Once he described death as the grim king.

The general's convictions were expressed best and most explicitly in his two inaugural addresses and his Farewell Address. In these public pronouncements, Washington did not refer to Jesus Christ but rather to the Supreme Author of all Good, a great and all-knowing providence, wise and just. It was a creator more than a redeemer that provided the model for his piety. In the First Inaugural Address, April 30, 1789, the first president reflected: "No People can be bound to acknowledge and adore the invisible hand, which conducts the Affairs of men more than the People of the United States. Every step, by which they have advanced to the character of an independent nation, seems to have been distinguished by some token of providential agency."[20]

While he served as commander-in-chief during the Revolutionary War, Washington had asked the Continental Congress for support for chaplains for his army. In the field, he encouraged his soldiers to attend worship services, believing that religion discouraged swearing, drunkenness, and carousing. For his own part, he both drank whisky and enjoyed gambling at cards. When he became president, Washington received a stream of congratulatory messages from a variety of religious bodies and their leaders. He often replied warmly and sincerely, acknowledging the contribution that the diversity of religious groups made to the national life.

Of special note is the new president's recognition of his Jewish fellow citizens and appreciation for their religion. In August of 1790, Washington wrote to the Hebrew Congregation of the town of Newport, Rhode Island:

> *May the children of the Stock of Abraham, who dwell in this land, continue to merit and enjoy the good will of the other inhabitants, while every one shall sit in safety under his own vine and fig tree, and there shall be none to make him afraid. May the Father of all mercies scatter light and not darkness in our paths, and make us all in our several vocations useful here, and in his own due time and way everlastingly happy.*

Washington did not wish to exclude religion from public life as much as did Jefferson, and on at least one occasion, he did suggest that citizens perhaps ought to pay taxes for the services they receive from the church.[21] No doubt, he would be dismayed at the later turmoil of sectarian challenges today as well as the attempt (on the other side) to develop a naked public square devoid of religious influence.

President James Madison—himself trained in theology at Princeton—appraised Washington correctly retrospectively in 1830 by saying that he did not suppose that Washington had ever attended to the arguments for Christianity, and for the different systems of religion, or in fact that he had formed definite opinions on the subject.

"But he took these things as he found them existing, and was constant in his observations of worship according to the received forms of the Episcopal Church, in which he was brought up."[22]

PRO AND CON

Holmes's charge is still researched and debated—was the first president a Deist? Novak says no by asking, *what is a Deist?* "Deists have generally subscribed to most of the following propositions, and have ranged widely from Christian rationalists to atheists." Novak lists the following beliefs as characteristically Deist:

1. That one and only one God exists.

2. God has moral and intellectual virtues in perfection.

3. God's active powers are displayed in the world—divinely sanctioned natural laws, both moral and physical.

4. General providence.

5. No miracles, no special providence.

6. Humans have a rational nature, can know truth.

7. Natural law requires leading a moral life.

8. The purest form of worship is to do so.

9. Immortality of the soul—endowed by God.

10. Retributive justice after death.

11. Critical views of all other religious beliefs and practices.

According to Novak, Washington believed the following:[23]

1. History is open to human initiative, imagination, and action.

2. Good intentions do not guarantee good results.

3. Much depends, too, on the excellence and efficacy of human actions.

4. Providence is not fate, not mere fortune. It is personal.

5. Providence is sovereign over all things.

6. Providence is not ... of material composition, but spirit and truth.

7. God is benevolent, but he is also sovereign, a just Judge.

8. To each nation He assigns a mission.

9. The mission assigned to America is an experiment in the system of natural liberty, of immense consequence to the entire human race.

10. The experiment in the United States might fail .... The favor of God is not unconditional, although His capacity for forgiveness and reawakening is.

11. Americans should act according to God's law in order not to turn away his favor. [24]

James J. Ellis, writing in *His Excellency, George Washington*, observes: "Looking back over two hundred years of the American presidency, it seems safe to say that no one entered the office with more personal prestige than Washington, and only two presidents—Abraham Lincoln and Franklin Roosevelt—faced comparable crises."

In Ellis's judgment, Washington's core achievement while president was similar to what he had done as commander-in-chief of the Continental Army, transforming the improbable into the inevitable. The historian quotes a French nobleman, visiting Mount Vernon in 1791: "it is less difficult to discover the North West Passage than to create a people, as you have done."[25]

SLAVERY

Ellis comments that slavery was the proverbial "ghost at the banquet" at the Constitutional Convention.[26] Slavery, of course, raised religious as well as political considerations. In February 1790, two Quaker petitions, the second of which was signed by Franklin in his last public act, were sent to President Washington. The chief executive, for his part, believed slavery to be a political anachronism. On three occasions in the 1780s, he had let it be known that he favored adoption of some kind of a gradual emancipation scheme. Warner Milton, a Quaker who knew his views, obtained an audience with the president. Washington listened carefully and refused to commit himself, saying that the issue might come back to him from Congress. Although Washington never publicly condemned slavery, he did provide for the liberation of his personal slaves in his will.[27]

Ellis concludes that what seems to moderns to have been a poignant failure of moral leadership was, in Washington's eyes, a prudent exercise in political judgment. Retrospectively, the moral question takes precedence. It is true that the first president on occasion had given priority to right and wrong in speaking about it. Ellis's judgment as a historian, however, is that while a political officeholder, he was characteristically obsessed with control. In his thinking about slavery, he exhibited "a relentlessly realistic insistence that ideals per se must never define the agenda." Indeed, Washington associated the idealistic agenda he rejected with sentient illusions—like the belief that American virtue was sufficient to defeat Great Britain in the war, or that the French Revolution would succeed because it was a noble cause. His earliest apprehensions about slavery, after all, were more economic than moral, namely that it was an inefficient labor system, ill-suited for the kind of diversified farming he had begun to practice at Mount Vernon.[28]

The historian judges further: "As both a symbolic political center and a deft delegator of responsibility, Washington managed to levitate above the political landscape. That was his preferred position, personally because it removed the presidency from the ... partisan battles on the ground."[29]

Ellis is confident about his own judgment that Washington most elementally was an ethical realist. Even though republican in ideology, he was of the opinion that the behavior of nations is driven by interests and not ideals.[30] "There can be no greater error to expect, or calculate upon real favor from nation to nation. 'Tis an illusion which experience must cure which a just pride ought to disregard," he reflected.[31] Nations always have and will act on the basis of interest. For his own part, Washington abhorred disloyalty and personal criticism.

When the first president retired from public life, Tom Paine, the author of *Common Sense*—still resenting Washington's opposition to the French Revolution—wrote a letter to him that included a prayer for the leader's imminent death, and wondering out loud "whether the world will be puzzled to decide whether you are an apostate or an impostor, whether you have abandoned good principles, or whether you ever had any."[32] The contrast between the American and French revolutions as they touched religion remained outstanding for the first president.

Washington, for his part, concluded that freedom of conscience was a right, not a privilege. Religious liberty must be fought for, and on this premise, he supported the movement for separation of church and state. Popularly, Washington's elevated person soon became part of the code, creed, and cultus of his nation's civil religion. He was revered as holding a place comparable with that of the biblical Moses. Actually, there was little secularism in the ethos of Virginia in Washington's time. In his version of Christian culture, hopefulness was supported by religious belief. He was convinced that Republicanism (as contrasted with populist Democracy) was the wave of the future, with attendant ecclesiastical consequences. In the closing years of his life, there was general foreboding in the nation about the religious anarchy that accompanied the French Revolution. Today, after the tragedies and nihilism of the twentieth century, Nazism, communism, and the rise of militant Islam, he would still adhere to faith in God.

THOMAS JEFFERSON

Will Obama prove to be a liberal, following in the Enlightenment pattern of Thomas Jefferson? Jefferson, author of the Declaration of Independence, was a unique pioneer, a champion of tolerance whom Obama memorializes for his many-sided contributions to democracy. Most important, the third president led in bringing about the separation of church and state. While chief executive, the Virginian was less successful than he had been as a revolutionary leader. When he left office after two terms, the country's economy was endangered and the international tensions that led to the War of 1812 were growing. Jefferson's most lasting achievement in the White House, many historians judge, was the negotiation of the Louisiana Purchase. By contrast, Obama is not an Enlightenment rationalist thinker, even though he holds great hope for the future. Rather, he is a careful lawyer realist whose life philosophy is much more carefully structured than that of Jefferson. The Founding Father's thought was like his house in Monticello, made up of assorted parts that never quite fit together logically. Obama is a mainline Christian, less optimistic than Enlightenment philosophers, more conscious of sin and salvation. Most of all, his heritage is African American, one that would probably have found him as slave if he had lived in North America in Jefferson's time.

THE APOSTLE OF LIBERTY

"When in the course of human events it becomes necessary for one people to dissolve the political bonds which have connected them with another, and to assume among the powers of the earth the separate & equal station to which the laws of nature and of nature's God entitle them."[1] These words from the preamble to the Declaration of Independence were written by Thomas Jefferson. On his tombstone, Jefferson asked to have inscribed the following words: "Author of the Declaration of American Independence, Of the Statute of Virginia for Religious Freedom, and Father of the University of Virginia." Together he regarded these two documents as embodying his greatest achievements.

As early as his draft for a constitution for Virginia in 1776, Jefferson proposed that "all persons shall have full and free liberty of religious opinion: nor shall any be compelled to frequent or maintain any religious institution." Tolerance was to be extended, to "the Jew, the Mahometan, and the Hindoo."[2] It was in the State of Virginia Act for Establishing Religious Freedom, passed by the legislature in 1786, that he set forth his conviction most firmly: "Almighty God hath created the mind free, and [willed] that free it shall remain." To attempt to enforce religious uniformity by "temporal punishments" or "civil incapacitations" is doomed to failure. It violates God's plan, "setting up fallible and uninspired men, civil as well as ecclesiastical in dominion over the faith of others," maintaining "false religions over the greatest part of the world and through all time, and resulted not in true agreement but in hypocrisy and meanness."[3]

Little would have been achieved in practice, however, had not Jefferson and Madison worked intensively to establish the highly revolutionary ideas of religious tolerance and freedom of conscience in their native state. While the Colonial Army under Washington was fighting for independence, they battled for more than political liberty. Of course, it would be simplistic to suppose that religious liberty was enacted into law in the new nation simply for abstract theoretical reasons. Diversity in the thirteen colonies was so great that any attempt to impose religious uniformity would have led to protracted civil strife.

It was not just questions of polity that engaged Jefferson. The

Enlightenment philosopher who led the fight for religious liberty saw himself as pre-eminently a man of conscience. For him, nothing was to be gained by the victory of the strong if they were immoral. Ever since the Emperor Constantine's acceptance of Christianity, the Founding Fathers knew, kings and other rulers had supported religion in the union of throne and altar. Following the Reformation, peace was established on the condition that the religion of the prince was to be the religion of the realm. Not only were Christian churches supported by the state with worldly goods and power, but there were legal penalties against heretics, even at times to the point of death. Wars were fought over religion, and rivers of blood had flowed over the centuries, Jefferson observed. All this was to belong to the past in the new United States.

ENLIGHTENMENT

Jefferson's outlook (like that of most of the other Founding Fathers) was premised on Enlightenment confidence in reason and nature, including nature's God. Bacon, Newton, and Locke were his mentors. A collector of books since his college days, he read widely, far beyond law, which was his profession, and was sensitive to the new and growing world of science. The third president of the United States reflected retrospectively in 1809, "Nature intended me for the tranquil pursuits of science, by rendering them my supreme delight. But the enormities of the times in which I have lived have forced me to take a part in resisting them, and to commit myself on the boisterous ocean of political passions."[4] Together, reason and nature attested to order and meaning in the world of God's creation. It was reason and not revelation (the latter was unnecessary) that yielded universal moral norms. Nature itself was not blind, tooth and claw, but in Jefferson's pre-Darwinian view, structured and purposeful.

It is not too much to say that Jefferson (along with Franklin) most of all among the Founding Fathers embodied the Enlightenment paradigm *par excellence*. His religious heritage was that of the Church of England, and he studied at the Anglican College of William and Mary. At this small institution, which he entered in 1760, it was the teaching of the professor of mathematics, Dr. William Small, who came from Scotland—the only non-clergyman among his teachers—that awakened him intellectually. A wider world opened before the young man as he became aware of the ferment that was going on among European intellectuals. From Small, Jefferson recalled, "I got my first views of the expansion of science, and of the system of things in which we are placed." When Small returned to Scotland, Jefferson read law with another faculty member, George Wythe, also a stimulating teacher and intellectual.

PERSONA

The young lawyer, standing six feet two inches tall and having red hair, began his practice of law and then was elected to the Virginia House of Burgesses. He entered the national scene when he was sent to the Continental Congress in Philadelphia. From 1784 to 1789, he represented the United States as its Minister in Paris. In France, he collected more books; his world view expanded as he encountered European culture directly. He was able to see firsthand the developments that led to the French Revolution.

Not caring for ceremony and not a moving public speaker, Jefferson rarely appeared in public during his time in the White House. However, as his colleagues in the Continental Congress recognized, he wrote brilliantly. A significant part of his influence as chief executive came from his ability as an effective political operator who often worked behind the scenes. His ability in this respect has been matched subsequently by very few of his successors, among them most notably Franklin Roosevelt.

Winning only the vice presidency in 1796, Jefferson was elected to the highest office in the land and began his two-term tenure in 1800. He saw his own elevation to the presidency as a victory for democracy and popular government; it was a step beyond 1776. "The Revolution of 1800 was as real a revolution in the principles of our government as that of 1776 in its form."[5] Jefferson's model was one of a republic of farmers; small towns and not cities. His differences with the Federalists, Hamilton and Adams, had become devastatingly sharp. Opponents labeled him a revolutionary, an anarchist, and an infidel. A Jeffersonian victory on Election Day could only accelerate unbelief, social chaos, and immorality, they argued.[6]

To say the least, Jefferson was slow in seeing what was coming in the course of the French Revolution.[7] The English historian Paul Johnson reflects: "He is fascinating because of the range of his activities, the breadth of his imaginative insights, and the fertility of his inventions. But his inconsistencies are insurmountable ...; he was a passionate idealist, to some extent indeed an intellectual puritan, but at the same time a sybarite, an art-lover, and a fastidious devotee of all life's luxuries."[8] In a biography entitled *American Sphinx,* Joseph E. Ellis argues that Jefferson no longer has the unambiguously high place as a Democrat that liberal historians earlier gave him. Four successive waves of thought have challenged his highly individualistic outlook— the Civil War, the closing of the frontier, the New Deal. and the cold war. "The third president's ideal of small town rural America had long since been displaced!"[9]

At the same time, Ellis acknowledges that only Jefferson among the revolutionary generation of political thinkers premised individual sovereignty, then attempted to develop government prescriptions for the protection of individual rights. This fact alone was enough to make him a giant in the land. "For better and for worse," the biographer concludes, "American political discourse is phrased in Jeffersonian terms as a conversation about sovereign individuals."[10]

What of Jefferson's family and sexual ethics? Like his predecessor, Washington, and a later successor who claimed his legacy, Jackson, he held slaves and did not always treat them benevolently. Jefferson had been widowed early in his career, in 1782, and did not remarry. Whether his alleged long-term sexual liaison with his slave woman, Sally Hemings, ever took place is debated by historians to the present; probably it did. It was a scandal made public by James Callender even while Jefferson was in the White House. Callender, himself of morally dubious reputation, had correctly reported Alexander Hamilton's affair with Maria Reynolds, a married woman.

What, if anything, went on in the case of the third president is less evident. Sally Hemings was in Europe with him, and he was at Monticello nine months before most of her pregnancies. A possible explanation is that it was Jefferson's nephew, Peter Carr, who fathered her mulatto offspring. Although Jefferson early in his career opposed slavery, his treatment later in life of some of his slaves—for example,

James Hubbard, whom he allowed to be severely beaten—has darkened his record. Did his accommodation to slavery and his sensuality blur his record as a believer in liberty?

The contemporary question is what remains of Jefferson's legacy of liberty—invoked by Jackson and Lincoln as well as Franklin Roosevelt, Reagan, and the two Bush presidents? The answer is—as these presidents recognized—that his model of civic virtue has ideological power to the present. Jefferson understood much better than most of his contemporaries, that freedom of religion is a foundational right without which all other claims for liberty, sooner or later, are compromised. Actually, he corresponded about his most intimate religious views in a guarded way and only with a few close friends and family. Jefferson, the religious liberal, believed theistically that God is the sustainer and director of the universe, not just creator and author of law and order. There was no gloomy existentialism about him, no search for theodicy.

THE PRESIDENT'S BELIEFS

Personally, Jefferson engaged in private prayer with the conviction that 1. There is one only God, and He is all-perfect. 2. That there is a future state of rewards and punishments. 3. That to love God with all thy heart and thy neighbor as thyself, is the sum or religion.[19] In his old age, Jefferson assured John Adams that in death, the true, immortal "essence" of the human individual would "ascend to an ecstatic meeting with the friends we have loved and lost .and shall love and never lose again." Both men died on the same day, July 4, 1826, a half century after the Declaration of Independence was signed.[11]

Described (unfairly) by his enemies as a howling atheist whom God surely would not allow to sit as head of the nation, Jefferson is an indispensable figure in American religious history. Praised by admirers as a Renaissance man, he did not draw back from championing criticism and innovation. The American historian Edwin S. Gaustad sums up his outreach by saying that he read widely in religious literature even while he denounced metaphysical and philosophical speculation as useless. "Religion mesmerized, tantalized, alarmed and sometimes inspired Jefferson."[12] Taught to pray by his mother, he read the Bible daily (in Latin and Greek) and prayed before bedtime. The third president attended church more often than Washington. Gary Scott Smith judges that Jefferson's faith was more a matter of the head than of the heart, in particular because he accepted Locke's empiricism.[13]

Critically, Gary Smith identifies the grounds on which the third president considered himself a theist: He not only premised a first cause that had produced the universe. Optimistically, he believed God had so constructed the universe that liberty would continually expand. Jefferson's deism, however, was evident in his denial of the Trinity. Breaking with orthodoxy in his anthropology, he repudiated the concept of the fall—but regretted that all people had elements of depravity. Still with deep conviction, he affirmed divine providence. The Great Ruler of the universe dispenses evenhanded justice, including a future state of rewards and punishments.

In a primitivist strain, the Virginian wanted most of all to go back to the plain and unsophisticated precepts of Christ. Smith notes that Gaustad views him as a religious reformer who wanted to substitute "morals for mystery, the unity of God for the Trinity, cosmic justice for the chaos of parochial self-interest."[14] Creeds, Jefferson believed, had been the bane and ruin of the Christian Church. Neoplatonism, Athanasius, and Calvin in particular were his targets. His conviction was that future life-after-death state depends on present action and not belief. Smith points out critically that Jefferson's own materialistic philosophy conflicted with his belief in life after death.

Smith concludes that Jefferson made his own synthesis of Lockean liberalism, Scottish common-sense realism, classical republicanism, and Christianity. The third president had significant reservations about Locke, however. Impressed by the moral philosophy of Francis Hutcheson, he took a communal approach as against Locke's "unbridled individualism," the historian concludes.[15] Jefferson's moralism was explicit: "Our Maker has given every person a conscience, as a 'faithful internal monitor.' Moral duties are [as] obligatory on nations as on individuals. It is strangely absurd to suppose that a million human beings, collected together, are not under the same moral laws which bind them separately."[16]

Paul K. Conkin, writing critically in *The Religious Pilgrimage of Thomas Jefferson*, emphasizes that the colonial North America in which

Jefferson lived was a largely Christian society; he was not, in fact, a secularist. "Religious issues were so pervasive and so important in his life that any ignorance of them precludes any holistic or undistorted understanding of either his character or his thought .... He spent a lifetime agonizing about the foundations of morality."[17]

Jefferson's methodological interest as an Enlightenment philosopher was in what Conkin calls the first level of religious substructure, natural theology premised on design in nature and the human mind. The second level of Christian superstructure—Christology, soteriology, ecclesiology, Conkin is convinced, he did not find believable. Simply put, "he repudiated Christian dogma and revealed religion but not the category of religion."[18] Jefferson "believed that most of the content in all revealed religions was irrational, but that his minimalist belief in a creative and providential and moral judgmental God was rational."

Conkin's analysis is that Jefferson in his criticism used the word "rational" in a number of different ways: Internal coherence as opposed to logical inconsistency, (God singular and unified). Also, verifiable cognitive propositions, clear enough to be tested by evidence—as in his view scripture was not. He believed that all references to a realm of pure mind or spirit—generally attributed to Plato, for example—are not negotiable.[19] Of course, his convictions had a history and developed over time.

Practically, Conkin argues, the seer of Monticello saw the highest goal of religion as the support of righteousness. Although superstition might remain widespread among the populace, he himself would find a different basis in conscience. As the authority of monarchs and priestly hierarchies receded in the face of Enlightenment rationalism, the Republican would replace them with conscience and self-discipline. Conkin observes that Jefferson believed that he was affirming the oldest, simplest forms of pure Christianity and opposing an impure Platonized religion. Where did the metaphysical materialism and corporealism that he espoused in attacking Platonism come from? His teachers included Joseph Priestly and Destrutt de Tracy among contemporaries, earlier Bolingbroke, and in antiquity, Epicurus. Against this background, he developed what Conkin describes as a theistic essentialism from his reading of Locke, Milton, and Shaftsbury. Jefferson was especially outspoken against the self-serving mystifications of priests and their schemes of salvation.

SOURCES

Jefferson learned about Unitarianism firsthand while he represented the new United States diplomatically in England and France. In London, the Virginian met Richard Price, a Unitarian minister, and personally attended some of his worship services. It was Price who helped acquaint Jefferson with Joseph Priestly, a fellow Unitarian clergyman who was also the discoverer of oxygen. Priestly had collaborated with Franklin in studying electricity. Jefferson read Priestly's 1782 tome on *The History of Corruptions in the Church,* and at the time of his own inauguration as vice president at Philadelphia in 1797, heard Priestly preach in the city.

Priestly was born in England in 1733 of Puritan dissenter parents, and because of his non-conformist religion, could not attend a major university in Great Britain. As a compensation, he turned to mathematics and natural philosophy. Not only was Priestly the first researcher to isolate oxygen, he also wrote the first history of electricity. While this was going on, he also composed a four-volume *History of Early Opinions Concerning Jesus Christ.* Not surprisingly, he sympathized with the French Revolution. While he was the pastor in Birmingham of the largest dissenting congregation in the country, his church, home, and laboratory were burned by a mob in 1790. To its credit, the city government in Birmingham actually paid him for some of the damages. Nonetheless, he decided to move to North America, and settled with his two sons in Northumberland, Pennsylvania in 1794, where he was greeted as a hero and martyr.

Jefferson found much to agree with in his friend's preaching and writing, although it is not fully clear how much of it he really understood. Priestly sided with early Judaism, in opposition to the Greek concept of a separate soul. Moreover, he believed in a wholly human rather than divine Messiah. Speaking of the Bible as the Word of God, Priestly was fascinated, as was Newton, with apocalypticism. Jefferson, by contrast, wanted a more rational universal standard. Conkin is right that Jefferson's reliance upon natural theology—the first level of his religious structure—was already crumbling in the larger intellectual world, more than he realized already in his lifetime.

Peter S. Onuf points out how much Jefferson hated priests who combine with "the magistrates to divide the spoils of the people" and are a barrier to republican progress.[20] In spite of religious liberty in the new United States, he feared that separation of church and state was not complete. Jefferson, for his part, presupposed connection between religious piety and republican virtue. His friend Benjamin Rush had told him, "I have always considered Christianity as the strong ground of Republicanism. It is only necessary for Republicanism to ally itself to the Christian Religion, to overturn all the corrupted political and religious institutions in the world." Jefferson believed that the clergy were almost always ambitious for political power. Still, after he returned home from France, he became concerned not only with a wall of separation between church and state but more positively with religious questions.

In short, Jefferson saw himself as a true Christian. "I am a real Christian, that is to say, a disciple of the doctrines of Jesus, very different from the Platonists, who call me infidel, and themselves Christians and preachers of the gospel, while they draw all their characteristic dogmas from what its Author never said nor saw."[21] His interpretation was that the Jesus of history saw himself as a reformer who brought the Jews "to the principles of true deism, and justice notions of the attributes of God, to reform their moral doctrines to the standard of reason, justice & philanthropy, and to inculcate the belief of a future state." Rejecting what he judged to be the blind faith of ordinary Christians, he would return to Jesus's intention "to reinstate natural religion, & and by diffusing the light of his morality, to teach us to govern ourselves."[22]

AUTHORITY OF PRIESTS SHATTERED

Onuf calls attention to Jefferson's self-imposed silence on religion in what he regarded as a very private matter and the progress he expected once it was freed from priestcraft and Platonism.

Onuf writes: "It was unthinkable to Jefferson that either republicanism or Christianity, stripped of their worldly corruptions, could provide fertile ground for the consolidation and expansion of the institution of slavery, although this is the best recent historiography." Onuf cites Charles F. Irons's research on "The Spiritual Fruits of Revolution: Disestablishment and the Rise of the Virginia Baptists."[23] He is convinced that Jefferson was not as far out of touch with contemporary developments as many recent historians have believed. Onuf writes further:

> *Our culture wars are not those of Jefferson's time, and not only because the real threat of religious establishments then [in Jefferson's time] still loomed so large. Faithful Christians of Jefferson's day did not cherish a sense of alienation or victimhood in the larger "secular" culture, nor did they define "faith" as against "science."*[24]

Onuf argues rather that the common ground that Jefferson proposed for republican Christians was not based on evangelical faith. He believed contrariwise that enlightened religionists, rejecting archaic and exclusive tests, needed to prove that republicanism and Christianity were compatible. Practically downplaying doctrinal tests, evangelical leaders of the Second Great Awakening often supported Jefferson's outlook.[25] The third president's major target remained "the reciprocal corruption of religion and politics in church establishments"—in short, unholy alliances with the state. He attacked theological mystifications with their leaps of faith, the renunciation of reason, and the abnegation of self. In terms of today's contemporary discussion of religion and politics, he was unsympathetic and temperamentally hostile to revivalist ideas. In the longer historical view, what was important is that he lived in an era in which traditional beliefs were being rethought.

Granted that the modern notion of the United States as a "Christian nation" would have appalled Jefferson, Onuf argues, still in part he bore responsibility for it in some measure. He sought most of all the autonomy of human persons, not a plurality of sects. His republican beliefs premised the individual's free and enlightened consent.[26]

Onuf concludes that it is only possible to construe Jefferson's beliefs as offering inspiration to modern advocates of the "Christian nation" theocracy by ignoring his republican faith as well as his abiding belief in the inevitable progress of reason and science.[27] Most of all the third president would be amazed at later anti-science sentiments. He wished for an enlightened democratic nation, not one of unreasoning faith! " Jefferson the self-professed 'Christian' who rejected the faith of the fathers, speaks to us in (at least) two voices, one ebulliently confident in a glorious Christian future, the other chronically anxious about assaults on individual liberty and autonomy, ever alert about the dangers of priestcraft."[28]

JEFFERSON'S TESTIMONY

Jefferson, seeking to hang on to a providential God of history and rewards in heaven, was explicit:

I hold the precepts of Jesus, as delivered by himself, to be the most pure, benevolent, and sublime which have ever been preached to man. I adhere to the principles of the first age, and consider all subsequent innovations as corruptions of his religion, having no foundation in what came from him. The metaphysical insanities of Athanasius, of Loyola, and of Calvin are to my understanding, mere relapses into polytheism, differing from paganism only by being more unintelligible. The religion of Jesus is founded on the Unity of God, and this principle chiefly, gave it triumph over the rabble of heathen gods then acknowledged. Thinking men of all nations rallied readily to the doctrine of one only God, and embraced it with the pure morals which Jesus inculcated. If the freedom of religion, guaranteed to us by law in theory, can ever rise in practice under the overbearing inquisition of public opinion, truth will prevail over fanaticism, and the genuine doctrines of Jesus, so long perverted by his pseudo-priests, will again be restored to their original purity. This reformation will advance with the other improvements of the human mind too late for me to witness it.[29]

Historically, it remains overwhelmingly clear that without the third president's curiosity and non-conformism of the heart, the American religious scene would have been much less creative and vital. Without his dissent intellectually, the evangelical revival of the nineteenth century would have been hemmed in by state control and might never have taken place. Jefferson's ethics must be seen in relation to the cataclysmic changes of the French Revolution. An older established order was overthrown, its leaders exiled or killed. The reign of terror was followed by the reign of Napoleon until his final defeat at Waterloo. The American Revolution was of a different sort, more Protestant and not anti-clerical. The English statesman Burke was not mistaken when he described it as a struggle for the rights of Englishmen. The old order of church and state, which Jefferson contested in North America, was not as entrenched as in Catholic France after the revocation of the Edict of Nantes; there was already pluralism of a limited sort as colonization progressed. Jefferson and Madison spoke realistically to problems; they did not just proclaim ideals. As a philosopher, Jefferson's zeal for science was magnificent. Still he never put his view of reality altogether as a system. His unfinished home building at Monticello symbolizes what went on in his questing, secular and religious. He was truly an educator of the nation as well as an adroit politician of integrity and conviction.

ABRAHAM LINCOLN

Obama praises and admires President Abraham Lincoln. But Lincoln was not a mainline Christian, although he ranks among the most religiously sensitive of all presidents as the Great Emancipator. Influenced by biblical prophetic insights, and knowing Scripture as well as Shakespeare in detail, he came to believe in human rights and condemned slavery. But he still was not sure that black and white could live together peacefully in the United States. Lincoln speculated about and at times advocated African colonization for liberated blacks. His moral genius was his ability to balance together a variety of values which at times conflicted, saving the Union and freeing the slaves. How effective he would have been if he had not been assassinated and had been able to serve out his second term is not known. One of the most insightful and authentically religious of all presidents, he remained a seeker. Obama shares some of the humility and authenticity that characterized his predecessor whom he seeks to emulate.

"I shall be most happy indeed if I shall be an humble instrument in the hands of the Almighty, and of this his almost chosen people." New Jersey legislators, February 21, 1861[1]

"We shall nobly save, or meanly lose, the last hope of earth."[2]

HISTORY AND MYTH: WHAT KIND
OF MAN WAS LINCOLN?

An evaluation from Reinhold Niebuhr: "Analysis of the religion of Abraham Lincoln in the context of the traditional religion of his time and place and of its polemical use on the slavery issue, which corrupted religious life in the days before and during the Civil War, must lead to the conclusion that Lincoln's religious convictions were superior in depth and purity to those, not only of the political leaders of his day, but of the religious leaders of the era."[3]

Elton Trueblood offered a reason for this judgment: Lincoln "could not abide the kind of religion which made a man interested only in the salvation of his own soul without any reference to human injustice, such as that of slavery. Lincoln had no admiration for citizens whose religion was political and nothing more." Trueblood concludes that although Jefferson was Lincoln's mentor in political philosophy, the Civil War president's perspective was the more concrete politically. The tragedy of his times required him to probe more deeply than self-evident truths "endowed by their Creator."[4]

Trueblood divides Lincoln's life into four chapters. The first ended and the second began in 1841, when he was thirty-two years of age, a time of change. The second included his time of broken engagement to Mary Todd, whom he later married, and it lasted for two decades, until he left for Washington and the White House. Trueblood divides his time in the presidency into a first and second part, the watershed being in the year 1862. What is important is how much the wartime president grew and developed in his spiritual insights.

Lincoln could not have brought the North to victory, saving the Union, if he had not been recognized as a leader with religious integrity. A thoughtful moralist, he was prepared to compromise when necessary—but not to rationalize away principle. There were too many causes to be kept together for anything else to be the case—abolitionism and saving the Union, for example.

President Lincoln's mythical elevation grew with Northern victory and then took off following his assassination. Pious eulogy pictured him ascending to heaven to join George Washington. The poet Walt Whitman offered a more "this-worldly" idolization when he wrote of the wartime president's "perfect composure and coolness—his unusual and uncouth height, his dress of complete black, stovepipe hat pushed back on the head, dark-brown complexion, seam'd and wrinkled yet canny-looking face, black, bush head of hair, disproportionately long neck, and his hands held behind him as he stood observing the people."[5]

Nathaniel Hawthorne pointed to the lasting stuff of dreams: "The whole physiognomy is as coarse a one as you would meet anywhere in the length and breadth of the state." He credited Lincoln with a great deal of native sense, no bookish cultivation, no refinement; honest at heart. Yet he found that and in some sly way he was "endowed with a sort of tact and wisdom that are akin to craft ... I like this sallow, queer, sagacious visage, with the homely human sympathies that warmed it ..."[6]

What of the Lincoln of history—the ethical realist? His wife Mary in the end evaluated her husband as an awkward but righteous statesman: "He was mild in his manner, but a terrible firm man when he set his foot down. I could always tell when, in deciding anything, he had reached his ultimatum. At first he was very cheerful, then he lapsed into thoughtfulness, bringing his lips together in a firm compression. When these symptoms developed, I fashioned myself accordingly, and so did all others have to do, sooner or later."[7]

Historians have a variety of reports about the president-to-be from the decade before he went to Washington and the White House. To Lawyer Whitney, for example, he appeared to have the air of "an ordinary farmer," a little slovenly, who for ten years wore the same short coat he had bought in Washington in 1849.

To Charles W. Marsh, a farmer and manufacturer of agricultural machinery who attended the Lincoln-Douglas debate at Ottawa, he was dressed simply in a suit of traditional cut with the air of "a kindly old fashioned, professional man who was making a good living but putting on no style." There was a paradoxical double image: Lincoln was a high-priced lawyer who often worked for the railroads and was among the most expensive in his profession. While on the circuit with ordinary people, he would whittle some wooden pegs with a pocketknife, pegs that he used to hold up his suspenders. Then he would launch into analysis of a document or into a plea couched in the "vocabulary of the people."[8]

What was clear from an early stage of Lincoln's career was that he had high intelligence and a remarkable memory. William Herndon, his law partner in Springfield, Illinois, described the president-to-be as follows: "He had no system, no order; he did not keep a clerk; he had neither library nor index, nor cash-book. When he made notes, he would throw them into a drawer, put them in his vest-pocket, or into his hat ... But in the inner man, symmetry and method prevailed. He did not need an orderly office, did not need pen and ink, because his workshop was in his head."

Eight months of the year, Lincoln the lawyer lived on Eighth Street in Springfield with his wife, in a modest but spacious and well-furnished house. The Lincolns gave lovely parties for Springfield society. The other four months of the year, he rode the "mud circuit" along the rutted and swampy roads, traveling in his buggy. At night he slept at an overflowing inn; the rooms were cold, roofs leaked, and there were bugs. People slept two to a bed, eight in a room; meals were not good. In the evening, Lincoln and accepted friends might meet in Judge Davis's court, generally at a back parlor. Present were the judge and his cronies, along with doctors, bankers, merchants, journalists, and prosperous farmers from the area—a mirror of the Illinois bourgeoise.[9] Here law and politics came together. Actually, the cream of coming Illinois leaders could be found on the circuit, sharing common thoughts and interests about harvests, investments, and natural calamities. "Illinois politicians were born in this fish pond of local worthies, landed proprietors, cattle raisers, doctors, schoolmasters, and, always and above all, lawyers who crowded into David Davis's 'orgmathorian' courts and into Masonic lodges."[10]

SLAVERY

In January of 1821, Thomas Jefferson wrote to John Adams about slavery: "The real question, as seen in the states afflicted with this unfortunate population, is, are our slaves to be presented with freedom and a dagger .... Are we then to see again Athenian and Lacedemonian confederation? To wage another Peloponnesian war to settle the ascendancy between them?" Slavery, Jefferson argued, had hung over the country like a black cloud for half a century. If he was as drunk with enthusiasm as Swedenborg or Wesley, he most likely would have seen armies of Negroes marching and countermarching in shining armor, he speculated, so terrified he was what was happening. "What are we to see, God knows, and I leave it to him, and his agents in posterity."[11] Religious enthusiasm, superstition and irrationality seemed to be largely all the same thing to the two former presidents.

Having served a term in the House of Representatives in Washington, it became clear all too soon to Lincoln that neither political compromise nor religious revivalism in the end could resolve the moral dilemma of the era, slavery.[12] Apologists on both sides quoted scripture. The president-to-be witnessed before his eyes the ties between North and South breaking down in the struggle about an institution that by all civilized standards was archaic. The appraisal is fair that unlike so many other politicians in North America and Europe (Emperor Napoleon III and Bismarck were his contemporaries) Lincoln did not seek power for its own sake. He entered politics in the end from a compulsive sense of duty rather than ambition as such, as he was convinced that slavery was an evil that uniquely threatened the United States.[13]

"Lincoln was conscious of great powers—had an inescapable duty to use them in the Union's defense."[14] His initial attack on slavery was legal and ethical, not religious in Greeley's sense; in short, he was not a crusader. He did believe, however, that the institution of slavery corrupted the slave owner and was morally destroying the South. Still he remembered what a Kentuckian had once told him: "You might have any amount of land, money in your pocket, or bank stock, and while traveling around nobody would be any the wiser. But if you have a darky trudging at your heels, everybody would see him and know you owned a slave. It is the most glittering property in the world."[15]

The young, successful lawyer aligned himself morally with future-looking forces, religious and economic, and the industrial power of the North in the end proved decisive in the war over which he presided. His own political party (originally), the Whigs, joined with evangelical Protestantism and European liberalism in appealing to reason and the economic rationalism of the market. Jefferson's rural America and its Southern slave culture held no promise for the future in Lincoln's view.

Still loyal to Whig ideas, Lincoln was called upon to give the adjournment convention speech at Bloomington, Illinois when the new Republican Party met there in May of 1856; along with his Cooper Union speech in New York city, it has been described as his best before becoming president. His law partner Herndon recalled: "His speech was full of fire and energy and force. It was logic. It was pathos,. It was enthusiasm. It was justice, equity, truth and right set alight by the divine fires of a soul maddened by the wrong. It was hard, heavy, knotty, gnarly, backed with wrath."[16]

During the Lincoln-Douglas debates, in August to October 1858, Lincoln made his case. Both men were candidates for the Senate. Douglas traveled dramatically by special train or coach, with a truck and field gun behind. In the election, he won the Senate seat but lost the presidency two years later. Central to Lincoln's argument was the fact that his opponent was never really prepared to say where he stood on slavery. It was Douglas's pantomime-horse approach that Lincoln attacked, destroying the politician's future career.

As a Whig, Lincoln had been committed to constitutional rights and a balanced government with limited executive power. His own policy turned out to be a very different one in the wartime emergency. Political scientist Clinton Rossiter characterized Lincoln's regime as a "constitutional dictatorship." In the course of the war, the president assumed far-reaching powers, some of which, in retrospect, appear to be in violation of the Constitution. He acted without prior consultation with Congress when he believed it necessary.

At the same time, it must be said that coming to the White House with a war to win, Lincoln combined humility with assertiveness and self-confidence. He exhibited a remarkable ability to weather the nastiness of politics without turning sour or striking back. Morally, he was inspired by a deep love of the Union as an almost religious ideal, rather than by abolitionism. Lincoln respected Jefferson but did not believe him to have been a strong president; Jackson and Polk he did not respect. The problems in Washington's time he judged to have been very different than in his own.

LINCOLN'S ETHICS AND RELIGION

Lincoln's attitude toward the presidency was summarized in a story to which he resorted when asked how it felt to be the chief executive of the nation. He told the tale of a man who was tarred and feathered and ridden out of town on a rail. When someone asked him how he liked it, he responded, "If it were not for the honor of the thing, I'd much rather walk." For Lincoln, the presidency was not a pleasant task. In the end, he would reflect, "I dreamt of power and glory, and all I have are blood and ashes."[17]

Seeking as a philosopher to clarify the wartime president's ethics, Ethan Fishman claims for him the classical virtue of prudence—in a tradition that dates from Aristotle, Thomas Aquinas, and Edmund Burke. Fishman points out that Aristotle made prudence (practical wisdom—*phonesis*) the archetypal moral virtue, and compares Lincoln's refusal of an absolutist abolitionism (that would end slavery and destroy the union) to Burke's rejection of the French philosophers who advocated violent revolution.[18]

What this means in contemporary terms can be brought up to date by reference to the categories of Max Weber.[19] Weber did not speak of prudence as much as of a dualism between a day-by-day morality of duty and a more far-reaching and inclusive morality of conscience. By a morality of duty, he referred to the continuing daily decisions that fall on political leaders, including presidents; perfection is not to be expected. Discharge of these responsibilities involves both power and compromise; Lincoln found this to be the case even in the midst of civil war.

On the other hand, Weber distinguished as well a morality of conscience, one that he judged to be indispensable in public life. Here imagination and wisdom are imperative. In speaking of a morality of conscience, Weber looked to a larger world view, for example, the principles of human rights, dignity, and self-government subsumed under the rubric of liberty and equality. An ethic of conscience, in the case of Lincoln, looked beyond compromise and refused to give up the right. With respect to both types of morality, duty and conscience, Weber believed that state power, including the use of force, is needed—as Lincoln found in the struggle to save the Union. The moral imperative is to act responsibly and to avoid the utopian fallacy.

Smith argues that Lincoln compellingly articulated the meeting of evangelicalism, republicanism, and common sense that had become the nation's world view and value system. "More than any other nineteenth century president, he became known for seeking to base public politics on scriptural principles and as a 'Christian' chief executive."[20] Smith also credits Lincoln with playing a pivotal role in the development of American civil religion. As he sought to discern the religious meaning of the Civil War, the president returned to an old theme in his early background and premised that God predestined events.

For biographers, there remain questions about the earlier pre-presidential Lincoln. William Herndon, Lincoln's law partner, said that he had never heard him utter any of the pieties that were attributed to him. Following the president's death, the Springfield associate spent years researching the matter. Joshua Wolf Shenk, writing in *Lincoln's Melancholy, How Depression Challenged a President and Fueled His Greatness,* reports: "Lincoln was raised in the thick of Old School Calvinism. In Kentucky and Indiana, his parents belonged to a fire-breathing sect called Separate Baptism, in which congregants heard—in the tradition of Jonathan Edwards's famous sermon 'Sinners in the Hands of an Angry God'—that they were bound for eternal hellfire, and nothing they could do or say or think would change their fate."

Frontier preachers were willing to allow that a saved elect had been foreordained by God for grace before the world began for salvation. One evangelist put the matter: "Long before the morning stars sang together… the Almighty looked down upon the ages yet unborn, as it were, in review before him, and selected one here and another there to enjoy eternal life and left the rest to the blackness of darkness forever. Lincoln for his part rejected such an 'out-Calvining of Calvin.'" When he left the rural life, he left religion as well.[21]

Records show that the Lincoln family belonged to the Little Pigeon Creek Baptist Church, which had been organized in 1816. Among Abraham's first scribblings was the Calvinist hymn, "Time what an empty vapor 'tis, and days how swift they are, swift as an Indian arrow fly, or like a shooting star."[22] In later life, Lincoln insisted to his campaign biographer, John Locke Scripps of the *Chicago Tribune,* that he came from nowhere. His early life could be "condensed into a single sentence from Gray's Eulogy, 'The short and simple annals of the poor.'"

As a young man, he had been forced to farm, as his family lacked money. But his father, Thomas, needed him for only four months a year, so he was "rented out" for the rest of the year. Actually, the relation between father and son was not cordial. Abraham lived in a different world and wished to escape from this setting. Young Lincoln had curiosity, intelligence, extraordinary energy, and insatiable ambition to move on. His way out was not that of alcohol; he did not turn to drink but to books. At the same time he participated in the whole range of frontier social events—political barbecues, house raisings, corn huskings and weddings.

Lincoln's intellectual depth is evident from his early writings and reading of poetry. His own poem, "My Childhood's Home I See Again," makes clear that he was anything but a romantic optimist about nature.[23] "Till every sound appears a knell, And every spot a grave. I range the fields with pensive tread, And pace the hollow rooms, And feel (companions of the dead) I'm living in the tombs." When Lincoln broke with his father in unbelief, looking for an escape from the family tradition of Calvinism, he turned to the Scotch poet, Robert Burns. Poe's "The Raven" was to become one of the future president's favorite poems. He was also fond of Byron and Longfellow, and cited in particular "The Haunted House" by Thomas Wood and "The Last Leaf" by Oliver Wendell Holmes. Lincoln also was fond of William Knox's "Mortality."

Amid Lincoln's unbelief, in about 1834 he is supposed to have composed "a little book on infidelity" of which no copies remain; it was destroyed by friends as they sought to protect his career in politics. Lincoln's friend Joshua Speed recalled the president-to-be's early skepticism about "the great truths of the Christian religion": "When all were idle and nothing to do Lincoln would talk about religion—pick up the Bible—read a passage—and then comment on it—show its falsity and its follies on the grounds of Reason."[24] At this stage of life, he looked to reason, cold, calculating, and unimpassioned, along with the basest principles of nature, to establish and maintain civil and religious liberty. Still he had acquired enough knowledge of the Bible to use it effectively as a public speaker, for instance in his metaphor of a house divided.

Lincoln's best-documented early statement in his own defense was made in 1846 as he ran for Congress against a Methodist circuit rider, Peter Cartwright. His opponent had accused him of infidelity. In reply, Lincoln produced a handbill that read: "That I am not a member of any Christian Church is true; but I have never denied the truth of the Scriptures; and I have never spoken with intentional disrespect of religion in general, or of any denomination of Christians in particular."[25]

No doubt, the image of the "populist Lincoln" cannot be taken uncritically at face value. When he ran for president, Lincoln's cousin, John Hanks, strengthened the frontier mythology by telling stories of the candidate's early life. He even showed off two fence-rails that he said were among the three thousand that the candidate had split three decades earlier. Whether this was the case or not, the truth was that the president-to-be had scarcely any formal education.

STEWART WINGER'S ANALYSIS

Stewart Winger finds that four elements of Whig belief coalesced in Lincoln's ethical and religious analysis: "Scottish moral philosophy, classical republican thought, common law and Protestant piety,"[26] "Whigs loathed the amoral and antigovernment tendencies both of utilitarianism and of radically liberal thought because they feared liberal thought hindered the workings of a positive moral state."[27] They posited a higher law above that of the state.

Winger argues that discussion of the Emancipator's beliefs often has ended in a mistaken choice between Lincoln as a conventional nineteenth-century evangelical and as a skeptic in the tradition of Thomas Paine. Winger himself proposes a third possibility: "Lincoln's use of religious language reflected a Romantic and poetic understanding of religion."[28] Although usually very skeptical of religious authority, Romantics often "found unorthodox ways to reaffirm surprisingly traditional, Christian descriptions of the human condition." Lincoln's religious rhetoric, Winger concludes, was part of "a broad Romantic quest to define America's purpose in a way that was morally and theologically winsome."

In short, Winger concludes that Lincoln was far more sophisticated than the figures of log cabin and rail splitter conveyed. Living in a predominantly Protestant culture—secularism had not yet set in—he used its symbolism powerfully and sincerely in his oratory. Winger places him as belonging to the earlier Romantic insurgency against the Enlightenment. For example, his fatalism was not that of traditional Puritan predestinationism but reflected the romantic and idealist epistemology which was widely dominant among the major religious thinkers in America at the time. This orientation was evident in Lincoln's oratorical Romantic description of Niagara Falls.

Lincoln was converted from what was often, for him, Enlightenment skepticism (or a less radical common sense approach) to a more Romantic and poetic relationship with nature. It was this shift that, in time, enabled him to reconnect with biblical and Augustinian ideas. Nature's ultimate meaning transcended both materialistic and utilitarian and bases. [29]

To the young lawyer, Niagara Falls called up "the indefinite past. When Columbus first sought this continent—when Christ suffered on the cross—when Moses led Israel though the Red Sea—nay, even when Adam first came from the hand of the maker—then as now, Niagara was roaring here .... Never dried, never froze, never slept, never rested."[30] In short, the president-to-be identified an image of God in the falls. His chronology was confused, but he nevertheless saw sign of divine watchfulness and superintendence. The ongoing miracle of creation impressed him.[31]

Although he was not a Protestant evangelical, the president's wartime statements resonated with many of the persons who made up his audiences. When he attended worship, even though not a church member, Lincoln went to Old School Presbyterian churches that opposed revivals as well as the international reform societies of the Second Great Awakening. As compared with Washington, for example, he knew the Bible extremely well and often read it. Concerning his non-affiliation, he is supposed to have said: "When any church will inscribe over its altar as the sole qualification for membership the Savior's condensed statement of the substance of both the law and the gospel, 'Thou shalt love the Lord thy God with all thy heart and with all thy mind and love thy neighbor as thyself,' that church I will join with all my heart."[32]

Lincoln rarely used Christ's name. He addressed deity rather with such titles as Almighty and Merciful Ruler of the Universe, Great Disposer of Events, Divine Providence, God of Right, God of Nations, Great and Merciful Maker, and Omniscient Mind. He told a delegation of Lutherans, "God determines the destinies of nations."[33] What Lincoln was not able to articulate to his own satisfaction and accept was the Christian concept of salvation. Not sanguine about evil, he was convinced that human beings were naturalistically egoistic. Slavery was founded on the selfishness of man's nature. Opposition to it rested on the love of justice. In his First Inaugural Address, he appealed to the better angels of our nature.

THE MEANING OF HISTORY

Lincoln's religious strength, Winger argues, was that he saw through the cultural optimism of persons like the historian George Bancroft, (Polk's secretary of the navy) as well as that of Stephen A. Douglas, who debated with him. The leading American scholar in the field, Bancroft (who had studied under Hegel in Germany) assumed in his ten-volume *History of the United States, From the Discovery of the American Continent,* that American politics was essentially untheoretical and practical.[34] Earlier terrors of religion as interpreted by a priesthood had been overcome. Living in the world of the Enlightenment, Americans no longer needed myths, only natural science and common sense. But this was not Lincoln's perspective; it was not what the Civil War was fought about, in his judgment. [35]

Winger attacks Bancroft sharply for making rhetorical bows to the national fathers while yet remaining ultimately conservative and demagogical. Bancroft's interpretation rested on a scheme of sacred history designed to flatter the electorate, he alleges.[36] At issue was the place of sacred history in the North American republic. "Lincoln and Bancroft both saw a 'last hope' in American democracy, but for Lincoln there was a real possibility that we might meanly lose it."[37] Before he issued his Emancipation Proclamation, the wartime president told his Cabinet that he had made a bargain with God, a covenant to do so after the tide of war had turned in the victory of Northern armies.[38] "I am under orders. I cannot do otherwise," he said.[39] Brought up to date, Lincoln's choice was more substantial than between a this-worldly social gospel and an anti-intellectual fundamentalism.

Winger interprets the Second Inaugural as a call to humility. For Lincoln, no man or nation could claim the right to triumph. America was no longer the culmination of world history; rather it remained under the judgment of God as merely one nation among many. He and his fellow countrymen must stand firm in the right, but they had not come to the end of times.[40]

Lincoln's close friend, Joshua Speed, concluded that Lincoln "tried hard to be a believer, but his reason could not grasp and solve the great problem of redemption."[41] The president is reported to have told the family of Henry Rankin, that "probably it is to be my lot to go on in a twilight feeling and reasoning my way through life, as questioning, doubting, Thomas did."[42]

Guezlo comments: "It was Lincoln's sense of being helpless and unworthy in the estimate of the glowering Father who offered nothing but demands for perfection Lincoln could not honestly claim for his own."[43]

Senator Paul H. Douglas from Illinois commented more than a century later:

> *The turning of the Union flanks and the defeat of the Union army at Gettysburg might well have meant the loss of the war with all the incalculable consequences which would have meant the creation of two hostile nations in the middle of North America, one dedicated to slavery and the other to freedom. North America would then have then become another Europe, fighting deadly wars periodically. Like Athens and Sparta would have been locked in internecine warfare. Gettysburg would have been but a prelude to still greater blood drenched struggles.*

In reflecting that both sides, South and North, pray to the same God, Lincoln was not unaware that piety and religion had made the Civil War even more intense and bloody. Maturing as a military leader, he eventually organized a powerful war machine. But this was not the end of matters for him. He probed questions of divine judgment, providence, forgiveness and redemption with an intensity that exceeded the Enlightenment rationalism of the country's Founding Fathers.[44]

Lincoln saw in Northern victory the guiding hand of Providence. Still the wartime president showed his stature and sincerely in his personal reflection on the theme of the judgment of God. Written out in September of 1862 for his own reflection, he had entitled it a "Meditation on the Divine Will." His secretary, John Hay, found the paper on his desk and preserved it. Lincoln, in fact, had never intended it for publication. "The will of God prevails. In great contests each party claims to act in accordance with the will of God. Both may be, and one must be wrong. God can not be for, and against, the same thing at the same time. In the present civil war it is quite possible that God's purpose is something different from the purpose of either party."[45] What was written was anything but a defense of the status quo. Enlightenment trust in reason and moral common sense had long since been compromised in the struggle over slavery. A simple, absolutistic perfectionism (as in abolitionism) did not exhaust the best insights of Christianity, he believed. Lincoln looked for reconciliation and reconstruction as peace dawned. Death cut short his ambition.

Lincoln had faced the nation's greatest tragedy to date in the Civil War. As he remained a religious seeker it was not ecclesiology that concerned him but destiny. More than six hundred thousand combatants were killed in a terrible, fratricidal war. Viewing his own role, Lincoln believed that he was not fully free but controlled by forces greater than himself—destiny. Assuredly, his language was more biblical than that of the Founding Fathers. A Westerner, a democratic nationalist, he held diverse values together: saving the Union and freeing the slaves. He did not speak with the idealistic dogmatism of a Wilson; no near-Manichean dualism seemed appropriate to the times. In short, he realistically distinguished ethics from ideology. It was a sign of his moral stature that under his self-criticism, American civil religion came of age.

If any president deserves the title of ethical realist, it is Abraham Lincoln. Patiently, he worked to hold the nation together, leading it carefully through civil war to the victory of liberty. He was right that the armed struggle was not just about slavery, but centered on national integrity and unity. No pragmatist, he still understood that morality has a cultural and historical context. The key to understanding Lincoln's ethics—and indeed his attitude toward institutional religion—was that he held together a diversity of values. In real life, they did not all fit together easily into a simplistic ideological pattern. Lincoln was too close to the tragedy of civil war to believe in easy human virtue. Retrospectively, it is clear that victory came not only because of Lincoln's integrity and strength of character, but due to the growing power of Northern industry. Protestantism and capitalism joined together in new and powerful synthesis, a development he participated in as a lawyer. Still, he would have been morally strong and wise enough to criticize it in its subsequent ruthlessness had he lived into the post-Civil War age of the robber barons.

WOODROW WILSON

Obama shares in much of Wilson's internationalism. The latter's attempt to make the world safe for democracy, however, did not include the end of racial segregation in the country. Rather, racism increased during Wilson's tenure in office. His father was a pastor in the South during the Civil War and defended slavery. Nor was the wartime president particularly thoughtful about religion. He was a Democrat and a Christian, he announced. Nothing else needed to be said! Wilson's culture Christianity, near modernist Calvinism, would seem of little relevance to forty-fourth president.

Joining the black church, Obama learned about a tradition of oppression that had been minimized while he lived with white grandparents and attended a privileged prep school in Hawaii. David Brooks reports that he has read Reinhold Niebuhr and does not believe that the world of politics can be saved by the practice of Wilson's version of democracy. Like Wilson, he is a lawyer but does not look for "once and for all solutions" to international problems. He is much more given to consultation than the former Princeton president, and has a very different sense of mission. Obama is more of an authentic populist who wants to remake the political and social world from below rather than from above.

"My life would not be worth living if it were not for the driving power of religion, for faith, pure and simple." January 3, 1915, Woodrow Wilson to Mrs. Crawford H. Toy.[1]

"There is a mighty task before us and it welds us together. It is to make the United States a mighty Christian nation and to Christianize the world." November 20, 1905[2]

INTERNATIONAL CHARACTERS IN WILSON'S WORLD

Wilson's political world was made up of a contrasting set of characters, both at home and abroad—some of whom he judged to be good and others evil. The situations in which he made decisions and the religious values he advocated are clarified by identifying these persons. His secretary of state, the Christian populist, William Jennings Bryan, had helped him to secure nomination as the democratic candidate at his party's convention. A pacifist, Bryan resigned from Wilson's cabinet when the president sent his note of protest to Germany, threatening war, following the sinking of the *Lusitania*. Himself a candidate for the White House three times, Bryan had been defeated in his last race by Theodore Roosevelt. By contrast with Roosevelt, Wilson's statements were more scholarly nuanced. He judged the former president to be often irresponsible and too belligerent.

Meanwhile, Kaiser Wilhelm ruled in Germany. Wilson saw him as dangerous and intransigent, as he refused to bring the European war to an end in a negotiated peace as the American president wished. Queen Victoria's grandson, the Kaiser had been born with a crippled arm. Like the monarchs of Austria-Hungary and Russia, he also believed that he ruled by the authority and grace of God. Wilson's piety and statecraft were antithetical to this claim.

On the Allied side, Wilson faced off against the revengeful strategy of the French wartime leader, Georges Clemenceau, an anticleric who did not believe in God and refused to join Wilson when the latter attended church in Paris. David Lloyd George, the English prime minister, cynically—as against Wilson's faith in progress—prophesied that the next world war also would be fought "to end all wars." Of course, no statesman at the time anticipated that the next global conflict would be concluded by the use of an atomic weapon. Even as the First World War destroyed European empires, it also altered the role and scope of the American chief executive. In a sense, the modern presidency began with Wilson.

Throughout the land, the war uprooted millions of citizens from their communities to participate in the hostilities in one way or another. That there could be a lasting return to normalcy turned out to be an illusion.

WHAT WILSON BROUGHT TO POLITICS

Wilson, looking ahead, had sought to prepare himself to participate as a Christian in American politics, even while he was a graduate student studying at Johns Hopkins University. Returning to teach at his undergraduate alma mater, Princeton, in 1902, he became an outstanding campus figure and was elected president of the university ten years later. Wilson had won his place by showing moral strength as well as intellectual gifts, but soon there were difficulties. When he left the school to run for governor of New Jersey, his administration was under siege because of his idealistic intransigence; he wished to redirect the university (away from privilege) to serve the nation and had been hemmed in by the trustees. He entered politics as a self-identified reformer.

The fourth gospel's version of the new birth was in the background of Wilson's political musings throughout his career, and he wished such an experience of redemption for the whole world. The lingering conversionist theme in Wilson's piety came from his conversion early in life. His twice-born experience took place at Columbia Seminary in Augusta, Georgia during the 1872–73 school year.[3] Wilson later linked it to the Christian moral principles that he believed would revive Western civilization. What he shared with his first secretary of state, William Jennings Bryan, (whom he came to regard as politically irresponsible) was the populism of a religiously based belief in the common man. Nonetheless, Wilson was not a commoner on the mold of Bryan. Wilson's life model was that of a university man, although he never found time to work out his political philosophy in the abstract fashion that he had wished. Enemies might call him a theocrat, but he was unequivocally committed to democracy and the legal separation of church and state.

Wilson's integrity was on display very early on, shortly after he entered New Jersey politics with the support of the party bosses. His moral sensitivity and conscience caused him to turn on them. "Gentlemen: a toast. I give you the Governor of the State of new Jersey, Woodrow Wilson—a liar and an ingrate."[4] These were the words of James R. Nugent, the chairman of the Democratic State Committee, who had hoped to control Wilson when he was elected governor of New Jersey; Nugent failed. Wilson had defied the bosses (although he had promised to let them have at least some of their turf) and had worked hard to destroy men such as the committee chairman. In fact, after this incident, in little more than a year, Wilson had been nominated for president as an anti-machine, anti-corruption politician. He explained of the New Jersey party bosses: "They did not believe that I meant what I said; and I did believe that they meant what they said"—that his word would always have to be the final ethical decision.[5]

Herbert Hoover, who accompanied the wartime president to Europe, defended the best in Wilson's moralism. Hate was rampant among the victorious allies, Hoover pointed out. At the peace conference, Wilson tried unsuccessfully to provide leadership to counter it, premised on his unshaken belief in democracy, Hoover claimed. Wilson's earlier-expressed principles were being expanded for an international setting. Earlier in his career, Wilson had observed that Congress—like state legislatures and party machines—frequently was dominated by "scheming, incompetent, political tradesmen whose aims and ambitions were merely personal." Strong leaders as well as clear goals were needed for reform, he argued. "No leaders, no principles; no principles, no parties," he reflected.[6] It was a conviction that he would carry over into international relations.[7]

One needs to go back to the early Wilson and his book, *Edmund Burke: The Man and His Times,* completed in 1893 while Wilson was still teaching, to understand his premises.[8] He emphasized, with Burke, that institutions are necessary to move politics forward. Wilson saw ruthless struggle as a fact of life but not as taking place in a spiritual vacuum. Like Jefferson, Wilson's judgments of principle were probably more historically conditioned than either man supposed. For both, relativism was not an alternative. "The history of liberty is the history of politics," Wilson argued, and added: "Sin is the transgression of the law, that is, of political progress."[9] *Is this all there is to sin?* theologians might ask.

Bringing his political science into his own era, Wilson argued that America's unique mission had been compromised in the gilded age following the Civil War, and more recently in the dollar diplomacy of his predecessor, William Howard Taft. During his first four years in office, Wilson's administration enacted more positive legislation than any other since the days of Alexander Hamilton. The reforming chief executive appeared in person before Congress in a new pattern, as previous presidents had not done, and championed the progressive causes he favored. Bills for the 1914 Clayton Antitrust Act and establishment of the Federal Trade Commission were passed—not with the expectation of breaking up industrial giants or even punishing wrongdoers, but to prevent wrongdoing such as abusive price discrimination. A child labor act was enacted, which was later ruled unconstitutional by the Supreme Court. The United States seemed to be a growing Christian society in the best sense of the term—to be sure, with the separation of church and state. In spite of all of his later championing of a new day, Wilson was not ahead of his time in his view of race relations. In his private notes, he observed that Negroes were not only ignorant people but also an "inferior" race. He also believed that women should be educated differently from men.[10]

Wilson's strong sense of rectitude tragically got in the way of what he wanted to accomplish internationally, and there were portents of what could happen early on during his time in the White House. The day after his election as United States president, when the Democratic national chairman asked to make suggestions about appointments, Wilson shot back: "Before we proceed, I wish it clearly understood that I owe you nothing. Remember that God ordained that I should be the next President of the United States."[11] In the face of press reports that Wilson was looking for a compromise on a particular piece of legislation, he assembled reporters and commented: "When you get a chance, just say that I am not the kind that considers compromises when I once take my position. Just note that down so that there will be nothing more of that sort transmitted to the press."[12] At the same time, Wilson's moral sense was reinforced by his almost rousseauean belief in the basic goodness of humanity. In particular, he believed in the wisdom of simple people to choose better than their supposedly more knowledgeable leaders.

WAR AND PEACE

Running for a second term, Wilson had allowed the election slogan, "He kept us out of war." In reality, his options were limited more than his words suggested; the Western allies—most of all Russia—were collapsing. Forces greater than himself had borne in on his presidency and precipitated American belligerency.[13] After the war, the Germans believed, Wilson did not keep his promises and betrayed democracy in their country. Depriving it of support, he left it to a declining fate that never ended until after Nazism. Practically, the American president's pronouncements weakened and shortened German resistance. His statements' vagueness became evident when he attempted later to make them the basis for a peace settlement.

> *An odd galleon was that which landed at Brest in early December, 1918, when the [ship] George Washington anchored. Down the gangplank walked this Yankee knight errant followed by a desperate crew of college professors in horn-rimmed glasses, carrying textbooks, encyclopedias, maps, charts, graphs, statistics, and all sorts of literary crowbars with which to pry up the boundaries of Europe and move them around in the interests of justice, as seen through [Woodrow Wilson's] ... Fourteen Points.[14]*

So reported the Kansas journalist, William Allen White. It was an impressionistic newsman's view, one which implied significant reservations about the liberal idealist's ability to remake the Old World.

President Wilson was convinced that a lasting peace was possible only if the old abuses of secret diplomacy came to an end. Authoritarianism was giving way to liberty; old monarchies were falling. The self-determination of nationalities was a requirement for a new world order, Wilson believed. At the Versailles Peace Conference, the map of Europe was redrawn and national boundaries changed. From the ruins of the Austro-Hungarian empire, the new states of Yugoslavia and Czechoslovakia were created; neither lasted until the end of the century. What would have been the result if the American leader's goals and strategies had been accepted by the Allies in Europe and at home by the United States Senate? Could the rise of Nazism and the Second World War have been prevented?

What remains remarkable is how much of Wilson's internationalism lived on in power in the American program at the beginning of the twenty-first century. His vision brought the reforming idealism and moralism of a still-young United States to a war-weary continent. The skepticism and pessimism that had already developed in parts of Europe were not in his view as he moved forward with a religiously supported sense of destiny. "We cannot turn back. We can only go forward, with lifted eyes and freshened spirit, to follow the vision. It was of this that we dreamed at our birth. America shall in truth show the way. The light streams upon the path ahead, and nowhere else."

WILSON'S RELIGIOUS PRINCIPLES

The president's "religious principles," as he called them, were not subject to intellectual challenge. Wilson once remarked to his White House physician confidant, Admiral Cary Grayson, "So far as religion is concerned, argument is adjourned."[15] The wartime leader held daily devotions with his family, reading the Bible and praying, and was sustained by the assurance that he was doing the will of God. Not surprisingly, his French counterpart, Clemenceau, at the Versailles Peace Conference dubbed him "a Protestant Priest."

Arthur Link, Wilson's prime biographer, evaluates the World War I president as "the prime embodiment, the apogee, of the Calvinist tradition among statesmen of the modern epoch."[16] Wilson's intent, he believes, was "to decide what faith and Christian love commanded." As president of Princeton University, he described Christianity as "a moral system based on high ideals," more than as a creed of form of doctrine. Link adds in qualification: "in matters of basic Christian faith, Wilson was like a little child, never doubting, always believing, and drawing spiritual sustenance from Bible reading, church attendance, and prayer." Taking the nation into hostilities in the war, he reflected that "the wise heart never questions the dealings of Providence, because the great, long plan, as it unfolds, has a majesty about it and a definiteness of purpose ... which we are incapable of conceiving."

Gary Scott Smith judges that the Christian in him cried out for a crusade and contradicted his call for nations' self-determination.

John A. Thompson, an English historian, reflects that Wilson's comment to his doctor had a slightly double-edged character. "Wilson came to maturity at a time when biblical criticism and Darwinism were raising serious questions about traditional theological axioms, and when many Anglo-American intellectuals were experiencing an agonizing loss of faith. His response to this situation, as he made clear in an entry in his confidential journal on his thirty-third birthday, was to fence his religion off from the ordinary working of his intelligence."[17]

Wilson wrote in his diary, "I used to wonder vaguely that I did not have the same deep-reaching spiritual difficulties that I read of other men having. I saw the intellectual difficulties, but I was not troubled by them: they seemed to have no connection with my faith in the essentials of the religion I had been taught ... I am capable, it would seem, of being satisfied spiritually without being satisfied intellectually."[18]

Much later in his life, he explained his position by the judgment that although some believe only so far as they understand—that seemed to him to be presumptuous—to make one's own personal understanding the measure of the universe.

Thompson finds that the barrier Wilson erected between his faith and his intellect worked in both directions. On the one hand, his religion remained a deeply emotional matter. In his own practice, he particularly valued hymn singing and the Communion service. On one occasion, he walked out of church when he found the speaker lacking in feeling and too academic. A longstanding friend expressed matters by saying that he "always took his religion very simply."

Thompson judges: "His father and the Presbyterian Church must be unquestionably right; having accepted these premised he dismissed theology from his mind and enjoyed his Bible, his God and his prayers without the least struggle with his intellect." Thompson is equally sure that the president's personal religious commitment did not compromise his thinking in other areas. He points out that Wilson's own writings in the field of politics were entirely secular in character. In a stance that was very different from that of his first secretary of state, William

Jennings Bryan, he did not view politics as an area for the realization of Christian values.[19]

Gary Smith's evaluation is that Wilson held "a progressive form of post-millennialism" (the belief that conditions will gradually improve until Christ's return). Inspired by Calvinism, he emphasized "order, structure and wholeness." Early on, in 1906, Wilson was outspoken that "Christ was not a reformer."[20] By 1910, he was ready to acknowledge that the church's task remained saving sinners, but it also had a direct responsibility to improve social structures and inspire reform. "In his later years, Wilson came to understand the ambiguous nature of moral decisions, but throughout his life, he tended to (sometimes simplistically) divide right and wrong, fight for moral ideals, and eschew compromise."[21]

In his own reflection, Wilson optimistically joined Social Darwinism with liberal Christian optimism: human beings are born inherently good! Smith argues that Wilson never explicitly repudiated the Calvinist doctrine of human depravity; rather "America was born a Christian nation," he argued. In the Princeton president's reflection, the kingdom of God was joined with nationalism. Critics accused him of "Messianism" and "missionary constitutionalism," of forcing United States institutions on others.[22]

PRO AND CON—WILSON'S CHARACTER

An English historian, writing at the end of the century and with greater distance from the past, reflects, "he was not, as might be supposed from his mature career, an example of the relentless drive which [has been] described as the 'Protestant Ethic' springing from 'Salvation Panic.'"[23] Wilson was a more reflective, many-sided person and among the most morally articulate of all presidents. The Jewish Boston lawyer, Louis Brandeis, whom Wilson appointed to the Supreme Court in 1916, described the president after their first meeting: "[He] has all the qualities for an ideal president—strong, simple and truthful, able, open-minded, eager to learn and deliberate."[24]

Wilson's Fourteen Points did not just fall from heaven—as was sometimes cynically quipped by his enemies. In fact, they had grown out of thoughtful consultation with internationalists and peace activists in his own country, which Wilson began even years before the crisis of war. As peace departed from Europe, the British foreign secretary, Sir Edward Grey, had issued his classic pronouncement: "The lights are going out all over Europe. I fear that they will not be relighted in our generation." It was Wilson's mission, the wartime president believed, to relight them. "Why has Jesus Christ so far not succeeded in inducing the world to follow His teachings in these matters?" This was the question with which Wilson once confronted his startled statesman colleagues when they met Paris to draw up a peace. Still carrying on his crusade, Wilson proceeded to supply the answer to his own question: "It is because He taught the ideal without devising any practical means of attaining it. That is why I am proposing a practical scheme to carry out his aims."

Personally, Wilson was not a fundamentalist but a low-church Christian in a tradition that dated back to the Lollards, followers of the reformer John Wycliffe in the fourteenth and fifteenth centuries. Wilson's version of the relation between religion and the state seemed strange to Anglicans and Lutherans, Roman Catholics, and the Orthodox alike. His question about Jesus was not one that would have been brought up at the Yalta Conference between Franklin Roosevelt, Winston Churchill, and Joseph Stalin as the Second World War came to a close, or by presidents Reagan or Clinton with the leaders of Europe after the fall of communism. As wartime leader of the nation, Wilson had described the American cause as so high that he "would be glad to die that it might be consummated."[25]

In hindsight, it is clear that there were many Wilsons, and all were not as innocent as the president himself supposed. One English historian, writing at the end of the twentieth century sees him as Janus-like and concludes, "No more complex personality ever ruled the White House."[26] For historians, political biography—even of honest men—is not simple. Lloyd George, the British prime minister who led his country's delegation at the Versailles Peace Conference, reflected in writing *The Truth About the Peace Treaties*: "All men have dual natures but Wilson's was badly mixed. There was his idealism and undoubtedly integrity; but there were his personal hatreds, his suspiciousness, his intolerance of criticism and his complete lack of generosity towards men who dared to disagree with him."[27]

The American satirist, Henry Mencken, caricaturized Wilson as "the perfect model of the Christian cad" who wished to impose "a Cossack despotism" on the country.[28]

Wilson ranks high on most historians' lists of American presidents. In Arthur Schlesinger, Sr.'s poll of experts on the presidency, taken in 1948 and again in 1962, Wilson rated first, far above all others in idealism, but he was lowest in flexibility. Among all presidents, Wilson ranked as the fourth greatest in Schlesinger's list, after Washington, Lincoln, and Franklin D. Roosevelt, and followed by Jefferson. Wilson described himself in the phrase, "a conservative as liberal." Diverging from his own religious tradition of Covenant Calvinism in the direction of Modernism, he reflected Jefferson's optimistic affirmation of liberty, nationalism, and faith (although he mistrusted Jefferson and opposed the tyranny of monarchs like the German Kaiser).

Actually, in many respects, Wilson's idealism continued the best aspirations of the nineteenth-century American reforming and populist tradition. Christianity meant justice, brotherhood, love, and peace—at times interpreted in utopian terms: a new day is possible. The kingdom of God in its fullness may be in the future, but it has to be struggled for courageously in the present—and it can be made real by human effort. His stance was post-millennial, with no sense of any impending eschatology as in fundamentalist dispensationalism. Although his view was not literalistic, he did not accept the pessimism about human nature espoused later by the Neo-orthodox Protestant theologians. Nor was he an ethical realist.

On the premise that personal biography is an unavoidable reference in any appraisal of a public figure, Sigmund Freud, the father of psychotherapy, and Ambassador William C. Bullitt collaborated in a psychological re-evaluation of the wartime president.[29] They were highly critical and negative. Most reviewers of what they wrote agree that they captured only part of the picture, albeit an important part. Wilson's low-church Protestant convictions contributed to the intolerant self-destructive aspects of his thought; at the end of his career, he convinced his followers in Congress not to compromise about the League of Nations, for example. In so doing, he defeated part of his own best achievement.[30]

At the same time, Wilson did believe passionately that human society had the potential for redemption from brutality and violence—as much as any Mahayana Buddhist championing the Buddha nature. His hearers only needed to be convinced; power politics was, at most, secondary. When Wilson came to office, a common belief in God and conviction about American destiny could be premised in public discussion. Liberal theists like Wilson affirmed progress under providence-- the growth of liberty and civilization—not the imminent soon-coming end of the age in an atomic holocaust or a religious eschatology.

The wartime leader, whose policies Freud and Bullitt so much despised, remained an academic, thinking in abstractions, even at the Paris Peace Conference. He is the only American president ever to have earned a doctoral degree. He completed it at Johns Hopkins University in 1886 and ranks among the most learned of presidents. The two Adamses, Jefferson, and Madison had represented a similarly high level of knowledge in the early history of the country. Wilson as a scholar was more specialized. He had first studied law at the University of Virginia and practiced briefly as a lawyer in Atlanta. Then he turned to political science in the new type of graduate school at Johns Hopkins, which allowed him a wider range of reflection. And although Wilson spent a major part of his career as a teacher and writer, he never intended to be merely an observer. Instead, he saw himself as a participant in the American dream as a man of action. Something could be done, he was sure. At the same time, his feelings of morality and duty in a number of respects were without the overpowering sense of expediency that characterizes most politicians, and this, no doubt, contributed to his stature.

By birth a Southerner, Wilson had passed his childhood in what had been the Confederacy. During the Civil War, his father had endorsed slavery. The younger Wilson had seen firsthand the hardship of the Reconstruction era. He remembered vividly how Jefferson Davis was taken in chains past the church where his father was pastor at the end of the war. Wilson, in his later political writings, accepted Northern victory, and with it Lincoln's ideology of freedom. He came to see the reunited Republic as making possible a new American nationalism, one that he joined with his version of civil religion—including democracy, liberty, and trust in God—in mission to the world.[30] Politically, of course, in defeat the South lost its earlier dominant place in the succession of American presidents. Wilson was the first (excluding Andrew Johnson) to come from the region after the Civil War.

Personally, Wilson had a strong marriage with his first wife, the one person the president "loved and trusted utterly." After she died of chronic kidney disease while he was in the White House, in August of 1914, Wilson wrote, "God has stricken me almost beyond what I can bear."[31] Soon he married a somewhat plump attractive forty-two-year-old Washington widow, Edith Bolling Galt. Passionately lovestruck, he wrote daily letters to Mrs. Galt that seemed more like those of an infatuated adolescent than a ruling President. "God has indeed been good to me to bring such a creature as you into my life. Every glimpse I am permitted to get of the secret depths of you, I find them deeper and purer and more beautiful than I knew or dreamed of."[32]

Gossip ridiculed Wilson as a college don who had become a lascivious skirt-chaser. It was Mrs. Galt, later Mrs. Wilson, who shielded the president from his critics when he became ill. She appeared at times to be virtually in control of the country. All correspondence with the ill president passed through her hands. Month after month, the government was left without direction as Wilson lay gravely sick in bed but refused to give up the farce of ruling. When Senator Fall told him, "We, Mr. President, have all been praying for you," Wilson answered, "Which way, Senator?"

WILSON'S FAILURE AND CONTINUING LEGACY

The peace treaty signed at Versailles perpetuated the fundamental economic arrangements of nineteenth-century Europe. John Maynard Keynes remarked that "the fundamental economic problems of a Europe starving and disintegrating before their eyes was the one question in which it was impossible to arouse the interest of the Big Four."[33] Nazism arose out of economic neglect as well as from ideological forces. In fact, Wilson misjudged a whole complex of potential developments as well as the impotence of moralism devoid of power. No one was prepared to forgive or forget in the pattern of Christian ethics. Why should they? In the Treaty of Versailles, all guilt was placed on Germany. How much was Wilson impaired psychologically as he debated the peace in Europe? Probably more than was evident on the surface, as he had already suffered at least two minor strokes. He was under strict care by his physician, Admiral Cary T. Grayson, and at times worked only a few hours a day at his desk, even while in Washington. Negotiations for peace in Paris exhausted the statesman, draining his energy away. His mission was interrupted drastically by health and personal collapse.

Barber, who specialized in researching different presidents' personality and character in the White House, describes the twenty-eighth president as "this century's brightest and most tragic moralizer in politics."[34] Freud and Bullitt give their own view on Wilson and the morality of power:

> *All the Allies were financially in his hands. His stern cable at the time of the armistice negotiations had made it seem certain that when he reached Paris he would say to Lloyd George, Clemenceau and Orlando: Gentleman I have come here to make peace on the basis of my Fourteen Points and on no other basis .... If you attempt to break your word and evade your obligations under the armistice agreement, I will under no conditions bind the people of the United States to guarantee the peace you make and thus involve them in the future wars an evil peace will ensure.*

Freud and Bullitt argue that if he had followed such a course, Wilson might possibly have obtained the "just and lasting peace" he had promised the world. Instead, he chose to fight for the peace he wanted, not with these male weapons but with the weapons of femininity. His tools would embody persuasion, not force. Never daring to have a fist fight in his life, he preached sermons to convert his hearers to the righteousness of Jesus's Sermon on the Mount.[35] Not surprisingly, members of the United States Senate had reservations about what Wilson had done in Europe. When the possibility of rejection of his peace treaty by that body was posed, Wilson snapped, "Anyone who opposes me in that, I'll crush."

While campaigning for the League of Nations on a cross-country tour, the president collapsed at Pueblo, Colorado in September of 1919. The outcome of history might have been different if he had died at the time; martyrdom could have helped his cause of internationalism.

Returning to Washington, he suffered a thrombosis that weakened his control of the left side of his body. Only a very few people were allowed access to the stricken president, and the White House became a sullen and quiet place. The cabinet met listlessly without the president, that is, until he fired Secretary of State Robert Lansing for having called it together. When the peace treaty came up for ratification in the Senate, Wilson insisted that his supporters vote against it. Enough of them did so, as it included the Lodge reservations, and along with thirteen Republican diehards, they defeated it.

Wilson's impotence—political and physical—was symbolized by an occurrence after he had left office. Continuing to live in the nation's capital, he still stood waving from an open window to some of his remaining admirers. Then, he tried three times to close its glass with his crippled arms but lacked the strength to do so. Yet after the Second World War, it became clear that the last word did not belong to his isolationist enemies.

The question remains outstanding as to whether President Woodrow Wilson was an ethical realist and/or an insightful apologist for Christianity. The answer is no on both counts. Wilson the ideologue set a pattern of unilateral presidential action as he led the United States into war in Europe. Certainly, there was genius in the plans he devised for a world organization following the coming of peace. The League of Nations was his major project. But his sense of what was possible on the ground was not clear-headed as he sought to support it, and he failed to win the confidence of his European allies or—in the end—of the American public. All this could have been different if Wilson had been more willing to compromise, less sure that God and history were on his own personal side. The power vacuum he left had tragic consequences, leading even to the Second World War. The Niebuhrs were right retrospectively in criticizing Wilson's weak appreciation of self-interest and power in appraising international relations. He came very close to identifying uncritically the Kingdom of God with democracy. A less liberal but pious Ronald Reagan, defending America's self-interest a generation later, would be much more successful in hastening the end of the cold war.

"In many ways Wilson was the greatest of the greats," President Harry Truman observed.[36] Truman believed that the charter of the

United Nations had at last vindicated the wartime idealist's program for the League of Nations. Smith points out, however, that more recently Wilson's detractors have argued that presidency contributed to "the demise of progressivism, the weakening of the Christian impulse to reform society, and the growing secularization of American politics and society." His linking of progressivism with the war effort helped make it politically impotent in the 1920s. As his term ran out, it was clear that the majority of the electorate had rejected the wartime president's claim that his country had a providential mission to spread "the blessings of democracy, capitalism and Christianity to the world." Americans were disillusioned by the war and fearful of communism at the same time that they were distracted by secularization and "the perils of prosperity." Pierard and Linder explain, "The 'unregenerate world' in the end did not accept Wilson's 'moralism and messianic vision.'"[37]

WARREN GAMALIEL HARDING

Warren Gamaliel Harding rates very low in professional historians' ranking of presidents. Obama receives a much higher standing, notably for his high intelligence and activism. A newspaper editor from Ohio, Harding was a confused, inactive leader whose indulgence and political impotence became clear only after his sudden and unexpected death. In his own household, Harding was dominated by his wife, whereas Obama is not. Initially, Wilson's successor had high popularity ratings in the country following his election. They grew significantly from the widespread disillusionment and reaction against the wartime president's failed crusade to make the world safe for democracy. But America did not return to normalcy under Harding's leadership. Scandal in his entourage became evident after his death. Obama also has come to power because of disillusionment with his predecessor's wartime legacy and failed domestic leadership. His integrity and activism are the antithesis of Harding's passivity and corruption.

THE POLITICIAN

Except for the very different weaknesses of Wilson and Harding, the United States could have played a more substantial role in international peace than it did when it was absent from the League of Nations. Harding would have had a top rating if public opinion polls had been in style while he was in office. His scandalous mismanagement became known only after he died in office. In his own way, he came to the presidency partly by luck, a naive and incompetent nihilist. In Harding's case, the populist strain misfired. He had a wonderful stage presence, but his "bloviation" oratory lacked substance and he simply did not know what to do in office. He won the nomination from the party bosses, as other candidates had more enemies than he did.

Harry Micah Daugherty—later to be the twenty-ninth president's corrupt attorney general—first saw Warren Gamaliel Harding as the latter was washing his boots at a school pump and preparing to speak at an evening political rally. Harding was running for the Ohio State Senate. The candidate's friendliness and suavity, as well as his statesmanlike qualities, impressed Daugherty who reflected that he "looked like a President. He was possible material."[1] Daugherty told Harding that he hoped that they would meet again. He was to become one of Harding's chief promoters for the presidency.

Later, when Harding had become a United States senator, Daugherty recalled having the following conversation with the advancing politician: "What would you do in my place?" Harding asked, and Daugherty replied, "I'd go into the big circus."

"And you think I'd have a fighting chance?"

"I think you have the best chance."

"Come down to brass tacks," Harding finally ordered. "Am I a big enough man for the race?"

Daugherty's answer was "Don't make me laugh! The days of giants in the President's Chair is passed [sic]. Our so-called Great Presidents were all made by the conditions of war under which they administered the office. Greatness in the Presidential Chair is largely an illusion of the people."[2]

"Bloviation," a word of Harding's own coinage, propelled the president-to-be's way in politics. "The word describes with onomatopoetic felicity the cheerful and windy expressiveness of the Harding oratory .... His fine presence, lush flow of verbiage, and partisan passion made a hit."[3]

Accepting the Republican Party nomination for the presidency, Harding promised that he would restore "party government as distinguished from personal government, individual, dictatorial, autocratic, or what not." In fact, he restored the parochialism and cronyism of small-town America as he had known it in Ohio—this in a world still reeling from world war. "Some men have greatness thrust upon them, some are born great, and some are born in Ohio," remarked Chauncey Depew. Harding was among the latter, from a state that supplied presidents Hayes, McKinley, and Taft—more than its share since the Civil War. Himself a thoroughly native type, handsome, genial, and kindly, he was fully the antithesis of the wartime president, Woodrow Wilson. Historian Richard Hofstadter describes him as also "complacent, and weak, a model of normal mediocrity."[4]

Certainly, there was an explanation for his rise to prestige and power. Following the end of World War I, Wilson's internationalism had gone out of style. The public mood was one of nostalgic longing for "the good old days." Citizens who had grown tired of Wilson's idealism responded to Harding's platform of "return to normalcy." The new Republican president won election to office by an unprecedented majority.

Harding had made his way up as an able public speaker, prominent in fraternal orders. He could be eloquent: "America's present need is not heroics but healing; not nostrums, but normalcy; not revolution, but restoration; not agitation but adjustment; not surgery, but serenity, not the dramatic, but the dispassionate; not experiment, but equipoise, not submergence in internationality, but sustainment in triumphant nationality."[5] Harding's voice was the voice of ease. One could relax while he spoke. Whereas Wilson's earnest oratory might evoke a frown from his hearers, Harding's platitudes washed gently like cool water over the mind! Critics have long charged that Wilson's successor symbolized a kind of nostalgic return to the past. Neither the president nor the nation was prepared to face the change that history had imposed.

The 1920 Republican Convention had become deadlocked among three conservative contenders. Most of its members were chosen by professional politicians, not yet by popular primary elections. In the end, it nominated Harding as a compromise candidate. Harding wrote, explaining the reasons for his choice as candidate:

*With Wood, Johnson and Lowden out of the way, I knew
I could count on friends in every one of their delegations,*

because I had followed in my pre-convention campaigning the rule that has guided me throughout my political career, which is not to hurt anyone's feelings or to step on anybody's toes if I could find foot room elsewhere. I figured that if politeness and an honest desire not to humiliate any rival just for the sake of winning a few votes were ever going to produce anything, this was the time. Other fellows, just as competent as I, or more so, had made enemies, and it looked to me that there was no one in sight that the convention could unite on except myself.[6]

A "front porch" campaign in which he said little and did not travel widely brought the candidate victory. Harding's election was made easier by his rapport and, at times, friendly intimacy with journalists; he even took time to play golf with some correspondents. They liked his frank, off-the-record talk. Harding had been editor and publisher of a small-town newspaper, the *Marion Star*, in his hometown in Ohio and had a good sense of press relations. At the informal press conferences held in a three-room cottage specially built near the Harding home in Marion to accommodate press representatives, his personality was warm and engaging. The Republican election victory was overseen by Will Hays and a brilliant campaign machine. The theme was America first, the slogan, "Let's be done with wiggle and wobble." Extreme nationalism was emphasized.

Samuel Hopkins Adams analyzed the ethos of the time: "It was a period of moral slump, the backswing from the idealism and sacrifices of war. Men's thoughts could not indefinitely maintain themselves on that lofty plane. Cumulative discontents blended in a savage resentment."[7] Citizens were unhappy and restless. A neurotically suspicious nation was prepared to blame everything on the leaders in power. With spreading unemployment and hard times—as wartime demands were no longer made on the economy—owners used the convenient excuse of "curbing the Reds" against labor causes.

THE PRESIDENT

Chosen as president of the nation, Harding's intent was to reign and not rule. Each day, the marine band would play on the lawn at 12:30

and the president would open wide the doors of the White House. He loved to shake hands with all comers in mass greetings. "I love to meet people. It is the most pleasant thing I do," he reflected. Administratively, his passivity brought confusion and deadlock. Harding remarked after he had been in office a year: "Curiously enough, most of the men whom I know, who have been seekers after the Presidency are those who care the least about encountering trouble, and if any of them ever comes to realize his ambition he will experience a rude awakening."[8] Initially, he made little effort to lead Congress. On the contrary, he expected Congress to legislate at its pleasure, and he was more than ready to compromise with party leadership in consultation. Harding's deference to party apparatus brought havoc to the federal workforce, about a quarter of whom were not protected by civil service. His appointments produced the worst corruption of any administration since the advent of civil service.

An attempt was made to meet postwar economic problems by lowering taxes and imposing higher tariffs, but it was not pursued vigorously. Soon a depression set in and Harding and his secretary of commerce, Herbert Hoover, concluded that it would have to be allowed to take it course. As the nation was dependent on international trade, protective tariffs generally made matters worse rather than better. It was inventiveness within the nation itself that seemed the most helpful and hopeful, and Henry Ford became more popular than the president. Harding showed little leadership in international affairs. "Really, I think we are getting along measurably well," the new chief executive reflected in mid-1921.[9] In the same year, he convened a naval disarmament conference with Great Britain and Japan, but not primarily on his own initiative. The conference took place only after Senator William Borah of Idaho had attached an amendment to a naval appropriation bill, requiring it.

Even during Harding's lifetime, there was known scandal in the Veterans' Bureau, as its director, Charles Forbes, sold items from the government's medical supply base in Perryville, Maryland to private contractors at low prices. Forbes also made undercover deals for hospital building contracts and sites. The Teapot Dome Scandal came to light only after Harding's death. It has been described as probably the most notorious political scandal in the country's history until its time.

Already before Harding's demise, Senator Thomas Walsh had started to gather evidence. Although the president did not profit personally from Teapot Dome, his political naïveté and lax administration remain notorious in the history of his office.

When Harding became president, a group of small-town cronies ran what was popularly called a "Department of Easy Virtue" from a little house on K Street.[10] The secretary of the interior, Albert B. Fall, persuaded Secretary of the Navy Edwin Denby to turn over management of the petroleum reserves to the Interior Department. Then he leased them to oil companies in return for gifts and loans. A Senate investigation, with a special commission appointed by President Coolidge, showed that Fall had given access to deposits at Elk Hill, California to Edward L. Doheny, and at the Teapot Dome in Wyoming to Harry F. Sinclair. After six years of legal maneuvering, Fall and Sinclair were sentenced to prison, but Doheny did not go to jail.

A measure of mystery surrounded Harding's death. He had set out on a "voyage of understanding" to Alaska. Obviously tired and disturbed, he could barely remain quiet long enough to sleep. On board ship sailing to Alaska, he asked his secretary of commerce, Herbert Hoover, "If you knew of a great scandal in our administration, would you for the good of the country and the party expose it publicly or would you bury it?" Hoover replied, "Publish it and at least get credit for integrity on your side."[11] When the secretary of commerce asked about the nature of the problem, the president mentioned rumors of irregularities in the Justice Department. Harding cut off the conversation when Hoover mentioned the name of Attorney General Daugherty. Later, a seaplane brought a long coded message from Washington, and the president appeared near collapse. Returning from Alaska, Harding fell ill of ptomaine poisoning, then pneumonia, and died of an embolism in San Francisco on August 2, 1923.

POST-HARDING JUDGMENTS

Harding's death brought an extraordinary outpouring of national emotion, with crowds waiting by the tracks to view the train carrying his body. It became clear how much the presidency symbolized the idealism of citizens. Virtually every town, city, and hamlet turned out mourners; they could be seen standing silently or kneeling by the tracks or on station platforms as the coach bearing the dead president's body passed. It was the death of a leader, barely two years in office, whom history would judge as one of the least successful in the White House. The growing importance of the presidency was evident. Thanks to the media, the dead leader was blown up to heroic proportions as his person was projected on the national scene.

The national mood changed with the disclosures of Teapot Dome and other scandals. William Allen White, the Kansas newspaper editor who had earlier eulogized Harding, now gingerly wrote: "The story of Babylon is a Sunday School story compared with the story of Washington from June 1919 until July 1923, and so far as that goes, considerably later. We haven't even yet got back to our Father's house. He can't see us even from afar off. Its invisible. And the whole thing is epitomized by the rise of Harding."[12]

Gazing at a stack of correspondence, Harding once reflected: "I am not fit for this office and should never have been here."[13] In a very different way than Wilson, Harding was a tragic failure, although his philosophy of life really had no category for tragedy. From time to time, he spoke of the United States as uniquely God's nation. Caesar, Napoleon, and Alexander Hamilton were his heroes, but he was—in contrast with them—not a strong man. Still, he had an emperor facade and satisfied the illusions of the populace. Isolationism would be again possible.

White reported: "He has no idea where to turn .... Some good friends would walk into the White House all cocked and primed with facts and figures to support one side and another would reach him with a counter-argument .... I remember how he came in here late one afternoon after a long conference ... weary and heartsick." White found that the president really wanted to do the right thing, but he did not know how. "I never knew a man who was having such a hard time to find the truth," White wrote. Then he reflected on how Theodore Roosevelt used to click into truth with the snap of his teeth! Wilson sensed it with some engine of erudition under the hood of his cranium! Harding, however, "pawed, wrestled, and cried for it and then had to take the luck of the road to get it," White concluded.[14]

In 1891, Harding had married Florence Kling DeWolfe, a strong woman who was ambitious for her husband's political career. After his death, the memory of their marriage was not allowed to rest in peace. A White House secretary quoted her remark, "Well, Warren Harding, I have got you the Presidency; what are you going to do with it?"[15] She was icy cold at his funeral. In retrospect, it may be said that a vacuum existed in the president's thought about the moral issues that surround the office. He lacked a significant and compelling religious model, and this in turn was projected on the life of the nation. "There must be some reason for everything he believed in odd moments when he thought about it—a God somewhere, an afterlife somehow in which we would not be judged too harshly for brass rails and poker games and the occasional midnight visit to the house by the railroad station."

Part of the Harding phenomenon, Barber believes, is to be explained from the way in which he seemed to typify the man in the street—rather than the university president. Charles Willis Thompson observed: "there was nothing in the man himself to arouse such a (grating) feeling—his perpetual smile and meaningless generality. It was only the incongruity between himself and his pretensions. If I had known him as a traveling salesman, a vaudeville actor, a nightclub entertainer or a restaurant keeper, I should have liked him very much."[16] "The bungalow mind," ex-President Wilson said once when he was talking of his successor.

William G. McAdoo, Wilson's son-in law, summed up Harding's person polemically: "The possessor of an adjustable conscience, which could be altered to fit every changing circumstance, Harding went through life with good cheer and gusto, believing thoroughly that a man can get along very well if he can fool some of the people some of the time."[17] McAdoo described Harding as a politician who spoke on every occasion he could with "a big bow-wow style of oratory." He often used rolling words that had no relation to the topic at hand, and "his speeches left the impression of an army of pompous phrases moving over the landscape in search of an idea." Sometimes when his meandering words captured a straggling thought, they would make it a prisoner until it died of servitude and overwork.

In 1931, Harding's secretary of commerce—who had later become president of the United States, Herbert Hoover—agreed to dedicate a hollow-centered memorial in Marion, Ohio, in honor of his predecessor. Harry Daugherty, who had been Harding's attorney general, was sitting in the audience, and Hoover had been advised to "aim at under rather than over-statement." Seeing his former associate in the Harding cabinet led him to be more outspoken. Harding, Hoover said, had weakened on his last Western trip not only "from physical exhaustion but mental anxiety .... [He] had a dim realization that he had been betrayed by the few men whom he had trusted, by men whom he had believed were his devoted friends. It was later proved in the courts of the land that these men had betrayed not alone the friendship and trust of their staunch and loyal mend but they had betrayed their country. That was the tragedy of the life of Warren Harding .... There is no disloyalty and no crime in all the category of human weakness which compares with the failure of probity in the conduct of public trust."[18] Most historians in their lists of presidents classify Harding simply as a failure.

Conclusions: Historians have described Harding as "an amiable fool, incompetent, inept, corrupt, immoral." He could not give leadership because most of the time he did not know what was going on. In his own mind, there might be a God in some faraway place, but the president's conscience did not trouble him about the matter. Midwestern small0town values, rooted in conformity and nepotism, were played out in corrupt cronyism. Only after his death did the nation come to recognize the moral vacuum he left as his legacy.

Societies are changed most powerfully by crises, and it was crisis that Harding and the American people wanted to avoid. As far as conscience was concerned, Harding never thought too much about it. In time, he learned that wicked men could threaten his tenure in office, but a vital understanding of evil, much less how individual righteousness strengthens democracy, was not in his purview. He was interested most of all in poker, bootleg bourbon, and willing women.

Harding seems to have had no understanding of any moral drama in history. His own view of its course related more to Caesar and Napoleon as powerful types. He lacked any larger ethical view comparable with that which Wilson derived from his personal religious conviction. Of course, to the public, Harding brought relief from the sermonizing with which his predecessor had wearied the nation. Statesmanship demands at least a minimum of ethical realism and sound judgment.

CALVIN COOLIDGE

Whatever else he was, Calvin Coolidge was honest. Americans wanted to return to "normalcy." Although he often spoke with the press, Coolidge was personally the antithesis of the energetic leadership that the times demand of Obama. The leader from Massachusetts embodied white Protestant culture. He governed in an era when the United States had embarked on a policy of isolationism, one that is no longer negotiable in the Obama era. Religiously he was a moralistic Yankee trained in neo-Hegelianism at Amherst College, and without any personally empowering religious experience. Tragically, the death of a son while Coolidge was president dimmed his enthusiasm for office during his second term. Both Coolidge and Obama were trained in law. The Republican from Massachusetts presided over an isolationist moralistic period. The former senator from Illinois has been, of necessity, bolder, an advocate of change. The New Englander probably never guessed that an African American would ever occupy the White House.

THE COOLIDGE REFORMATION

Old patterns of New England Puritan decency were back in the White House with Coolidge, following the Harding administration's scandals. Considered and determined in his judgment, he allowed no Watergate-style cover up of the abuses of his predecessor's regime. The new president remarked, "Some people think they can escape purgatory. There are three purgatories to which people can be assigned: to be damned by one's fellows, to be damned by the court, to be damned in the next world. I want these men to get all three without probation."[1] In two years, all of Harding's corrupt retainers were dead, disgraced, or at least out of office.

Coolidge affirmed a Puritan belief in hard work, but an even greater strength of character was his patience. His motto was "Let well enough alone." To his patience was added a strain of mystical resignation. "I am in the clutch of forces that are greater than I am," he wrote, despite being the most powerful man in the world.[2] The dedicated man, he explained in his newspaper column, "finds that in the time of need some power outside him directs his course."[3] But this was not all of the president's outlook. Finally, he added, "The ways of Providence are beyond our understanding."[4] This affirmation made clear that Coolidge was not a fundamentalist!

Morally it was a strange interregnum—after the First World War and before the second one, before the Depression. "Cool off with Coolidge" was the campaign slogan. The president was moral to the core but at times as inactive as a quietistic ancient Chinese philosopher. "If you see ten troubles coming down the road, you can be sure that nine will run into the ditch—before you reach them." Barber classifies Coolidge as belonging to the passive-negative withdrawn type of president.[5] In fact, Coolidge was shrewd as well as self-contained. His White House rhetoric and style were compartmentalized according to his audience: witty banter with reporters, high-minded addresses to the nation, silence at social occasions. On the one hand, Coolidge's personal relations were coolly detached. On the other hand, he held a record 520 press conferences, 7.8 per month compared with Franklin Roosevelt's 6.9 per month. The Republican president enjoyed banter with "lithe boys" who came along on his vacations—as he referred to newspaper reporters.

Topics of Coolidge's addresses to the nation revealed his common-sense moral stance: "Doing the Day's Work," "The Genius of America," and "Religion and the Republic," and their character and tone were carefully formal.[6] Whether campaigning or as president, he often spoke of general principles more than details. As a Vermonter by birth who attended college in Massachusetts and then remained to practice law in that state, the president often turned back in reflection to his past. Describing his home place and his father, he expressed faith in providence. Life had been harsh and demanding in his youth and had taught him standards and patience. Speaking later from the White House, his theme was that "the chief ideal of the American people is idealism."[7]

Coolidge was not a New England Brahman of the Boston type, nor did he come from new immigrant stock. Instead, his family came from the limited and diminishing group of citizens who still bought at crossroad stores, often earning their money from farming small, stony fields. It was said that they seldom could see very far beyond the next ridge of farmland; many of their ideas were prosaic. Not surprisingly, Coolidge appeared at times to be a "a Puritan in Babylon." Proud and unimaginative but trusted by the American middle class, he was seen popularly as embodying the responsible and moral.

BIOGRAPHY

Calvin Coolidge was born in Plymouth, Vermont on July 4, 1872. His family had been citizens of his native village for five generations. His mother, who died when he was twelve years old, left a lasting mark on his idealism, and following her death, he was sent for education to Black River Academy. He failed his first attempt to pass the entrance examinations for Amherst College, but after a year of further study at St. Johnsbury Academy at Ludlow, the best preparatory school in the state, he was accepted at Amherst. Coolidge's college preparatory curriculum had included Latin, Greek, French, ancient history, geometry, rhetoric, and American literature. He was religious in the tradition of his hometown.

When Coolidge came to Washington after Harding's death, he asked the pastor of Washington's Congregational church to be the first to see him. He attended its services but did not immediately become a member. One Sunday after the president took communion, the pastor announced his name for membership without consulting him. Coolidge's explanation for the delay was that he might not be worthy enough. Good works but not justification by faith seemed to be his understanding of Christianity.

Coolidge had been educated in a Congregational Church college. At Amherst in 1891, some 336 students made up the school, the majority from rural and small-town backgrounds, and only about a third from outside New England. It was a closely knit community. Coolidge was not elected to a fraternity until his fourth year. Most of the time, he lived in a boarding house as he received a good classical education; he was a quiet, frail person. His transition to a more positive role was in part accidental. Only upperclassmen could carry canes and wear high derbies. It was the tradition that, clad in topper and stick, they raced from one end of the athletic field to the other each fall. Coolidge was among the last seven across the line and so had to provide entertainment as well as dinner for the others. His speech, "Why I Got Stuck" was an outstanding success. Turning all his pockets inside out in silence to show how he had lost all his money on the race, he exclaimed, "You wouldn't expect a plow horse to make time on the race track or a follower of the plow to be Mercury!"[8]

In his senior year, he was asked to give the "Grove Oration," which followed the more formal addresses and ceremony at graduation. Held in a nearby grove with students smoking corncob pipes and seated on the grass, it was an occasion for in-house humor about faculty and students. Coolidge's performance was judged a smashing success, and it revealed the dry wit that was to remain with him throughout his career. Amherst alumni later helped Coolidge on his way, giving him political connections at decisive times, although he probably could have made his way without them.

Coolidge began his professional life as a lawyer in Northampton, Massachusetts, the city of Jonathan Edwards, the colonial preacher theologian. The president-to-be became a clerk in the office of John C. Hammond and Henry P. Field, both Amherst graduates, and they supported his admission to the Bar. In early October 1905, he married Grace Goodhue, a vivacious, outgoing woman as compared with Coolidge, who was dull and cranky in spite of his wry wit. Coolidge made his way up in his profession step by step, as city councilman, chairman of the Republican City Committee, the state House of Representatives, mayor of Northampton, and state senator. He was responsible, shrewd, and very honest—a powerful practicing politician. After two terms in the state Senate, Coolidge was elected its president.

His address at his installation, "Have Faith in Massachusetts," summed up his philosophy: "This Commonwealth is one. We are all members of one body. The welfare of the weakest and the welfare of the most powerful are inseparably bound together. Industry cannot flourish if labor languish .... Men do not make laws. They do but discover them. Laws must be justified by something more than the will of the majority. They must rest on the eternal foundation of righteousness .... The people cannot look to legislation generally for success. Industry, thrift, character, are not conferred by act or resolve .... Ultimately, property rights and personal rights are the same thing .... Expect to be called a stand-patter, but don't be a stand-patter. Expect to be called a demagogue, but don't be a demagogue .... Don't hurry to legislate. Give administration a chance to catch up with legislation."[9]

Coolidge was elected lieutenant governor in 1916 and governor in 1919. It was a police strike in Boston in the latter year that brought him to national attention. Although he was not alone in settling it, his words were much admired and widely publicized: "There is no right to strike against the public safety by anybody, anywhere, any time."[10] In short, he came on to the scene with a law-and-order platform and became the most popular figure in his state. In June 1920, he was nominated at the Republican National Convention as vice presidential candidate. His name had been shouted from the floor, touching off demonstrations. It was the first time since 1880—when Garfield was nominated—that the delegates and not the bosses had decided. When Harding died suddenly and unexpectedly, Coolidge came to office.

Coolidge derived at least part of his conviction at Amherst College, a bastion of optimistic-culture Protestantism. He was most impressed by his teacher, Charles Garman, the professor of philosophy, of whom he wrote: "His course was the demonstration of the existence of a personal God; of our power to know him, of the divine immanence and of the complete dependence upon him as Creator and Father. Every reaction in the universe is a manifestation of his presence. Man was revealed as son and nature, the hem of his garment."[11] In short, the Victorian synthesis of natural and revealed theology dominant in nineteenth-century Protestant America lingered on. But different from

Wilson, in this case its moralism supported the president's belief in non-entanglement in Europe, as well as laissez-faire economics.

Garman's ethic provided the rule of life for Coolidge, who said, "I knew that in experience it had worked. In time of crisis my belief that people can know the truth, that when it is presented to them they must accept it, has saved me from many of the counsels of expedience."[12] Garman urged his students to carry all issues back to fundamental principles, weighing them carefully. Although his ethics had a rational bent, he did not take his question-raising method to the end; in short, there was a practical side to his neo-Hegelianism. The premise was that the question of "how" answers the question of "what"; process and not product is what matters.

There was a sad side to Coolidge's personal life, in spite of all of his ironic humor. On July 7, 1924, his favorite son and namesake, Calvin, Jr., died from blood poisoning at the age of sixteen. Coolidge said of the event, "the power and glory of the Presidency went with him."[13] Calvin, Jr. had played tennis on the south grounds of the White House. He had worn sneakers without stockings, and when a blister developed on one of his toes, he did not report it in time. It was an infection that could have been cured by antibiotics later. After his son's death, Calvin Coolidge, Sr. is reported to have slept long hours in the White House in the latter part of his time in office. The president recalled poignantly: "In his suffering he was asking me to make him well. I could not."

EVALUATION

Coolidge's moral model was clearly laissez faire. Considered money honest, he deferred to the economic system. As president, he vetoed farm relief bills; a bonus for World War I veterans was finally passed only over his veto. Regulatory agencies became primarily places for the assistance of business; tax reductions favored capital, and a there was a high protective tariff. In foreign affairs, the president showed no wide vision. The era of Coolidge prosperity came to an end shortly after he left office, as the stock market crashed in 1929. The ethic that business is business and success in it is the ultimate goal of life proved shortsighted. Savings were lost in bank failures, and homeless, hopeless job seekers walked the streets or rode freight trains. Professor Garman's philosophy of a tidy moral universe—already called in doubt by the First World War—was challenged practically by the Depression.

As an administrator, Coolidge made a point "to recruit men of sufficient ability so that they can solve all the problems that arise under their jurisdiction." His intent, explicitly, was to lighten his own major responsibility, and he rarely interfered. "One rule of action, more important than all others, consists in never doing anything that some one else can do for you." The president was known not to discuss politics with his wife Grace at the White House. Together as hosts, they entertained a great deal. His long, impenetrable silences, along with his poker face even on social occasions, became notorious. In part, it was a defensive stance: "Can't hang you for what you don't say," Coolidge explained.[14] His dinner table silences and mild insults turned on his role as a poker-faced clown that had brought him attention as an undergraduate at Amherst College. The President's comments could touch the heart while leaving the political brain and brawn of the nation relaxed. In principle, his abstract pseudo-Hegelian fatalism had little clear connection with classical Christianity.

Donald R. McCoy concludes his carefully written biography by describing Coolidge as "a statesman of the later nineteenth-century kind" who was unable either to look forward or to comprehend satisfactorily the tendencies of his time. Not a cynic, his gentle political realism was limited. "He thought he was presiding over the renovation of society, when, in fact, he was floating on top of a nation that was drifting into a new era."[15] Almost inevitably, a more activist president would come to office.

Lenin and Mussolini were the leading chiefs of state in the era, McCoy reflects. Coolidge did not have their flair for leadership, but neither did he possess their megalomania or instinct for terror. McCoy labels Coolidge a failure because he did not look ahead or fight to head off the problems of the future. Any other leader available probably could have done little more. Still, the nation would have been morally and intellectually better for the attempt.

Conclusion: Coolidge was sincere in his reverence and belief in God—but not a very living God. The moralism that he preached to the country fit his personality. There was a pantheistic strain about his view that worked against any radical view of human wickedness, and he espoused a gentle sense of spiritual progress. One wonders whether biblical religion with its drama of salvation and redemption, including eschatology (last things), ever crossed his imagination. Coolidge, like his contemporaries, was interested most in the American past and bracketed world history. A self-righteous isolationism was in vogue against Wilson's wartime internationalism, and the White House did not challenge it. Retrospectively, Kennedy observed, the British slept while German democracy was being savaged.

HERBERT CLARK HOOVER

Hoover had little sense of what was going on along Main Street in America as the Depression engulfed the nation. Obama, the activist, is the opposite, using virtually every weapon at his disposal to end the widespread agony of financial collapse. Hoover was a religiously inactive Quaker and had been a member of Wilson's staff at the Versailles Peace Conference. A mining engineer trained at Stanford University in California, he was widely popular when he came to the presidency. He had used his professional skills to save thousands of civilian lives, efficiently leading international relief efforts (especially in Belgium) during the First World War. Soon after he became president, however, the 1929 stock market crash undid his administration. The Depression was a crisis of the same sort that Obama faced when he came to the White House. Hoover, however, in contrast to his later successor, failed to enlist popular support and bring the crisis to an end. Fate dealt him a bad hand. One must hope that Obama and his program for change will have better luck.

BIOGRAPHY

The English economist, John Maynard Keynes, wrote in his 1919 book, *Economic Consequences of the Peace:* "Mr. Hoover was the only man who emerged from the ordeal of Paris with an enhanced reputation."

Hoover accompanied President Wilson to the peace conference that followed the First World War. The president-to-be had the habitual air of a weary Titan, Keynes observed, or as one might put it, an exhausted prizefighter. Hoover's vision was firmly fixed on the essential facts of the European situation. In Keynes's judgment, he brought to the peace conference the atmosphere of "reality, knowledge, magnanimity, and disinterestedness, which if, they had been found in other quarters also, would have given us the Good Peace."[1] He was a mining engineer and not a lay theologian like Wilson.

Born in 1874 in West Branch, Iowa, Herbert Hoover was the son of a blacksmith and farm implement salesman. The family was Quaker, and his mother—who was seminary trained—traveled from one Friends meeting to another, preaching. The early death of his parents—his father when Herbert was six years old and his mother two years later—changed the childhood setting of his life dramatically. At the age of ten, young Hoover was sent to Oregon and given over to the care of his mother's brother.

At the age of fifteen, when he went with his uncle to an open Quaker land- settlement business in Salem, he first heard about the new Stanford University in California. Over his family's objections, he took the entrance examination. His native ability was evident, in spite of the limitations of his background; he was given special tutoring in the summer and admitted to the university.

At Stanford, Hoover was trusted and encouraged by the eminent geologist, John Branner. Throughout his lifetime, he was not an eloquent speaker; words were not his best resource. Work was, however—intensive even compulsive work on details.[2] His career as a mining engineer and then in public service exemplified the American ideal of a self-made man, including a strong sense of conscience.

Hoover in explanation of himself observed: "I come of Quaker stock." Then he added: "I never worked very hard at it."[3] This remark made clear his anchorage in a secular world. Still the early pattern of action and belief persisted. Later in life, Hoover described his childhood as one of nature and games, somewhat minimizing Quaker discipline. Quakers sat together in their plain meeting houses and emphasized inner light and equality. And there was discipline. Queries were read out at the monthly meeting, asking about members' behavior and reminding them of their duties. Just before he entered the White House, Hoover is reported to have explained to a Washington neighbor:

> *A philosophy of rules telling you what to do in given circumstances is a philosophy which you can sometimes escape from because, if circumstances arise which are not among the given circumstances, then there are no rules, and you can do as you like. But if your people make you believe that the "Inner Light" would light everything, then you keep trying to expand that "Light" to cover every new circumstance that happens and every new problem that arises, and you are never through. You keep getting new rules, from inside, all the time.*[4]

Before being elected president, Hoover was widely hailed as the great wonder-working engineer. His service with the American Relief Administration after the war was in the best tradition of Quaker good works. He wrote: "Never was a nobler work of disinterested goodwill carried through with more tenacity and sincerity and skill ..." Little thanks was asked or given. Often in the teeth of European obstruction, Hoover avoided an immense amount of human suffering and indeed, the breakdown of the European system.[5] In fact, this was not the first of his projects.

It was during the Boxer Rebellion in China at the turn of the century that Hoover first began his career in organizing relief, in this case for foreigners. In the early period of World War I, the Belgian civilian population was starving, as the country was cut off from food supplies with armies on all sides of its borders. Generals and politicians alike were concerned primarily with military victory. Hoover persuaded the belligerents to allow food supplies to enter the country and even found funds to pay for them. In relief activities after the war, Hoover had become familiar with the Bolshevik Revolution. To his credit, he recognized it as an act of reaching out for the dream of a better life. In answer, he advocated a more valid sense of individuality as well as "true cooperation" between individuals. Communism could not be contained by force alone, he believed.

The Friends' ethic of social service was a sectarian one, judged sociologically. Martin L. Fausold, in his biography of Hoover, points out the longstanding division between the absolutists and relativists among Quakers.[6] The former were rigid in principle, preferring to risk all rather than to compromise and weaken their stand. The latter more flexible party developed after William Penn died and the Friends lost political control of Pennsylvania. This second party understood itself as a "Divine Lobby" in an imperfect world. Practically, Hoover belonged to the second.

In his book, *American Individualism*, published in 1922, he expressed his Quaker sentiment; it was much more secularized, in his case, than Wilson's Presbyterianism.[7] Such modernist piety could and did inspire and undergird moral and religious movements. Practically, its goal was to bring cooperation, voluntarism, mutual self-help, philanthropy, and individualism. In Hoover, the moral heritage was joined with a first-class mind.[8] This was clear from Hoover's point of view at the Versailles Peace Conference where he was attached to President Wilson's staff,. Hofstadter describes it as being as much like that of a nonbelligerent as possible. He was experienced enough to see through the propaganda of both sides and knew, for example, that many of the atrocity stories recounted in propaganda were untrue. Hoover himself reflected: "I dealt with the gaunt realities which prowled about outside."

Hofstadter speculates that Hoover might have been elected president in 1920, but the Republican Party passed him over for Harding. Becoming secretary of commerce in the Harding and Coolidge cabinets, he won respect as an efficient bureaucrat, as well as the most liberal member of the cabinets in which he served. In his biography, *Herbert Hoover, a Public Life*, David Burner finds that the president was strongly influenced by sociologist Thornstein B. Veblin's "instinct of workmanship"—industrial precision, professional creativity, rational economics, moral imperatives, and public well-being.[9] Politically, his outlook was one of ordered freedom, communality, and productive work. Arthur Schlesinger, Sr., writing as a historian, remarked that Hoover in the presidency "transmuted all adventure into business ...." It was a hallmark of his later career and temperament that he took no joy in dealing with politicians or the public." He once groaned about the presidency: "This office is a compound of hell."

CHARACTER

Barber, classifying Hoover as an active-negative person, notes the difficulty: "The rise of Herbert Hoover coincided with an immense expansion in the mass media, particularly newspapers and radio."[10] But soon he began to restrict reporters, often leaving for his forest camp in Virginia without giving notice to the press. Not surprisingly, reporters turned against him. Hoover became known as one of the presidents who have been most burdened and worried while in office. H. G. Wells, the English historian, found him a "sickly, overworked and overwhelmed man." His workload as president was eighteen to twenty hours each day. It was said that he never laughed aloud and always had a frown on his face.[11]

Still, in his own way, Hoover exemplified a deeply felt presidential morality. "The presidency is more than an executive responsibility, it is an inspiring symbol of all that is highest in American purpose and ideals," he reflected.[12] But he did not see it in terms of public relations. "This is not a showman's job, I will not step out of character and you can't make a Teddy Roosevelt out of me."

He added, "I have never liked the clamor of crowds. I intensely dislike superficial social contacts. I make no pretensions to oratory." Hoover disdained "the crowd," which only feels; it has no mind of its own that can plan. "The crowd is credulous, it destroys, it hates and it dreams—but it never builds. I hesitate to contemplate our country if the preoccupation of its officials is no longer the promotion of justice and equal opportunity but is to be devoted to barter in the markets ... it is degeneration." With this stance, he could not intervene successfully against the growing economic collapse. He was no match for Roosevelt's charm or the rising Great Depression,

Barber gives attention to the question of personality, charging that Hoover's demeanor did not allow him to enter into genuinely cooperative relations with other persons, especially when such relations required compromise. The engineer-president simply did not have appreciation for the irrational in politics, and it was not surprising that he failed to engender an enthusiastic response by oratory.[13] Characteristically, Hoover believed in economy and efficiency as ends in themselves. His capitalist model has been judged critically to be that of an unregulated profit system. In 1930, Hoover did concede that over-speculation was causing depression, but it was not the only factor, he said. The crisis was worldwide, and the major forces fueling the depression were outside the country.

At home, he opposed relief: "I am opposed to any direct or indirect government dole. The breakdown and increased unemployment in Europe is due in part to such practices." For the federal government to give money for relief "would have injured the spiritual responses of the American people .... We are dealing with the intangibles of life and ideals .... A voluntary deed is infinitely more precious to our national ideals and spirit than a thousand fold poured from the treasury." Newsreel men photographed him feeding his dog on the White House lawn.

Writing as a historian, Hofstadter observes that "Within little more than a decade the story of Hoover's wartime career was all but forgotten. The man who had fed Europe had become a symbol of hunger, the brilliant administrator a symbol of disaster."[14] Hoover left under a cloud of rejection without parallel since the time Andrew Johnson gave up the presidential office. Did Hoover ever really see that rugged individualism had ceased to be virtue in the economy? Nor was it as Christian as he believed. The day of the robber barons was past. An unmanaged capitalism had become self-defeating. Although the Quaker engineer championed the old virtues of religious faith, integrity and incorruptible service and honor in public affairs, these were not in themselves enough to meet the crises of the time. An old order had broken down, domestically and abroad. His successors imposed a new, more socially active presidential morality.

What happened was not a sudden personal failure but the collapse of a whole world and its moral paradigm. What Hoover believed in—efficiency, enterprise, opportunity, individualism, substantial laissez faire, personal success, material welfare—had all been recommended by Jefferson, Jackson, and Lincoln. Earlier, these ideals had seemed fresh and invigorating. Hofstadter concludes that "Hoover was the last presidential spokesmen of the hallowed doctrines of laissez-faire liberalism."[15]

Initially when he ran for the presidency, Hoover had a good relationship with the press. His publicity assistant in the Commerce Department, George E. Akerson, facilitated the relationship. Hoover's opponent in 1928 was Alfred E. Smith, who refused to accept the dry pro-Prohibition plank in his own Party's platform. Disadvantaged nationally by his Roman Catholic stance, Smith did manage to win many of the larger cities. Following his own election victory, Hoover made a goodwill trip to South America. Not friendly or a hail fellow well met, he leaned toward impatience and pessimism. The stock market crash of October 23, 1929, Black Thursday, and still more what happened on Tuesday the twenty-eighth, the day the bubble burst—challenged his dominant premise, which linked prosperity and liberty.

There was an explanation in over-speculation at home, as well as depression in the world abroad, the president conceded. Hoover characteristically opposed radical solutions, as when the head of General Electric called for a special session of Congress and issuance of bonds to fight the Depression. Hoover sought out bankers and asked them to arrange a pool of half a billion dollars to ease the large financial crush on the nation—without too much success. When Congress adjourned in the spring of 1931, he instituted a one-year moratorium on war-debt payments from Europe. His other weapon against the Depression was the Reconstruction Finance Corporation. Hoover wanted an increase of taxes, and it was passed by Congress, but without an unpopular sales tax that was at first part of the package.

Then there was the question of Prohibition; it stood in the way of discussion of more important economic questions. The Wickersham Commission was appointed by the president to investigate whether it should be repealed as the Massachusetts State Senate asked. Throughout the country, there was a breakdown of law enforcement. Hoover himself had had a wine cellar while in London and knew the ban against alcohol was not working. Still he felt a constitutional responsibility to enforce the law that had been established democratically. He gave in for resubmission of the Eighteenth Amendment to the states only shortly before his Party's national nominating convention.

LIMITED SOCIAL VISION

With the Depression came domestic unrest, and the military under McArthur drove bonus marchers out of Washington on November 5. The general himself supervised the operation in boots and uniform.

Hoover later remarked, "Thank God you have a government in Washington that knows how to deal with a mob."[16] Tanks, tear gas, and guns were used against women and children as well as men. Actually, McArthur—against Hoover's orders—drove the veterans' group across Anacostia Bridge and reckoned that he did not "want himself or his staff bothered by people coming down and pretending to bring orders."[17] Hoover in his memoirs twenty years afterwards still believed "as abundantly proved later on, the march was in considerable part organized and promoted by the Communists and included a large number of hoodlums and ex-convicts determined to raise a public disturbance."[18]

In campaigning, Hoover lacked most of all what Roosevelt had: charisma. In the period between his defeat in the fall election and the latter's inauguration, Hoover tried to involve Roosevelt in politics and was largely unsuccessful. One of his major concerns was to preserve the gold standard. After Roosevelt came to power, he remained an outspoken critic of the New Deal, objecting to the federal government's interference in personal liberty, lack of congressional work on legislation, and the mass of administrative procedures that were developed without legislative review. Harlan Fiske Stone, a longtime friend of the ex-president, replying to Hoover's book, *The Challenge to Liberty*, wrote "the necessities of an increasingly complex civilization, in which every individual and group within the state becomes interdependent," requires "restrictions on individual liberty. The issue [of industrial depression] cannot be settled by an appeal to the eighteenth-century philosophy of individualism in the abstract, for that philosophy cannot be completely adapted to the twentieth century."

Internationally, Hoover remained a non-interventionist and strict anti-communist who, from the outset, opposed Roosevelt's realistic recognition of the USSR.[19] Later, after the Second World War, he suggested that the United States withdraw from the United Nations and join up with other "God-fearing countries." Much that he defended in economic and international policy would have been more than acceptable in less strenuous times. His morality was fundamentalist, both in looking to the past and in its rigidity—of course, not in terms of his religious ideology, which remained vague. Historians to the present day debate the effectiveness of Hoover's principles. If re-elected, could he have overcome the Depression or would there have been civil war inspired by unemployment? Hoover's fine attributes and services notwithstanding, the larger party of historians agree with the verdict of the majority of Americans when he was defeated in his bid for a second term in office: his policies were a failure.[20] The goal of government should be not only ordered freedom but the economic and social welfare of its citizens.

Hoover long resented what he regarded as the facileness of his political opponent, Franklin Roosevelt. The contrast between the two men was clear. Hoover was more organized and often correct in principle. But he did not see clearly enough the desperate needs of the nation.

Conclusion: Hoover believed in God, but a gentle Quaker deity and not the Calvinist one of Woodrow Wilson. He was, in fact, a technocrat engineer caught in the quagmire of the Great Depression, and not a politician with charisma. No fanatic, he had recognized that both sides invoked morality for their own ends during the First World War. Ruling later, when the stock market collapsed, he was "a humanitarian caught in the wrong place when the lightning struck." The dominant national mood was one of laissez faire when Hoover came to office. Initially, he spoke of ending poverty in the nation by economic progress. Instead, he got Depression. His social ethic continued to be unqualifiedly capitalist and left no place for the social welfare of Roosevelt's New Deal.

Hoover appraised positively the Quaker belief in human nature based on a divine inner light in each individual person. But for him, it was largely secularized. The symbolism of the corruption of original sin did not belong to his outlook. He was courageous and prudent within his own perimeters and was scrupulously honest. John Nance Garner, Franklin Roosevelt's first vice president, observed: "I have never reflected on the personal character or integrity of Herbert Hoover. I have never doubted his probity or his patriotism." In many ways, Hoover was superbly equipped for the presidency; his failure to win re-election marked the watershed end of an era. The presidency took on new activism and ethical realism under his successor.

FRANKLIN DELANO ROOSEVELT

Justice Louis Brandeis commented after meeting Franklin Roosevelt personally that the new president had "a first rate temperament and a second rate mind." The latter could not be said of Barack Obama. He is a first-class intellectual. Both men studied at Harvard. Both came to office in a time of national financial collapse. Whereas Roosevelt's first task internationally was one of patience, waiting out isolationist sentiment until the country was prepared to enter the Second World War, Obama has a much more complicated and many-sided responsibility in combating international terrorism. There no single foe, no enemy generals to sign off on unconditional surrender. Obama's family life is happier than that of the Roosevelts, his religion more evangelical. Franklin Roosevelt held back from the racial integration that his wife Eleanor championed in deference to the Democratic segregationist South, whose votes he needed. He probably never thought long about a black successor.

Who was Franklin Delano Roosevelt?

"Philosophy? I am a Christian and a Democrat—that's all." Quoted in Francis Perkins, *The Roosevelt I Knew.*[1]

"We must all unite in labor and prayer to achieve victory and to bring back to the world an international order dominated by true

Christian principles." Roosevelt to William Cardinal Dougherty, October 19, 1942[2]

Carlo Levi, in *Christ Stopped at Eboli,* tells how in this remote Calibrian Italian village, Levi found pictures of neither the fascist dictator, Benito Mussolini nor of the nation's king in Rome. But portraits of two other figures were present: the Virgin Mary and Franklin D. Roosevelt. They seemed to divide the universe between them: "The Madonna appeared to be a fierce, pitiless, mysterious ancient earth goddess, the Saturnian mistress of this world, the president a sort of all-powerful Zeus, the benevolent and smiling master of a higher sphere."[3] Roosevelt had become an international mythological figure, even in his own lifetime.

Roosevelt was an Episcopal vestryman, not a crusading Presbyterian elder on the pattern of Woodrow Wilson, under whom he had served as assistant secretary of the navy. Roosevelt's goal was not to redeem the world, as Wilson seemed to hope to do, but only to keep liberty alive long enough for civilization to survive. Domestically he crusaded for what theologians have designated as the "social gospel."

Even before American intervention in the Second World War, Franklin Roosevelt wrote to Pope Pius XII in 1939, emphasizing the faith of the masses: "They know that unless there is a belief in some guiding principle and some trust in a divine plan, nations are without light, and peoples perish. They know that civilization handed down to us by our fathers was built by men and women who knew in their hearts that all were brothers because they were children of God. They believe that by His will enmities can be healed; that in His mercy the weak can find deliverance, and the strong can find grace in helping the weak."[4] Whatever else he was, the president was not a religious sectarian.

Psychologically, at home the president achieved "a close feeling of communion with the voters" unparalleled since Jackson's day. The following incident from the 1936 presidential campaign is an example: in New Bedford, Massachusetts a young woman broke through the Secret Service guards and passed the president a note.[5] A textile worker who received the minimum wage of eleven dollars a week, she recently had suffered a 50 percent wage cut. "Please send somebody from Washington up here to restore our minimum wages because we cannot live on $4 or $5 or $6 a week." Brought up with wealth and privilege to feel like a young prince, Roosevelt could identify with others of lesser social standing, making them feel that he understood their needs and suffering.

Seeking to understand Roosevelt's ethics, a biographer invoked the mixed image used by the often cynical Italian political theorist Machiavelli—the lion and the fox. He saw the lion side as embodied in a muscular Victorianism, steady values energetically advanced. At the same time, the new president took a fox-like leap into the new age, following along whatever trail of policy looked most effective, even dashing down it.[6] In short, there was both idealism and opportunism in his strategies. He thought empirically and impressionistically.

The Roosevelt myth was achieved in part at the price of "a necessary deception," one that continued throughout the campaign for office and later in the administration from the White House. The president's crippled physical condition (that he could not use his legs) was concealed from the public from the beginning to the end. The pretense made was that it simply did not exist. The White House imposed a ban on photographs and newsreels showing Roosevelt's braces or depicting him sitting in a wheelchair, or being lifted out of his car.

At the outset, feigning good health and vitality, the candidate flew to Chicago in 1932 to accept his party's nomination. The presidential historian, Forrest McDonald, sums up his own historical evaluation of Roosevelt by saying that he was the most wily and gifted of presidential imagemakers.[7] Psychologically, Franklin Roosevelt was a success. A reporter once remarked that he "must have been psychoanalyzed by God," as he appeared so calm and free of care—never flustered but amiable and urbane.[8] What this meant was sorted out by Barber, the researcher of presidential character, who classified Roosevelt as an outstanding example of the active-positive type. Presidents in this category have had a conviction of their own capability, that they are fully able to meet the challenges of the job. Barber sums up his own evaluation simply: Roosevelt was "healthy minded." One sign of it was that he laughed. A new journal, Common Sense, claimed that the election in which Roosevelt defeated Hoover was a contest between "the great glum engineer from Palo Alto" and "the laughing boy from Hyde Park."[9]

Shortly after his first election victory, the new president had explained his understanding of his relation to his predecessors: "The presidency is not merely an administrative office. That is the least of it. It is pre-eminently a place of moral leadership. All of our great Presidents were leaders of thought at times when certain historic ideas in the life of the nation had to be clarified. Washington personified the idea of Federal Union. Jefferson practically originated the party system as we now know it by opposing the democratic theory to the republicanism of Hamilton. This theory was ... reaffirmed by Jackson. Two great principles of our government were forever put beyond question by Lincoln. Cleveland, coming into office following an era of great political corruption, typified rugged honesty. Theodore Roosevelt and Wilson were both moral leaders, each in his own way and for his own time, who used the Presidency as a pulpit. That is what the office is—a superb opportunity for reapplying, applying to new conditions, the simple rules of human conduct to which we always go back. Without leadership alert and sensitive to change, we ... lose our way.'[10]

THE HISTORICAL SETTING

Roosevelt's religion and ethics will be misunderstood unless they are seen in the setting of his times. He is listed as second greatest in the ranking of presidents, after only Lincoln in the second Riding-McIver poll of historians. An aristocrat, Roosevelt did not belong to the Evangelical Empire; nor was he a Victorian. Alley makes clear that Prohibition and Protestant sectarianism became outdated when he came to power. "Though an Episcopalian, he espoused an a-Protestant, a-ecclesiastical position. This was a personal matter with him, not something to be demonstrated at a prayer breakfast or through religious friends and associates. The Bible he saw in essentially ethical terms, and the manifestation of his biblical insights was often militant, possibly as a result of the profound influence of the headmaster of his prep school at Groton, Endicott Peabody."[11]

Alley concludes that Roosevelt's was not a God who endorsed nationalism, but one who could be trusted to bind up the planet's wounds. The wartime president issued a call to a universal faith for the world, rather than the cry for nationalist faith to galvanize the nation for a titanic struggle against the forces of evil. Unilateralism was the antithesis of what he stood for!

Without Roosevelt's international leadership in the Second World War, fascism might well have triumphed. At the outset of his term in office, he drew the United States out of the most dangerous economic catastrophe the nation ever experienced. "This great Nation will endure as it has endured, will revive and will prosper," he said.[12] In the first hundred days of his administration, Congress, looking to Roosevelt for leadership, enacted legislation of major change—some of it in weeks, others in a few hours. His strategy was a flexible rather than a dogmatic or ideological one.

American historian Richard Hofstadter describes the New Deal as more a series of improvisations than a far-reaching, far-seeing plan, and concludes that it showed little regard for the wisdom of economics. Roosevelt brought an outlook and approach to his office, more than a carefully crafted program. The new chief executive himself observed: "The country needs and, unless I mistake its temper, the country demands bold, persistent experimentation. It is common sense to take a method and try it. If it fails, admit it frankly and try another. But above all, try something."[13] They were the words of a pragmatist rather than an ideologue.

The fresh administration espoused no single philosophy but an attitude. At one of his earliest press conferences, the man from Hyde Park compared himself to a quarterback in a football game. As leader, he knew what the next play would be, but beyond that, he could not predict or plan too rigidly because "future plays will depend on how the next one works." Chance thus had a large role in what was to develop.[14] The skeptic and satirist, H. L. Mencken, quipped of Roosevelt's pragmatism: "If he became convinced tomorrow that coming out for cannibalism would get him the votes he so sorely needs, he would begin fattening a missionary in the White House backyard come Wednesday."[15]

In fact, Roosevelt's piety, while a personal matter, was real.[16] Judge Samuel Rosenman wrote: "While the President was not a regular churchgoer, I always thought of him as a deeply religious man. That he should turn to prayer instead of oratory on the most important day of the war [D-Day] since Pearl Harbor was not surprising; Roosevelt felt a veneration for his Creator which expressed itself often. It was this feeling that made him ask for special church services on particular occasions, such as inauguration days. He was deeply moved during those services, and you could see the effect of them on his face as he left the church to go to the Capitol to take his oath of office. His reference to God, so frequent in his speeches, came naturally to him; they were prompted by the same feeling."

Rosenman concluded that he had often thought that the wartime president's deep concern for citizens whose social and financial situation was the meanest and the lowliest had religious roots in his conviction about the innate dignity of every human being. Roosevelt's gospel, in antithesis to the individualism of his immediate predecessors in the presidency, was the social gospel. Laissez faire individualism had led to an impasse.

Roosevelt, unlike Hoover, genuinely enjoyed public relations. A significant part of his appeal lay in his inclusiveness, his Anglican catholicity. Reaching out, he included the Irish Roman Catholic, Tommy Corcoran, and the Jew, Ben Cohen, among his advisors. A key to Roosevelt's morality is in the simple fact that as an extroverted political leader whose vision was outgoing, he had little time for introspection.[17] He was a fixer, a non-theorist, far more interested in making things work than in understanding their deeper meaning. Roosevelt did not go into politics simply to pursue some "damned duty," as Secretary of State Stimson once said of Hoover.

Practically, there were negatives. The United States recovered only slowly from the Depression, in spite of the New Deal. City bosses benefited, as Roosevelt recognized the reality of power. His leadership had to function in a pluralistic setting, and he was forced to parcel out benefits between national farm organizations, labor unions, and businessmen. Critics argued that although he had concluded his first inaugural address by urging the importance of discipline, he himself propounded no disciplined program. How much was this a fault of character or a necessity of his experiment of the New Deal? Roosevelt himself was the personal embodiment of liberalism, and after him, it found no comparable leader. No one of similar stature took his place as its chief ideologue. His foreign policy in the end became messy, and he left a heritage full of peril for the future as the cold war with communism dawned.

In terms of personal heritage, the second Roosevelt to be president was proud of his aristocratic wealthy family and Harvard background. Moderate Anglicanism came with his side of the family line. Franklin was raised in a religious home not a theologically inquiring one: it could be said that his Christianity was believed in but not mulled over. Holding a similar view at Groton, Endicot Peabody, the master of the prep school Roosevelt attended, was of the opinion that boys should not think too much. The confirmation class the master led and in which Roosevelt shared was more practical than intellectual. Franklin's father had been anti-politics in the style of much of his social class; his son was the reverse.

At Groton, in prep school, "Christianity, character, and muscle" had been the program. This modernist legacy remained throughout FDR's lifetime, his friends believed, although probably the majority of aristocrats in his class questioned it.

In his junior year at Harvard, the young man announced to his stunned mother that he was engaged to his cousin, Eleanor Roosevelt. A personality in her own right, she contributed to his social conscience and her greatest disappointment later in life was his marital infidelity. To her credit, she refused to let him become an invalid after his polio in the pattern his mother suggested. Before his crippling illness, Roosevelt practiced law for five years and found it dull; then he was elected to the New York State Senate. Soon he became assistant secretary of the navy. At the end of Wilson's term in office, he ran with James M. Cox against Harding and Coolidge and lost. Polio may have kept him from another unsuccessful political race.

For Roosevelt's own career, suffering and finitude became most real in the injury polio wracked on his body beginning in August of 1921. It raised religious questions, even for the unintrospective lawyer. Vacationing at Campobello Island, New Brunswick, he became overheated and then immersed in the icy Newfoundland sea. Although he predicted that he would soon regain use of his legs, he was mistaken. Later he was to realize that the first stages of treatment had been muffed by his doctors. Still he fought back. Day after day, the politician aristocrat would haul his dead weight up the stairs by the power of his hands and arms, step by step. As sweat poured off his face, he would tremble with exhaustion. Beginning in 1924, he swam in the mineralized water at Warm Springs, Georgia. In 1927, he founded the Warm Springs Foundation for the care of other poliomyelitis victims. Roosevelt's mother urged him to retire to the family's Hyde Park estate along the Hudson. If he had done so permanently, American history might well have taken a different turn.

Max Lerner reflects admiringly: "The command of his illness became a form of self-command, which, in history's own due time, was translated into the command of a nation." Roosevelt once explained to Francis Perkins that he felt, when he was stricken down, that God had abandoned him, and he was plunged into black despair, in rare explanation of his own inner struggle.[18] There was "the jagged alternations between hope and despair; the necessity of giving blind trust to a physician even when the physician, cruelly pressed, could scarcely trust himself, which had to be ministered to with the utmost firmness, subtlety and tenderness." Still the extroverted optimist a month later could joke: "I have renewed my youth in rather unpleasant manner by contracting what was fortunately a rather mild case of infantile paralysis." Together with his wife, Eleanor, he slammed the door on expressions of despair.

After the president's death, Mrs. Roosevelt reflected: "He had to think out the fundamentals of living and learn the greatest of all lessons—infinite patience and never-ending persistence."[19] Had there been a moral and religious lesson? Asked whether she thought that her husband's illness had affected his mind, she replied, "Yes, I think it did. I think it made him more sensitive to the feelings of people. "

THE NEW DEAL

Before becoming governor of New York, he had supposed that public ills could be cured by laws—legislation that would deal more with the effects than the causes of unemployment, bad housing, and the crisis in agriculture. However, as president, he soon came to understand intuitively that this was not enough, as the Depression was settling in with power. In 1933, the new administration's legislation embodied the social program for farmers and the unemployed that had successfully been a part of Roosevelt's strategy as governor of New York. On the suggestion of Samuel Rosenman, the new leader established his Brain Trust, headed by Raymond Moley. Intellectuals from the university, more than wealthy businessmen, determined government ideology. The Brain Trust included Rexford Tugwell, Lindsay Rogers, and Adolf A. Berle, Jr., most of them professors from Columbia University. H. L. Mencken wrote: "You Brain Trusters were hauled suddenly out of a bare, smelly classroom, wherein the razberries of sophomores had been your only music, and thrown into a place of power and glory almost befitting Caligula, Napoleon I, or J. Pierpont Morgan, with whole herds of Washington correspondents crowding up to take down your every wheeze."[20]

Although strategies changed tactically and in substance, FDR gave the impression that he was always fully in command, offering programs that would work. John Gunther described his news conferences with the word "educational." He "was like a friendly, informal schoolmaster conducting a free-for-all seminar."[21] As it became clear that editors saw him differently than reporters and even disliked him at times vehemently, the president's response was to use radio to bring his message. Robert Sherwood, who polished the script and often gave it drama, remarked that he had never seen a better actor. The presentations were well rehearsed and beautifully executed. Roosevelt's memorable lines in his speeches included the words at his first inauguration: "The only thing we have to fear is fear itself,"—a theme that joined morality and psychology.

"No series of events in modern history is surrounded by more mythology than the New Deal, inaugurated by the 'Hundred Days,'" historian Paul Johnson argued in revisionism at the end of the twentieth century.[22] Johnson believes that Roosevelt really had no program, and what he did was very slow in arresting the Great Depression, although it did change the public mood into one of confidence.

The national government was to do more than just offer guidelines and referee disputes, a strategy that Hoover had already begun. The person who helped Roosevelt most to overcome the Depression, according to Johnson, was the Houston banker, Jesse H. Jones, his secretary of commerce, who ran the Reconstruction Finance Corporation, and was, in effect, the New Deal's banker. A Texan, swearing and hard-drinking,

Jones despised the Eastern banking establishment and advised Roosevelt to call a bank holiday. Then, when the banks re-opened, he insisted on more generous lending policies to stimulate the economy. Uncle Jesse, the Economic Emperor of America, was "the first financial pirate to realize that the new field of opportunity lay in public service" and became secretary of commerce.[23] In Johnson's judgment, he incarnated the state capitalism that Hoover had already attempted and Roosevelt carried further. The Federal Deposit Insurance Corporation, which Roosevelt at first opposed, was organized behind his back by Jones and Vice President Garner.

Johnson is not complimentary in his description of Roosevelt's attempt to keep the American gold price ahead of the London and Paris markets: "He delighted in his deviousness. He told his colleagues: 'Never let your left hand know what your right hand is doing.' Morgenthau, Secretary of the Treasury asked: 'Which hand am I, Mr. President?' 'My right hand, but I keep my left hand under the table.' The downside of FDR's useful cheerfulness in public was what was often an unseemly levity, not to say frivolity, in private, when serious business was to be done."[24]

In fact, Roosevelt was a complex person, and his invocation of religion was more than expediency. "Christian sentiments reverberate throughout New Deal political rhetoric, a reminder of the pervasive influence the Social Gospel has traditionally played in American reform. But when Roosevelt invoked these sentiments in the 1930s, they hit their targets with the authority of Jesus Christ himself."[25]

Roosevelt used religious metaphors to stigmatize the earlier leadership in the Republican era of the 1920s. He would cleanse the temple of the "money changers." Faced with the irresponsible populism of Huey Long and Father Coughlin, he would reach out "to the forgotten man at the bottom of the economic pyramid" in his own way. Roosevelt explained: "There have been administrations in the life of the country which have represented only a part of this great union of interests, and, unfortunately, at times, a very special and narrow interest ... Any neglected group, whether of agriculture, industry, mining, commerce, or finance, can infect our whole life and produce widespread misery."[26]

Roosevelt was a practicing politician concerned with the reality of power; the moral and indeed the religious question is how one orchestrates power. Abe Fortas explained: "Roosevelt was a master at controlling action and making it constructive. He was a real Toscanini. He knew how to conduct an orchestra and when to favor the first fiddles and when to favor the trombones. He knew how to employ and manipulate people." However evaluated, Roosevelt's approach was not as simply occasionalistic, as opponents charged. Charles A. Beard, the American historian who was at times a Roosevelt critic, went so far as to say eulogistically that Roosevelt "discussed more fundamental problems of American life and society than all the other presidents combined."[27]

STRATEGIES

The mature Roosevelt, soon to be deceased, in his last State of the Union message of January 1944, affirmed clear moral conviction about the world, both at home and abroad: "The Republic had its beginning, and grew to its present strength, under the protection of certain inalienable political rights—among them the right of free speech, free press, free worship, trial by jury, freedom from unreasonable searches and seizures .... We have come to a clear realization of the fact that true individual freedom cannot exist without economic security and independence. 'Necessitous men are not true men.' People who are hungry and out of a job are the stuff of which dictatorships are made".[28]

Roosevelt listed as human rights the right to a useful and remunerative job in the industries or shops or farms or mines of the nation, adequate food and clothing, a decent home, adequate medical care, sickness and unemployment protection, and the right to a good education.

Roosevelt had named the lion's goals, to use Burns's figure. But the president remained fox-like in seeking to achieve them. Schlesinger argued of Roosevelt: "His favorite technique was to keep grants of authority incomplete, jurisdictions uncertain, charters overlapping. The result of this competitive theory of administration was often confusion and exasperation on the operating level, but no other method could so reliably insure that in a large bureaucracy filled with ambitious men eager for power, the decisions and the power to make them would remain with the president."[29]

There were other fox-like traits. A significant part of Roosevelt's success grew out of the way he thoroughly seduced the press and its representatives, the reporters, and they went along with him. More open than his predecessors, he allowed any subject to be discussed at his press conferences, and his replies were characteristically lucid and candid. For example, his explanation of the banking crisis in 1933 had such clarity that reporters broke into applause. Still, when necessary, Roosevelt could be evasive, and from time to time he "put a spin on the news," making events sound different than they first appeared to be. There were off-the-cuff remarks as well.

In his second inaugural address, reflecting on the dominant values of the nation, Roosevelt remarked that "one third of a nation [is] ill-housed, ill-clad, ill nourished." Speaking of an improved moral climate in America, he posed as an ethical test "whether we provide enough for those who have too little." Asserting ethical conviction, Roosevelt came out in his second term for a federal anti-lynching law with great rhetorical fervor. But more than two-fifths of the Democrats in Congress were from the racially segregated South, and the proposal was defeated with their support. Actually, as Francis Perkins, his secretary of labor observed, Roosevelt took the capitalist economy for granted as much as he did his family. With the onset of World War II, Roosevelt remarked that he had changed from "Dr. New Deal" to "Dr. Win the War." Franklin Roosevelt, from his wheelchair, was thrust into unique responsibilities and wielded unprecedented power. To his credit, he was not crusader in the mold of Woodrow Wilson. Avoiding fanaticism and wartime panic (such as the persecution of conscientious objectors), he exercised moral leadership in the war against fascism.

WOMEN IN ROOSEVELT'S LIFE

Franklin Roosevelt's relationships with women—his wife, Eleanor; his mother, Sara Delano Roosevelt; his secretary, Missy LeHand; Crown Princess Martha of Norway; and his great love, Lucy Mercer—have become better known as numerous historians have researched and written about them. Whether he remained virile after his polio attack is not known for sure; his sons circulated conflicting rumors about him.[30] It is clear that his political partnership with Eleanor made for a creative presidency, and he knew it. Yet ever since Lucy Mercer came into the Roosevelts' lives, in many respects it was more lawyerlike than on the pattern of deep family affection. Eleanor would not ruin her husband's political career. But she refused to return to their marriage bed after she discovered Franklin's first infatuation with Lucy Mercer, and she mourned until her death the trust that she judged had been lost forever by his betrayal.

Eleanor lived on a long seventeen years after her husband and died in 1962. On her bedside table, she left a faded copy of Virginia Moore's poem, "Psyche." It showed how deep her hurt had been.

> *"The soul that has believed And is deceived Thinks nothing for a while, All thoughts are vile. And then because the sun is mute to persuasion, And hope in Spring and Fall Most natural, The soul grows calm and mild. A little child, Finding the pull of breath better than death... The soul that had believed And was deceived ends by believing more than ever before."*[30]

A single word notation had been written across the top of the poem by Eleanor, "1918."[31]

EVALUATION

Summing up Franklin Roosevelt's character, McDonald reflects that the New Yorker knew better the craft of maneuver. At the same time he was less serious, less deliberate, and less responsible. It would not have been his mode to seek to smooth over the conflict between Stalin and Churchill as to how captured Nazis should be treated with a joke about how many would have to be killed.[32]

Roosevelt never seems to have put utopian trust in the League of Nations or its successor to be, the United Nations. His concern was more for a concert of the great powers able to keep the peace. At the Yalta Peace Conference with Churchill and Stalin, his realism failed him. Eastern Europe fell under communist dominance for nearly half a century.

Like Wilson, under whom he served as assistant secretary of the navy, Roosevelt had a sense of destiny. But it was less legalistically moralist or determinist than that of Wilson. "Roosevelt's reputation, however, will remain greater than Wilson's, and in good part because the circumstances of his martyrdom were more auspicious. Wilson died only after his defeat was a matter of historical record; Roosevelt died in the midst of things .... Further, the very lack of confidence in the American future and a positive program of ideas increases faith in the wonder-working powers of the great man ..."[33]

Roosevelt's ethical model was not bourgeois, and he never would have pampered the middle class as Nixon did. Nor was he as introspective or morose. Instead, his healthy-minded morality has been characterized as a "thou shalt," which supported in principle what Roosevelt wanted to do anyway. At the outset, as early as 1932, Roosevelt stated the conviction that remained throughout his time in office: the presidency is pre-eminently a place of moral leadership. He understood what Americans believed and lived for—their common democratic conviction and the morality implied in it. Human rights and religious freedom were defended to the death against Nazism as well as Japanese emperor worship. The national community and the world were given a new chance through his career and faith in liberty and justice for all.

Alley's judgment is that "Religion gave Roosevelt a sense of destiny not bound to legalistic determinism but a destiny to be worked out in freedom .... His religion had no exclusionist overtones and did not contribute to American Messianism or Christian nationalism ...." as in the case of Wilson. In short, he avoided a Calvinistic strain.[34] Alley argues that what he calls Roosevelt's relativism made it possible for him to view communism rationally. Refusing to stereotype it as a demonic force, he was not ideologically enmeshed. His religion was a universalism that respected God and at the same time did not make intolerant black-and-white distinctions about right and wrong. The wartime president did not crusade against particular evils fanatically, a trait that the German martyr Dietrich Bonhoeffer criticized in Americans

Smith concludes: "Interested much more in the moral, character-building, and social emphases of Christianity than its theological or devotional aspects of Christianity, Roosevelt's faith was sincere but not intellectually sophisticated."[35]

"To the extent that Roosevelt embraced a theological perspective, he largely affirmed the tenets of early twentieth-century liberal Christianity. He most highly valued the Bible's ethical teachings and stressed God's goodness and love, the Ten Commandments, and Christ's Sermon on the Mount. Like other theological liberals, he rejected he doctrine of human depravity." Max Lerner puts the matter clearly. Roosevelt did not believe in evil; in particular, he failed in dealing with the communists at the end of the Second World War.

Even before he was inaugurated, FDR had a close call with death. Returning from a fishing cruise in February of 1933, he stopped at Bayfront Park in Miami, Florida. An unemployed bricklayer, Giuseppe Zangara, fired a revolver at the president-elect from point-blank range. The would-be assassin's bullet missed, as the wife of a Miami physician deflected his arm. Instead, the mayor of Chicago was hit and fatally wounded. What would have been the course of events if Roosevelt had not been so fortunate? The question makes clear how large Roosevelt's contribution turned out to be. He himself refused to speculate about such iffy questions.[36]

HARRY S. TRUMAN

Harry Truman was Franklin Roosevelt's vice president and came to office on the death of the wartime president. Whatever he lacked in education (he did not go to college), he made up for by courage and common sense. Southern Baptist and a Freemason, the president from Missouri was his own man, but on a very different pattern than Roosevelt or Obama. He was anything but a sophisticated Harvard-educated lawyer. The eras of both Truman and Obama rank as watershed times, but in very different settings. Truman's decisions to drop atomic bombs on Japan and to recognize the state of Israel echo on even to Obama's time in the White House. The forty-fourth president seeks to plan ahead more comprehensively, even amid uncertain times. Truman was obliged to respond to crises on short notice (with the airlift to Berlin and war in Korea). He did not confront an economic depression of the intensity faced by Obama. Politically he proved to be a great popular campaigner when he ran on his own for a second term of office. "Give 'em hell Harry" did not move with the finesse of the senator from Illinois, but he did not dodge responsibility or hard decisions. Neither does Obama.

MIDWESTERN "CULTURE PROTESTANTISM"

Harry S. Truman's Midwestern "culture Protestantism" was reinforced by his Freemason affiliation. He was a high-ranking member of the Masonic Lodge in Missouri. He has been described as a bridge figure between the New Deal and the age of Eisenhower. His emotions were on the side his predecessor, "the Boss," Franklin D. Roosevelt— his religious and ideological base closer to Ike. Truman frequently acted from instinct and was often—but not always—vindicated later. His most crucial ethical decision was the atomic bombing of Japan, one that he never regretted. Still it was the most controversial from a Christian point of view. In 1949, Truman told a group of visiting Anglican bishops that the Sermon on the Mount was "what America was living by!"[1]

After his election victory over the Republican candidate, Thomas Dewey, in November of 1948, the Man from Missouri expressed his conviction in detail: "Democracy is, first and foremost, a spiritual force; it is built upon a spiritual basis—and on belief in God and an observance of moral principle. And in the long run, only the church can provide that basis. Our founders knew this truth—and we will neglect it at our peril."

Earlier, in two speeches during the previous year, Truman had said:

> *Religion should establish moral standards for the conduct of our whole nation, at home and abroad. For the danger that threatens us in the world today is utterly and totally opposed to all these things [spiritual values]. The international Communist movement is based on a fierce and terrible fanaticism. It denies the existence of God and wherever it can it stamps out the worship of God .... Our religious faith gives us the answer to the false beliefs of Communism .... I have the feeling that God has created us and brought us to our present position of power and strength for some great purpose.*[2]

The thirty-third president was first of all a realist—and very different in character than Roosevelt's second vice president, Henry Wallace. Soon it became clear that there was a paradox about him: in being a realist, Harry Truman was also a moralist with common-sense religious convictions, unambiguously concerned to do his duty—"his damnedest" as he said. His task was a singularly formidable one.

American foreign policy was at an impasse, as Stalin had been allowed to occupy most of Eastern Europe. His predecessor, Franklin Roosevelt, had never chosen or groomed a successor. The vice president—soon to become president—was not a close friend of the leader he identified as "the Boss," and there were no common plans between them.

It was "the most extraordinary political arrangement of the present century." So Truman's biographer, Robert H. Ferrell, described the Missouri politician's nomination for vice president of the United States. Why did a great power like the United States, at the end of two world wars, bring a Prendergast machine figure to its highest office? Of course, part of the explanation lay in the party leaders' rejection of Wallace. "Truman was a slightly jowly man with a straight mouth and friendly eyes," and he spoke with a twang, his biographer reports.[3] Formerly a county judge—an administrative position— much of Truman's life had been otherwise occupied with American Legion activities and Masonic initiations. But he was no womanizer!

Elected to a second term in the United States Senate, Truman had come to national attention when he successfully initiated and organized an investigation of wartime waste and corruption. From an early age, in his family, he had heard "the muckraking cadences of Progressivism and the militancy of Populism." His parents had revered William Jennings Bryan and Woodrow Wilson as champions of the people against special interests. Whereas Franklin Roosevelt attended Harvard and Wilson had been president of Princeton University, Truman was prevented from attending college because his father had gone into bankruptcy. Along with Andrew Johnson, he was the least formally educated chief executive since Lincoln. "I am just an ordinary American citizen but I am also the President of the United States .... There may be a million other Americans who could hold this office as well as I, but I am holding it and I intend to fill it to the best of my capacity. I'll be darned [he may have said something else] if I will turn this office over to my successor with its prerogatives impaired by an American general [Douglas MacArthur]."[4]

Truman once reflected: "The presidents made the highlights of American history, and when you tell about them, you've got it."[5] In fact, he was from the outset much more than a reflection of the diverse forces left in play by the New Deal. Truman told the British foreign secretary, Anthony Eden, about a month after becoming president: "I am here to make decisions, and whether they prove right or wrong, I am going to make them."[6] The sign on his desk, "The buck stops here!" was his acknowledgment that he had to make unpopular ones. He was interested in the facts and not an ideologue.

Almost as soon as Truman took up residence in the White House, critics had labeled him a man far too small for the job. Truman lacked the charisma and public speaking ability that had contributed so much to Roosevelt's success. Southern Democrats condemned him for his liberal civil rights program. Truman reflected in his diary: "I wonder how far Moses would have gone if he'd taken a poll in Egypt? What would Jesus Christ have preached if He had taken a poll in the land of Israel? Where would Martin Luther have gone if he had taken a poll? It isn't polls or public opinion alone of the moment that counts. It's right and wrong, and leadership—men with fortitude, honesty and a belief in the right that make epoches in the history of the world."[7]

Polls were taken, although not as often as they were in later years. In 1948, advance sample polls predicted that Truman would lose to New York Governor Thomas E. Dewey in the November presidential election. Truman denounced the "Republican do-nothing 80th Congress" and carried on a "give 'em hell" campaign. His moral as well as political victory over Dewey gave him an independent stature of his own. The Truman Doctrine and the Marshall Plan brought aid to Europe as it resisted a communist takeover. When South Korea was invaded, Truman responded with force, acting through the United Nations. In particular, because China had been lost to Mao's Marxism, the last period of his presidency was the era of paranoid anti-communism led by Senator Joseph McCarthy. Actually, Truman's acceptance of General Marshall's advice and withdrawal from China probably saved the United States from a catastrophe as great or greater than the Vietnam debacle.[8]

Whatever else he was, Truman was a sincere patriot. Before the Second World War, following the passage of the Draft Act of September 16, 1940, already a senator, he asked to go on active duty. He dressed in the uniform of a colonel of the field artillery and presented himself at the headquarters of General George C. Marshall, army chief of staff. "General, I would like very much to have a chance to work in this war as a field artillery colonel," he said.

Marshall pulled his spectacles down on his nose and asked, "Senator, how old are you?"

"Well, I'm fifty-six years old," was the answer.

"You're too damned old," was Marshall's answer. "You'd better stay home and work in the Senate."[9]

When he was first approached about the vice-presidential nomination, he played the stubborn Missouri mule when it was nearly in his grasp. The explanation seems to be that the prospect of the presidency scared him.[10]

MORAL PARADIGM

No biographer credits Truman with being an abstract ethical or religious thinker, but to his credit, he never relativized or psychologized good and evil or faith in God. For him, there was right and wrong, and that was the fact of it. "From his parents, especially, he received a set of simple, traditional values, internalized them and held steadfastly to them for ever after…. Harry Truman's world view shaped itself first around the religion-of-the-deed he imbibed at home."[11] Honesty, duty, loyalty, and the Victorian paradigm of moral behavior were what he believed in. Debates about doctrine did not excite or interest him. Like Lincoln and Wilson as well as many other presidents, the moral panorama of the Bible was a source of moral idealism and a concern for social justice. By his twelfth birthday, Truman had read the Bible through twice and could cite chapter and verse as necessary. "I spent a lot of time on the 20th chapter of Exodus (the Ten Commandments) and the 5th, 6th and 7th chapters of Matthew's Gospel (the Sermon on the Mount)," he explained.[12] In fact, Truman reported that he was not interested in "the religious thing" but gave priority to the Bible as the source of moral guidance.

Unlike other Baptists, he seldom used "born again" language. Rather he judged that many of the world's tensions come from differences over religion; hubris was one of its explanations. "It is all so silly and comes of the prima donna complex again."[13] Like George Washington and Franklin Roosevelt, Truman was a Mason. The Enlightenment legacy of the Masonic order complemented his Bible Belt background. He became Masonic Grand Master of Missouri in 1940.

A populist in political background but not an ideological liberal, Truman was prepared to continue the progressive direction of Roosevelt's policies. In race relations, for example, he recognized that blacks wanted justice and not just kindness or charity. Urging continuation of the Fair Employment Practices Commission, the president argued, "Discrimination in the matter of employment against properly qualified persons because of their race, creed, or color is not only un-American in nature, but will lead eventually to industrial strife and unrest. The principle and policy of fair employment should be established permanently as part of our national law."[14]

Truman's counterparts at the Potsdam conference, held at the conclusion of the Second World War, asked him to preside. Joseph Stalin and Winston Churchill found him self-confident and decisive, not halting or reticent. Churchill noted: "He takes no notice of delicate ground; he just plants his foot down firmly on it."[15]

Churchill's physician, Lord Moran, explained further: "His method is not to deploy an argument but to state his conclusions."[16] Truman had no time or interest in ideas and theories simply for their own sake. The new American president was most comfortable with concrete "facts" and did not enjoy abstract discussions of current events or even of history.

Critics complained that Truman's "values were very much those of the business-minded middle classes. George F. Babbitt (if he were a Democrat) would have been a valued member of Truman's poker group, the Harpie Club."[17] It was a one-sided judgment that overlooked his ability to grow in office. His social outlook did expand with experience. In piety, Truman was a country Baptist whose views were close to fundamentalism, although that was not where he came out in the end. He was not impressed with sentimental piety.

The little man from Missouri with a politician's sense of reality was outspokenly frank as well as honest. Fortunately for historians, he wrote letters to himself from time to time, venting his feelings and resentments—and then when he had cooled off, did not send them. Biographers have an especially good picture of what went on in his mind from his diary. Blunt and simple, he was not easily fooled. An example of his evaluations of persons he encountered in different parts of his career has been preserved:

Gas Welch—a thug and a crook of the worst water

Joe Shannon—hasn't got an honest appointee on the payroll

Mike Ross—just a plain thief

Willie Ross, who had recently died—I suspect his sales of rotten paving have bankrupted the government of hell by now

Edward Stettinius (State)—a fine man, good looking, amiable, cooperative, but never an idea new or old

Henry Morgenthau, Jr. (Treasury)—block head, nut

Henry L. Stimson (War)—a real man—honest, straightforward and a statesman

Francis Biddle (Justice)—make your own analysis

Frank Walker (Post Office)—my kind of man, honest, decent, loyal—but no new ideas

Frances Perkins (Labor)—a grand lady—but no politician. F.D.R. had removed every bureau and power she had

Henry Wallace (Commerce)—no reason to love me or to be loyal to me

Harold Ickes (Interior)—never for anyone but Harold, would have cut F.D.R.'s throat or mine for his "high-minded" ideas—and did

Claude Wickard (Agriculture)—a nice man, who never learned how his department was set up

James Forrestal (Navy)—Poor Forrestal ... He never could make a decision.[18]

This outlook carried over into Truman's religious judgments. He alone among incumbent presidents overtly resisted Billy Graham's offer of counsel. The evangelist did gain entrance to the Oval Office, and while he was there, asked the chief executive if he would like to pray with him. "Couldn't do any harm," was the reply. Truman had seen too much of revivalists in his own youth to welcome Graham back to the White House.

Later, after his term was over, the Baptist Mason reflected: "He claims he's a friend of all the presidents, but he was never a friend of mine when I was President. I just don't go for people like that."

Graham had told Truman: "I follow political trends carefully and would be delighted at any time to advise you on my findings among the people." The man from Missouri was not interested![19]

Barber credits the thirty-third president with being an active-positive type and cites William Hilllman who, in *Mr. President,* quotes Truman: "So I don't let these things bother me for the simple reason that I know that I am trying to do the right thing and eventually the facts will come out. I'll probably be holding a conference with Saint Peter when that happens. I never give much weight or attention to the brickbats that are thrown my way. The people that cause me trouble are the good men who have to take these brickbats for me."[20]

After a brisk walk early in the morning, he went at his job with all his might, cheerfully, and he relished it, Barber emphasizes. His first memory was of his laughter while chasing a frog across the backyard. His grandmother once said of him: "It's very strange that a two-year-old has such a sense of humor." He could become angry but was seldom depressed. The White House staff called him "Billie Spunk." Barber notes that when spirits hit bottom in 1948, Truman said: "Everybody around here seems to be nervous but me." And he played the piano. Truman did not hesitate to compare the compound criticism directed against him with the "vicious slanders" against Washington, Lincoln and Andrew Johnson.

Barber's eulogistic evaluation of Truman's character has been challenged by other biographers. Alonzo L. Hamby, for example, finds him to have been much less secure in his own person than Barber alleges.[21] There was a downside to his outlook—in cultural history. Notoriously, Truman was not at home in modern art, music, theater, or architecture—all of which he in part associated with "the crackpot variety of liberals." His diary contains an entry after he visited the Mellon Gallery to view works by Rembrandt and other traditional masters: "It is a pleasure to look at perfection and then think of the lazy, nutty moderns. It is like comparing Christ with Lenin. May there be another awakening. We need an Isaiah, John the Baptist, Martin Luther—may he come soon."[22]

FAMILY AND EARLY CAREER

Truman's parents had financial difficulties while he was growing up, and he also had problems with his eyes. He was told at home to avoid fights, as the family could not afford to replace his heavy-lensed glasses. Even running for a second term as president, he saw himself as the underdog. It was the First World War that called forth Truman's strongest qualities of courage, liberated him for leadership, and gave him maturity. Before his service in the army during the First World War, Truman had been a bank employee and a farmer, had joined the Masons, and had fallen in love with Bess Wallace, whom he later married. He had know her since childhood, and their marriage was a warm and faithful one without a touch of scandal.

Still unmarried, Truman volunteered for National Guard duty when the United States entered the First World War; he was already a member of the organization, and he was assigned the rank of lieutenant.[23]

At the front in France, he was put in charge of a field-artillery battery largely made up of boisterous pranksters. Earlier, two of their commanding officers had broken under the strain of attempting to lead them. When the troops under Truman's command collapsed and ran under enemy fire, he called them every name he knew. "The curses that poured out contained some of the vilest four-letter words heard on the Western Front .... 'It took the skin off the ears of those boys. The effect was amazing,' [the chaplain] Padre Tiernan recalled with pleasure. 'It turned those boys right around.'"[24]

Patrick Anderson reflects in his biography on Truman: "It was as an army captain under fire in France that Harry Truman first learned that he was as brave and as capable as the next man. He learned, too, the rule that says that an officer must always stand by his men. Perhaps he learned that rule too well."[25]

Truman himself explained: "We don't play halfway politics in Missouri. When we start out with a man, if he is any good at all, we always stay with him to the end. Sometimes people quit me but I never quit people when I start to back them up."[26] Truman's style continued to be one of intense loyalty, centered on interpersonal relations. The stick-togetherness pattern of imperfect allies, and a for-me-or-against-me pattern continued into Truman's presidency. He commented to Admiral Leahy: "Of course, I will make the decisions, and after a decision is made, I will expect you to be loyal."

Margaret Truman reflected on her father's philosophy: "the friends thou hast and their adoption tried, grapple them to thy soul with hoops of steel."[27]

Max Lerner writes admiringly of Truman's integrity: "It was a heritage of intense individualism, with disdain for rank, ceremony, 'side,' one that stressed the authentic selfhood of the person, beyond the distortions of success, happiness, fulfillment, power that have attached to individualism in our time." Lerner concludes that it was not just the Benjamin Franklin ("Poor Richard") acquisitive type nor the Walt Whitman "Leaves of Grass," "I sing myself" gender. Rather it was a Mark Twain individualism, "scornful of pretense, stubborn, somewhat perverse, fiercely asserting the authenticity of the natural man."[28]

In the meeting of Truman's small-town Baptist morality and practical politics, first in the local Missouri setting, then in the United States Senate, and at last in the presidency, Truman's ethical paradigm served him well as a leader. Its biblical sources have already been identified, but they did not stand alone. As a boy and then a young man, he had read about and then, he believed, had thoroughly studied history. Actually, his judgments were simplistic, even though he dabbled in world history. President Truman continued to hold a great man theory and even tried to carry it over into his own judgments. At times, in his moral outlook, there were grays, but more often than not, only good and evil with personal relations divided between friends and enemies. Still his ethical model was not projected as overtly on a cosmic scale as much as in the case of Wilson.[29]

THE USES OF POWER

The politician from Missouri understood the reality of power and was not prepared to give it up unnecessarily when he became president. At times, Truman felt he could administer even better than Roosevelt, it is alleged. The new president assuredly was more frank. Patrick Anderson, in *The Presidents' Men,* writes critically: "Presidents owe a loyalty to the nation that transcends any allegiance to erring friends. Roosevelt understood this instinctively; Truman would not recognize it." A further difficulty, according to Anderson, was that Truman was more sentimental than most other presidents. Anderson concludes: "It is often helpful for a President to be a ruthless s-o-b, particularly in his personal relations; this, for better or worse, Truman was not."[30]

In spite of his critics and amid continuing congressional opposition,

Truman's domestic achievements were considerable. "At the end of his nearly eight years in office, housing and full employment acts had passed Congress, as had extended social security coverage and increased benefits, raised minimum wages, and there were limited gains in civil rights as well as consolidation of other New Deal programs."[31] In short, Roosevelt's legacy had not been betrayed. But Roosevelt and Truman were realistic practicing politicians with different motivations and moral models.

One of the greatest achievements of the post-Roosevelt presidency, as Winston Churchill gratefully acknowledged, was the Truman Doctrine, which extended active multilateral participation to nations threatened by Soviet communism. The Marshall Plan, NATO, the Berlin Airlift, as well as the Point Four Program of aid to underdeveloped countries all were initiated in the Truman years. Saner than McCarthy's ravings, they helped to protect Western Europe from Russian power. Retrospectively, these policies were positive and exemplified the new role of American leadership in which Truman believed. The president's long-range goal was to stay ahead of the Russians. It was Truman's decision not only to drop atomic bombs on Hiroshima and Nagasaki, but to proceed with development of hydrogen weapons. In Washington, Eisenhower questioned the wisdom and the necessity of the atomic bombing of Japan, on the grounds that the nation was already virtually defeated. Truman decided to use it to impress the communists as well as to deter a foe.[32]

Will history record that he was equal to the revolution in warfare in which he was a prime actor? The wartime president justified the dropping of the atomic bomb on Japan (opposed by many religious leaders) from the judgment that at least a half million American soldiers' lives would have been lost in an invasion of Japan. Dean Acheson, his secretary of state, wrote that he was totally without "that most disabling of emotions, regret." Yet the tragedy remains. Truman's world was circumscribed, even though his intelligence was sharp. For example, at times he dismissed the Russians as Orientals and accepted the claim that the United States would have at least twenty years' monopoly on atomic weapons. It is too simplistic to suppose, as some of Truman's critics have claimed, that he provoked the cold war. Stalin was ruthlessly oppressive, and by 1949, the Soviets had the bomb, and the arms race was spiraling.[33]

As late as October of 1945, Truman was capable of racial remarks. His "conversion" may have come in September of 1946, when a group of blacks met with him in the Oval Office and gave an account of racial attacks in the South during the past year. A black veteran, Isaac Woodard, wearing his uniform, was taken off a bus in Batesburg, South Carolina, and blinded by policemen who jabbed their nightsticks into his eyes, Truman's visitors reported. Hearing about the incident, Truman was shaken and said, "My God! I had no idea it was as terrible as that! We've got to do something." Finding difficulty in obtaining congressional action, he issued Executive Order No. 8981, which looked toward desegregation of the armed forces.[34]

During the 1948 presidential campaign, a group of Dixiecrats promised to subdue a budding Southern revolt against the Democratic Party if Truman would weaken his civil rights stance. The president's response, related by his daughter, was, "My stomach turned over when I learned that Negro soldiers, just back from overseas, were being dumped out of army trucks in Mississippi and beaten. Whatever my inclinations as a native of Missouri might have been, as president I know this is bad. I shall fight to end evils like this."[35]

At the end of Truman's term in office, January 12, 1953, Roy Wilkins wrote to him: "[N]o Chief Executive in our history has spoken so plainly on this matter as yourself and acted so forthrightly [on segregation] .... Yours was sheer personal courage, so foreign in the usual conduct of political office, high or low."[36]

Truman's relationship with his secretary of state, Dean Acheson, was an especially productive one, as different as the two men were. Truman had his own homespun diplomatic efforts as well. In fact, he once envisaged organizing a moral crusade against communism throughout the whole world. He wrote to Lewis Strauss: "I have had special representatives call on the Patriarch of Istanbul, and I myself have talked to the Chief Rabbi of Israel, as well as a great many of the religious leaders of all sects and opinions in this country."[37] The president explained that he had also met with the chief bishop of the German Lutheran Church, as well as with American Roman Catholic cardinals. Indeed, he had corresponded with the pope. An attempt to establish diplomatic relations with the Vatican was part of his effort. It was blocked by religious leaders as well as politicians. Truman wrote of an American Anglican leader: "Sorry he couldn't see anything but the Totalitarian Church of Rome as ... a menace to free religion! What a travesty!"

SECOND TERM ACHIEVEMENT AND FAILURES

Confronting possible defeat in the 1948 campaign for the presidency, Truman's whistle-stop campaign has been characterized as "exaggeration, hyperbole boisterous, a shouting piece of excitement ... the sort of thing that would have amused Andrew Jackson ... brought laughter to Abraham Lincoln ... and even (though he would have winced at the source of the commotion) produced approval from Franklin Roosevelt."[38]

For example, Truman commented: "You remember the Hoover cart ... the remains of the old tin lizzie being pulled by a mule, because you couldn't afford to buy a new car, you couldn't afford to buy gas for the old one .... By the way, I asked the Department of Agriculture at Washington about the Hoover cart. They said it is the only automobile in the world that eats oats."[39]

Unfortunately, Truman's victory over Dewey, when he won the presidency on his own, did not translate fully into political capital with Congress or the electorate. He could begin but not end hostilities in Korea, and in spite of the heroism of projects like the Berlin airlift, the nation drifted into McCarthyism. In a speech at Wheeling, West Virginia on February 9, 1950, Senator Joseph R. McCarthy of Wisconsin claimed that he held a list of Communists working for the federal government. Truman himself believed that Alger Hiss was a conspirator and remarked to a friend, "The s.o.b. is guilty and I hope they hang him."[40] Of course, he disagreed with McCarthy and his charge that Truman's own State Department was infiltrated with communist agents.

Truman simply did not have the finesse of Roosevelt, as anyone could see. But would the long-term results have been better if Roosevelt's earlier vice president, Henry Wallace, had been in the White House? Fortunately, Truman was concerned with patterns of power—not just good will or altruism. He was firm in his decision about West Berlin: "I'd made the decision ten days ago to stay in Berlin. Jim (Forrestal) wants to hedge—he always does. He's constantly sending me alibi memos, which I return with directions and the facts. We'll stay in Berlin—come what may .... I have to listen to a rehash of what I know already and reiterate my 'Stay in Berlin' decision."

The underlying philosophical question is how much a president is free to control circumstances and events; how much does he respond to them? Critics attacked Roosevelt's successor for believing that United States democracy—seen on his own self-righteous and uncritical terms—was to become the worldwide pattern; his reason was that it is true and right. But unlike Wilson, he was not out to save the world but only seeking to protect his own country, even as in principle he accepted Wilson's internationalism. The verdict of the majority of American historians now is that although he was neither Roosevelt nor Eisenhower, Truman had an efficiency of his own, a moral sense, as well as self-confidence.

Essentially a controversialist, Truman yet saw himself in the tradition of presidents Jefferson and Jackson.[41] Ferrell's judgment is that Truman's greatest virtue was his ability to keep himself separate from the presidency, his sense of self from becoming the role he assumed. Farrell argues that to win, a candidate must be sincere and believe in his own vision of what the country should be. He must "consider himself—to use a seventeenth century phrase well understood in Puritan theology—a chosen purpose for that grand purpose. In that single respect Truman made a superb candidate." [42]

His fellow countrymen came to recognize his virtues more clearly only after several more presidents. "Today, it seems that his plain ways were a throwback to the Puritan fathers' meaning of the world plain: the unadorned life that is stripped of excesses in appearance so that it exists as a testament to the principles beneath."[43]

It is part of Truman legacy that he was much more successful than Harding had been after the First World War or Grant after the Civil War. One reason was that his political common sense was much stronger than that of either of his predecessors. His faith in God was expressed in Baptist and Masonic loyalties. It was his reading of the Old Testament that evoked his immediate support for the state of Israel at the time of its founding— a crucial decision. From his own moral and religious vision, he made a number of watershed choices whose influence remains to the present. Much of his success grew out of the fact that he was not a perfectionist when realism was called for. Truman's influence on history—which he loved to study—was enormous, more than he could ever have expected. For the man from Missouri it was about more than just power—but a contest of world views and moral principles.

DWIGHT D. EISENHOWER

Eisenhower was a distinguished general with a record of major achievements before entering the White House. Older than Obama, and less daring in his administration, Eisenhower made the presidency his second career. Ike had stability and character, as does Obama. At heart, Eisenhower was a conservative Republican, not a reformer seeking change. His religion was more vague than that of his African-American successor. Critics labeled it: "Piety Along the Potomac." The cold war had settled in when Eisenhower came to power, and he sought to control the arms race and prevent an atomic holocaust. Obama needs to do more in a hurry. He does not play a hidden hand (declining to reveal his intentions) as the general did from time to time, for example, in refusing to attack McCarthy directly. The forty-fourth president's battles were political and not military before he took over the White House. Coming to office, he immediately faced a crucial test of armed power in Afghanistan and responded using both traditional military and psychological weapons.

"I am the most intensely religious man I know." *New York Times,* May 4, 1948[1]

"Application of Christianity to everyday affairs is the only practical hope of the world." *Life* magazine, December 26, 1955[2]

Like generals Washington, Jackson, and Grant, Eisenhower was virtually unbeatable once he became a presidential candidate. Even though he appeared to be an amateur as a politician, his political skills were well honed. At the same time, he seemed to be a smiling father figure but had a fierce temper.[3] So the paradoxes of his presidency were identified by a careful biographer who argues—as against the judgment that his personality was one-dimensional—that Eisenhower was perhaps one of the most complex men ever to occupy the White House. His approach to office only appeared to be simplistic. Eisenhower had accomplished a singular fete, leading the Allies' forces that crossed the English Channel and conquered the Nazi army; it was a crossing that neither Napoleon nor Hitler had been able to carry out.

Though seemingly modest, Eisenhower was excited by the adulation of crowds when he returned to the United States. He described his welcome home after the Second World War: "I was amazed at the number of people who met us in the streets and the wild enthusiasm of their greeting. The trip to Washington was so overwhelming, I thought everything to follow would be anticlimax. When we went to New York, however, the entire city seemed to be on hand. Hour after hour, we traveled avenues jammed with people, with incalculable others hanging out the windows of towering office and apartment buildings."[4]

Beginning his first inaugural address, the commander-in-chief of the Allied forces in Europe during the struggle against Hitler offered the following prayer: "Give us, we pray, the power to discern clearly right from wrong and allow all our actions to be governed thereby and by the laws of the land. Especially we pray that our concern shall be for all the people regardless of race or calling."[5] That Eisenhower believed in God and thought religion important for morality was not surprising, in view of risks he had taken in the face of suffering and death, in order to win his great victory on the battlefield. It was not the ritualistic but the civil aspects of faith that were most compelling to him, with his low-church family heritage. He attended Sunday worship as the leader of the free world.

A joining of idealistic and patriotic themes ran throughout Eisenhower's pronouncements in office. His speeches contained more religious rhetoric than virtually any other president. Only a few academics dared to disparage the new "Piety along the Potomac" as too vague and too indefinite. The general had seen the human cost of battle and knew the suffering that modern warfare brings to soldiers and civilians on both sides. America, he assured his audience, "is the mightiest power which God has yet seen fit to put under his footstool." Eisenhower's morality had been instilled from a sectarian revivalist religious conscience. Actually, Piety along the Potomac, his acknowledged beliefs, had little connection with New Testament salvation by faith: "He that conquereth his own soul is greater than he who taketh a city"; "Forget yourself and personal fortunes"; "Belligerence is the hallmark of insecurity"; "Never lose your temper except intentionally."[6]

BIOGRAPHY

The president was named after the famous evangelist, Dwight L. Moody. The Eisenhower family belonged to the River Brethren, a group loosely connected with the Mennonites, one of the traditional peace churches. In typical Anabaptist fashion, River Brethren did not receive believers into the church until they had reached adulthood. Eisenhower left home before he was eligible for baptism and church membership. He was baptized (not by immersion, as was the practice of the River Brethren) and joined the Presbyterian Church in Washington, D.C. after becoming president. He had been brought up a Protestant sectarian with a perfectionist separatist ethic. Now he turned to the Puritan heritage, one more clearly associated with government, and became affiliated with a denomination in the Calvinist tradition. Of course, its theological outlook did not engage him as deeply as it had the Presbyterian, Woodrow Wilson. He did not speak in Wilsonian abstractions, but this did not mean that he was not shrewd or a successful negotiator.

Eisenhower was born in Denison, Texas on October 14, 1890, one of six brothers. The family moved to Abilene, Kansas, where he grew up. Eulogistically, he described his mother, Ida Stover from Virginia, as "by far the greatest personal influence in our lives." In school, he showed such an interest in generals and battles that his high school yearbook predicted a career in the teaching of history. But it developed otherwise. Eisenhower ranked near the middle of his graduating class at West Point, in part because of discipline problems. At the military academy he entered in 1911, he became a heavy smoker and was in rebellion against rules that he believed to be unnecessary. After graduation, while he was stationed at Fort Sam Houston in San Antonio, Texas, he met and married Mamie Doud, a native of Iowa whose family lived in Denver. Eisenhower was not in battle during the First World War. The November 1918 armistice went into effect just a week before he was scheduled to go overseas.

Probably undervaluing Eisenhower as a passive-negative president, Barber (classifying presidential personality) reflects on chief executives in this group: "They were performing their duty under duress, not crusading after some political Holy Grail ... one senses in their attitude an assumption that merely occupying the office of President provided justification enough ... and that their responsibilities were limited primarily to preserving the fundamental values by applying them to disagreements no one else in the system could resolve."[7] A parallel is with Andrew Jackson, who also had a violent temper but was publicly disciplined.[8]

Theodore White, who had reported on a whole series of presidential campaigns, observed:

> *I had made the mistake so many observers did of considering Ike a simple man, a good, straightforward soldier. Yet Ike's mind was not flaccid, and gradually, reporting him as he performed, I found that his mind was tough, his manner deceptive, that the rosy public smile could give way, in private, to furious outbursts of temper; that the tangled rambling rhetoric of his off-the-record remarks could when he wished be disciplined by his own pencil into clean, hard prose.*[9]

In keeping with the Puritan heritage—so often secularized in American politics—Eisenhower linked morality inextricably with the dignity and freedom of individuals. His intention was to reassert a traditional Republican theme. However, unlike Ronald Reagan, his Republican moralism was not exclusively conservative but revived earlier progressive themes as well. Politically, he supported the extension of social security coverage, health insurance, and government-built housing.[10] Eisenhower understood that in spite of the Allied victory, America must struggle for its place, even with its great power antithesis.

Russia was spied upon with high-flying planes and more atomic and hydrogen weapons stockpiled.[11]

MILITARY CAREER

It was Eisenhower's interest in the new weapons called tanks, which he shared with George S. Patton, that earlier started him on the way to national prominence. An article recommending their development as a means of overcoming trench warfare and the slaughter it brought in the First World War was published under his name in 1920. It did not agree with Eisenhower's superiors' views, but he was supported by General Fox Connor, and his career continued with Connor's endorsement. Eisenhower became an aide to General John Pershing and subsequently was assigned to study at the Army War College. In 1929, he was made a personal aide to the chief of staff, General Douglas MacArthur. Eisenhower recognized that without this assignment under MacArthur, he "would not have been ready for the great responsibilities of the war period."[12]

The young military leader served on MacArthur's staff for seven years. It was there, especially, that he learned his skill in administration. Older structures of military command based on the pattern of hierarchy were giving way to a system less like a pyramid, more like a floating crap game. Interdependent functional specialties, organized in teams, had to be brought together around new technological and strategic concepts. Eisenhower was skillful personally in this "game," and its central coordination pattern carried over into his presidential administration. Personally, he was disappointed in MacArthur's political partisanship and disapproved in particular of his superior's conduct in putting down the Bonus March of 1932. Commanding the operation, MacArthur supervised the removal of the unemployed veterans camped near the Capitol, even branding them as communist revolutionaries.

After serving with MacArthur in the Philippines, Eisenhower returned to Fort Sam Houston in mid-1941. Marshall called him to Washington five days after Pearl Harbor and would have liked to keep him there. However, when Eisenhower was sent to London in May 1942 as a liaison between American and British strategists, his performance so impressed Winston Churchill that he was assigned to command the Allied invasion force. Eisenhower skillfully dealt with military and political leaders of diverse countries, bringing harmony out of chaos. At the same time, he was firm and even blunt with military in the field, for example, George Patton, whom he finally removed from command for insubordination in the occupation period.

Earlier, he had written to Patton: "Dear General Patton: You first came into my command at my own insistence because I believed in your fighting qualities and your ability to lead troops in battle. At the same time, I have always been fully aware of your habit of dramatizing yourself and of committing indiscretions for no other apparent purpose than that of calling attention to yourself."[13]

Eisenhower was not an uncritical militarist. He did not love war as Patton did. When told of the imminent use of atomic weapons against Japan by Secretary of War Henry L. Stimson, he opposed it on the grounds that Japan was already nearly vanquished. For a period after the war, he served as head of the Joint Chiefs of Staff in Washington, and eventually as the Allied commander of NATO in Europe; the latter he regarded as "the most important job in the world."[14] Between military assignments, he accepted the presidency of Columbia University in October 1948. His ties with the academic world never were very strong.[15] "No intellectual, he was not at home in the world of ideas."[16]

Yet Eisenhower's presence was more decisive and pervasive than it first appeared to be to many observers. Richard Nixon said of his predecessor that he was a far more devious man than most people realized, and in the best sense of those words. Not shackled to a one-track mind, he always applied two, three, or four lines of reasoning to a single problem, and he usually preferred the indirect approach where it would serve him better than a direct attack on a problem.[17] But there were also unhappy mistakes, the Faubus and U-2 affairs, the McCarthy contagion, and Dulles's brinkmanship.

As against the dominant piety in Washington, the United States Supreme Court was already enforcing the non-establishment clause of the First Amendment in a way that it had not been imposed before. Under Eisenhower's watch, it declared racial segregation in the public schools unconstitutional during his second year in the White House. When Governor Orval E. Faubus attempted to obstruct the integration of a high school in Little Rock, Arkansas, the president handled the matter by sending in a thousand federal troops. White resistance continued into the administrations of his successors, with Martin Luther King, Jr. leading in crucial change.

In foreign affairs, Eisenhower refused to intervene when uprisings occurred in East Germany in 1953 and Hungary in 1956, although his secretary of state, John Foster Dulles, had spoken of "liberating" captive peoples in communist countries. Religious persecution went on at a large scale behind the iron curtain. The president did not support the British and French invasion of Egypt—one of his most crucial decisions. Not surprisingly, Americans felt threatened when the Soviet Union launched the first man-made satellite ever to orbit the earth in October of 1957. The National Aeronautics and Space Administration was established in July of 1958, and funding for scientific research increased.

MOTIVATION

Barber justifies the passive-negative classification he assigns to Eisenhower as follows: On multiple occasions, the president "asserted himself by denying himself."[18] That is to say, Eisenhower took a stand against the suggestion that he should take a strong stand. Barber explains:

> *Eisenhower would not get down in the gutter with Joseph McCarthy nor stop the Cohn and Schine hi jinks. He thought that Franklin Roosevelt had usurped congressional powers and said when 'those damn monkeys on the Hill' acted up, he would stay out of it. Press conferences were another Roosevelt mistake. Eisenhower did not like them. Was he under attack in the press? "Listen," Eisenhower said, "anyone who has time to listen to commentators obviously doesn't have enough work to do."[19]*

Barber points out that President Eisenhower did not so much select problems upon which to concentrate as he selected an aspect of all problems—the aspect of principle. It was a self-conscious morality that at times he claimed to be apolitical. In self-denial and refusal, he was not attacking or rejecting others but simply turning away from them. That

Eisenhower had achieved distinction before being elected president gave him a very different outlook than occupants of the White House who had yet to establish their image.[20]

Why then did he run for president? There was an important moral dimension. Barber identifies it by saying that Eisenhower was a sucker for duty. The general reported that "A decision that I have never recanted or regretted [was the decision] to perform every duty given me in the Army to the best of my ability and to do the best that I could to make a creditable record, no matter what the nature of the duty."[21] From home Bible reading to the West Point creed, he felt that duty was a certainty. Still, his duty was not to save the world or to become a great hero. Barber is correct that the great strength of such character is its legitimacy: "It inspires trust in the incorruptibility and the good intentions of the man."[22] But the difficulty lies in its inability to produce results. Passive-negative type presidents often preside over drift and confusion amid the apparent orderliness of formalities.

Finally agreeing to run for the presidency, Eisenhower's platform emphasized the inadequacy of the nation's response to communist threats to freedom around the world. He opposed what he regarded as the debilitating influence of the federal government's domination of the economy, and he rejected centralization. The candidate called for restoration of initiative to states and local communities, along with reliable internationalism. However, he was not in favor of the dismantling of the complex of federal social welfare agencies; in short, he still supported much of Roosevelt's social strategy. Although Truman had been friendly toward him, in the end, Eisenhower did not reciprocate.

McCarthyism, along with the Korean War, had become an issue in his first campaign for the presidency. Eisenhower himself accepted the Wisconsin senator's goal of removing subversives from the federal government. Still, as a military man and colleague of General George Marshall, he resented McCarthy's denunciation of his mentor as a traitor who had abandoned China to the communists. Campaigning in Denver, Eisenhower offered a measured defense of Marshall, one that he planned to repeat when he spoke in Milwaukee with McCarthy on the platform. Meeting personally with McCarthy, Eisenhower gave the Minnesota senator a stinging rebuke. But at the urging of the governor of Wisconsin, Eisenhower removed the defense of Marshall from his speech. Enough had been said, he was counseled. Critics saw indecision in the stance, which continued virtually to the end of the McCarthy episode. Eisenhower never took on the smear tactics and lies directly. Was it cowardice and moral weakness?

In September of 1951, the Republican senator from Ohio, John W. Bricker, proposed a constitutional amendment forbidding executive agreements in foreign relations without the consent of Congress. The proposed amendment was directed especially against the Yalta Conference accords made by President Roosevelt. Eisenhower's strategy was typical, as in the McCarthy case. Privately, he voiced the opinion that such an amendment to the Constitution would "cripple the Executive power to the point that we [would] become helpless in world affairs." Still he tried to avoid public controversy and played for time. Finally forced into direct opposition, his cause won by only one vote in the Senate. Eisenhower had once commented: "Rich organizational experience and an orderly, logical mind are absolutely essential to success. The flashy, publicity-seeking adventurer can grab the headlines and be a hero in the eyes of the public, but he simply can't deliver the goods in high command. On the other hand, the slow, methodical, ritualistic person is absolutely valueless in a key position. There must be a fine balance .... In addition ... a person in such [high] position must have an inexhaustible fund of nervous energy ... and to force them [subordinates] on to accomplishments, which they regard as impossible."[23]

The president's personal papers give evidence of a logical and critical mind, and historians have upgraded their rating of him. Still, he often gave a different impression. There were awkward and confusing moments at news conferences, marked by uninformed and even garbled sequences. On occasion, the answers to questions were dense by design, and he could say, "I'll have to look that up." It could be a strategy for avoiding the issue. The view that Eisenhower was a figurehead in his own government was set forth in the 1958 bestseller by Marquis Childs, *Eisenhower: Captive Hero*. With a flaring temper, the general could be moody and temperamental with his advisors.[24] Culturally, his tastes were not sophisticated. He read light escapist Westerns and whistled the theme song from the film *High Noon* for months. The Eisenhowers relaxed with a group of wealthy friends called "the gang."

Eisenhower finally decided to run for a second term, even after a heart attack. During his second term, he put his prestige on the line as he attempted to limit federal spending, especially on defense. United States defense efforts had brought new problems. Returning home from a summit meeting with Eisenhower in September 1959, Nikita Khrushchev spoke positively about prospects for peace. Then U-2 spy plane pilot, Francis Gary Powers, was shot down near Sverdlovsk. U-2 spy planes had been flying over the Soviet Union since 1956 at an altitude of 60,000 feet. Eisenhower's most recent authorization had been that flights be made not later than May 1. In two weeks, Macmillan, de Gaulle, Eisenhower, and Khrushchev were to meet in the Elysee Palace in Paris. Khrushchev was informed of the overflight during the May Day celebration in Moscow and went public on May 5 and 7. Eisenhower at first authorized continued lying about the project, and Khrushchev was relentless in his polemic at the Paris meeting of the big four. Subsequently, Eisenhower in a fit of temper, described the Russian as a "son of a bitch ... completely intransigent and insulting to the United States."[25] He authorized the CIA to proceed with plans to overthrow Castro, even though he had earlier pledged non-intervention.

LEGACY

Eisenhower did show sound common sense; he was not a moral relativist. He explained:

> *Difficulties arise, of course, when we begin to apply basic truths to human problems .... While in the field of moral truth of basic principle the statement tends to be black or white, the task of the political leader is to devise plans among which humans can make constructive progress. This means that the plan or program itself tends to fall in the "gray" category, even though an earnest attempt is made to apply the black and white values of moral truths. This is not because there is any challenge to the principle*

or the moral truth, but because human nature is far from perfect. The principal objective is to make progress along the lines that principle and truth point out. Perfection is not quickly reached; the plan is therefore "gray" or "Middle-of-the-road." But it is progressive![26]

In his last weeks in office, the retiring president's farewell speech showed his statesmanship at its best. His remarks about the dangers of the garrison state have been the most widely quoted of all. The "conjunction of an immense military establishment and a large arms industry is new, in the American experience. The total influence—economic, political, even spiritual is felt in every city, every State house, every office of the Federal government .... In the councils of government, we must guard against the acquisition of unwarranted influence, whether sought or unsought, by the military-industrial complex."

The magazine *Nation* wrote that for eight years, he had seemed to be unable to grasp the problems of the time; now he spoke like the leader its editors had longed for.

Patch and Richardson believe that Eisenhower would have been especially pleased with the assessment of his presidency that dominated the historical literature during the Eisenhower Centennial Year of 1990.[27] "Eisenhower deserves high praise for framing defense issues not just in economic, but in moral terms. Security to him meant preservation of fundamental values, and he never forgot that weaponry was simply a means to that end."[28] In these terms, he is credited with a rare blend of strategic competence and principled reflection. But as principled he was too rigid and aggressive, and he could never admit that anti-American hostility was at times unconnected to the cold war. Eisenhower's greatest failures, Patch and Richardson conclude, came not from lethargy or ineptitude but lack of vision. He contributed little if anything to abating the growing tensions of race and class, even as his outlook became more and more outdated. "To a great extent Eisenhower achieved what he wanted. He was not able to ask for more."[29]

Writing of what he views as "the misfortune of Eisenhower's presidency," Patrick Anderson concludes in *The Presidents' Men*, the misfortune "is that a man of such immense popularity and good will did not accomplish more. All the domestic problems that confronted the nation in the 1960s—the unrest of the Negro, the decay of the cities, the mediocrity of the schools, the permanence of poverty—were bubbling beneath the surface in the 1950s, but the President never seemed quite sure that they existed, or if they did, that they were problems which should not concern him."[30]

Paradoxically, Eisenhower later became a hero to the new left. William A. Williams, a specialist in United States diplomatic history, argues that the general had an instinct for the visceral: understand who you are and be true to that knowledge. "Play no games. Do not scramble around on a bean stalk reputed to top out among the upper class."[31] Williams praises Eisenhower as one who could recognize and accept the limits of power in a way that General Douglas MacArthur could not.

Williams finds Eisenhower to have been a great soldier, at least in a professional sense. He understood that the war against Germany would be an extremely bitter struggle and opposed all peripheral campaigns. His strategy could be regarded as cautious and hesitant only by those who did not understand the situation. Eisenhower had recognized the importance of tanks and planes long before MacArthur. Lacking the overwhelming force that is required to be ruthless, he applied the force available in steady pressure. In time, he maneuvered the Germans into defeat and surrender with a limited army.

Williams concludes that the same characteristics came through in the cold war. "He alone cooled it down. The boy from Kansas may not have been properly ruthless, and no doubt failed to force through all the reforms that were desirable, but at crucial moments he could and did speak two very important words, 'Enough' and 'No.' No doubt, he should have said them more often; and then gone on in other matters to cry 'Yes' and 'More.' But he turns out to have been saner than his immediate successors in the White House."

RELIGIOUS EVALUATION—IDENTITY AND IMAGE

Writing in *Presidential Greatness*, Thomas Bailey reflected of Eisenhower: "He was a conciliator and accommodator, an apostle of the middle way, rather than a critic and crusader; a tranquilizer rather than a stimulant. American soldiers are trained to defend things, not to uproot them; the Army does not ordinarily produce flaming liberals."[32]

Neither a political scientist nor a biblical scholar, he held the nation together in moral idealism against isolationism more effectively than Wilson. In terms of long-term vision, Bailey concludes, the president's program and outreach left something to be desired regarding love of neighbor and care for the needy. He lived in an era of Billy Graham's rising revivalist piety. Paradoxically, it was in the same period that the Supreme Court secularized the public schools by banning prayer and Bible reading. Billy Graham, moved by Eisenhower's "sincerity, humility, and tremendous grasp of affairs" had urged the general to become a candidate for the presidency. Eisenhower reciprocated, saying that the evangelist was "remarkably gifted and had accomplished much good." Graham would tell Eisenhower, "Like Lincoln, you have put a spiritual emphasis in the White House, and like Lincoln you have been dedicated to a cause."[33]

Lincoln had as his goal that he himself was on God's side. He was not always sure that God was on his. Eisenhower and Graham were more confident that God was their ally, critics alleged. Graham would write, urging the wartime hero to run for a second time: "I realize that this is a hard thing to say—you have already given so much of your life to your country—yet in probably the most unique way in American history you have been placed in the office of president, not only by the overwhelming confidence of the American people but also by Divine Providence."[34]

Writing from a more critical perspective, Alley sees Eisenhower's elevation to the presidency as the restoration of American Messianism.[35] "It was not prophetic religion set on the cutting edge, but affirmation of the status quo. Dwight Eisenhower was the marvelous champion of the Goldilocks Era, that Everything will work out all right if one takes the cards which are dealt to him and plays them properly." The leader of the war in Europe was convinced that soldiers and clergymen are in the same business—defending the dignity of man and the glory of God. He was fervent but vague about religion. His brother Milton explained that the president took membership and was baptized in the Presbyterian church in Washington, D.C.—to provide spiritual simulation and to protect American freedom and democracy in the world. It was not an evangelical "twice born" experience.[36]

In all fairness, it needs to be said that Eisenhower's premise had already been espoused by his predecessor, Harry Truman. It was that democracy is founded on biblical values and on the belief that each individual human person has worth in the sight of God. Smith enumerates the signs of his faith: commitment to prayer, view of the Bible, attitude toward death, belief in God's providential direction of history, and conviction that the United States rested on a firm religious foundation. His hope was to help solve "the fearful atomic dilemma." The pursuit of peace is "our religious obligation and our national policy."[37]

Eisenhower, in fact, said little about Jesus. "I believe in democracy." This had been his confession of faith, issued with the intent of rallying all "faiths" to endorse the American system as God's way.[38] In Alley's judgment, Eisenhower embodied the secular religion described by Will Herberg, Reinhold Niebuhr's Jewish friend and admirer, as "being serious about religion but not taking religion seriously."[39] There was a domestic move to the right, a return to the ethos of the pre-New Deal Harding, Coolidge, Hoover era—but in a very different time, not just copying it. It was as humorless as the culture in which it carried on. The Norman Vincent Peale and Billy Graham line was being advocated from the White House. Smith concludes: "Clearly, Eisenhower did not have a well developed biblical worldview grounded in extensive study of the Scriptures and Christian literature …. Although his faith was authentic, not hypocritical or pretentious, it appears not to have been as central to Eisenhower's philosophy and persona as he apparently believed or wanted others to think."[40]

JOHN F. KENNEDY

Obama—like Kennedy—has drawn great crowds of admirers inspired by semi-religious motivation. Like Kennedy, he champions social change and wants action—to begin to get something done now. He is probably less cynical and more personally religious than the martyred president. Kennedy had the opportunity to bring some of the best social insights of Roman Catholicism to America's common life during the papacy of Pope John XXIII but failed to do so. Instead, it was his funeral that most reflected the country's common patriotic civil religion in relation to his person. Although Kennedy had contact with Martin Luther King Jr., he moved slowly on questions of integration. Kennedy's progressive social program was not enacted by Congress in his lifetime, but later, under Lyndon Johnson, his successor. One must hope that Obama is more effective in working with the legislature. He is not a rich man's son (as was Kennedy), has better health, is not sexually indulgent, and has set very high goals for himself in a time of national crisis.

"I am not the Catholic candidate for president. I am the Democratic candidate for president who happens to be a Catholic." —John F. Kennedy, to the Greater Houston Ministerial Association, September 12, 1960

Kennedy died too young. At forty-three years of age when he was sworn into office at the beginning of 1961 he was, by contrast, strikingly younger than his predecessors. His coming to the White House, admirers believed, would put an end to intellectual, cultural, and moral stagnation. "The Kennedys seemed young, vital, happy, warm, and caring. Their physical attractiveness was surely a powerful factor in the polls; numerous studies have shown that Americans tend to equate good looks with intelligence, sensitivity, sincerity, self-confidence, independence, poise, competence, and good character."[1]

The image that Kennedy created on the day of his inauguration was so powerful that no failure or disaster—not even death itself could ever finally dim it for his admirers. The new White House family was the equal of movie and television stars in glamour, and the symbolism of the utopian dream of Camelot—a musical the president loved to hear—came to be associated with the Kennedys.[2]

Arthur Schlesinger, Jr., the American historian who worked for Kennedy and later wrote a history of the young president's time in office, remembered: "Washington positively fizzed in 1961. [It] seemed engaged in a collective effort to make itself brighter, gayer, more intellectual, more resolute. It was a golden interlude ... One's life seemed almost to pass in review as one encountered Harvard classmates, wartime associates, faces seen after the war in ADA conventions, workers in Stevenson campaigns, academic colleagues, all united in a surge of hope and possibility."[3]

John F. Kennedy's presidency lasted only 1,037 days. Following his assassination in Dallas, Texas on November 22, 1963, he was mourned worldwide. The young president's death evoked the potent mythology of kings and martyrs. What would his achievement have been if he had not been martyred? Citizens mourned his assassination with a deep sense of America's national destiny. Kennedy had brought a gaiety and grace to his office that had been lacking before in many of his more ordinary predecessors. Mary MacGregor reflected: "That lightsome tread, that debonair touch, that shock of chestnut hair, that beguiling grin, that shattering understatement ... He walked like a prince and he talked like a scholar. His humor brightened the life of the republic."[4]

Only Lincoln and Franklin Roosevelt had aroused comparable grief following their deaths in office. At first, among historians, Kennedy's reputation skyrocketed. Schlesinger and Theodore Sorensen championed the young president's reputation, establishing what has been called a kind of pro-Kennedy orthodoxy. Disclosure of his ever-present marital infidelities, together with his role in encouraging military action in Vietnam, caused his image to plummet. In one historian's list, he was rated above average but only as thirteenth in performance. Critical negative biographies continue to appear, putting Kennedy's admirers on the defensive.

It cannot be said that the first and only Roman Catholic president brought very much positively from his religion to public life, even though it was the creative era of the Second Vatican Council. He has been recognized retrospectively as not too religious, although he had been taught by his parents to attend Mass. Sorensen, one of his intimates, reflected that he cared "not a whit for theology." Herbert Parmet referenced a close friend's judgment when he said that Kennedy had "no sense of piety as an internal characteristic."[5] Gary Wills, himself a Roman Catholic, reflects: "It is an old story: for 'one of your own' to get elected, he must go out of his way to prove that he is not just one of your own. The first Catholic President had to be secular ... in Catholic ... supererogation."[6] What did he really believe about good and evil? How was he motivated morally? A critical, calculating, "hard cold warrior," his ideology was primarily a pragmatic trust in reason joined to the quest for power.

Beginning with his inaugural address, Kennedy espoused the nation's enlightenment-based faith in liberty with rhetoric that has outlived his foibles: "I have sworn before you and Almighty God the same solemn oath our forebears prescribed nearly a century and three quarters ago ... And yet, the same revolutionary beliefs for which our forebears fought are still at issue around the globe—the belief that the rights of man come not from the generosity of the state but from the hand of God."[7] Enlightenment optimism was joined with a secularized Puritan sense of manifest destiny in Kennedy's patriotic language, although he himself was not in any sense a Puritan: He concluded: "With a good conscience our only sure reward, with history the final judge of our deeds, let us go forth to lead the land we love, asking His blessing and His help, but knowing that here on earth God's work must be truly our own."

Kennedy ranks with Lincoln, Roosevelt, and Wilson as motivating his followers. His personal tastes were middlebrow, but he associated with the highbrow. Intellectuals, artists, and musicians attended his presence at the White House. Still there was an evident paradox in Kennedy's inspirational capability; it was not overtly emotional. He affected a cool style and favored rational arguments. Beneath the surface, he held an ironic and fatalistic view of life, one accompanied by an irreverent wit and a wry sense of humor. Characterized by his wife as "an idealist without illusions," he invoked moral idealism in support of his political goals.[8]

The president-to-be's election strategy made obsolete many of the accepted rules of traditional campaigning. Old political lore and established precepts fell before his determined and powerful drive for the White House. Kennedy's action has been compared to a badger's savage instinctive plunge for his victim's jugular--ruthless, and direct. It went on through some fifteen years with undeviating purpose and ended in a breathlessly narrow final victory. Kennedy's world view was more activist and intellectual than that of Eisenhower, more skeptical than that of Truman. Whereas Eisenhower had viewed politics with disdain, Kennedy participated gladly in the political process. Skeptical of causes as well as strategies, his own resources for winning were more important than any ideology.

The young leader's world view was more activistic and intellectual than that of Eisenhower and more skeptical than that of Truman's ideology. Kennedy's own deepest concerns were singularly pragmatic, and his ruthlessness was only partly concealed. His was a time when the national ethos was one of a still vital hopeful liberalism—not the cynicism and despair of the later era after the Vietnam War and Watergate. Unlike other more careful, experienced members of Congress, Kennedy made no secret of his ambition, even as his philandering was carried to the point that would have threatened his career if it were disclosed in the press. Ideology and power, as tools of politics, were used every waking moment in traits of character learned most of all from his father. Under pressure from the latter (who was a friend of McCarthy's), John Kennedy was the one senator whose vote was not on record to censure him.[9]

BIOGRAPHY

Kennedy, in his realism, understood correctly that the roots of the Soviet-American conflict were so deep that it could not be settled easily. A cold warrior, he recounted Winston Churchill's question, "If this is what they do in the green wood, what will they do in the dry?" Bored by Secretary of State John Foster Dulles's moralistic rhetoric, Kennedy rejected the Eisenhower-Dulles massive retaliation military policy as dangerous and outmoded. Still, he conceived of America's role as necessarily one of militant leadership in the cold war. This stance was evident in the Bay of Pigs invasion, which he authorized as well as in his negotiations with Khrushchev.

Like every other president, his biography explained a great deal about him. Kennedy was Irish Roman Catholic by birth and tradition. His paternal great-grandfather, Patrick Kennedy, immigrated to the United States from Dunganstown, a small village in southeast Ireland in 1848. President Kennedy's father, Joseph Patrick, born forty years later in 1888, attended Harvard rather than a Roman Catholic college or university. Practical-minded, he cared little for books or ideas but he did manage to marry the Boston mayor's daughter, Rose Fitzgerald. "Honey Fitz," as the mayor was called, was long a popular figure in the city.

Still resenting that he was not allowed to join the old Boston Brahmans, Joseph Kennedy had become a millionaire by the age of thirty-five. Roosevelt appointed him as ambassador to the Court of St. James in England because he was one of the few businessmen to support the New Deal in 1932. Kennedy Senior's suggestion that the English give in before the Nazi threat ended his own chances for the presidency. Nonetheless, it seems a fair surmise that without his father's riches, John F. Kennedy would never have become president, and the elder Kennedy helped to chart shrewd political strategy all the way to the White House for his family. He not only cleared the way, it was said, he paved it.

Never fully accepted by Boston's socially prominent Brahmans, Joseph Kennedy moved with his family to New York in the mid-1920s. He was almost certainly involved in illegal liquor smuggling in the Prohibition era; he subsequently turned to investment in motion pictures. Kennedy Senior had made much of his money in the stock market in the Roaring Twenties. "It's easy to make money in this market," he once remarked. "We'd better get in before they pass a law against it."[10] He was a clever, tireless, tight-lipped, and ruthless manipulator in a time when the market was often "the closed preserve of tipsters, insiders, and manipulators." Joe and his fellow traders would take options on selected idle stocks, causing market activity. When prices went up far enough, they would take their profits. They sold and left gullible suckers to take the losses when the stocks declined again over time.[11]

The Kennedys' second son, John Fitzgerald—nicknamed "Jack"—had a record of illness from childhood. A physician noted that he was born with an unstable back, and he suffered from it terribly, even while president. Later in life, he was diagnosed with Addison's disease, and he also became infected with venereal disease from his carousing. John F. Kennedy's rise to the White House required deception comparable to that used about Franklin Roosevelt. In many respects, his illnesses were more life-threatening than Roosevelt's crippled legs.

Jack went to Choate, a prestigious prep school, and in 1936, entered Harvard. He graduated cum laude. His senior thesis, "Why England Slept?" was edited by Arthur Krock of the *New York Times* and was later made into a book. Promoted by his father, it had major sales and won a Pulitzer Prize.[12] For a brief time, it was on the bestseller list. In response to a question about it from Ambassador Kennedy, the English political scientist, Harold Latski (under whom John F. Kennedy was alleged to have studied but did not), replied: "I don't honestly think any publisher would have looked at that book of Jack's if he had not been your son, and if you had not been ambassador."

The future president wanted most of all to go to war after the Japanese attack on Pearl Harbor. Because of his unstable back, he easily could have avoided military service but chose not to do so. He also had an ulcer and asthma. During his time in the navy, he often wore a corset and slept on a board. For the first three months of service in the navy, the future president held a desk job in the Office of Naval Intelligence in Washington. J. Edgar Hoover, the FBI head, held records of his affair with Inga Arvad, a twice-married Danish woman who was suspected of being a German spy. Biographers have speculated that she was the only woman with whom he was ever really in love. Arvad, for her part, described young Kennedy as self-centered and having a great disrespect for structures along with much self-centeredness. She reflected that the elder Kennedy's authoritarianism had warped his son.[13]

As the navy was short of skippers for its eighty-foot PT boats (which carried a ten-man crew), young Kennedy was put in charge of this type of small vessel. It was a position that did not require a physical examination. In battle on August 2, the Japanese destroyer *Amagiri* rammed his PT 109 about 2:00 AM, causing a gasoline explosion on board. Kennedy was courageous after the crash, and he bravely helped to rescue some of his men from the water.[14] A naval review board gave him a medical discharge at the end of 1944.

At home, there had been the worst possible news for the family: the death of Joe Junior. An experimental bomber designed to knock out V-1 "buzz bomb" launching ramps in France had exploded and killed the Kennedys' first son. At Christmastime in Palm Beach, their father gave the next youngest brother the assignment of taking Joe Junior's place in a career in politics. In order to campaign, Jack moved to Boston and began preparations to run for the congressional seat from the Eleventh Massachusetts District. James Michael Curley, the incumbent, planned to run for mayor. Young Kennedy won by a large majority. Speaker of the House Tip O'Neill later wrote, "Looking back on his congressional campaign, and on his later campaigns for the Senate and then for the presidency, I'd have to say that [JFK] was only nominally a Democrat. He was a Kennedy, which was more than a family affiliation. It quickly developed into an entire political party, with its own people, its own approach and own strategies."[15] The Kennedys always operated with a close clan hierarchy, Garry Wills argues in his book entitled *The Kennedy Imprisonment, A Meditation on Power;* there was an inner circle.[16] To those who belonged by birth were added the honorary Kennedys. No one was allowed to break step.

Jackie, whom John F. Kennedy married in September 1953, had studied at Vassar and the Sorbonne and graduated from George Washington University in 1951. Her husband-to-be thought of her as a woman of "class" and was impressed with her knowledge of foreign languages as well as of ancient history.[17] A model of good looks, taste, dignity, and poise, Jackie played a vital role in Kennedy's image-making. Crowds were larger when she went along. Jackie got along well with Jack's father but not with his mother, Rose Kennedy, and there was strain from the start. She was realistic in accepting her husband's philandering. As bills came in from Jackie's spending sprees and her extravagance (probably in part revenge), they soon became a point of controversy between the couple.

OUTLOOK

As the question of Kennedy's Roman Catholicism became an issue in his political campaign for the presidency, his religion turned out to be an asset rather than a liability. The problem of tolerance came out into the open in the West Virginia primary, where his principal opponent was Hubert Humphrey. A crucial hurdle in Kennedy's drive for the presidency was passed when he defeated the senator from Minnesota in this predominantly Protestant state. Rose Kennedy came to West Virginia and campaigned for her son. In practical political fashion, supporters were recruited financially as well as by rhetoric. Funds were distributed widely in what opponents regarded as bribery. Still, the candidate was personally convincing.

The reporter of presidential contests, Theodore H. White, described Kennedy's speech the night before the primary vote as the best he had ever seen a political candidate make. Implying that his opponent was both intolerant and incompetent, Kennedy looked straight into the television camera and defended his religion eloquently: "So when any man stands on the steps of the Capitol and takes the oath of office of president, he is swearing to support the separation of church and state; he puts one hand on the Bible and raises the other hand to God as he takes the oath. And if he breaks his oath, he is not only committing a crime against the Constitution, for which the Congress can impeach him—and should impeach him—but he is committing a sin against God."[18]

Richard Reeves has concluded that Kennedy had little ideology beyond anti-Communism, along with his faith in active, pragmatic government. Still there was about him an attitude or a way of taking on the world. He substituted "intelligence for ideas or idealism, questions for answers. If some would call that cynicism, he would see it as irony. 'Life is unfair,' he said, in the way the French said, 'c'est la vie.' Irony was as close as he came to a view of life: things are never as they seem ...."[19] Reeves's judgment is that Kennedy was a compartmentalized man who had much to hide and was comfortable with secrets and lies.[20]

"Why had he aspired to the presidency?" James Macgregor Burns asks. "Not for ideological reasons—Jack did not think ideologically. He was not pursuing an overriding cause or even an arresting new program—that was not his way."[21] Instead, he spoke of a new frontier: "The old era is ending, the old ways will not do." It was time "for a new generation of leadership—new men to cope with new problems and new opportunities .... We stand today on the edge of a new frontier—the frontier of the 1960s, a frontier of unknown opportunities and perils, a frontier of unfulfilled hopes and threats ... A whole world looks to see what we will do. We cannot fail their trust."[22]

The new president was a personal friend of Columbia University professor Richard Neustadt, who in his study of presidential power had given priority to personal leadership over institutional power; he followed this lead. Crisis followed crisis, as he governed alone, reacting, improvising. Burns concludes: "By Kennedy's own design, the decision-making process centered squarely on him. He had abolished the checks and balances within the White House that might have produced a more searching evaluation" (as in the Bay of Pigs). The political scientist's evaluation is that "for all of the heat generated in the 1960 campaign, there was remarkably little distinction between Kennedy and Nixon on the issues."[23]

The novice occupant of the White House did not long escape critical scrutiny by biographers. In September of 1963, Victor Lasky published *JFK: The Man and the Myth;* it attacked Kennedy's character as morally obtuse, calculating, vain, cold, and superficial. His indictment was so biting that it was withdrawn from print after Kennedy had been assassinated.[24] By contrast, Arthur Schlesinger, Jr., in *A Thousand Days: John F. Kennedy in the White House,* lauded the martyred president's character as a "combination of toughness of fiber and courage." The historian attributed a long list of virtues to him: intelligence, moral courage, self-awareness, intelligence, learning, style, empathy, vitality, humor, detachment, discipline, and compassion.[25]

Michael Novak, a conservative Roman Catholic social ethicist, has praised Kennedy as a rhetorical radical, a liberal, fiscal conservative, and institutional Tory.[26] Whatever else can be said, it is clear that Kennedy was very different than the myths about him would suggest. He was a pragmatist who, in spite of all rhetoric, most of all followed his father's non-ideological approach to government. He expected little from institutions but was ready to work within them. Coming to office, Kennedy showed disdain for formal organizations. Instead, he was most of all concerned to identify interesting people and then tried to get them "plugged in" organizationally. His administration depended more on charisma than on regularized patterns of administration. Using a loose structure, he relied for counsel in particular on his brother Robert, whom he appointed attorney general. His political success was greatly enhanced by his liking and affinity for the press.[27]

Part of Kennedy's distinctiveness, of course, was that he was the first Roman Catholic president of the United States. Novak credits the Catholic tradition as contributing to his style: "The cold eyes that had looked in the abyss ... the excitement in his mind about words like 'burden' and 'sacrifice' ... a high sense of liturgy, a sense of rapidly passing time against an eternal backdrop ... 'not in the first one hundred days, nor in the first one thousand days, nor in our lifetime on this planet' ... and an undisguised love of power and politics—all these were signs of a distinctly Catholic, even Irish Catholic, sensibility."[28]

The tragedy was that Kennedy brought none of the wisdom of the Roman Catholic intellectual tradition to his office, at a time that his church was making major accommodations to human rights and democracy. His ambition was in another direction. Other presidents often had set dramatic goals—many of which have remained unrealized. Kennedy set a new goal: to land a man on the moon before the end of the decade, and it was reached.

Kennedy had called Martin Luther King, Jr. during the election campaign, assuring him of support. Once in office, he delayed taking action for months. It was only amid a spiraling civil rights crisis (that he could no longer avoid) that a politician—often calculating and motivated by expediency—finally took a stand of principle. Kennedy announced:

> *The heart of the question is whether all Americans are to*
> *be afforded equal rights and opportunities, whether we*

*are going to treat our fellow Americans as we want to be
treated. If an American, because his skin is dark, cannot
eat lunch in a restaurant open to the public, if he cannot
send his children to the best public school available, if he
cannot vote for the public officials who represent him,
if, in short, he cannot enjoy the full and free life which
all of us want, then who among us would be content to
have the color of his skin changed and stand in his place?
Who among us would then be content with the counsels of
patience and delay?*[29]

Kennedy's assassination contributed in a major way to the passage
of the Civil Rights Act of 1964 under his successor.

THE PRESIDENCY

Initially, when he came to office, Kennedy did not exercise due
diligence over the nation's foreign intelligence services. The new
president's quest for power contributed to the debacle of the Bay of
Pigs. He allowed the invasion of Cuba—planned before he came to
be chief executive—to be carried through. Foreign affairs professionals
have criticized him for a tendency to accept too many "givens" in
defense matters. After the Bay of Pigs fiasco, it did become clear to
Kennedy that he must install his own trusted appointees in positions
of responsibility. In the Cuban missile crisis (which he helped to
precipitate; the Cubans claimed the Russian missiles were defensive),
Kennedy did demonstrate genuine statesmanship. "He looked at things
from the Soviet side, compromised on secondary issues, did not play
politics, and when he succeeded in getting the missiles removed, did
not gloat or boast .... The missile crisis ... impel(led) Kennedy to take
new initiatives in seeking a reduction in Soviet-American tensions."[30]

Popularly, Kennedy's charisma made him a star. Reporters spoke of
a frenzy that swept through audiences and of female jumpers, leapers,
clutchers, touchers, screamers, and runners who worshiped the new
celebrity.[31] Publicly, Kennedy gave the image of a culturally committed
liberal who admired intellectuals and would turn to them for wisdom. To
say the least, he was more interesting than the bourgeois Nixon.[32] Reporter
Theodore H. White observed that to be transferred from assignment to

Nixon's to Kennedy's campaign tour was "as if one had been transformed in role from leper and outcast to friend and battle companion."

VALUES AND MORALITY

Kennedy's campaign against his political opponent, Vice President Richard Nixon, alleged that the Republican values were all wrong and that his own election alone would set things right. Stated in sweeping generalities, the claim was repeated again and again. James Reston, a sympathetic commentator, observed: "Above all, Kennedy made promises—scores of them daily, telling people wherever he went that he and big government would cure their ills ..."[33] Farmers, laborers, and the old all were to be cared for. The candidate was getting away with murder on his domestic program, Reston judged. Nixon, his opponent, estimated the cost of what was promised at between 13 and 18 billion dollars; Kennedy replied that the figure was "wholly fictitious."[34]

Lincoln, Washington, the Roosevelts, Wilson, and Jefferson all were eulogized by Kennedy; character was associated with political greatness in each case. Kennedy not only celebrated their integrity but linked himself to them. Reeves notes that each of these presidents were leaders of considerable rectitude, even though on occasion, they compromised for expediency's sake. "But unlike the nation's most admired presidents, Jack in fact lacked a moral code embracing the virtues cherished for centuries by those who linked character and leadership ..."[35]

"Beneath the surface, however, Jack was pragmatic to the point of amorality; his sole standard seemed to be political expediency ... he lacked a moral center, a reference point that went beyond self-aggrandizement."[36]

In his first and only term, Kennedy's legislative achievement was not large. His proposals for school reform and an increased minimum wage failed. The first was blocked by the hierarchy of his own church, which at the very least wanted low-interest building loans for its own school projects. For the second, Kennedy characteristically found weak support in Congress. Gary Wills argues that the Kennedy attitude was an expression, in an exaggerated form, of a characteristically American attitude in the postwar period. The United States had overwhelming nuclear resources, so it could dispose of the world benignly, as it wished, without resistance. As Philip Marlowe remarked: "When a man has a gun in his hand, you are supposed to do what he says. We had a nuclear gun in our hand—and to our amazement, people still refused to do what we told them to,"[37]

Persons whom Wills calls "the best students of power"— Machiavelli, Hume, Clausewitz, and Tolstoy—have always placed its source not in the will of the commanding, but that of the commanded, Wills argues. Political power means an ability to get others to do the conqueror's will. If they do not, they can be destroyed. The question is whether such destruction is real political power. "Conquest is not automatically control .... We can, at present, blow up the world with our nuclear weapons; but that does not mean we can rule the world."[38] Wills claimed that Machiavelli carefully distinguished between the two concepts: "Anyone comparing one of the countries with the other will recognize a great difficulty of conquering the Turks, but great ease in governing them once conquered ... But it is just the reverse with realms governed like that of France." The key factor is not the resources of the conqueror, but the disposition of the conquered. "The docile Turks resist well, but easily conform; the French are easily divided by their conquerors, but rarely if at all were united by their rulers."[39]

Wills also cites Tolstoy's *War and Peace:* "Power, from the standpoint of experience, is merely the relation that exists between the expression of someone's will and the execution of that will by others."[40] It is the second—not the first—factor that is most determinative.

Richard Reeves concedes: "There was gallantry to Kennedy's consistent lying about his health and his success in persuading the press and public that he was a man of great energy."[41]

"Kennedy's health continued to be excellent." This was the statement released to the press by Dr. Eugene Cohen, his internist, and his back doctor, Dr. Janet Trvell. It was a lie! "I'd rather be dead than spend the rest of my life on these goddamned crutches!" the president had exclaimed to one of his doctors. Still Kennedy benefited from one great stroke of good luck medically. In 1939, doctors discovered that cortisone could maintain those suffering from Addison's disease in a rather normal lifestyle. For his son's protection, in 1947, his father started to put caches of cortisone and other medications in bank safety deposit boxes worldwide. The simple truth is that Kennedy did not have the "vigor" he claimed.

Wills's judgment is that Kennedy was a prisoner of his own taste for crisis, a passion for being in the midst of action.[42] In Wills's view, the Eisenhower years were characterized by a tacit acceptance of limits; Kennedy's aspiration of universal control was not present. "Eisenhower understood power, its meaning and limits."[43] For Kennedy and his teachers about power, acknowledgment of limits would have meant sanction of a failure of nerve. The issue was not *can* you do everything, but *will* you do everything? "The American resources were limitless: brains, science, talent, tricks, technology, money, virtuosity. The only thing to decide was whether one had the courage to use all that might …"[44]

Wills reminds his audience that another leader was killed in the 1960s. "Dr. [Martin Luther] King [Jr.], more radical in his push for racial justice, was more peaceful in his methods … King, though more revolutionary in some people's eyes, was not 'charismatic' in the sense of replacing traditional and legal power with his personal will. He relied on the deep traditions of his church, on the preaching power of the Baptist minister; and he appealed to the rational order of the liberal state for peaceful adjustment of claims advanced by the wronged."

Wills points out that the speeches of John F. Kennedy are studied by scholars who seek to trace out their unintended effects in Vietnam as well as other regions. In contrast, the oratory of Martin Luther King is memorized at schools as alive and powerful. It was King's achievement to have rallied broken men, transmuting an imposed squalor into the beauty of chosen suffering. No one did it for his followers. In helping them, the African-American leader exercised real power, achieving changes that dwarf the moon shot Kennedy championed. Wills concludes that the "Kennedy era" was really the era of the black preacher. "He [King] was young at his death, younger than either Kennedy; but he had traveled farther. He did fewer things; but those things last. A mule team drew his coffin in a rough cart; not the sleek military horses and the artillery caisson. He has no eternal flame—and no wonder, he is not dead."[45]

The category of American civil religion has been used widely to interpret the public response to the assassination of President Kennedy.[46] The designation of civil religion in this case is not intended in an ecclesiastical sense. Rather, it is used to describe the symbolism of life and death, rituals and meanings evident throughout the nation. Although Kennedy himself was a Roman Catholic, the response to his death was not simply on confessional lines. The entire nation grieved at the young president's premature end, regretting the loss of his vitality and promise. Suddenly, Americans turned inward to a deep existential level of response about life's meanings. As appraised by sociologist Robert Bellah, civil religion draws some of its symbolism from major religions; in the United States, it is drawn primarily from Judaism and Christianity. But its mythos is a distinctive one. Most of all, it encompasses the experiences, the inner history of Americans through wars and crises in their life together.

Historically, religion has had a defensive as well as a prophetic character as it has attempted to bring human beings in touch with the realm of the sacred. In primitive life and even in the great national religions (of Egypt, the Fertile Crescent, India, and China, for example), in what has been called archaic religion, the major concern has been for the survival of the tribe or nation. The defeat of the enemy and victory at all costs has been the goal. On the other hand, the major Western theisms—Judaism and Christianity at least, along with Hinduism and Buddhism from India—have not been so single-minded. They have allowed a place for tragedy and a good beyond tragedy. More is at stake than the survival of the tribe or even the nation. The watershed between the defensiveness of archaic religion and the "international faiths" needs to be distinguished in appraising Kennedy's legacy. The question with respect to his death—as the whole culture for a moment moved into the religious sphere—is to which kind of outlook, to the archaic or to less self-defensive forms of religion. Both tendencies, the archaic and the prophetic, were present at the death of Kennedy. In the former position, the nation's destiny is identified with the deity, without any sense of the self-criticism that a person such as Lincoln, for example, envisaged. Kennedy's own career and outlook evoked a largely archaic national response, even though there were more deep meanings in his own Roman Catholic tradition.

CONCLUSIONS—SUMMARY

There was a great contrast between Kennedy and Eisenhower: youth and age. In the younger man's case, there was less government support for religion and less influence of religion the in chief executive's thinking and policies. Smith judges that Kennedy is one of the most difficult presidents to analyze. Apparently believing in God as a supernatural force, he quoted the Bible frequently and did not offend Jews or Protestants. But he considered church teaching irrelevant and had little personal faith. To the Protestant church historian, Martin Marty, Kennedy appeared "spiritually rootless and politically almost disturbingly secular."[47] This was unfortunate, as he lived in the era of Pope John XXIII and the Second Vatican Council, while three American Jesuits—John Courtney Murray, Gustave Weigel, and Robert Drinan—were leading the fight for religious tolerance in their church internationally. Still, Reinhold Niebuhr praised him as working harder than any other contemporary leader to avoid nuclear catastrophe.

Andrew Greeley protested that Kennedy "did not seem to perceive any connection between the teachings of his religion and his social and political commitment, nor much relationship between the morality of his church and the problems he faced in the world's most important office."[48] Bored by abstractions, he never took ideology very seriously. In fact, he had little philosophical orientation beyond anti-communism and faith in active, pragmatic government. "Kennedy seemed to believe that people could control their own destiny and that the traditional moral standards did not apply to him."[49] Smith notes that he strove to be strong and appealed to some of the messianic impulses that Woodrow Wilson had. Eventually driven to take a stand on civil rights for blacks, his appeal to the nation was still set in pragmatic terms. Reeves labels him a reluctant spokesman for social justice. "There was a radical difference between public image and personal behavior—hundreds of sexual trysts with women, many of whom were total strangers."[50]

Campaigning, Kennedy asked: "Are we going to admit to the world that a Jew can be elected mayor of Dublin, a Protestant can be chosen foreign minister of France, a Moslem can serve in the Israeli Parliament—but a Catholic cannot be president of the United States?" Part of his greatness was that he achieved a wonderful breakthrough against prejudice to become the first Roman Catholic to lead the nation. Political scientist James MacGregor Burns observes: "Polls in the late 1950s showed that many Americans would not vote for a Catholic presidential candidate. It was not only the rank bigotry of rural nativists that Kennedy had to overcome. Liberal Protestants, a strong force in the Democratic party, clung to the notion that the Catholic Church was pursuing political power to impose its conservative dogmas on the country through its authoritarian command over a dedicated army of tens of millions of believers."[51]

Old barriers of intolerance dissolved as Kennedy fought against prejudice. In Morgantown, West Virginia, he told his audience: "a country which disqualified Catholics from its highest office wasn't the country that my brother died for in Europe, and nobody asked my brother if he was a Catholic or a Protestant before he climbed into an American bomber plane to fly his last mission."[52] The irony President Kennedy so often expressed was negative in its own way, and carried with it a sense of fatalism on his part. Ironically, he spent much of his foreign policy energy on an effort to extricate the nation from the danger he engendered by supporting the Bay of Pigs invasion of Cuba.

Theodore White writes: "The magic Camelot of John F. Kennedy never existed ... The knights of his round table were able, tough, ambitious men, capable of kindness, also capable of error ... Of them all, Kennedy was the toughest, the most intelligent, the most attractive—and inside, the least romantic." White sees the assassinated president as a realistic dealer in men, a master of games who understood the importance of ideas. "To his credit, he posed for the first time the great question of the sixties and seventies: What kind of people are we Americans? What do we want to become?"[53]

James MacGregor Burns sums up his own political evaluation: "With his startling success in 1960, Kennedy invented a new brand of political campaigning. He engineered a new route to the presidency. After him, most candidates would no longer see party leadership as essential to their ambitions."[54] Others wearing party labels would follow Kennedy's example of hunting for votes wherever they could be found. Similarly, they would ignore party platforms when the occasion called for it, tailoring messages narrowly to reach vulnerable constituencies. Like Kennedy, they would develop personal, transient electoral coalitions with the one purpose of getting them elected to office. Burns argues that this legacy has had grave consequences for American election polity.

LYNDON BAINES JOHNSON

A POLITICIAN AT LARGE

Lyndon Johnson left a wheeler-dealer record in the Senate that Obama did not try to match. The Texan had a masterful knowledge of legislative detail as well as the personal lives of his colleagues. Obama, for his part, was less visible when he represented Illinois in Washington. However, while aspiring to the presidency, he ran a brilliant election campaign that was carefully planned and detailed. Johnson, "a good old boy," did not trust university intellectuals. Obama, by contrast, comes from the academic elite. Johnson grew up among the patterns of Southern revivalism and changed denominations while still a teenager; Obama comes from a very different strand of evangelicalism and has been deeply inspired to social action by its preaching. His goal is not to become as bogged down in Afghanistan as Johnson was in Vietnam.

KENNEDY'S SUCCESSOR

"As bound to the society as it was, Protestantism [in the South] lacked vigor and vitality respecting political and social issues—most notably race. Southern politicians became extreme caricatures of the region. The church did not find a way of making that faith relevant to societal needs any more than did the politicians who represented the section in Congress. The exceptions were few and Lyndon Johnson was one of them."[1] Alley describes the president with this praise. He judges Kennedy's successor to have been an outwardly religious man who could quote the Bible as needed. With respect to the popular piety of the time, he made common cause with Billy Graham along with the Prayer Breakfast movement, but was not deeply moved by either.

Johnson's grandfather was a Baptist preacher. Personally, Christian doctrine meant little to the grandson during his public life. In its place, his primary loyalty was to civil religion. Alley judges that LBJ did not use religion cynically, "though use it he surely did," campaigning across the country for the war in Vietnam with a kind of counter-Wilson strategy. He finds Johnson to have been obsessed with a patriotic Messianism.

"All I have, I would have given gladly not to be standing here today." So Lyndon Johnson proclaimed when he addressed Congress for the first time after he came to the presidential office following John F. Kennedy's assassination. The new president reflected more informally: "The president carries heavier burdens than I ever envisioned. You feel little goose pimples coming up your back because it's such a frightening, terrifying responsibly." From his staff, he would ask honesty, frankness, loyalty, dedication, and diligence."[2] They should give "carefully considered judgments and advice" but not withhold information or differences of opinion. To his credit, Johnson did not develop a full-fledged "Texas Mafia" comparable with his predecessor's family. Claiming the Kennedy legacy, he had a program of legislation which he fought for vigorously. By contrast with the young president, he was successful with Congress. Johnson believed that "Those who would carry on great public schemes must be posed against the worst fatiguing delays, the most mortifying disappointments, the most shocking insults, and worst of all, the presumptuous judgment of the ignorant upon their designs."[3]

Johnson hung this quotation from the English statesman, Edmund Burke, on the wall of his Capitol office while serving as United States senator from Texas. As Senate majority leader, he was known as an expert middleman and wheeler-dealer, successful in personal relations and capable of bringing legislation to enactment. In contrast, as president, he again and again humiliated and bullyragged his lieutenants, even as he raged against the Kennedy clan. Eventually, the pressures of high office exhausted him. Barber's criticism (as a researcher of presidential character) is that Johnson showed the disorientation of an expert middleman who had been elevated above the ordinary political marketplace.[4] When he became president, Johnson no longer was surrounded by a circle of senatorial barons, each of whom had his own authority and independence. He had instead a circle of subordinates whom he dominated even as he commanded: "all you fellows must be prudent about what you encourage me to go for." His problem was knowing what is right! Practically, Johnson knew his way around the leadership of the Senate, and at times, even of the country. In the world at large, he misjudged the power of nationalism and was defeated in Vietnam.

The future occupant of the White House graduated from high school in 1924 in rural Texas as president and the youngest member of a senior class of six. He enrolled at San Marcos College, then an unaccredited school. As an undergraduate, his political initiative was evident almost at once. Blackballed for membership in the leading campus fraternity, Johnson organized another, the White Stars. Working as an assistant in the school president's office, Johnson did not confine his activities to the responsibilities delegated to him. San Marcos College president Evans once remarked: "I declare you hadn't been in my office a month before I could hardly tell who was president of the school—you or me."[5] At college, the young man participated in debate where a flip of a coin often determined which side he was to take and learned skills which were still evident in his later life.

Johnson became editor of the school newspaper and expounded his own practical philosophy in its pages:

> *The great men of the world are those who have never faltered. They had the glowing vision of a noble work to inspire them to press forward, but they also had the inflexible will, the resolute determination, the perfectly attuned spiritual forces for the execution of the work plans. There are no tyrannies like those that human passions and weaknesses exercise. Ambition is an uncomfortable companion many times ... Restless, energetic, purposeful,*

it is ambition that makes of a creature a real man. Personality is power; the man with a striking personality can accomplish greater deeds in life than a man of equal abilities but less personality.[6]

The vision was typically rural Texas—pragmatic, optimistic, and not particularly religious, even though he was nurtured in the Baptist and Disciples of Christ traditions. It seems fair to conclude that he was basically a secular person. Historian James Reston wrote of him: "He is fiercely patriotic. He genuinely believes that God looks out for Uncle Sam. He has no doubt that this nation was set apart to achieve good and noble purposes ... He believes in the American System." It was culture Protestantism, nationalism on the Texas pattern.[7] Alley writes: "The unvarnished patriotism was an honest function of the man, but the 'Messianism' was the same." Reflecting on the politician's later career, he judges, "The façade that covered the Johnson rationale for the Vietnam conflict was far less sophisticated that that which shrouds the Nixon policy."[8]

At the age of twenty, in 1929, Johnson became principal of an elementary school in Cotulla, Texas, where there was a large group of Mexican students. He was a hard worker who showed energy and determination, and at times, he was high-tempered and aggressive but also creative. Barber reflects on Johnson's style as it blossomed into what he did later: "I think Johnson's character infused this stylistic pattern with a compulsive quality, so that he was virtually unable to alter it when it proved unproductive."[9]

Johnson came to Washington at the beginning of the New Deal and worked in the office of Congressman Richard M. Kleberg. The frontier individualism that Wilson eulogized in theory lived on in power in Johnson's presidency. His design for the Great Society was based on the deeply felt conviction that there should be enough nourishing food, warm clothing, decent shelter, and education for everyone's children— as well as an end to racial discrimination. When his moment of destiny came with Kennedy's assassination, the new president emphasized continuity and institutional authority as he took over the symbolic trappings of the head of state. Kennedy had articulated goals; Johnson, honoring his memory, would marshal support for them, political and moral.

Johnson's rhetoric and utopian vision reflected the changes of the post-World War II era, one in which blacks in particular were in revolt against earlier oppression. "This great, rich, restless country can offer opportunity and education and hope to all—all black and white, all North and South, sharecropper and city-dweller. These are the enemies—poverty, ignorance, disease. They are enemies, not our fellow man, not our neighbor, and these enemies too, poverty, disease and ignorance, we shall overcome."[10] Johnson proposed legislation to provide medical care for the aged, education, housing, urban development, and conservation. Unlike his predecessor, he saw it enacted. There were problems of details, but he knew the direction the nation needed to go to solve its problems. As majority leader of the Senate, he had been largely responsible for steering through the civil rights bills of 1957 and 1960.

Barber speaks of Johnson's style—the whirlwind energy, the operator-dominated personal relations, the idealistic rhetoric, and the use of information as an instrument—as powerful tools. "Obviously personal relations was the core of his style."[11] The variations were Johnson-on-the-make and Johnson-in-charge. In the first, he was expanding his influence through energetic social manipulation. In the second role, he dominated and forced subordinates into conformity.

Johnson wanted to persuade every citizen that his goals were in their interest. Utilitarianism and patriotic dedication were blended in his ethics. In his world view of populism, there was no place for class struggle. "I do not want to be the president who built empires or sought grandeur, or extended dominion. I want to be the president who educated young children to the wonders of the world. I want to be the president who helped to feed the hungry ..."[12] In his own way, Johnson's vision reflected his moral idealism even as a "wheeler-dealer." His open-armed gestures, his tone of millennial promise, and the euphoria with which he spoke all reflected the Southwestern frontier symbolism of his native region. Johnson's shrewdness in judging men, his drive to succeed, his understanding of the governmental process, were all factors that shaped his remarkable career.

After he reached the White House, Johnson asked Professor Eric C. Goldman of Princeton to assemble a group of the best minds, "a quiet brain trust," and consulted former presidents for advice. The idea of the war on poverty developed while he was in Texas during Christmas week of 1963. In his first State of the Union speech (January 8, 1964), he did not link it directly to Kennedy's program. Johnson's motto was "Strive for the impossible; settle for the possible." In an interview, he explained, "the satisfaction one gets out of life is really what you live for."[13] Johnson later mused: "There was no magic formula. We had to try a wide variety of approaches. Some worked better than others. Some failed completely. I heard bitter complaints from mayors of several cities. Some funds were used to finance questionable activities. Some were badly mismanaged. That was all part of the risk."[14] Criticisms from activists pointed out that the scale was not great enough to match the rhetoric with emotional over-promising of results as well as bold statements on the extent of deprivation.

In defense of Johnson, Milton Eisenhower (who knew him personally) observed: "There is no question that when Johnson became president, he became the most militant civil rights leader in the history of the country. He was now obviously doing what he felt the people of the United States wanted done or that he felt the people ought to want to have done." After all, "what one stands for at any time in his life depends a good deal on what the responsibility is."[15]

THE WHITE HOUSE CHARACTER

Johnson was not mistaken in his judgment that there was a crisis in race relations. Four days after the 1965 Voting Rights Act was passed, Watts—a suburb of Los Angeles—broke into riots. The president responded: "We must not only be relentless in condemning violence, but also in taking the necessary steps to prevent it." The assassination of Martin Luther King, Jr. on April 4, 1968 showed how deep opposition ran.[16] Congressional legislators speeded the passage of the Civil Rights Act of 1968. Earlier civil rights legislation had outlawed the poll tax and literary tests for voting. The second Civil Rights Act prohibited discrimination in the sale or rental of housing. Joseph Califano (who later served Carter as secretary of health, education, and welfare) observed that Johnson "devoted a staggering amount of his time, energy, and political capital to breaking the Senate filibuster and passing the act."[17]

Johnson's program in the area of education retrospectively appears utopian. He knew that something needed to be done. How to do it was another matter, and his administration became involved in projects that Johnson used from time for his own election benefit. American society would not be great, he said, "until every young mind is set free to scan the farthest reaches of thought and imagination."[18] The president envisaged a time when nobody in this country is poor, "no child will go unfed and no youngster will go unschooled." In the large, his unrealistic exaggeration raised false hopes. "Seldom from responsible public figures even during an election, does one hear balderdash such as this."[19] Sociologist S. M. Miller observed that the Great Society was based on belief in "cost-free liberalism," which held that improvements could be financed out of economic growth, not taxpayers' pockets. "That mistaken judgment, coupled with the failure of some programs to achieve results commensurate with their rhetoric, prompted public disillusionment."[20] Of course, at the beginning of the next century, George W. Bush would attempt a much more faith-related social program.

Nominated as candidate for the presidency on his own at the Atlantic City Democratic Convention in 1964, Johnson proclaimed that the strength of the nation "is greater than the combined might of all the nations, in all the world, in all the history of this planet. And I report our superiority is growing."[21] Was it hubris? Victory over Goldwater was made much easier because the Republican candidate made recklessly militaristic threats. At the same time, he agreed not to make either the Vietnam War or civil rights an issue. Winning by a strong margin, Johnson claimed a popular mandate and linked himself to the legacy of Wilson, Roosevelt, Truman, and Kennedy. Again, he was organizing task forces with leaders from academia, business, and labor to advise him on legislative programs as he characteristically asked that they remain secret. A remarkable amount of legislation was passed with effective support from Johnson's office, most new ideas coming from people outside the government. Medicare, for example, became law. The timing of Johnson's legislative proposals was excellent, and he consulted with congressional leaders, Mansfield, Albert, and Dirksen.

Goldman reflects that "Johnson tried too hard to win over press and TV people during his first month in office."[22] He knew that relations with the press was a key issue but a credibility gap grew over time. His press secretary, George Reedy, concluded: "His manners were atrocious—not just slovenly but calculated to give offense."[23] James Deakin observed: "Somehow, Lyndon Johnson as president has seldom been able to state a major position or make an important announcement in a straightforward and unequivocal way. Somehow his pronouncements turn out later to have been full of weasel words or hidden meanings or downright deception." Many reporters viewed the president as the great American yahoo, "a big talker whose specialty is the off-color joke." Johnson's language was so grossly crude that often it was unprintable.[24] Personally, Johnson judged that the media was to blame for their poor relations, and he invoked secrecy against it in small as well as larger matters.

Johnson's character was summed up in part by his relations with women. His wife, Lady Bird, showed endless patience with his philandering. Robert Caro, in his *Path to Power*, describes the young Johnson's affair with Alice Glass, the beautiful and sophisticated mistress of Charles Marsh. Marsh, a Texas tycoon, owned the only newspaper that covered Johnson's entire congressional district. The Texan had built Longlea, his estate in northern Virginia, for her. Johnson's relationship with Alice had to be kept secret from her husband. She was blonde, tall, well read, and traveled; she knew the arts, as well as architecture and landscaping. When their affair began, Johnson was a young Congressman of twenty-nine and she was twenty-six. Marsh was twice her age. Soon, Johnson began spending weekends at Longlea. Marsh (who later married Alice) did not know what was going on—but Lady Bird may have. Lerner describes it as the only time when Johnson risked his political career, not simply serving his own self-interest. It shows his complexity, Lerner argues. "The contrast between Lyndon and Alice was almost absolute. Gangly and awkward, he slopped his food into his own mouth at table—was vulgar and crass with his long nose and ears. Still his lack of knowledge about poetry and philosophy opened him to her charms and he longed to possess her physically. The scoundrel politician became her lover ... Alice Glass was the sex dream and culture dream suddenly made real." The couple talked of divorce but knew it would wreck both of them. A turbulent relationship between the two continued even after she married Marsh and was not just his mistress. She and Marsh divorced and then she married again. She finally broke off contact with Johnson because of the war in Vietnam; his role in it enraged her."[25]

JOHNSON AND BILLY GRAHAM

Following the Kennedy assassination, when Johnson first entered the White House, Billy Graham gave his blessing to the new president: "As God was with Washington at Valley Forge and with Lincoln in the darkest hours of the Civil War, so God will be with you. There will be times when decisions come hard and burdens too heavy to bear—that is when God will be nearest to you."[26]

Johnson replied with a pious answer: "Pray for me, too. I cannot fulfill this trust unless God grant me the wisdom to see what is right and the courage to do it. I want to be the president of all the people."[27]

Kennedy had once remarked of his vice president that he was "a very insecure, sensitive man with a huge ego."[28] Graham gave Johnson what he most craved: love without strings. "Not many people in this country love me,"[29] Johnson confided in Walter Cronkite. "When I was being called a crook and all, he'd invite me over and we bragged on each other. I told him he was the greatest religious leader in the world and he said I was the greatest political leader." The Graham pastoral call was like "a new injection" during hard times.

The University of Chicago church historian, Martin Marty, rightly evaluated Johnson's place as that of "a man in transit between epochs and value systems."[30] The liberal Protestant social action agenda seemed to be in decline, at least for those in Johnson's circle. The New Deal Democrat turned to Graham's more traditional message of saving souls rather than reforming society, and it offered him protection from the burden of office. Lady Bird explained, "Lyndon had a very strong sense of need, to be sure he was on the right path ... a need for an anchor. Billy was a comfort—and if ever there is a position in the world where you feel need all the help you can get, it's the presidency."[31]

"Nobody could make Johnson feel he was right about Vietnam like Billy Graham could," Bill Moyers said.

In 1967, Graham reflected, "I do know that President Johnson had little choice." The evangelist's conviction was that Johnson was right because he was in authority.

Johnson could roar like a lion on one side and talk as gently as if he was talking to a little child. Johnson had grown up relishing "long, tall preaching," and he was pleased to find an old-fashioned preacher around for both political and personal counsel. Graham reported: "He'd go into the First Bedroom late at night and see the great stack of papers that the president was determined to get through before he slept. He'd lie in bed and read three newspapers and watch his three television sets," the evangelist said. "Every time I'd ask him to have prayer, he'd get out of bed and get down on his knees in his pajamas."[32] When the evangelist asked him if he had received Christ as his personal savior, the president replied: "You know Billy, I know that I've received Christ, I'm not sure in my heart that I'm really going to heaven ... I did it as a boy at a revival meeting. I guess I've done it several times." Johnson was always a little bit scared of death, Graham concluded.

Graham cited scripture. "No matter what the law may be—it may be an unjust law—I believe we have a Christian responsibility to obey it. Otherwise you have anarchy."[33] Graham always stayed behind the pulpit, cautious and conservative.

At home at his Texas ranch after he had left office, Johnson stood under the oaks, next to his parents, where he was to be buried. "Billy," he asked, "will I ever see my mother and father again?"

"Well, Mr. President, if you're a Christian, and they were Christians, then someday you'll have a great homecoming." Would Billy preach at his funeral?

"I want you to look in those cameras and just tell 'em what Christianity is all about. Tell 'em how they can be sure they can go to heaven. I want you to preach the gospel. But somewhere in there, you tell 'em a few things I did for this country."[34]

VIETNAM WAR

The tragedy of Lyndon Johnson was primarily in his escalation of the war in Southeast Asia. He leaped before he looked! From the outset, there was opposition in private by Senate majority leader Mike Mansfield, who in particular criticized the concept of neutralization.[35] But Johnson simply would not be deterred; in naive optimism long, he believed that eventually he could carry the day. Bornet writes: "What the president got from the outset was very bad news. But bad news only spurred him on." The historian concludes: "The point is that the new president clearly did not think his way through his Vietnam inheritance in November and December of 1963. His knee-jerk decision was made in hours—not even in days."[36]

Johnson's pronouncements sounded more like those of a dictator than of a democratic leader. A secret National Security Action memorandum (implemented on November 26, 1963) was clear: "The president expects that all senior officers of the government will move energetically to insure the full unity of support for established United States policy in South Vietnam. Both in Washington and in the field, it is essential that the government be unified.[37] Bornet criticizes the president for making unqualified public and private promises of support to South Vietnam from the outset, even while it was clear that its government was in a state of chaos. The American public was given no idea in the winter of 1964 that their future had already been committed. Johnson gave such reasons as "America keeps her word" and "our purpose is peace." What was going on was not just a jungle war but a struggle for freedom on every front of human activity, he believed.

The Gulf of Tonkin incident off North Vietnam in the summer of 1964 was, in part, a contrived one. There remains the moral, and indeed the religious question of truth-telling. Johnson deliberately misled Congress and the American people; they were not told about the covert raids being carried out by South Vietnamese gunboats. On direct order from the president, the bombing of North Vietnam was begun February 7, 1965. In spite of Senate majority leader Mansfield's private criticism, the administration won in the passage of a congressional resolution. Senator William Fulbright from Arkansas, in particular, gave leadership and support, and directed it through the legislative branch of the government without any declaration of war. Mistakenly, Johnson and his advisors supposed that escalating military pressure "scientifically" would ultimately induce Hanoi to stop supporting the Viet Cong. They further believed that the use of force could be carefully controlled and turned off and on as they wished. They were confident that diplomatic signals and military action could be coordinated so as to send particular "messages to the enemy."

Johnson mistakenly decided to follow Kennedy's lead and acted against Eisenhower's earlier refusal to interfere militarily in Indochina. Had he done otherwise, he might have remained popular and honored. But he misunderstood the power of nationalism in Southeast Asia and wrongly saw the Vietnam War as a parallel to President Roosevelt's struggle against totalitarianism and Roosevelt's leadership in taking the country into the Second World War. Fearing the Russians, Johnson limited the escalation of the war in Vietnam. The strategy simply did not work; Johnson tried to negotiate, offering a program of regional development in the area. The North Vietnamese refused. Retrospectively, critics have judged that the war was one which Indochina's people's own loyalty would have to decide. The Americans simply could not win it on an anticommunist program (as against nationalism) in spite of massive military intervention.

Johnson identified communist ideology with evil and greatly feared any concession to adversary powers who espoused it. Eisenhower and Dulles had drawn back in Hungary, Suez, and Vietnam. Johnson lacked enough intimate knowledge of foreign affairs to judge whether such a strategy was appropriate under his tenure in office. Certainly, most of the intellectual establishment recommended intervention in Vietnam. Still, the fact remains that Johnson's own qualities contributed to his decision to escalate the war in Vietnam. Relying on others' judgments, he spoke of goals and principles more than available means.

Barber reflects that "Johnson's remarkable effectiveness in situations where the social environment provided directions is not to be doubted."[38] In the Senate, he was successful as a consensus builder, as he caught issues at the right stage of their development. As Senate Democratic leader, he mapped the range of senatorial opinion, appealing to members' expectations and perceptions. "The raw materials were given: Johnson did not take a stand; he worked with the range of stands he found among other members, pushing here, pulling there, until he had a workable configuration of votes."[39] Of course, one must distinguish between the Johnson of the first and second terms. Only as he defeated Goldwater, running for the presidency, did he become deeply involved in the Vietnam debacle. As he took the reins of power, following Kennedy's assassination, there was great optimism as the deceased president's program was enacted in Congress in a war on poverty. In his second term, as the war in Vietnam dragged on, James Reston concluded that what was proved again was "once more that truth is the first casualty of war and that war corrupts good men."[40] Foreign policy was a different matter than domestic affairs. As his troubles grew, he dominated his advisors to the point that they could help him very little. Instead, the imbalance and exaggerations of his own inner struggle grew.

The president's deepest fear was that the Vietnam War would be escalated into hostilities with Russia and China. He was haunted by the possibility of escalation—even to the point of atomic hostilities—in the cold war. As the violence and tragedy of Vietnam could be seen on national television, anti-war sentiment strengthened rapidly. In time, the president found himself at war with the Christian conscience of the nation and with religious leadership. When he attended church during the fall of 1967, in Williamsburg, Virginia, at Bruton Parish Church, the church of Washington, Mason, and Henry, the presiding minister used the occasion to put the question of the war to him.

Johnson simply was wrong in his belief that the public would support an undeclared no-win war of attrition thousands of miles away. Students for Democratic Society organized and protested on college and university campuses. The Coordinating Committee to End the War in Vietnam eventually came to encompass thirty-five organizations. Among those fighting the war, the limitations Johnson imposed on the armed services were resented deeply. For example, in Air Force Operation Rolling Thunder, no strike was to be made without the administration's prior approval; no pre-strike photography and no second strike were allowed. In the end, General Westmoreland criticized the president: "Johnson hoped the war would go away, so he could concentrate his energies on building a 'Great Society' at home, but his key Vietnam decisions were destined to drag out the war indefinitely."[41]

What was the religious question? In this situation, theologies of a just war seemed obsolete. This traditional theory has its requirements: that it be a war of last resort, declared by competent authority, with a reasonable chance of success, warfare to correct wrongs in which non-combatants are immune and destruction not out of proportion to achievements. Vietnam in the end did not qualify. Most of all, the

American public was not convinced that it did. In the end, Johnson could not avoid recognizing this fact. He had not been a fully well man since his 1955 heart attack. Overwhelmed by events, he announced on March 31, 1968, "Accordingly, I shall not seek, and I will not accept, the nomination of my party for another term as your president." Actually, his announcement was overshadowed in the news by the assassination of Martin Luther King, Jr. and the riots that followed in Washington, D.C. and elsewhere. A little more than two months later, Robert Kennedy was killed in Los Angeles on June 5. In the summer of 1968, the Soviets invaded Czechoslovakia, repressing the Prague Spring.

Worst of all, Johnson decided to let the public know as little as possible about the nature and extent of the war in Vietnam. In a half-war and half-peace situation, he could not measure fully or control, his presidency began to crumble. "Suspicions congenital to his nature became delusions, calculated deceit became self-deception, and then matters of unqualified belief." The Tet Offensive made clear his misjudgments and self-delusions. Defeated, Johnson withdrew from the presidency, having shed blood on a terrible scale without success while ever fearing Russian intervention and an atomic holocaust. "Why do you want to destroy me? I can't trust anybody! Everybody is trying to cut me down, destroy me!" he mused.

Barber views Johnson's manipulation, his maneuvering, his penchant for secrecy, his lying, his avid interest in himself, his sense of being surrounded by hostile forces, and his immense anger all as signs of profound insecurity. There was a moral and even a religious question at the base of his difficulties. He had tried to be an idealist and pragmatist at the same time—with only ideological guidelines. As an expert political middleman and wheeler-dealer, Johnson had long sought out visions of the past, present, and future, not for their accuracy but for their utility. The credibility gap grew even wider in the later part of his administration. His religious reference had been Billy Graham whose personalistic revivalism was dominant in the era.

In *The Tragedy of Lyndon Johnson,* Goldman calls attention to the role of Bill Moyers in the articulation of Johnson's presidential goals. "Moyers was for civil rights, against poverty and concerned with better education … He had all the gestures of liberal intellectualism while never having been immersed in its tradition … His religious orientation was a clue; he was a product of the reformism of Billy Graham, not of Reinhold Niebuhr."[42] To Goldman, the Eastern University professor, Johnson—even as president—appeared as a polished cowboy who drawled out so much buncombe and bawdiness. Yet he concludes, "After years of meeting first-rate minds in and out of universities, I am sure I have never met a more intellectual person than Lyndon Johnson."[43] "In terms of sheer IQ, he had a clear, swift, penetrating mind, with an abundance of his own type of imagination and subtleties."[44]

Barber observes psychologically: "Johnson, in the midst of struggle, developing a secret arrangement or pumping hands in a crowd, could feel a burst of elation, but not for long."[45] Success in gaining power gave him no pause. He felt compelled to go on at a fantastic pace. "Let's go, let's go," he said even as he pretended he wished that he were lying quietly under a tree. His friendship with Protestant evangelists did not answer his spiritual needs or give him peace of soul. In the defeat in Vietnam, the United States lost its first war and went through a deeply wrenching experience of the type that it had not known even in the Second World War. The shadow of a hydrogen holocaust remained.

Johnson's support for Hubert Humphrey (his vice president) when Humphrey ran for the presidency in the fall of the year was not strong—at least until the campaign for his successor neared its end. Johnson was alleged to have said, "Nixon is supporting my Vietnam policy stronger than Hubert." So why should he whistle-stop Texas? In the end, Humphrey lost by only seven-tenths of a percentage point in the popular vote.[46] Liberalism had met its defeat in Vietnam, riots, and the political assassinations of King and Kennedy. At Richard Nixon's inaugural ceremony, Henry Kissinger observed Johnson as he came down the aisle to the strains of "Hail to the Chief" and reflected: "I wondered what this powerful and tragic figure thought as he ended a term of office that had begun with soaring inspiration and finished in painful division. How had this man of consensus ended up with a torn country? Johnson stood like a caged eagle, dignified, never to be trifled with, his eyes fixed on distant heights that now he would never reach."[47]

George Reedy, Johnson's press secretary, wrote: "He may have been a son of a bitch but he was a colossal son of a bitch. He also possessed the finest quality of a politician. It was a sense of the direction of political power—the forces that were sweeping the masses." Reedy concludes that most important of all, Johnson knew how to make the country's form of government work. "This is an art that has been lost since his passing and we are suffering heavily as a result ... not merely content himself by getting ahead of those forces ... he mastered the art of directing them ..."[48]

RICHARD MILHOUS NIXON

Nixon is in a negative class by himself. Probably the most intelligent president of his era, he was also its most tragic moral failure—the antithesis of Obama. Nixon despised Eastern intellectuals; Obama is one of them. Still, Nixon's visit to communist China was a brilliant achievement and has left a lasting positive historical legacy. Watergate was his ethical debacle. Clearly, Obama has his personal demons more under control; Nixon did not. Nor will the forth-fourth president so blindly engage in irresponsible international warfare as did his predecessors in Vietnam and Cambodia. Nixon's career surely raises crucial issues about good and evil. He was as secretive as Obama is public, and his religion gave him little or no moral help!

WHO WAS RICHARD NIXON?

"As biographers assessed and reassessed Richard Nixon in the years after his resignation from the presidency, they variously labeled him a right-wing conservative, Republican moderate, secret liberal, a warmonger, and peace maker, but he was always one thing: a supreme opportunist. He was consistent mainly in his inconsistency. He not only seized opportunities as they offered themselves—he created opportunities that he then exploited."[1]

Religiously, there was an opportunity in the friendship with evangelist Billy Graham, and the putative Quaker from Whittier, California seized upon it. The problem was that it provided him with no social ethic, apart from Graham's refusal to hold segregated revival meetings in the South. The religionist's message was primarily one of personal salvation, not of social justice. When consulted about issues of war and peace, he most often chose belligerency.

Max Lerner called attention to the paradoxes which he identified in Richard Nixon's character. "He saw himself as a Mr. Christian, in John Bunyan's Pilgrim's Progress, constantly beset by enemies, trials, and testings, always having to prove himself to men and history … He saw life in the purest life-and-death terms of Social Darwinism." Lonely on the mountain, striving for some Superman role beyond good and evil, Nixon in his own strange way was a Nietzschean spectacle. Like the ill-fated magus of legend, the genie he released from the bottle in the end became a whirlwind that destroyed him.[2]

Nixon was the only president of the United States to resign while in office. He departed from Washington, D.C. on August 9, 1974 after the House Judiciary Committee had drawn up articles of impeachment against him. White House tapes of presidential conversations exposed not only the hypocrisy of Nixon's public moralism and religious pretensions. They proved that he had lied to the American people. A wag remarked: "If Dick Nixon ever wrestled with his conscience, the match was fixed." Enemies called him "Nick's son."[3]

Still, Nixon was in many respects one of the most outstanding and capable presidents of the second half of the twentieth century, towering over other occupants of the White House. His achievements were many and great. Elliot Richardson (who, as attorney general, resigned rather than follow Nixon's panicky order to fire the Watergate special prosecutor) reflected retrospectively later: "Richard Nixon had it within his grasp to be our greatest post-World War II president."[4] What happened to make it otherwise?

Does the explanation lie in what biographers have appraised as Nixon's fatalism and pessimism, his substitution of technique for value? There was also his distrust of political allies as well as the energies lost in controlling aggressive feelings. What was beneath it all in life attitude—more than this in religious belief and ethical commitment? Nixon ought not to be demonized; he was a complex character. "When you compare the Nixon of the Hiss case, the Checkers speech, and the post-California outburst, with the Nixon of the Peking trip and the China policy turnabout, there is an undeniable growth. But it was growth on the cognitive, not the emotional level."[5] With the exception of Lyndon Johnson, no one had come to the White House with so much political experience. Nor did anyone come so psychologically damaged to the highest office in the land. What religion he had lay on the top of his mind, not in the depths of his being.

Nixon claimed the idealism of the American dream in his second campaign for the presidency. "Tonight I see the face of a child ... He hears a train go by. At night, he dreams of faraway places where he'd like to go. It seems like an impossible dream. But he is helped on his journey through life ... A gentle Quaker mother with a passionate concern for peace quietly wept when he went to war. A great teacher, a remarkable football coach, an inspirational minister encouraged him on his way."[6] So Nixon addressed the Republican National Convention at the beginning of his first successful bid for the highest office in the land.

What was his Quaker background in the traditional peace church community of Whittier, California? Nixon came from a family of moderate means. There had been a middle-class struggle for survival. Two of his brothers died in youth and the family had money problems while he was growing up. Completing college, he was accepted at Duke Law School. After graduation, he sought and failed to find a position in New York or Washington. Instead, his mother made arrangements for him to work in a small Whittier, California firm, and he practiced divorce and criminal law. Married in 1940, he joined the navy as a lieutenant junior grade after Pearl Harbor. Had he followed the Quaker pattern of pacifism as a conscientious objector, he would never have become president.

Part of the paradoxes of Nixon's character lay in the differences between his two parents, Hannah, his patient, saint-like mother, and his bullying, politically minded but brooding Irish father, Frank Nixon. Hannah Nixon gave him a sense of idealism and moral values; Frank Nixon laid the basis for his son's ruthless tactics and value-free language, which emphasized interests, power, and the determination to win at any cost. Outraged at the excesses of the New Left as well as the media elite, the aspiring politician based his electoral strength on the non-intellectual classes as he appealed to the "silent majority."

"His critics saw a fraud and a demagogue, a gut-fighter who pretended to be a preacher. Nixon's backers, like ... Herbert Hoover, saw a preacher often pretending for reasons not of his own making, to be a politician."[7] Although an honorable, dedicated man, he had been sometimes forced by public opinion to campaign ruthlessly. Critics protested that, in the end, the result was a mixture of virtue bordering on piety and alley-fighting tactics.

As a young lawyer after the war, while he was completing a case in Baltimore, Nixon, thirty-two years old, received a telephone call from a Whittier banker who asked him to run against the congressional incumbent, Jerry Voorhis. "Voorhis's conservative reputation must be blasted," Nixon said, and he showed pictures of himself in uniform. He won with an aggressive rhetorical performance while still calmly answering questions, and with little help from anyone else. Then he rode on to power—in Congress, the Senate, the vice presidency, and at last to the White House—as a cold warrior and anti-communist crusader. Former president Hoover credited Nixon with exposing "the stream of treason that has existed in our country."[8]

Gary Wills has dubbed Nixon, paradoxically, the "last liberal."[9] Wills finds him typifying a belief in automatic progress that ignores the tragic flaws of the American character and political system and believes uncritically in the American dream. Without the Alger Hiss spy case, in all probability, he would not have made it to the White House. Nixon did owe some debt to the Quaker moral vision. Even in the most intense period of the cold war, he described himself as an internationalist: "I'm not necessarily a respecter of the status quo in foreign affairs. I am a chance taker in foreign affairs; I would take chances for peace. The Quakers have a passion for peace, you know." While the liberal utopian vision was fading with the war in Vietnam, Nixon sought replace it only with the brutality and the cynicism of realpolitik. He reflected the worst in his age, eaten up with ambition and hungry for power.[10]

Early in his career, a journalist tried to explain Nixon's political appeal: "as a person and as a personality, he embodies much that is held to be precious by a large and growing number of Americans—that segment of the middle class to which he belongs ... He is young, he is enterprising, he is successful."[11] Exuding earnestness and frankness (but lacking a sense of humor), his style of life had appeal for middle-class citizens who shared his aspiration for a ranch house, furs for the wife, and pets for the children.

Nixon professed religious faith—and faith in religion. Patriotism and love of family ranked first among his values. Publicly, there was devotion to hard work and free enterprise. Praise was given to the people, citizens of a democracy. Respect for military might was combined with a quest for peace. Nixon testified to firm faith in America's destiny as a nation highly favored by God. Still, as early as the Eisenhower presidential campaign, Adlai Stevenson envisaged a place called "Nixonland—a land of slander and scare, of sly innuendo, of a poison pen, the anonymous phone call, and hustling, pushing, shoving—the land of smash and grab and anything to win."[12]

IDEOLOGY AND PRESENCE

Nixon's ideology has been evaluated as a peculiar blend of a (secular) Protestant work ethic, liberal optimism, and power politics. Theoretically, he accepted Keynesian economics, supporting national health insurance, a minimum income, wage and price controls, as well as deficit financing.[13] Nixon's political instincts were not simply parochial or isolationist; to his credit, he was a strong advocate of assistance to underdeveloped countries. He also supported the SALT talks on disarmament. As vice president, he made one of the key rulings that led to the Senate passage of the 1957 Civil Right Act.

With his shadowed face, eyes set protectively beneath lowering brows, and rather sour mouth turned down at the corners, Nixon did not present an attractive (much less charming) presence. His gaunt appearance and uneasy manner were most evident in his first television debate with Kennedy, and indeed may have cost him the presidency. In the second debate, he did better; he had prepared himself more fully, he explained later. For years earlier, Nixon had taken on a heavy responsibility, speaking from the rear platform of trains and stumping for congressional candidates in Eisenhower's presidential campaigns. Overall, he simply was not a hail fellow well met. Once during the

1956 Eisenhower campaign, Nixon's staff and reporters were cavorting in the hotel swimming pool. The vice presidential candidate appeared in his bathing suit, dived in, and swam the length of the pool a couple of times, and then climbed out and departed without saying a word or even smiling at anyone.[14] The personal isolation that was later to haunt his presidency was already evident.

Lacking a real foreign policy strategy when he himself came to the White House, Nixon, at the beginning of his first term, sought advice from a Harvard professor, Henry Kissinger. Together, they achieved the dramatic moments that led to Nixon's re-election. It was a first-rate odd-couple partnership. Nixon had the office, and the scholar-diplomat would instruct him about what to do with it; what united them was a common sense of the power principle. The spokesman for the right reversed his anti-communism; his visits to Moscow and Peking led to detente. The treaty controlling anti-ballistic missile building, signed with the Russians, was significant but limited in consequences.

The lists of failed presidents between 1840 and the 1870s generally include Tyler, Taylor, Fillmore, Pierce, Buchanan, and Andrew Johnson. These chief executives were followed later by Harding and Hoover in the 1920s. Nixon was a different type, a crisis manager who said that he couldn't understand why people won't take risks. Retrospectively, it can be said that he was a transitional president who faced the forces of the past and the requirements of the future in an exceptionally difficult period of United States history. Joan Hoff is correct in arguing that Nixon was more than Watergate (and Watergate was more than Nixon). Lerner casts him mythologically as a Titan who had rebelled against the reigning divinities of the liberal Olympus, a Prometheus-type figure stealing—if not fire, then sulfur—from the gods.[15] How does Hoff's view that Nixon was ethically apricipled play in terms of the conservative political and religious program Nixon espoused publicly?

Hoff's evaluation is that an "unprincipled person is one who consciously lacks moral scruples and is presumably aware that standards are being violated. In contrast, the apricipled person [like Nixon], seldom reforms his behavior or expresses remorse for transgressions against societal norms because there is no conscious admission of wrongdoing."[16] Hoff's conclusion is that in the end, Nixon became so confused that he could not tell right from wrong or national security from the obstruction of justice. Nixon was not simply the exception, standing alone. Kennedy and Johnson had been his precursors—a Roman Catholic and a Bible Belt Protestant—and both were pragmatists. The constantly changing postures and positions so characteristic of the aprincipled person, "describe more politicians in the United States during the last fifty years than is usually acknowledged."

Nixon knew that middle-class values were threatened by change—most of all, they had been threatened in the Depression which had impacted so strongly on his family. Good people, along with less responsible ones, had suffered. Nonetheless, he himself would rely on character.[17] In his memoir book, *Six Crises*, written after his first failed attempt to win the presidency, Nixon observed: "Courage—or putting it more accurately, lack of fear—is a result of discipline. Any man who claims never to have known fear is either lying or else he is stupid. But by an act of will, he refuses to think of the reasons for fear and so concentrates entirely on winning the battle."[18]

Nixon did have a well-thought-out political ideology, which he could relate to middle-class Protestant Christianity and even to his friendship with Billy Graham. Whereas Eisenhower emphasized what the middle class had gained, Nixon stressed what it was in danger of losing. He encouraged the middle-class belief that the country's fate was being manipulated by a communist conspiracy. "Three words describe my life in Whittier: family, church, and school," Nixon wrote.[19] At the Republican Party Convention in 1952, Eisenhower hailed his running mate as one "with special talent and an ability to ferret out any kind of subversive influence where it may be found and the strength and persistence to get rid of it."[20]

One of the president's favorite teachers while he was an undergraduate at Whittier College reflected: "Nixon had an analytical mind rather than a philosophical mind. He gave all of what was asked. But he didn't vouchsafe much beyond that."[21] The conclusion seems a fair one: "The portrait that emerges ... is of a young man whose greatest character strength was that he could make himself do almost anything he felt needed to be done to reach his goals."[22] "Only a thin line separated his single-minded determination from unscrupulousness and lawlessness, and he stepped over that boundary when he felt himself under siege."[23]

WARTIME PRESSURES

A wartime atmosphere dominated in Washington as well as across the country when Nixon took office in the White House. Vietnam was the first war since the Civil War that seriously divided public opinion as well as that of the elite opinion makers. After he had nominated Patrick Gray to become permanent head of the FBI, Nixon told him in February of 1973: "with the media against you, with the bureaucracy against you, uh, with the professors, uh, with the church people and the rest, let alone Congress, it's a hard damn fight."[24] His paranoia was not corrected by idealism or simple realism.

Nixon's wiretaps and secret domestic surveillance may well have come directly out of his conduct of the war in Vietnam. Kennedy, Johnson, and Nixon all failed to understand that from the beginning, it was Saigon's war to win or lose. But still pursuing it, Nixon claimed to be acting for the silent generation in the United States, as he again and again trampled on human rights in the United States and abroad. The IRS was employed to support his strategies as soon as Nixon came to office and the plumbers used its records. Instead of trusting the course of events, the chief executive nurtured resentments that led him into blatantly illegal acts which eventually he could no longer conceal. "He maneuvered, at Watergate, to steal an election he was almost certain to win anyway; in the process, he stole the presidency from himself."[25]

Nixon was calculating in his attempt to win the support of the South and its religious conservatives for his policies. He criticized desegregation, and twice tried to fill Supreme Court vacancies with a conservative Southern judge whom the Senate rejected. Then he fulminated against malicious character assassination by the Senate and called upon "the millions of Americans living in the South" to testify against "this act of regional discrimination."[26] He himself was for "law and order," and he told a group of Pennsylvania Republicans that "If I am president, I am not going to owe anything to the black community."[27] Billy Graham, it needs to be noted, had refused to hold racially segregated crusades in the South or anywhere else.

When Nixon's strategy to win the war in Vietnam was not effective, he reflected: "Once I realized that the Vietnam War could not be ended quickly or easily and that I was going to be up against an anti-war movement that was able to dominate the media with its attitudes and values, I was sometimes drawn into the very frame of mind I so despised in the leaders of the movement. They increasingly came to justify almost anything in the name of forcing an immediate end to a war they considered unjustified and immoral. I was similarly driven to preserve the government's ability to conduct foreign policy and to conduct it in the way that I felt would best bring peace."[28]

Even as Nixon realized that the war could not be won, he wanted to make its end part of a larger global transaction. His capriciousness in foreign policy ran over into the domestic. As the 1972 election approached, Nixon observed: "Democratic presidents, since FDR, had excelled—and reveled—in flexing the formidable political muscle that goes with being the party in the White House ... So I ended up keeping the pressure on the people around me to get organized, to get tough, to get information about what the other side was doing ... I told my staff we should come up with the kind of imaginative dirty tricks that our Democratic opponents used against us and others so effectively in previous campaigns."[29]

RELIGIOUS CONSIDERATIONS

Nixon's campaign reference to an inspirational minister cited at the beginning of this chapter was part of an intentionally projected image. The candidate's advisors had modulated it in code words to give it the widest possible impact; moral and religious references can serve to help avoid the issues. Nixon spoke boastfully of his own moral goals: "I will work increasingly to halt the erosion of moral fiber in American life, and the denial of individual accountability for individual action."[30] But in contrast to such public pronouncements, Nixon shared with his intimate associates a special world with a very different sense of reality. Viewing the unfolding story of American politics without any abiding moral or religious reference, they prided themselves on their own special form of pragmatism. Politics was reduced to power and technique. The word ***power*** was heard frequently; it was often spoken as if it were reality's fundamental ingredient.

Michael Novak, writing as a Roman Catholic ethicist, is especially critical, arguing that there was not simply a dangerous expansion of executive power at the expense of the Congress, the courts and the press. In Nixon's "corporate presidency," the image of Technopolis—a high technological organization—was substituted for the Constitutional system. Novak designates the stand as "more rational than fascism but none the less centripetal, similarly faceless, similarly banal." Nixon's associates were expected to relinquish their humanity to meet the abstract impersonal needs of efficient management. After his second electoral victory he instituted mass staff resignations. "In the self-effacement of his remote control government, Nixon's personality was satisfying his own needs by the kind of men he permitted around him and the style he encouraged them to adopt."[31]

Nixon's self-proclaimed faith in America rested in the final analysis on a belief that there is no limit to what human beings can achieve if they will only make use of their intelligence, their technology, and their ideals. Simplistic and rigorously moralistic in public, he had no self-critical ethical or religious perspective from which to judge his own policies as provided either by religion or traditional morality. There was a crass violation of the First Amendment of the Constitution; the president established what Reinhold Niebuhr called "The King's Chapel." National religious leaders were invited to conduct Sunday services in the White House. Implied endorsement of the president's policies, not prophetic criticism, was given the sanction of the holy.

Novak observes that the set of circumstances which arrested the slide toward Technopolis was chancy.[32] Trivial accidents, lucky flukes like the Watergate arrest, reduced a seemingly irresistible juggernaut from triumph to humiliation as they broke down secrecy. The June 23 tape in particular was evidence that Nixon had lied. Still, he resigned without repentance or making any acknowledgment of guilt. In his judgment, the mistakes he had made were primarily political rather than moral. His appointed successor, Gerald Ford, subsequently destroyed his own chances for re-election when he gave Richard Nixon a complete pardon the month after he had resigned.

Publicly pious and moralistic, Nixon sought cover under the

righteous mantle of leaders such as Billy Graham. Privately, the White House tapes revealed him to be vain, profane, and cynical. The contradiction was glaring. A doctrine of fate rather than of providence was at the heart of Nixon's conviction. Human beings and their wills, he was convinced, operate in a predetermined context. Up there, an unknown flow of fate rolls on into eternity. The universe is mysterious and incalculable. Down here, man is seen as crouched and waiting, prepared through effort to catch the sudden sign for action. Nixon's view was that circumstances rather than individual ambition place a leader in the right time and the right place. There was a practical difficulty: such a view tends to eliminate middle-ground progressions.

Historically, one should not underestimate Nixon. He was the most profound and influential among the presidents of his era. His breakthrough in relations with China by itself gives him an enduring place in the presidential succession. Henry Kissinger—the great realist—and Nixon—the lingering idealist—worked together. He faltered at home over what was at first a somewhat minor matter that need not, if handled otherwise, have brought him down. He failed to destroy the tapes as he might have done at the outset and saved his presidency. But characteristically, the loner did not do so. His defective ethics and theology leave lessons to be learned. But they do not tell the entire story. He has his lasting place in American history as a "bad guy," but he was not just that.

BILLY GRAHAM

It is clear that Nixon appeared attractive to Billy Graham, and he promoted the Californian for the presidency more than any other candidate. Graham, in fact, lent his own personal prestige to the former vice president when Nixon ran for the White House. Senator Mark Hatfield reflected: "See a picture of Billy speaking in a great crusade. Everything is religious in this atmosphere—Billy speaking, Billy praying, Billy reading the Bible. Billy is one of the most admired and respected men in our country, Billy with the Pope, Billy with Madame Nehru, Billy with kings and queens, Billy with the president."

Christians would begin to conclude: "Billy's close to God. Billy's close to Nixon. Therefore, God must have ordained Nixon a to be president and he's getting his message through Billy."[33]

Graham went so far as to excuse if not defend Nixon's ruthless Christmas bombing of Cambodia: "Like all Americans, I thought a cease-fire was imminent. I think that was what caused the reaction across the nation. I deplore the suffering and the killing in this war, and I pray it can be ended as soon as possible, but we also have to realize that there are hundreds of thousands of deaths attributed to smoking ..."[34] Graham claimed a basic biblical message: "human sin is everywhere; tragedy is with us always, a mark of our fallen nature, and to focus on one sin or sorrow over another is to miss the larger point that we are all in need of grace."[35]

NIXON'S DOWNFALL

Reflecting on Nixon's betrayal of public trust in Watergate, the evangelist explained: "I did misjudge him. It was a side to him that I never knew, yet I'd been with him so many times. He was just like a whole new person. I talked to Julie about that and she felt that about her own father. I almost felt as if a demon had come into the White House, and had entered his presidency, because it seemed to be sort of supernatural. I mean it was so ugly and so terrible, especially the cover-up and the language and all that. It was just something I never knew."[36] "I wonder whether I might have exaggerated his spirituality in my own mind."[37]

Nixon's presidential statements, spiced with references to the Puritan ethic and pietism, centered not on a transcendent God who judges both men and nations, but only on Nixon's own personal vision of what the nation should be. The self-interest that corrupts even the best intentions, at times in hubris, remained unrecognized. Of course, it is a position evident in a host of American political figures. The question is not whether Nixon recognized the reality of political power; he did. But why did he not see beyond it in the kind of conscience which transcends particular administrations and their problems? Did he really believe his own ideological propaganda? Faith in God brought no judgment to his life. For him, religious faith had not moved beyond nationalism. It carried no critical or prophetic judgment.

From the time of McCord's letter to Judge Sirica describing a cover-up and offering to testify if he were given a shorter sentence, Nixon was a man desperately trying to save himself; he could not function effectively as a president. Still, there was the challenge of the Yom Kippur War in Israel. The Jews desperately needed supplies, but there was no transport. Nixon himself finally cut the knot: "Send the stuff on anything that moves."[38] Then as the Israeli forces won, the Egyptians sought American help in arranging a truce. Nixon had still played the statesman, even though he was falling apart mentally and as a man. The night before he left the White House, knowing that he would resign in the morning, he knelt in prayer with Kissinger. Fate was not enough— and to whom did they pray together? Nixon left the White House with a rambling, sentimental speech. In it, he was full of self-pity, but he nonetheless believed that history would justify him. But Nixon was not finished. His career did continue and he emerged influential again, writing and recommending strategy for his successors.

There was tragic loss, not just for the president, but for the nation in his collapse and departure from his central place on the national and international scene. Stephen F. Ambrose has written careful, balanced biographies of both Eisenhower and Nixon. Ambrose concludes his third volume on Nixon, Ruin and Recovery 1973-1990, with:

> "Because Nixon resigned, the full promise of his opening to China has not been realized …
> Because Nixon resigned, his program for an energy policy that would lessen American dependence on foreign oil was abandoned.
> Because Nixon resigned, the Republican Party moved to the right, bringing a majority of the voters in the country along with it …
> Because Nixon resigned, the welfare reform he proposed that was so badly needed died. So did his program providing health insurance for Americans. Who can measure the misery endured by millions of poor Americans as a result?
> Because Nixon resigned, revenue sharing died. This came just at the time the cities were losing their factories and tax bases. The result was visible poverty in the cities, in the

*form of homeless men, women, and children, such as had
not been seen in America since the Depression ....*"

Ambrose's debatable conclusion was: "Because Nixon resigned,
what the country got was not the Nixon Revolution but the Reagan
Revolution. It got massive, unbelievable deficits. It got Iran-contra. It
got the savings and loans scandals. It got millions of homeless, and
gross favoritism for the rich. None of that was any part of the proposed
Nixon Revolution. When Nixon resigned, we lost more than we
gained."[39]

In the end, Nixon turned out to be a flexible, pragmatic conservative
who was not a dogmatist. The career of Richard Nixon makes clear
the perils of power politics and the pursuit of statecraft without moral
absolutes.

GERALD RUDOLPH FORD

Ford was a good and pious congressman whose colleagues' recommendation elevated him to vice president and put him on the road to the White House. Inheriting the highest office in the land after Nixon resigned, he faced a crucial responsibility in deciding what to do about the legacy of the Watergate scandal. Invoking his own piety, Ford granted the ex-president an unconditional pardon. In so doing, he probably acted too quickly, and his honeymoon in the White House was short-lived. By contrast, Obama might well have proceeded less on intuition, analyzing matters in a more step-by-step way. As later in the case of the forty-fourth president, Ford inherited a colonial war from his predecessor. Congress forced him to withdraw American troops from Vietnam. Relying on Henry Kissinger for foreign policy advice, he did manage to advance human rights in the Helsinki negotiations with the Russians. Debating Jimmy Carter when he ran for the presidency on his own, Ford blundered about Poland and lost to the first president from the Deep South since the Civil War.

BIOGRAPHY AND RECORD AS A LEGISLATOR

"He knows how to listen to Simon or Usery, how to get from them what he needs to know ... I think he is the kind of person who plays a good poker hand ... You can't guess what he wants—that's good. It not only encourages debate … It is my judgment that it would offend him if he thought you were trying to guess what he wanted. He doesn't like yes-men."[1] So Gerald R. Ford was described by one of his close advisors. In these and other characteristics, he was the antithesis of the man whom he replaced in the White House. His religion, Anglican evangelical, was a deeply held faith which he refused to flaunt in public.

Ford was the first and only person to hold the highest office in the land without being elected either president or vice president. He was appointed vice president and confirmed by the Congress, following the resignation of Spiro T. Agnew late in 1973. For a quarter of a century, he had served in Congress, representing Grand Rapids, Michigan. After Nixon's fall from power, Ford became heir to the presidency, and he took the oath of office on August 9, 1974. To his credit, he strove to heal the wounds of the Watergate scandal that had cost Nixon the White House. The new leader said that he wanted to be the president of all the people and promised openness and candor.[2]

"Raised in the Calvinistic milieu and staid social setting of Michigan's Grand Rapids, Gerry Ford absorbed the community's reserved cultural outlook on manners and morality through the tutelage of his parents." So Edward L. and Frederick H. Schapsmeier, in Gerald R. Ford's *Date with Destiny: A Political Biography*, characterize his values.[3] They add: "he did regard himself as a quiet and persistent spokesperson for the middle class of America. Representing that segment of society of which he was a product, Ford reflected its endemic brand of Mid-American conservativism."[4]

The president was born in Omaha, Nebraska on July 14, 1913 and was christened Leslie Lynch King, Jr. The name Gerald Rudolph Ford came from his stepfather. After her marriage to the son of a wealthy millionaire broke up only sixteen days after his birth, his mother moved to Grand Rapids, Michigan. There she married her second husband, whom she had met at Grace Episcopal Church. Ford's three half-brothers were born to the couple. Actually, Gerald did not know about his own background until the age of seventeen. One day, while he was working as a waiter and fry cook at Bill Skougis's Dairy Shoppe, in fall of 1930, a stranger approached him and said, "Young fellow, my name is Leslie King, and I'm your father." Ford recalled later, "I was stunned and didn't know what to say." Only then did he learn that Gerald Rudolph Ford, Sr. was not his real father. Ford's natural father had come to Detroit to pick up a new Lincoln. He handed his son twenty-five dollars and said, "Buy yourself something you can't afford otherwise."

Ford reflected later: "Nothing could erase the image I gained of my real father that day, a carefree, well-to-do man who didn't really give a damn about the hopes and dreams of his first born son. When I went to bed that night, I broke down and cried."[5]

The future president played football at South High and then at the University of Michigan. He reflected about the value of athletics: "Football has been and is my first love. The lessons I learned from football have helped me along in political competition. Both politics and football reflect unique qualities in the American character—rough, tough, total competition within well-defined rules; rugged individualism tempered by team spirit and sacrifice; self-discipline that doesn't degenerate into blind obedience; willingness to accept the final score when the gun goes off or the last ballot is counted."[6]

Ford had been accepted for the football team at Harvard as well as at Michigan, but in the end, he decided to stay in his home state. The 1935 Michigan yearbook gave him a place in its Hall of Fame with the citation: "Jerry Ford ... because the football team chose him as their most valuable player; because he was a good student and got better grades than anyone else on the squad; because he put the DKE House back on a paying basis; because he never smokes, drinks, swears, or tells dirty stories ... and because he's not a bit fraudulent and we can't find anything really nasty to say about him."[7]

After graduating at Ann Arbor, Ford went to Yale to help coach football, and through his own persistent efforts, was admitted to Yale Law School, graduating in 1941. Following the outbreak of World War II, Ford joined the navy in April of 1942 and served on a light aircraft carrier, the U.S.S. Monterey. By the end of the war, he had had two years of battle experience, first commanding a 40-mm anti-aircraft battery on the fantail of his ship, and then doing duty on the bridge. He explained the change that wartime service brought to his political conviction: "Before the war, I was a typical Midwest isolationist. I returned understanding we could never be isolated again. We were and are one world. It was clear to me, it was inevitable to me, that this country was obligated to lead in this new world. We had won the war. It was up to us to keep the peace."[8]

Having returned to Grand Rapids in 1946, Ford was elected president of the Home Front, a reform-oriented Republican organization whose goal was to unseat GOP boss Frank McKay. In fact, it had been organized with his friends before Ford went into the navy. Supported by them, he was elected to the House of Representatives. The new congressman explained: "First, I had to make sure I would have the endorsements of a number of Dutch leaders. The Dutch made up 60 percent of the population of the district, and 90 percent were Republican. There were two rival groups, the Dutch Reformed Church and the Dutch Christian Reformed Church ... I'm Irish, Scotch, and English, and have no Dutch background. Fortunately, Dr. Ver Meulen, my friend from the Home Front, got a group of Reformed leaders to be on my side."[9]

Ford won over a four-term incumbent congressman, Bartel L. Jonkman, a Christian Reformed leader whose allegiance was to the McKay machine. The larger target, of course, was Boss McKay. Jerald terHorst of the Grand Rapids Press described him as a "stocky, secretive man who affected a pince-nez and a pearl stickpin, maintained a fancy automobile, but was seldom seen in public places. Lacking formal education, he spoke in short, explosive phrases, usually profane."[10] When he did speak, however, things happened in one part of the state or another.

Jonkman, McKay's man in Congress, a member of the House Foreign Affairs Committee, was an outspoken opponent of U.S. membership in the U.N. and had opposed both the Marshall Plan and aid to Greece and Turkey. Senator Arthur Vandenberg (the head of the Senate Foreign Relations Committee, whom Ford admired) wanted Jonkman defeated. Two years later, Ford, known as hard-working with a pleasant personality, was made a member of the Appropriations Committee.

Attempting to understand what made Ford what he was, Shogan observes that political loyalty has several levels: there is not only mutual allegiance to shared principles but also loyalty of one politician to another and to the party. Ford embodied not only the first but the second. Loyalty "was a political golden rule based on mutual trust and need that served not only to nurture ambition but also to protect against risk and error."[11] Shogan adds: "And no one in memory, not even Eisenhower, tried so hard to like people as Ford did. It was part of a creed he consciously adopted as a youngster.[12]

Ford remembered: "By the time I entered seventh grade, I was becoming aware of the deep emotions that rivalries can stir ... hating or even disliking people because of their bad qualities was a waste of time ... everyone had more good qualities than bad. If I understood and tried to accentuate these good qualities in others, I could get along much better."[13] Ford's motto when he first came to the White House was: "We can disagree and still be friends."

Ford has been described as a pragmatic conservative in the sense that he tended to rely "on experience and inherited belief rather than on precisely formulated doctrines—a true Burkean."[13] The same admirer saw him as an "insider attuned to the whirligig of politics, he did not envision himself either a political reformer or as one to engender some kind of social regeneration in the country." His was the traditional "Horatio Alger Cluster" of American values, antithetical to the Great Society and the liberal philosophy that attempted to alleviate poverty through massive welfare programs. Ford believed in patriotism, peace through strength, social advancement via meritocracy, fiscal responsibility, personal morality, and civic virtue. He supported programs for the future, based on free enterprise and private endeavor. Although a member of NAACP, the president-to-be nonetheless argued: "I happen to think it is far wiser timewise for kids to be in their neighborhood schools than to spend a lot of time traveling from their home to a school which may be three, four, five, or ten miles away."[14]

After he had served as a member of the Warren Commission (which investigated John F. Kennedy's assassination) with Jack Stiles, Ford wrote Portrait of the Assassin, a book on Lee Harvey Oswald, whose character interested him.

A lifelong Episcopalian who lived in Alexandria near Washington, Ford was a member of the Immanuel-on-the-Hill parish. At the Capitol, he was the fifth of the so-called "five sisters" who met each Monday at 7:30 am in the prayer room of the House: John Rhodes of Arizona, Les Arends of Illinois, Charles Goodell of New York, and Albert Quie of Minnesota. Even though a practicing Episcopalian, Ford was an evangelical but not a fundamentalist. His special religious counselor was Billy Zeoli, a former Youth for Christ director. Zeoli preached to professional football and baseball players as well as to teenagers. While he was still minority leader of the House of Representatives, Ford is reported to have "accepted Christ." His conversion experience occurred during a service that Zeoli conducted in 1971 before the Washington Redskins/Dallas Cowboys game. Ford wrote to Zeoli, "Because I have trusted Christ to be my saviour, my life is his." He thanked the evangelist for leading him to his faith. Zeoli in turn promised he "would never comment on a political decision" made by Ford. But while Ford was in office, Zeoli sent him a prayer memo each week.[15]

When the Supreme Court decision Engle v. Vitale invalidated the New York Regents school prayer, Ford commented: "Already we have gone too far in establishing a religion of secularism in the United States. While many still do profess to believe in God, they act as if He did not exist. We need to use all the forces at our command in the family, school, the church, and our society to strengthen rather than weaken our spiritual and moral values."[16]

Ford was coming more and more to public attention, and there were premonitions of his future role. The May 1964 issue of the *Congressional Quarterly* listed him as the only member of House included by its members in their preferences for the presidential nomination. There were limits to Ford's conservativism. Ford was anti-Goldwater in sentiment, even as he opposed Johnson's Great Society as a shambles of contradictions. He supported Johnson's goals in Vietnam but strongly disagreed with his strategy. Johnson attacked him personally for his opposition, describing him as "dumb." "Jerry played football too many times without a helmet. Jerry can't walk and chew gum at the same time."[17]

VICE PRESIDENT—THE WAY TO THE PRESIDENCY

When he took the oath of office as vice president in the House chamber, early in December of 1974, he remarked: "I am a Ford, not a Lincoln. My addresses will never be as eloquent as Lincoln's. But I will do my best to equal his brevity and plain speaking."[18] One of his greatest assets was that he had a working knowledge of the legislative process, knew the value of long-range goals, and believed in rational compromise. Unlike Nixon, his psychological make-up was totally devoid of paranoid tendencies against those who opposed him. He was not obsessed with attaining power and had the capacity to grow in office.

How Ford came to the vice presidency and then the presidency tells much about the times as well as about the man. After his nomination by Nixon as successor to Agnew, Senate confirmation hearings began in the Senate Committee on Rules and Administration.[19]

10:05 *am*, November 1, 1973:

> Ford commented at the outset: *"Gentlemen, I readily promise to answer your questions truthfully. I know you will not pull any punches ... Through my testimony, it is my intention to replace misunderstanding with understanding, and to substitute truths for untruth."*[20]

> The chairman of the committee, Senator Howard Cannon, queried: *"Do you believe that a president can legally prevent or terminate any criminal investigation or prosecution involving the president?"*

> Reply: *"I do not think he should. I hope there will never be a president who will take such action. If a president resigned his office before his term expired, would his successor have the power to prevent or to terminate any investigation or criminal prosecution charges against the former president? I do not think the public would stand for it. Whether he has the technical authority or not, I cannot give you a categorical answer. The attorney general, in my opinion, with the help and support of the American people, would be the controlling factor."*[21]

THE NIXON PARDON

Ford's presidential political style reflected his attempt to restore the moral integrity of the presidency. He invited in business and labor leaders along with governors, mayors, and county officials. Soon after, before a Veterans of Foreign Wars group in Chicago, Ford announced he would offer an amnesty for 50,000 Vietnam draft evaders and deserters, but not an unconditional pardon, as he had for former president Nixon. Ford's changes in symbolism and administration initially brought him considerable good will. The press celebrated his folksiness, telling how he toasted his own English muffins in the morning and at the end of the day took a swim to relax. His manner was self-effacing and brought a positive report of a 71 percent approval rating in the Gallup poll shortly after he took office. All of this changed when on Sunday, September 8, 1974, four weeks in office, Ford granted Richard Nixon "a full, free, and absolute pardon." Actually, the new president had only a month of good will and popularity.

The background of the Nixon pardon merits attention. On August 1, 1974, Nixon's chief of staff, Alexander Haig, phoned Ford and asked to meet with him.[22] The vice president asked his chief of staff, Robert Hartmann, to be a part of the meeting. In the latter's presence, Haig did not speak freely; then he requested a second meeting the same day. Haig asked if Nixon "could agree to leave in return for an agreement that the new president [Gerald Ford] would agree to pardon him."

Ford's answer was: *"Well, Al, I want some time to think."*

When Hartmann was told about the conversation, he exclaimed angrily to Ford: "You should have taken Haig by the scruff of the neck and the seat of the pants and thrown him ... out of your office!" He judged that Ford "had not yet grasped the monstrous impropriety" of Haig's inquiry. On the next afternoon, Ford called Haig and told him he had "no intention of recommending what the president should do about resigning" and added "that nothing we talked about yesterday afternoon should be given any consideration in whatever decision the president may wish to make."

Ford always insisted that there had been no deal. Only one of his advisors, Phil Buchen, advocated pardoning Richard Nixon. The new president's pardon of his predecessor "for all offenses against the United States that he might have committed while in office" aroused immediate controversy. It probably cost him a second term when he ran on his own for the White House. A key sentence in the pardon explained Ford's motivation: "I do believe with all my heart and mind and spirit that I, not as President, but as a humble servant of God, will receive justice without mercy if I fail to show mercy."

There were two themes in Ford's comments in the document: the powers of the presidency—first, the historic office, the Constitution, "this desk," and Harry Truman's plaque that says "The Buck Stops Here." He referred to himself as president eight times. Secondly, he spoke of "conscience" six times. Ford believed it was the right thing to do, although a short time earlier, he had remarked to Congress that the American public would not stand for such a thing. Ford was the first of a succession of three chief executives, all of whom claimed an evangelical born-again experience: Ford, Carter, and Reagan. That he belonged to this group (including his successors) explained the way in which his pardon was phrased.

A commentator in the magazine *Christian Century* responded: "Ford's statement has got to be sincere, because the theological justification for his presidential act is the only one that clarifies it. As a political act, it has already brought the President nothing but trouble and doubtless will continue to do so."

Commonweal, the Roman Catholic lay magazine, commented: "To talk of mercy while ignoring justice is to make a mockery of morality, and this is what Mr. Ford has done. Ford's pardon represented bad theology and even worse politics ... The President's desire to heal national wounds and show compassion is commendable; his fatal mistake, however, was his abysmal failure to appreciate that the American people also deserve compassion."[23]

The Protestant liberal, Robert McAfee Brown, observed: "in trying to show mercy to Richard Nixon, the President acted with cruel injustice to John Dean, H. R. Haldeman, John Mitchell, and over 30 other close associates of Mr. Nixon who will probably go to prison for crimes with which their boss cannot—due to Mr. Ford's action."[24]

Political scientist Roger Porter, who served in the Ford administration, summed it all up retrospectively: "For many Americans, this single act overwhelmed the aura of openness, accessibility, and candor that he [Ford] had so successfully begun to establish."[25] Hartmann comments that it was the real Gerry Ford; the decision embodied his beliefs and values. Reflecting later on his action, Ford did not express any regret. The action he took was necessary to get on with his own presidency: "It was an unbelievable lifting of a burden from my shoulders."[26]

Hartmann argues that different from all other recent presidents, Ford lacked truly national experience. It would have been out of character for other presidents to have pardoned Nixon in the way Ford did.[27] Hartman speculates that Eisenhower, in the pattern of response to McCarthyism, would have looked for a behind-the-scenes scenario; a pardon would have been granted for an explicit admission of guilt in an agreement between Nixon and the special prosecutor. Moreover, Eisenhower probably would have used a go-between intermediary, Hartmann thinks. Truman would have viewed a pardon for Nixon as an affront to the underdog, and he certainly would not have viewed Nixon as an underdog.

If Kennedy—rather than Ford—had been in office, he most likely would have sought a greater public airing of the issue. Any other course of events would have been seen as contrary to the leadership principles he espoused. Johnson, Hartmann speculates, probably would have looked for a negotiated settlement, with himself as the mediator. But he probably would not have acted as abruptly as Ford, not wishing to risk his own consensus. Nixon himself would have been quick to realize that a pardon would outrage middle-class values—as it did in the case of Ford's generosity.

ACHIEVEMENTS IN OFFICE

Barber notes that the appointed president made his hard choices early on. "He had no positive announcements to make about peace or prosperity; on the other hand, he decided to make two very controversial announcements, which reminded the nation of Watergate and Vietnam."[28] In terms of the positions he took on legislation, Ford was more active than Eisenhower or Nixon. "Presidents who want to maximize their popularity could take Ford as a kind of negative model and reverse everything he did."[29] Ford's moral stance was primarily inner directed in an attempt to do what he thought was right. Like Truman, he was not overly concerned with the polls. In short, Ford combined morally motivated activity with a refusal to be led by public opinion.

Throughout his two years in office, Ford had to face the difficulty of working with a Democrat-controlled Congress. He had some success in securing legislation on deregulation and tax cutting, but in all made sixty-six vetoes, mostly against spending bills. Legislators would not give him the funds he requested for emergency assistance to the disintegrating government of South Vietnam. The American armed services under his command were forced to evacuate Saigon. However, Ford did not consult Congress when he sent troops to recover the merchant ship *Mayaguez* after it was seized in Cambodia. In this short military action, he proceeded on his own. His request to lift an embargo on aid for Turkey, and his plan to help the anti-Marxist guerillas in Angola also were refused.

Barber praises Ford's love of teamwork and his speeches of conciliation when he first took office, and he makes them the basis of classifying Ford as an active-positive president. Still, when Ford called a summit meeting of economists and declared war on inflation—a war complete with WIN buttons ("Whip Inflation Now"), the strategy had little positive impact. Soon, a recession developed. The new president's reputation slumped, and the media bore down on him.

Not all commentators agree with Barber's classification or with his view of Ford's inner sense of conviction as well as his combativeness. After all, he played football before turning to politics. Some have called him an active-negative type. Neustadt observes that he had unquestionable decency, but he blurred this in a month. He needed to assume the continuity of the office by his demonstration of difference from his predecessor. Ford's dramatic action symbolized the reverse. "The pardon seems a matter less of newness than of conscience [and] sympathy ... Nixon, he reportedly was told, seemed suicidal."[30]

Ford retained Henry Kissinger as secretary of state. Kissinger helped to organize the 1975 Helsinki Conference, participated in by thirty-four nations. His statesmanship has been criticized for its recognition of the status quo of borders in Europe. In retrospect, it is significant that the Helsinki documents were cited repeatedly by dissidents in Eastern Europe. Ford summarized their contents: "They affirm the most fundamental human rights ... They call for a freer flow of information, ideas, and people ... They offer wide areas for greater cooperation ... They reaffirm the basic principles of relations between states ... The United States gladly subscribed to this document because we subscribe to every one of these principles." Ford added: "History will judge this conference not by what we say here today, but by what we do tomorrow—not by promises we make, but by the promises we keep."[31]

"Gerald Ford's biggest continuing problem in the White House," Ron Nessen noted, "was the portrayal of him in the media as a bumbler."[32] Ford fell on the slippery steps of *Air Force One* while embarking in Salzburg, Austria on June 1, 1975. In full view of television cameras, his unsteady knees let him down while skiing. Once, he bumped his head while getting out of a cramped helicopter.

Within his own party, Ford had to struggle for the nomination against Ronald Reagan. Ford argued, "My record is one of progress, not platitudes, specifics not smiles, performances not promises. It is a record I am proud to run on."[33] Campaigning on his own for the presidency, he represented himself in a Truman mold, attacking the do-everything 94th Congress. It was not just Ford's record that was at issue in the campaign. Watergate was in the background, as well as the pardon of Nixon. Carter reminded voters (as against Nixon) "You can trust me" and "I will never lie to you."

Ford was gaining in the polls against Carter until the televised debate from the Palace of Fine Arts in San Francisco, October 6. 1976, Max Frankel, associate editor of *The New York Times,* referring to the Helsinki accords, asked Ford whether "the Russians have dominance in Eastern Europe." Frankel followed up his question: "Did I understand you to say, sir, that the Russians are not using Eastern Europe as their own sphere of influence and occupying most of the countries there and making sure with their troops that it's a Communist zone?"[34]

Ford's answer was a major political gaffe and contributed to his loss of the presidency: "I don't believe, Mr. Frankel, that the Yugoslavians consider themselves dominated by the Soviet Union. I don't believe that Romanians consider themselves dominated by the Soviet Union. I don't believe the Poles consider themselves dominated by the Soviet Union. Each of these countries is independent or autonomous. It has its own territorial integrity, and the United States does not concede that those countries are under the domination of the Soviet Union."[35] The debate took place in the period in which the Solidarity protest was at its peak in Poland. Carter, of course, condemned the policy of accepting a Soviet sphere of influence. In the election, Carter won 40.1 million votes and Ford only 39.1.

At his inauguration, Carter praised his predecessor: "For myself and for our nation, I want to thank my predecessor for all he has done to heal our land." Ford rose and shook Carter's hand. Speaking out later, he commended Carter for completing negotiations for SALT II, the Camp David agreement, his settling of the Panama Canal issue, and handling of both the embargo on Turkey and diplomatic relations with China. With respect to domestic policy, Ford judged: "I think on economics, the Carter administration has been a disaster."[36]

Like the Democrat who defeated him, Ford remained a deeply religious person; in fact, a "twice-born Christian." Giving the commencement address at Gordon-Conwell Seminary (the evangelical school from which his son Michael graduated in 1977), Ford reflected: "My presidency led to a great reliance on God." The two attempts on his life, he said, made him realize how tenuous mortality was, and daily grappling with affairs of state made him conscious of "how limited man's wisdom is." He added, "some of the problems were so complex we didn't always immediately understand them."[37]

Ford died in 2007, condemning Bush II's invasion of Iraq—a conviction that was announced by his own wish only after his death. His religion did not solve all the dilemmas that he hoped it would. But he was sound morally and psychologically, a decent kind of ethical realist who had firm convictions by which he lived and died—but was not a reformer, much less an agitator or fanatic.

JAMES EARL CARTER

Jimmy Carter aroused popular enthusiasm and came into office announcing his "born-again" Christian motivation. Morally, he promised, "I'll never lie to you!" He was running more against Nixon than against Ford! Carter had come to national attention as a representative of the New South when he championed desegregation at his inauguration as governor in Atlanta. Critics described him a Puritan and Yankee from Georgia. Obama, by contrast, comes from the Land of Lincoln and another part of the evangelical church, the black rather than the white. The Georgian from Plains left a lasting legacy by courageously championing human rights; he eventually became the nation's most respected ex-president. He has undertaken remarkable social service (in Habitat for Humanity) since leaving the White House. Carter is widely evaluated retrospectively, however, as a presidential individualist, a pietistic Baptist Christian who "never got inside Washington." Obama is much more community oriented, and is a highly skillful political operator with remarkable self-discipline and control. Unfortunately, he faces some of the same problems of violence with Muslim fanaticism that bedeviled Carter.

"There is no way to understand me and my political philosophy without understanding my faith." —Carter, December 28, 1983[1]

"The most important thing in my life is Jesus Christ." —Carter, Kenosha, Wisconsin, April 2, 1976[2]

THE PERSON

He was a "wheeler-healer," riding to power on the promise of national reconciliation; so the commentator, Eric Sevareid, characterized Jimmy Carter. American historian Robert A. Rutland observes that "the short, soft-spoken former governor of Georgia ... was the longest of long shots for election to the presidency."

"There's a lot of things I will never do to get elected," Carter told a crowd in Concord. "I will never tell a lie, make a misleading statement, or betray a trust. If I should ever betray a trust, don't support me ... I'm a businessman, I'm a farmer, I'm a planner, I'm an engineer, I'm a nuclear physicist, I'm a politician, I'm a Christian."[3] Carter's coming to office was the result of American populism in the post-Watergate setting.

Attacking the Nixon legacy (sometimes by implication but more often explicitly), Carter defended moral absolutes—in his case, based on religious faith. Barber explains: "The moralizing story comes up as a reaction to the battle story, which, like a war gone on too long, seems to degenerate from adventure to butchery. The moralists ... seek to recapture innocence in the person of an outsider who will clean up the Capitol."[4]

"Carter is difficult to evaluate as a president because his rise was so quick and dramatic and his fall, though not as quick, was clearly a stunning failure."[5] So observes Erwin C. Hargrove in *Jimmy Carter: the Politics of Public Goods.* Hargrove viewed Carter as a legatee of the vanished tradition of Southern progressivism. This tradition opposed machine politics, political corruption, and unethical business practices; it preached a gospel of efficient, honest government. Largely middle class and drawn from the professions and commerce, its advocates were concerned for social reform and to protect the weak and unfortunate. Hargrove judges that their outlook was characterized by a minimum of emotion, an attitude reflected in Carter's interest in engineering-like competence.

Carter broke politicians' longstanding balance of politics and religion as a deliberate campaign strategy; he was an evangelical and near fundamentalist, but not a hard-shell fundamentalist.[6] To say the least, he was not simply bland about religion like so many other candidates. It was a deliberate campaign strategy on his part, premised on the belief that his use of moral language made his case more appealing. Addressing the Democratic National Convention on July 15, 1976 in New York, Carter argued: "We feel that moral decay has weakened our country, that it is crippled by a lack of goals and values … Our country has lived through a time of torment. It is now a time for healing. We want to have faith again. We want to be proud again. We just want the truth again."[7] The presidential candidate concluded by quoting the rock musician, Bob Dylan, "We have an America that is busy being born, not busy dying." Carter was preaching morality as against expediency and nihilism.[8]

No longer in the White House, having lost to Reagan, Carter turned out to be one of the most distinguished of all American ex-presidents. He surpassed at least in some of his achievements even John Quincy Adams and William Howard Taft. His intervention in Haiti prevented hostilities and made singularly crucial contributions to peace. While in office, his greatest achievement probably was the Camp David Peace Accord between Israel and Egypt. The accord was slow in implementation because of fundamentalist opposition in Israel, and Carter's defeat for re-election as president came significantly from Iranian Shi'ite fundamentalists' taking of American hostages.

From an explicitly religious point of view, there was an acceptance of limits; there could no longer be unrestrained power abroad. In his inaugural address, Carter said: "We have learned that 'more' is not necessarily 'better,' that even our great nation has its recognized limits, and that we can neither answer all questions nor solve all problems."[9]

Carter's openly religious stance—characteristic in part of his region—drew bitter attacks from critics as well as eulogy from his supporters. The rural South in which he grew up has a more homogeneous cultural tradition than the North. His political base was made up of a broad constituency of rural residents, suburban conservatives, blue-collar workers, inner-city blacks, and practical liberals. Peter Meyer, in his *James Earl Carter, The Man and the Myth*, asked somewhat cynically: "Was he seeking a council seat in the City of God or the City of Man? … Even if one believed in his sincerity, the lingering doubt was whether a vote for Carter was a vote for a president or a priest."[10]

Harper's magazine editor Lewis Lapham attacked the Georgian by observing that "He was elected to redeem the country, not to govern it."[11] Meyer also spoke against Carter's Southern Baptist affiliation, describing the denomination as a "religious sect that has always seemed to live on the outer banks of the mainstream of American culture." What needs to be clear is that religious themes, earlier intentionally muted in politics, became vocal in Carter's attack on the abuses of Watergate.

Carter himself had not always been unambiguously frank or principled. Early on in his political career, he did a radical about-face. Elected governor in Georgia on a conservative platform, he surprised his hearers by announcing outspokenly his new liberal premise in his inaugural address: "the time of racial discrimination is over."[12] His presidential campaign vocabulary included words like *decent, honest,* and *filled with love,* as well as *compassionate* and *competent.*" It also reflected his personal temperament, his regional background, and his religious inheritance. He believed in doing what was *right.*" [13]

Carter's world view was Wilsonian, in that it placed high value on cooperation among nations. Both presidents defended human rights and worked to achieve lasting peace. Carter was disappointed in his hopes for cooperation between the USA and the USSR (even as Wilson was disappointed at the Versailles Peace Conference and with congressional rejection of the League of Nations). Dumbrell appraises Carter's position ethically as distinguished from Wilson's as a "kind of optimistic Niebuhrism." Carter frequently quoted Paul Tillich: "Religion is a search." It was foreign policy problems that showed Carter at his best as a problem-solver, determined personally to deal with longstanding unresolved situations such as the Panama Canal and the Middle East. His four major accomplishments—the Panama Canal treaties, the normalization of U.S. relations with China, the Camp David agreement between Egypt and Israel, and the negotiation of the SALT II treaty with the Soviet Union—took shape significantly on his initiative.[14]

Politically, Carter's elaboration of a human rights ethic in the 1976 presidential campaign did help to unify the fragmented Democratic Party coalition. Whatever else was the case, Carter was not as naive or without guile as his enemies or his friends charged. Hamilton Jordan, his campaign advisor, had mapped a strategy as early as 1972: "As Jordan saw it, 'a highly successful and concerned former Governor of

Georgia and peanut farmer' had more than a good chance of satisfying the nation's 'thirst for strong moral leadership'—a thirst which, Jordan predicted, 'will grow in four more years of the Nixon administration'"[15] Carter, in his inauguration address, promised an absolute commitment to human rights.

Jody Powell declared, *"If we can't be for that, what the hell can we be for?"*[16]

Elizabeth Drew commented on it: "The human rights issue helps him with the Jews if he has to bring pressure on Israel; it helps him with the right; it helps him in the South; it helps him with the Baptists, and he also happens to believe in it. And he won't be deterred."[17]

The Russian dissident, Andrei Sakharov, sent telegrams and letters to Carter both before and after his election. He was at least speaking out clearly for fundamental human and democratic values in "a world wrapped in lies" as a group of Russian dissidents pointed out. In 1979, a Moscow cab driver was reprimanded for displaying a portrait of the president.

Carter did better legislatively than he is often given credit for. The Panama Canal Treaty and reform of civil service were enacted on his watch. His policy advisers, Cyrus Vance and Zbigniew Brzezinski, both wished to modify what Brzezinski described as America's "hysterical preoccupations" with communism. Eventually, there were tensions between Vance and Brzezinski, and in the Iran crisis, the latter won out. Professionals in the foreign service from time to time questioned the absolutism of Carter's idealism. Increasingly, his strategy was not one of new legislation but enforcement through the provisions of the Helsinki Final Act which had been negotiated during Ford's administration.

GROWING PROBLEMS

The consensus of Carter's first two years began to unravel late in 1978, and then disintegrated during 1979. The crisis began in earnest when Carter allowed the Shah of Iran into the United States for medical treatment for cancer; in retaliation, a group of Americans were seized as hostages. The occupant of the White House was only trying to do what he considered to be right. Assistant Secretary of State for Near Eastern Affairs Harold Saunders observed that the president was "simply acting as Jimmy Carter—an outraged and concerned American who happened to be president."[18] Anything less than an all-out unrelenting public commitment to the hostages seemed to the country's leader to be morally unacceptable. With the failure of the helicopter rescue mission, his re-election effort was doomed.

At times, the Georgian seemed to share a "good-man-above-politics" stance with a president like Eisenhower. By comparison, however, he was much more specific, well-read, and articulate about his personal moral convictions. He used them as a basis to criticize domestic social injustice such as racial discrimination as well as abuse in foreign policy, in a way that Eisenhower did not. No doubt, Carter's twice-born pietistic language was an endless source of confusion. An orthodox Lutheran would speak more paradoxically of the Christian life as a state of being a thoroughgoing sinner and a forgiven saint. A traditional Roman Catholic thinks of Christian existence as a process of growth nurtured by the Church with its visible and tangible sacraments. In the Baptist view, ritual and holy office are not as central. The Church—the community of born-again Christians—is made up of the regenerate. Persons need to be converted "in the heart." The proof text is John 3:16. However, the further question of the voluntary responsibility of Christians for a sinful world—if not ignored intentionally—often remains secondary.

One difficulty Carter soon had after taking office was that he had campaigned as a moral person who would clean up things in Washington more than on the issue of leadership. He sought to demystify the "imperial presidency," carrying his own luggage and banning "Hail to the Chief." What seems to have happened is that he created a public persona of morality rather than of power. Carter's dogged tenacity also made him oblivious to the negative effect of one issue on another. To his credit, he did not hesitate to tackle hard problems by showing vision and tenacity. But his ambition and naiveté were two sides of one coin, critics argued.[19]

Religionists like Carter have been criticized, in his case unfairly, for lacking social concern and being interested in only personal religion. He was a Baptist who wished to carry conversion, second birth, into society. Of course, conversion is prepared for by a sense of moral failure and sin. In mid-summer of 1977, Carter had labeled energy problems as a crisis of confidence. It was part of his long lament which eventually would play into the hands of Reagan's ideological optimism. The president's rhetoric seemed to fall flat. The claim of a crisis, however true, detracted from Carter's charisma and positive image as a leader. Too often he had "cried wolf" about an emergency.

SUCCESSES

Carter believed that social transformation can be achieved, a position more radical than most of the Southern Baptists, many of whom traditionally have tended toward quietism. Although he probably attempted too much with a lack of clear priorities, he had an exceptionally able mind and was capable of factual analysis of specific problems, and he was ambitious. Hargrove charges, to the contrary, that as an engineer, Carter lacked a political philosophy. Assuredly, he was not a philosopher; his campaign biography, *Why Not the Best?* was in a number of respects naive—for example, in its "great man" theory of history. But Carter did have conversionist moral convictions that guided his actions as he sought to realize a number of specific goals.[20]

The high point of the Carter presidency came when his personal efforts brought about the Camp David agreements. Appearing with President Sadat of Egypt and Premier Begin of Israel, Carter commended them both before a joint session of Congress. Then, using the words of Jesus, he identified himself as a Christian and quoted the Sermon on the Mount: "Blessed are the peacemakers." His position was the antithesis of realpolitik or cynicism.

Speer evaluates Carter's Baptist background and its influence on his presidential morality sympathetically. "Baptists have traditionally emphasized voluntarism and consensus, a fact that has implications for their view of power and their understanding of the structure and process of government."[21] The Baptist commitment to the principle of consensus is basic in the voluntarism of local church life. Of course, it influenced Carter's paradigm consciously and unconsciously. E.Y. Mullins, a leading Southern Baptist theologian of the last century, explained Baptist polity as a "consensus of the competent."[22] Speer reflects that Carter's ideological problem was that voluntarism and the ideal of consensus remain in tension with the exercise of authority and power. "Baptist perceptions and sensitivities bring to special clarity the moral dimension of power," Speer writes. He identifies consensus as the ideal pattern of decision-making among Baptists; it requires action between parties on the basis of primary moral agreement. In fact, this explains the Baptist bias against power, as it directly conflicts with voluntarism. Each "power holder must judge that his or her perception of the rightness of an action is correct, regardless of the wishes of the power subject, thus contravening the latter's moral freedom."[23]

Low-church Protestant voluntarism claims a scriptural basis, as Mullins pointed out: "Because the individual deals directly with his Lord and is immediately responsible to him, the spiritual society needs to be a democracy."[24] Simply put, the local Baptist church is the town meeting of the Kingdom of God. Its premise is not representative government but direct government by the people, Speer concludes. He argues that this kind of social model played itself out in Carter's actions as president when, for example, Carter was asked about political bargaining early in his time in office, and replied: "I am not much of a trader. That is one of my political defects for which I have been criticized a great deal. We will be receiving the report on the analysis of water projects about April 15. I am not sure if that exact date will be met. And I'll assess each one of those projects on its own merits ... I am not inclined at all to trade a water project that's not needed or my approval of it in return for a vote on a tax refund."[25] Congressman Morris "Mo" Udall recalled: "Back in November [we Democrats] could hardly wait to cooperate ... You'd sit in a meeting with Carter, and he felt this compulsion to remind you that he also had your constituents as his constituents, and that he wouldn't hesitate to take Congress on."[26]

CRITICS

Barber comes to the point: "The modern skeptical story of conscience fumbles after character in the Campaign Street Test—the totally unrealistic assumption that he who is good at running for president will be good in running the presidency. At the center of a politics of conscience [Carter's outlook] is the priority of character. What is missing in this line of political philosophy," Barber judges, "is that political values are contingent."[27]

"Values are not irrelevant; a politics without values reduces the democratic adventure to a dismal pull and tug among interests. But politics is not theology. There is no salvation in it. At its best, it sets the conditions for a virtuous life. Its arena is a messy middle ground between the best and the probably."[28]

Initially, at the beginning of a president's term in office, he often is seen as one resolved to keep the enemy at bay. Eventually, however, there comes a cracking stage, followed by one of collapse of values that a leader seems helpless to prevent. A change in mood and appraisal is generally triggered by a particular series of events that is described as a crisis. In Carter's case, it had to do with the fall of the Shah of Iran and the taking of American hostages. This unexpected sequence of events—paradoxically with Reagan's capture of much of the conservative religious vote—insured Carter's defeat when he ran for a second term in office.

As Carter's power waned, at the beginning of 1980, Dom Banafede attempted to analyze for the *National Journal* why the earlier populism that had supported Carter had dissolved. "Carter's cardigan sweater has been stored in mothballs, and he stopped carrying his own luggage a long time ago."[29] Carter saw the United States as a society polarized by single-interest politics. Congress was ridden by reform and fragmented in leadership. An overzealous press was in pursuit of the sensational and the unsavory. Carter himself had become aware not only that the nation's resources are finite, but that government assistance by itself will not bring salvation.[30]

In the longer perspective, it needs to be pointed out that the Carter administration did not solve America's post-liberal debate. Pat Caldwell discerned in 1977 that Carter "understood and shared the frustrations of most Americans" with the liberal versus conservative debate inherited from the 1960s. The debate offered little guidance … toward fundamental solutions of problems like energy, the economy, cities, welfare reform, government efficiency."[31] Carter's answer lay in populism and transcendence of special interests, in fiscal conservatism, inexpensive domestic human rights policies, and competence and compassion. His populism was refreshing, but failed to establish a new consensus or build coalition. In fact, Carter's post-liberal foreign policy floundered amid the shocks of 1979. Still, it must be judged that his attempt to achieve a foreign policy of leadership without hegemony was a worthwhile effort; he wished to transcend anti-communist containment. The difficulty was that it did not bear fruit soon enough and he felt forced to jettison it in the face of Russian militancy by 1979.[32]

To his credit, historically, the "uncharismatic Jimmy Carter," the advocate of human rights, was responsible in a major way for a global wave of democratization, moving the United States away from the crippling hypocritical and counterproductive legacies of the cold war. He and his foreign policy advisors understood that they were working in a world in which ideological labels were declining in importance. Liberal democracy was moving ahead of both communism and rightist dictatorships.[33] As an evangelical Christian, Carter understood the religious dimensions of life better than most chief executives. In his realism, he identified long-term problems of justice and freedom that still haunt the country and the world.

RONALD REAGAN

Obama has a popular appeal of semi-mythical character; it is of much the same type that Ronald Reagan evinced in his campaign to reach the White House. The difference between the two presidents is that the first African-American leader in the White House is a lawyer rather than a movie actor. He is a "hands-on" administrator by contrast with the former free enterprise-oriented television spokesman for General Electric Corporation. It was Reagan who began the tradition of "hands-off" government that led to financial collapse at the end of the Bush era. In the economic crisis of 2009, Reganomics succumbed to its antithesis, "Obamanomics." Obama, the community organizer, has shown a richer sense of social solidarity. He has championed collective responsibility and government activism. Both presidents exhibited authentic religious motivation. The nationalistic culture Protestantism that Reagan championed has not belonged as much to the black church.

PATRIOTISM WITH RELIGIOUS CONVICTION

"We can work to reach our dreams and to make America a shining city on a hill." (Ronald Reagan to national religious broadcasters, January 31, 1983)

"My daily prayer is that God will help me to use this position so as to serve him." (Reagan's letter to Greg Brezina, October 25, 1982)

"Reagan does not argue for American values; he embodies them. To explain his appeal, one must explore the different Americas of which he is made up ... It is our movie. He is an icon, but not a frail one put away in the dark ... He is a durable daylight 'bundle of meanings' ... called myth."[1] The forty-first president had been a motion picture actor in the new world of mythmaking on the West Coast. Twice elected governor of California, he brought Hollywood to the Potomac. It was not a tired or cynical Hollywood, but a patriotic and even a religious one: "America is the 'A-Team' among the nations, bursting with energy, courage and determination."[2] Reagan spoke patriotically of loyalty, faithfulness, courage, and the ability to make the crucial moral distinctions between right and wrong in each new generation. They had a religious basis: "When I read the writings of our Founding Fathers, who designed our system, I always note how openly they gave praise to God and sought His guidance. And I just can't believe that it was ever their intention to expel Him from our schools."[3]

On his own terms as a right-wing conservative, the California governor made an "end run" around Carter's piety, affirming "I too am a twice-born Christian!" Not a critical, probing mind, but not a hypocrite, the anti-communist sincerely believed in God and country. Traveling the land as a spokesman for General Electric, the former Hollywood actor launched a crusade against big government and welfare, as well as against the communist evil empire. Opportunity was what mattered. Private initiative must succeed. The former New Dealer turned Republican practiced the power of positive thinking as he campaigned for moral renewal. Eulogizing the country's past history, he espoused Christian conservative causes such as the pro-life movement and advocacy of school prayers. Critics might call him "a con man," "a popular sleepyhead," and "an emperor with no clothes," but there was no second Reagan behind a façade—as in the case of Nixon. To his credit, the cold war came to an end on his watch.

Reagan's Roman Catholic White House communications director, Pat Buchanan, judged the president to be "a self-taught Christian ... a very simple Christian," one who focused on his personal relation with God. Later in life, he had "become more and more an outspoken believer in God. He talks about it often."[4] Baptized by immersion as a youth and not as an infant, he was brought up in the tradition of the twice born. Pat Robertson reflected, "He is probably the most evangelical president we have had since the founding fathers." D'Souza credits Reagan with having what Edmund Burke called moral imagination, the belief that there was right and wrong in the world. On this premise, Prime Minister Margaret Thatcher could say, "Ronald Reagan won the cold war without firing a shot."

Religious leaders' endorsements, not just politicians' responses, helped to bring the ex-movie star to the highest office in the nation; they enhanced his legitimacy. Late on the night of his first national election victory, Pat Boone called Reagan's home. Boone asked if the president-elect remembered the day, a decade earlier, when "we joined hands and prayed, and we had a sense of being called to something higher?"[5] Reagan did remember that Boone had brought a small party of religious leaders to Sacramento to visit Governor and Mrs. Reagan. Before leaving, they joined in a prayer circle with all seven people holding hands. "I was just sort of praying from the head," the Reverend George Otis said. "I was saying those things you'd expect—you know, thanking the Lord for the Reagans, their hospitality, and that sort of thing." So it went on for ten or fifteen seconds, and then it changed. Everything shifted from my head to the Spirit—the Spirit," Otis recalled. "The Holy Spirit came upon me and I knew it. In fact, I was embarrassed. There was this pulsing in my arm. And my hand—the one holding Governor Reagan's hand—was shaking … And I made a great effort to stop it—but I couldn't."

As this was going on, the content of Otis's prayer changed completely. His voice remained essentially the same, although the words came much more rapidly and intently. They spoke specifically to Ronald Reagan and referred to him as "my son." They recognized his role as leader of the state that was indeed the size of many nations. Otis described Regan's "labor" as "pleasing" to the Lord. "The foyer was absolutely still and silent. The only sound was George's voice. Everyone's eyes were closed. If you walk before me, you will reside at 1600 Pennsylvania Avenue."

Otis later learned from Herbert Ellington, who had been on the right side of Reagan, that the governor's other hand had been shaking similarly to Otis's. Ellington himself recalled years later that he somehow felt a "bolt of electricity" as he clasped Reagan's hand. It was a phenomenon in the tradition of ecstatic Pentecostal type piety, rather than ethical criticism or judgment. Garry Wills observes that if such a story had been told about Jimmy Carter, it might have prevented his election. "There was an initial suspicion of Carter's religion as 'kooky.'"[6] But with Reagan, matters seemed different. In fact, both men found personal piety to be to their own political advantage when they ran for the presidency. Reagan, in the end, was more successful in expressing it as he defeated Carter. The zeal of the new political right was joined with that of the New Religious Right.

We miss the point of what went on if we suppose that there was only manipulation on Reagan's part any more than on that of his predecessor. Reagan "brought passionate conviction to right behavior, without much awareness that rights can ever be in conflict or in doubt. He was trained to rectitude, not to questioning. He was what the period (of his youth) called a muscular Christian, an independent disciple, the Paul Revere of piety."[7]

An intriguing question must remain unanswered and hypothetical: Could Reagan have won his popular election victories if he had not run against Jimmy Carter (and Carter's former vice president, Walter Mondale) as he joined religion and morality? Carter had won earlier, defeating the incumbent president, Gerald Ford. But the peanut farmer from Georgia had really run against Nixon and his heritage— the distrust engendered by Watergate. Carter's Christian faith made him honest, he said; he would not lie. Reagan, practicing the power of positive thinking, developed a more powerful symbolism and overcame Watergate more buoyantly.

If the movie actor turned presidential candidate had offered only a secular approach, he might not have been able to win, in spite of all his charm. Instead, his piety eased any suspicion of his Hollywood background. Carter's argument was only that his religion made him personally trustworthy. It belonged primarily in private life, in his view. (Only as a private citizen and not as president had he invited his Sunday school class to the White House.) Reagan championed a more comprehensive myth, identifying with the nation's religion from the time of the Founding Fathers.[8] He would restore America's unique role of leadership as a city set on a hill.

The Yale political scientist Stephen Skowronek, writing in *The Politics Presidents Make,* observes: "Whatever the limits of the Reagan reconstruction, no president in recent times has so radically altered the terms in which prior governmental commitments are now dealt with or the conditions under which previously established interests are served."[9] Many past occupants of the White House have sought the highest office in the land primarily for the power that it brings. In the case of Nixon, for example, power was separated from ethics in his deepest motives. Not so with Reagan. He sought public office in order to lead in the fulfillment of America's destiny in the world. Historians have documented the collapse of political liberalism in the sixties. Religious liberalism had long since lost its appeal amid the crises of the Second World War. Against all cynics, Reagan caught the trend of the time—to the right.

WHAT REAGAN STOOD FOR

"He starts from where people actually are—slipping away from but still held by religious faith—and helps them move to where, roughly, they want to go: an enlightened community of vision justifying pride in the republic, a vision akin to, yet distinct from, religious faith. The remains of religious sentiment—ideality, yearning, spiritual earnestness—thereby become the grounding for a high public culture."[10] Irving Howe's description of the New England cultural leader in the nineteenth century, Ralph Waldo Emerson, could be applied as well to Reagan. The new Republican president's central conviction, as he came to office, was simple: individual freedom is the highest good and government is the enemy. For him, this was an unequivocal moral stance, devoid of cynicism.

It is the relativists and deconstructionists who are wrong—as they are against moral common sense. Reagan explained in his autobiography, *Where's the Rest of Me?:* "The original government of this country was set up by conservatives, as defined years later by Lincoln, who called himself a conservative with a 'preference for the old and tried over the new and untried.' Either we believe in our traditional system of individual liberty, or we abandon the American Revolution and confess that an intellectual elite in a far distant capital can plan our lives for us better than we can plan them ourselves."[11]

Earlier a Franklin Roosevelt admirer, in national politics, Reagan's goal was to reverse the New Deal. Committed to checking the power of the federal government at home by cutting taxes, he wanted to turn as many as possible of its responsibilities over to local governments. With respect to foreign affairs, Reagan was unequivocally committed to checking communist power. Intellectually, the president was never an abstract thinker but drew on his own intuition and common sense. Campaigning for office in 1980, the candidate's performance was the reverse of Carter's malaise, melancholy, and sense of limits. "Our optimism has again been turned loose. All of us recognize that these people who keep talking about the age of limits are really talking about their own limitations, not America's."

The Republican candidate's ideology was expressed in the story and symbol of folk piety. He eulogized the "everyday heroes of American life" in semi-religious, mythological terms: "parents who sacrifice long and hard so their children will know a better life than they've known; church and civic leaders who help to feed, clothe, nurse, and teach the needy; millions who've made our nation and our nation's destiny so very special—unsung heroes who may not have realized their own dreams themselves but then who reinvest those dreams in their children."[12]

Testifying openly as a Christian, Jimmy Carter had promised to renew the integrity of the highest office in the land, appealing to his own twice-born religious experience. Reagan would allow no less. He, too, claimed the experience of the new birth from his youth in the Disciples of Christ Church. His mother had been a devout woman of faith and good works, although his father was a drunkard. Reagan's ideology would renew the whole nation ethically—not just a sub-group of Baptist Christians—and Americans would again stand large and tall.

Running on such a vision, very few observers thought that it was possible for the ex-movie actor turned politician to win election. They were mistaken. At his first inaugural, Reagan added hard work to the divine mandate of the nation's exceptionalism: "It does require, however, our best effort and our willingness to believe that together with God's help we can and will resolve the problems which now confront us. And after all, why shouldn't we believe that? We are Americans."[13]

As a movie star, Reagan had depicted his own moral model in a number of films. One of them (which he liked most of all) told a story of the Notre Dame football team under Knute Rockne; the coach urged his squad on to victory by the words of a dying player. The account was largely apocryphal, a fabrication about the career of George Gipp.[14] From it, Reagan became known as "the Gipper." As an actor, he knew the dramatic persuasion of "border situations" of injury, life, and death. In another film, he depicted an accident victim who had lost both legs and woke up in the hospital, asking the question, "Where's the rest of me?" Reagan made the question the title of his autobiography.

Growing up in a Midwestern small-town religious setting, the president-to-be had attended the church-sponsored Eureka College, a Disciples of Christ (Christian Church) institution. Already, his dramatic talents were evident. After graduation, he had become a radio sports announcer, showing remarkable ability to depict games and bring them alive for listeners, even as they remained unseen in the pre-television era. Reagan's professional career in radio, motion pictures, and television gave him experience in using symbolic language and actions, including those of religion. In time, he had gone to Hollywood and married Jane Wyman, and they had been eulogized as Hollywood's ideal couple. But she later divorced him because she did not share his interest in politics. As a screen star, Reagan had won high-paying parts but was never really a great actor. When his motion picture career slowed down, he was employed by General Electric in public relations. Praising the efficiency and power of its corporate leadership—as against government bureaucracy—he espoused General Electric's free-enterprise philosophy on television and in speeches throughout the nation.

Reagan reported: "For eight years [1954-1963] I hopscotched around the country by train and automobile for GE and visited every one of its 139 plants, some of them several times. Along the way, I met more than 250,000 employees of GE. Looking back now, I realize that it wasn't a bad apprenticeship for someone who'd someday enter public life ... Those GE tours became almost a post-graduate course in political science for me ... by 1960, I had completed the process of self-conversion."[15] Reagan added, "I enjoyed every whizzing minute of it. It was one of the most rewarding experiences of my life."[16]

Nancy's response was positive. Reagan was sponsored by Lemuel Boulware, GE's vice president from 1944 to 1960, a spokesman for capitalism and free private enterprise, whose program was one of reduced taxes and getting government out of the business world. Boulware was a father figure for the future president.

Between marriages, Reagan had a reputation of being somewhat of a man about town. He was suspected of relations with a variety of women. The image faded after his second marriage to another actress, Nancy Davis. (Their first child was born only seven months after their marriage.) Nancy helped to solidify and channel Reagan's growing conservative political conviction. He shifted from Democrat to Republican, voting Democratic the last time for Truman. Reagan's fight against communism in Hollywood set the pattern for his later thought and ideology; communism embodied the antithesis of all that he stood for. He testified before the Congressional committee that investigated red influence in Hollywood without naming names. To the FBI, however, he did tell more privately. Its file about him included very negative reports about the organizations he joined in 1945 and 1946, but then noted with approval his subsequent anti- communist stance.[17] In the end, as head of the Screen Actors' Guild, he seems to have espoused the position taken by the leadership of the motion picture industry: the United States government should outlaw the Communist Party and then proceed to prosecute its adherents.

Martin Anderson, senior fellow at the Hoover Institution at Stanford University, helped organize Reagan's first campaign for the presidency, and remained with him for a period to help develop the new president's programs. Anderson asks about the Reagan phenomenon: "How did it happen? How did an aging, ex-actor from Hollywood rise to power in the United States and preside over the greatest economic expansion in history? How, by spending more on military weapons than anyone ever had, did that bring us closer to eliminating the scourge of nuclear-tipped intercontinental ballistic missiles? How did Ronald Reagan, with a reputation for being lazy and not too bright, manage to stay in political power so long—and to succeed as well as he did?"[18]

Anderson's answer in sum is the new capitalism that he describes as "a powerful intellectual movement that is still rising ..."[19] "The fundamental changes in national policy still occurring in the United States and in virtually every country of the world are the inevitable result of intellectual changes that have already occurred."[20] Anderson, of course, refers especially to the demise of communism, socialism, and "any other form of dictatorship statism (that has) ... proven to be intellectually bankrupt." His claim is that Reagan saw the tide of events much more clearly than his press and intellectual critics. Capitalism and democracy, morality and religion, were the cornerstones of Reagan's ideology.

Once elected president, Reagan's goal was to reverse the Great Society program announced by Lyndon Johnson—restoring private initiative. A capitalist ethic of reciprocity—but not dependence on the federal government for handouts—was to pervade every aspect of life. Reagan's ideology of freedom was clearly distinguished from a political philosophy of equality.[21] There were to be no more free and irresponsible handouts. American democracy was to be conceived in terms of free enterprise and as one of give-and-take, a voluntary and reciprocating association between parties. The goal was the return of the Republic to its initial moral starting point.[22] Clearly, one of Reagan's chief targets was the New Left, and its very rise helped to bring him to power. Facing off as governor against rioting students at the University of California in Berkeley, Reagan protested that freedom ought not to be equated with nihilism: "That educator is wrong who denies there are any absolutes—who sees no black and white or right and wrong, just shades of gray."[23]

The president had a specific strategy that was designed to bring about his goals, both morally and religiously. The movie actor turned politician would make all fifteen members of his Cabinet messengers to carry his ideals throughout the bureaucracy and the nation. He would enlist the help of two of its leading institutions, the courts, and the churches; the new leader in the White House saw both as crucial to the revival of the moral life of the nation. He sought to control the courts over a long period of time by appointing judges sympathetic to his right-wing outlook. This he significantly succeeded in doing with influence to the present. To carry his message through religious institutions was a more difficult challenge because of the separation of church and state. But religious television was controlled largely by evangelists whose support Reagan had sought on his own initiative as early as the 1980 campaign.

NATIONALIST AND RELIGIOUS RHETORIC

Addressing a prayer breakfast held in the Dallas Convention Center on August 23, 1984, the morning before his re-nomination, the president affirmed: "I believe that faith and religion play a critical role in the political life of our nation and always has."[24] Historically, candidate Reagan was correct. The question was "how?" Of course, his claim that the United States was founded on explicitly Christian principles (rather than Enlightenment rationalism) brought criticism from a number of sources. Still, his campaign utterance was put in non-sectarian language: "I believe that George Washington knew the city of man cannot survive without the city of God, that the visible city will perish without the invisible city. Religion played not only a strong role in our national life, it played a positive role."[25]

In campaigning, Reagan went beyond the generalities of civil religion to affirm an explicitly Christian loyalty.[26] Clearly, his allegiance was to the New Religious Right and not simply to Christianity, much less religion in general.[27] Jerry Falwell was his best ally among the clergy, and Reagan opposed abortion more than he had while he was governor of California. Pat Robertson attributed the Republican victory in the 1980 election to providence. Less than a decade after Reagan, Newt Gingrich—author of the "Republican Contract with America"—was explicit that the New Religious Right remains a major power in the Republican Party. He compared its role with that long held by organized labor in the Democratic Party.

Gary Smith evaluates Reagan's personal faith as genuine and very meaningful to him and judges that it was essential to his political philosophy.[28] As president, he presented his own Disciples of Christ tradition in a broad-minded way as having "little hard and fast dogma but based on a literal interpretation of the New Testament." He was a believer who at the same time suspected that "an all-wise and loving father" would not "condemn any of his children to eternal damnation." To be sure as an evangelical, he had twice invited Billy Graham to speak to the state assembly, but Graham was not his sole point of orientation; he might flirt with but he was not a legalistic or sectarian. After he was shot and wounded by John Hinckley Jr., nine weeks after entering the White House, with serious danger to his life, he wrote afterward: "Whatever happens now, I owe my life to God and will try to serve him in every way I can." His favorite scriptures were John 3:16 and II Chronicles 7:14: "If my people ... shall humble themselves and pray, and seek my face, and turn from their wicked ways, then will I hear from heaven ... and will heal their land." Reagan did seem to have had some mystical experiences, as we noted at the outset.

The Reagans' personal religious observance drew mixed reviews while they occupied the White House; they were not regular churchgoers like the Carters. Donald Regan, the second chief of staff who served at the outset of Reagan's second term, is emphatic that the White House schedule was dominated by the advice of Mrs. Reagan's astrologer.[29] Very soon, he learned that March 4 and March 5, the time of the Reagan's wedding anniversary, were very good days. But the president was not allowed to address the nation about the Tower Committee's Iran-Contra report on March 9, 1987, as March 7–14 was an especially bad period according to Nancy Reagan's astrologer. Other bad times included January 20: nothing outside WH-possible attempt. March 10–14: no outside activity, March 16: very bad, March 12–19: no trips or exposure, March 19–25: no public exposure, April 21–28: stay home.

Donald Regan was also bitter about his experience as Reagan's secretary of the treasury during the president's first term: "From first day to last at Treasury, I was flying by the seat of my pants. The president never told me what he believed or what he wanted to accomplish in the field of economics. I had to figure these things out like any other American, by studying his speeches and reading the newspapers ... I found this disembodied relationship bizarre."[30] Regan refused to speak to the president after resigning. Actually, the astrology that Regan found so annoying while chief of staff was only one side of Reagan's life after his marriage to Nancy Davis, who was a Presbyterian rather than a member of the Disciples of Christ Church. The president-to-be and Nancy attended Bel Air Presbyterian Church in Los Angeles. Its pastor, Donn D. Moomaw, offered the invocation at both inaugurals, and from the White House, Reagan referred to him as "my pastor."

Moomaw came immediately to Washington when he heard that the president had been shot. "I went to the White House ... Nancy asked Carolyn and me if we would accompany her that evening to the hospital ... I went in expecting to see a very ill man, and he was ... but he was like resilient steel. He wanted to talk about the Church. He was very open to talk about the faith. So open that I said to him, 'Ron ... are you ready to meet God?' He said, 'No. I have a lot more I want to accomplish before I meet God.' I said, 'Oh, no. That's not what I mean. If the bullet had taken your life, would you have been okay with God?' And after he thought, he said, 'Yes.' And I said to him—to the dismay of my wife that I was pushing so hard—I said, 'How do you know?' I expected that he would probably give me an answer on the basis of some works [that] the plus side of what he had done was winning. He didn't. He looked me in the eye and he said, 'I have a Savior.' You can say a lot of other things ... but if you don't say that you don't have the first clue. A profound understanding of salvation."[31]

THE END OF THE COLD WAR

Would what he designated as "the Evil Empire" have collapsed in Eastern Europe without Reagan's morally and religiously inspired anti-communism? At this point, he achieved his goal and left his name on the record for posterity. Having confronted the issue of communism head-on ever since he had encountered it as a labor union leader in Hollywood following the Second World War, Reagan would allow no compromise whatsoever with its evil. If the Russians would not bring the arms race to an end, he had said, he was prepared to develop a new massive defense with laser beams and weapons in space—fantastic as it all seemed. As president, he negotiated personally with Gorbachev in Iceland, and might have given up all United States ballistic missiles (his staff feared) were they not a part of his Star Wars strategy. But Star Wars weapons at the time existed only in the president's imagination as he fantasized them. As in so many of the moralistic stories he told, the facts were secondary to the lesson.

Eugene D. Genovese, distinguished scholar-in-residence at

the University Center in Georgia, observed: "The pros and cons of Reaganism and the depth of the changes it has introduced will take a long time to sort out ... What has been happening in Eastern Europe and the Soviet Union is, in actual fact, the most sweeping example of a counter revolution known to modern history."[32]

In good fortune, Reagan was blessed with halcyon weather in international politics. Carter's luck ran out in less than three years, whereas Reagan's lasted six years and then revived after Irangate. The most active conflicts in which he invoked force concerned small (in terms of population) countries: Libya, Nicaragua, Lebanon, and Grenada. Carter's belief that power relations could and should be downplayed as an element in international politics had been given up. Still, Reagan—like his predecessor—interpreted international politics largely in moral terms—but with his own judgments about good and evil. United States exceptionalism meant that America was to be a beacon for the world, a shining city on a hill. At the same time, he demonized the communist world.

The background of the Iceland meeting with Gorbachev (not scheduled as a full-scale summit) was crucial. Reagan was harassed by a problem that had brought down the Carter administration, international hostage-taking. "Reagan's hostages, fewer than Carter's, less visible, taken sporadically, killed selectively, had become permanent facts of life ... But this did not make them less an irritant or long-term danger."[33] In the fall of 1986, the FBI arrested Gennedi Zacharov for spying. In reprisal, the Soviets imprisoned a United States journalist, Nicholas Daniloff, on trumped-up charges. The American hope was that the situation could be clarified in conversations with Moscow. When the invitation came for the American president to meet the Russian leader on short notice, he was prepared to accept it.

At the same time, a new aggressiveness on the president's part had frightened the Russians. They saw him correctly as outspokenly and belligerently anti-communist (if not mad). Of course, there were multiple causes for the Soviet's desire for disarmament and peace. The Russians' unsuccessful war in Afghanistan (their Vietnam), the atomic catastrophe at Chernobyl, and a bankrupt economy checked earlier militancy. Reagan and Gorbachev, the personalities involved, were not incidental to what happened. Without the latter, the cold war might not have ended. Gorbachev later reflected on his own feelings in a long letter to Reagan, in which he wrote in part: "Our relationship is a dynamic stream and you and I are working together to widen it. A stream cannot be slowed down, it can only be blocked or diverted. But that would not be in our interests."[34] Reagan achieved more than he ever had expected—the end of the cold war.

When he gave his farewell address to the American people at the conclusion of his second term in office, the ex-movie actor reflected: "I was not a great communicator but I communicated great things. The Reagan Revolution," he said, "always seemed more like The Great Rediscovery, a rediscovery of our values and our common sense ... We meant to change a nation, and instead, we changed the world ... All in all, not bad, not bad at all."[35]

SUPPLY-SIDE ECONOMICS

Reagan was as confident of his approach in domestic affairs as he was in foreign affairs. After he was shot and nearly bled to death from a would-be assassin's bullet, the Democratic Congress enacted his program of supply-side economics. The elder statesman had showed courage, humor, bravery, and leadership, even in the face of possible death. Without the incident, legislative passage of Reaganomics would have been more difficult. The president also advocated his own economic program with moral enthusiasm and fervor. David Stockman, his budget director, wrote: "The tax cut was one of the few things Ronald Reagan really wanted ... The only thing behind which he threw the full weight of his broad political shoulders ... [O]ne of the few episodes in domestic policy and legislative bargaining in which he firmly called the shots."[36] Reagan had been interested when he heard about the Laffer Curve, as it showed how revenues would increase if taxes were reduced. The conclusion was as dubious as theory and did not work practically. The long-term result of Reagan's policies was that an enormous indebtedness was left for future presidencies, although he continued to advocate the reduction of deficits to the end of his time in office. In the short run, there was an economic boom; the economy recovered in spurts but remarkably much more quickly than it did under Roosevelt's New Deal. Still, it was the enormous budget deficits, initiated under Reagan, which led to the Perot phenomenon and George H.W. Bush's defeat when he ran for a second term.

IRANGATE

There were dangerous limitations in the fact that Reagan was not a hands-on activist president. Indeed, he was the reverse. He delegated responsibility and did not work long hours. Some of his aides, ideological like himself, thought in generalities; others working on details were more pragmatic. A number of the president's trusted advisors disappointed him during his second term in office. "There is bitter bile in my throat," Ronald Reagan told *Time* magazine. "I think we took the only action we could have in Iran. I do not think it was a mistake ... This whole thing boils down to a great irresponsibility on the part of the press."[37] Associates claimed that Reagan had been told about the arms for Contras project. Did he forget? He had a perennial tendency to remember things his own way.

Was the Irangate episode Reagan's Watergate? An expert on the Middle East estimated that as much as a billion dollars worth of arms may have been sold to Iran. The funds earned from the deal were to be used to supply the Nicaraguan Contras. Disclosure of the pattern of events brought an inevitable dramatic decline in the president's popularity ratings, and he seemed to lose much of his "Teflon character." There was a widespread impression that his policy had been a double one: he said one thing in public and did another secretly. The Iranian arms sale took place even while Reagan urged American allies to refuse to send weapons to the region.

Garry Wills concluded: "The Iranian episode radiates incompetence—in its substance, execution, and apologies. The aides in close contact with President Reagan today are the least distinguished such group to serve any president in the postwar period."[38] The Irangate scandal in a sense went beyond Watergate, as it reached over into foreign policy and was international. Of course, it was Nixon's attempted cover-up—so clearly revealed in the tapes—that drove him from office. By contrast, Reagan repeatedly attempted to go public, and his attorney general asked that a special prosecutor be appointed by the courts. Yet the uproar continued and cast a shadow over the conclusion of Reagan's presidency.

SYNTHESIS: A SUMMING UP

Wilbur Edel sums up his criticism of Reagan, citing in particular his intellectual shallowness and sophomoric interpretations of history. The president adopted a religious mantle, alleging that he would lead the country back to the precepts of the Puritans—exemplified by John Winthrop—and a "higher law." Instead, he encouraged a grasping, money-hungry trend in society "that put personal ambition above the general welfare and economic aggrandizement above all other human rights."[39] He made a blatant emotional appeal for support in the name of what he called the New Patriotism. There was a betrayal of his election promise of openness in office as well as lack of control over subordinates to whom he gave almost unlimited authority to carry out his politics.

In the climax of his March 8, 1983, Orlando, Florida, so-called "Evil Empire" speech attacking communism, Reagan had emphasized: "We must never forget that no government schemes are going to perfect man. We know that living in this world means dealing with what philosophers call the phenomenology of evil, or, as theologians would put it, the doctrine of sin. There is sin and evil in the world, and we're enjoined by Scripture and the Lord Jesus to oppose it with all our might."[40]

Historian Michael Beschloss argues that Reagan was in fact a determined Christian, due largely to his mother, who instilled in him the belief that "everything was part of God's 'Divine Plan." The president's Los Angeles pastor, Don Moomaw, recounts how he and the chief executive "spent many hours together on our knees," with Reagan part of "the total experience—the sadness, the rejoicing, the singing." Apart from belief in God, he would have been scared to death, he said. The former movie actor Reagan accepted the pre-millennialist premise that Jesus's second coming would be preceded by Armageddon, bringing the end of the world. The Apocalypse is near. "In private, Reagan insisted that recent 'signs and events' showed the immanence of Armageddon, such as 'wars fought to no conclusion' and earthquakes, storms, volcanic eruptions. When the Apocalypse came, there would be 'armies invading the Holy Land' and a plague in which 'the eyes are burned from the head.'"[41]

Garry Wills, in criticism, is not prepared to take all of Reagan's oratory at face value. He argues that the leader missed decisively what the Christian tradition affirms about good and evil in the myth of the fall. "In Reagan's campaign and presidency, the principal accusations against Democratic predecessors and rivals has been that they were guilty of pessimism ... 'little men with loud voices cry doom.'" When Reagan was asked to discuss his own religious experience, every instance he could think of was a matter of seeing the bright side to death or disaster. Unfortunately, modern society lives from the symbol of the market, Wills reflects: "The market thus produces a happy outcome from the endless miseries, a sinless product of countless sins and inadvertencies. Eden ... rises again, unbidden, by the automatic engineerings of the market."[42]

Wills does allow that Reagan at times acknowledged that the biblical tradition makes clear that there is no "clean slate" of nature unscribbled on by all one's forebears. This may be Christian realism. Human beings are entangled in each other's errors. Wills finds, however, that Reagan actually believed energetically in the counter myth to the Fall, one of the perfectability of human nature. Instead of respecting the longer tradition, he made his own happy world of pleasant stories. Wills describes it as "a fragile construct that had to be protected from the challenge of complex or contradictory evidence, from any test of evidence at all." In short, the movie actor was guilelessly guiltless. A possible answer to this charge would be that Reagan was many-sided and not always consistent. Many of his evangelical friends characteristically mixed the myth of the fall with cultural optimism.

The legacy remains: Reagan embodied a particular type of approach to morality and religion—evangelical, patriotic, and pietistic, and at the same time, inclusive. Its roots are deep enough in the American tradition to enhance a candidate's stature very powerfully with the electorate. Details could be left to others in religion as well as in politics. The fact is, however, that on Reagan's watch, the cold war came to an end. Without his decision not to compromise with communism, this might not have come to pass.

GEORGE H. W. BUSH

Bush I took office in the shadow of his predecessor, Ronald Reagan. Obama won with a different campaign, a forthright attack against Bush II and the war "W" initiated from the White House. The Bush presidents, like Reagan, enlisted the support of politically conservative evangelicals. Obama by contrast has found a major electoral base in the black church. To his disappointment, Bush I lost when he stood for re-election because of intervention in the presidential race by another Texan, Ross Perot. The forty-first president's major achievements were in the foreign policy area. Much to his credit, he was wise enough not to go on to Baghdad after liberating Kuwait. Less successful in controlling economic policy at home, he broke his "read my lips" campaign promise not to raise taxes. Obama will have to get more done domestically than did Bush I if he is to win re-election to a second term. If he can handle foreign wars in Iraq and Afghanistan with his predecessor's adeptness, he will have had good fortune.

THE BUSH LEGACY

George Herbert Walker Bush came to office at a time of unique opportunity: The cold war had come to an end. The threat of an atomic holocaust seemed in his time to have largely dissolved. Where would the new president take the nation after Reagan's crusade? "America is never wholly herself unless she is engaged in high moral principle. We as a people have such a purpose today. It is to make kinder the face of the nation and gentler the face of the world."[1] So Bush I reflected in his inaugural address. The new leader asked for help and support from the Democrat-controlled Congress. For its part, it carried on largely in a pattern of politics as usual.

Accepting his party's nomination for the presidency, candidate Bush had reflected on his own propensity to take risks: "To achieve something in this world, you've got to be willing to take risks ... I should have gone to college at eighteen, but I joined the navy; I should have stayed back East and worked in my father's prosperous business, but I went West and started out on my own ... President Ford offered me an ambassadorship to England or France—pretty glamorous duty. I opted for China. Advisors warned me against going to the CIA; it was supposed to be a political dead end ..."[2] As a young naval aviator, even before he entered college, he had a distinguished military record, taking life-threatening risks as he flew in the Pacific during World War II.

When he ran for the presidency with Reagan's endorsement, Bush proclaimed: "We don't need radical new directions, we need strong and steady leadership. We don't need to remake society, we just need to remember who we are." In January 1989, as he took office, Bush announced, "We're coming in to build on a proud record that has already been established." A Bush staff member explained: "It was awkward to follow Reagan and claim success. We couldn't say we'd be cleaning up the Reagan mess. We would just have to do it without talking about it." Bush himself said, "We are the change."[3]

Of course, journalists did not leave matters there. The editors of *Time,* not sparing in their criticism of Reagan's successor, did their own media-style take on his qualifications: "More than most other politicians, he was a paradox. A brave war hero, he was mocked as a wimp. Modest and ingratiating, he was at times downright nasty. A Phi Beta Kappa student at Yale, he could sound incoherent and sometimes even goofy."[4]

But it was important that Bush was not to be classified with fixated types such as Lyndon Johnson or Richard Nixon. Still, he was not even faintly comparable with Reagan in dramatic power and charisma. Nor did he have Reagan's knack for turning a catchy political phrase, although like his conservative mentor, he spoke out against the "L-word"—liberalism. Rhetorically, Bush was not remembered except for two phrases: "voodoo economics," that he applied to Reaganomics before becoming a candidate for vice president in 1980; and "read my lips" in his own 1988 campaign for office. Nonetheless, he came to power in the White House in happy circumstances. The contrast between the very tension-ridden phase of international politics in 1981 (at the beginning of the Reagan era) and the prospective world of 1989 (when Bush took office) was candidate Bush's best selling point when he ran as the Gipper's successor. Of course, he had to deal with the remains of the Irangate scandal. A special prosecutor was at work deciphering a train of events that might have toppled a less-popular president than Reagan. How much Bush was "in the loop" of information about it is still disputed.

The earlier moment in Bush's political career of which he said he was most proud occurred while he was still a congressman from Texas. As a member of the House of Representatives, he had voted for the Civil Rights Act. Returning home to Texas, he attended a meeting in which it was denounced because it "will lead to government control of private property, the Communists' number one goal." Following this denunciation, it was Bush's turn to speak, and he gave his argument: "I did what I thought was right. We agree on most issues. This one we don't agree on. I hope I still have your support. But if I don't have your support, I hope I still have your friendship. If I don't have your friendship, I'm sorry, but I have to vote with my conscience."[5] The congressman received a standing ovation. In his autobiography, he remembered: "More than twenty years later, I can truthfully say that nothing I've experienced in public life, before or since, has measured up to the feeling I had when I went home that night." Characteristically, Bush observed later: "You can make decisions that people don't like without incurring their wrath. Often how you do something is more meaningful than what you do."[6]

Bush did bring an outstanding major asset to the office of the presidency from his earlier career. He was singularly well experienced and knew personally most of the decision-makers of the leading nations of the entire world. For Europeans, he was the kind of American with whom established foreign-policy makers liked to deal, a knowledgeable insider in diplomacy with experience in intelligence work; he was an East Coast establishment person, upper class, and Ivy League. Internationally, he was mildly "hawkish." Bush appeared as a career politician of a high quality and not an ideologist. As vice president, he had kept a low profile in exercising his office amid Reagan revivalism.

Bush first came to Washington to serve two terms in the House of Representatives. Then Nixon asked him to run for the Senate from Texas, and he was defeated. Bush was regarded as fanatically loyal to the president. Charles Coulson once remarked in characteristic Nixonesque: "He takes our line beautifully."[7] Nixon had promised Bush an ambassadorial appointment if he lost. Bush was ambassador both to the UN and to China in a period that required tact in diplomacy. He did his brief period as CIA director under Ford, working to re-establish good relations between the agency and Congress. Bush served as Republican Party chairman in the difficult years of the 1970s; loyalty to Nixon and to his party had been his defining characteristic. Kenneth Duberstein, Reagan's last chief of staff, put the change of command in the White House in the best possible light: "If Reagan's was a 'defining' presidency that in bold strokes and grand ideas set the tone of the present political order, Bush's promises to be a 'refining' administration that in pastel colors and day-to-day steps will consolidate the gains of the Reagan years."[8]

More than in the case of Carter, Bush was disciplined and selective about what he believed the country should undertake. His nationalism was clear from his statements: "I will never apologize for the United States of America. I don't care what the facts are. I am a practical man. I like what works. I want to offer the hope of freedom to countries around the world because that's the basis of our very being in this country, our own freedom. As president, I mean to work toward a new harmony, a greater tolerance, an understanding that this country is a partnership."

It was Bush's good fortune that he came to office at a time when the prestige of the presidency had been greatly improved. Positively, he did take risks with his popularity, for example, in dealing with the budget deficit and most of all, he stood firm against Saddam Hussein. He believed that the Gulf War was necessary and right, and acted accordingly. Bush's national security advisor, Brent Scowcroft, defined the crucial question in the Gulf War: "Can the U.S. use force—even go to war—for carefully defined national interests, or do we have to have a moral crusade or a galvanizing event like Pearl Harbor?"[9] Bush retrieved Kuwait from Hussein's army but did not go on to topple the Iraqi president.

WAS BUSH'S A GUARDIANSHIP PRESIDENCY?

David Mervin, senior lecturer in politics at the University of Warwick in England, has written a research study of George Bush Sr.'s time in the White House entitled *George Bush and the Guardianship Presidency*.[10] He did so after interviewing some two dozen members of Bush's high-level staff while he was president—including Andrew H. Card, Jr., Bush's former deputy chief of staff, C. Boyden Gray, his legal counsel, and General Brent Scowcroft, his assistant for national security affairs. Mervin's primary thesis is that Bush did not share the activist presumption of presidents such as FDR, Wilson, Truman, Kennedy, Lyndon Johnson, and Reagan. On the contrary, like Eisenhower earlier, he was a conservative rather than an advocate of change; in short, a guardian president who did not seek to extend the outreach of government. Bush Senior refused the model of an expansive, omniscient leader who has a solution at hand for a wide range of problems. It was out of conviction that he poured scorn on the social engineering of liberal activist presidents.

Vice President Bush told the Ripon Society: "I am a conservative. I voted along conservative lines when I was in Congress. I took conservative positions before assuming this job. I take conservative positions now."[11] In his autobiography, Bush writes: "I supported much of Harry Truman's foreign policy in the late 1940s. But I didn't like what he and the Democratic Party stood for in the way of big, centralized government—the attitude that 'Washington knows best' and the policies and programs it produced. I considered myself a conservative Republican."[12] The stance, of course, has roots in the president's early experience as the second son of an investment banker, born in Massachusetts and spending his childhood at Greenwich, Connecticut—the son of a senator. Like his father, Bush was born to wealth and privilege; he saw the world through this lens: "Dad taught us about duty and service."[13] Prescott Bush was fifty-five when he first ran for the Senate. The family pattern of conservativism was moderate, non-confrontational, and relatively non-ideological; it included civility, compassion, and a sense of community.

Mervin emphasizes that Texas conservativism, in the region where Bush went after finishing at Yale, was characteristically different than New England. Rough-and-tumble, untrammeled capitalism was king in the Southwest's individualistic political culture. The dominant role model was not that of well-born and well-connected citizens (as it was in Prescott Bush's Connecticut) but of lucky individuals coming from inauspicious beginnings, who had made vast fortunes suddenly. When George H.W. Bush ran for the Senate in 1964, he unsurprisingly endorsed Goldwater's agenda, denouncing the pending Civil Rights Act and opposing Medicare as well as foreign aid. America ought to withdraw from the United Nations if the People's Republic of China was given membership in the international agency.[14]

For the Yale Skull and Bones fraternity member, leadership required honor, integrity, and a sense of public service and experience—the right training and intuitive sense to make correct decisions as problems come up. As compared with his predecessor and successor, these had a higher priority than overarching vision. His ambassadorship to the United Nations and then to China, and directorship of the Central Intelligence Agency were presidential appointments.

Even while he worked loyally for Nixon, Kissinger kept him ignorant of the forthcoming changes coming in United States policy toward China. As Reagan's vice president, Bush was loyal, deferent, self-effacing, and self-abasing—but not really overly well prepared for his jobs. Mervin judges that it fair to say that when he became president, unlike Reagan, he had no overall program or goal, no dominant ideology. "We don't need to remake society. We don't need radical new directions."[15] The premise was that the less the government does, the more the people will prosper and progress. Bush remained skeptical of what could be accomplished by passing laws. Mervin's point is that a guardian president finds little opportunity to be an innovator. "I believe that the solution to this grave problem lies in the hearts and goodwill of all people and that sweeping federal legislation can never fully succeed."[16] Johnson's Great Society Crusade was a crusade that failed, he suspected, and for his part, he would not make the situation worse.

Reagan had an ideological edge to his conserativism, and like his predecessor, Jimmy Carter, came as an outsider to Washington. Bush was an insider. At the beginning of his 1988 campaign, he reflected, "I do not hate government."[17] When he became president, he made longstanding personal loyalty to the president the reason for appointment to office. The *New York Times* observed, "Loyalty is his ideological vision."[18]

Although at first, he appointed almost exclusively old friends, in time, persons more oriented on policy were needed. More often than not unsuccessfully, he sought to cultivate Congress. "To my friends— and yes,—I do mean *friends*—in the loyal opposition—and yes, I mean *loyal*—I put out my hand. I'm putting out my hand to you, Mr. Speaker. I am putting out my hand to you, Mr. Majority Leader ... The American people want action. They didn't send us here to bicker. They asked us to rise above the merely partisan."[19] It was a kindler, gentler style of leadership not based on power alone.[20]

When he was not effective at home as he had hoped, Bush Senior turned to the larger world abroad. He was attacked by critics who argued that his foreign policy strategy was one of not having a strategy. Lawrence Eagelburger, secretary of state after Baker, defended administration policy: "There was a strategy behind the president's conduct of foreign policy ... [it] was characterized by pragmatism and flexibility ... [Admittedly] our approach was often ad hoc [but] a certain ad hockery is a virtue, not a vice, when you are dealing with a world in crisis, and in chaos, one in which it is impossible to be certain of anything six months ahead."[21] In the Gulf War, Bush personalized policy making, managing but not charting a new course, Mervin believes. Of course, the president was concerned about public opinion and won it overwhelmingly to his side. For his part, Bush did not run a constant presidential election campaign in the style of Reagan and Clinton.[22] One aide commented: "What he was saying to the American public was 'I have just done a heck of a good job as president of this country; I deserve a second term and I shouldn't have to go through all this hassle to get there. The American public ought to be able to perceive that I have done a fine job ...' He just didn't feel that he should be compelled to go and present his case before the American public in a campaign setting."[23]

RELIGION

Chase Untermeyer noted: "The irony is that in looking at the 1992 voting results, the Christian Right was the most loyal element to George Bush ... For three years, Bush had failed to recognize the signs of evangelical disillusionment, nearly losing that constituency by the time he got into a campaign mood. Had Bush maintained better liaison with the Religious Right and been more attentive to its concerns during his first three years in office, the overcorrection at the last hour would not have been necessary, and more time could have been spent reaching out to Republican moderates, who ultimately deserted George Bush in favor of Bill Clinton or Ross Perot."[24]

Pat Robertson ran against Bush, making a strong showing in some of the primaries. Falwell, not a Pentecostalist like Robertson, stayed with Bush from the beginning of the primaries. Bush explained:

> *I guess some people think that Jerry and I are sort of an odd couple. He has had friends criticize him for his strong support of me and I've had people telling me, 'Don't you know that Jerry Falwell hurts you politically?'... Jerry Falwell has been an absolute gentleman to me. He's never asked for a thing, and he has only given encouragement and friendship.[25] When we went to Sudan, we visited Jerry Falwell's hospital. Here was the private sector, individual Christians, reaching out to deprived Muslims. I took Pat Robertson along on that trip, and it was very instructive, since his organization was also involved ... They are religious leaders who represent thousands of constituents. They have every right to offer input from their particular vantage point, though we don't agree on every issue ... But certainly, I want to be sensitive to their concerns.[26]*

Bush's growing appreciation of the Religious Right is an interesting story. It was in February of 1985 that he first met the thirty-eight-year-old author of religious and inspirational books, Doug Wead. Bush was

278

en route to speak at the National Religious Broadcasters' convention. When Wead saw a copy of the speech he was planning to give, the new friend recognized at once that Bush did not know the language of the "born-again" evangelical experience. The vice president notoriously was wise enough to engage Wead as his own religious liaison. Wead—who already had authored a book about Reagan's religion with sales of half a million copies—had blundered when he addressed a group of pastors convened by Dr. James Kennedy at the Chicago Airport Hilton Hotel. "What did it mean to be born again?"; "How can one know that he is really saved?"; "Can a person be born again without knowing it?" he had been asked. Queried about his personal religion, he had denied that he was "twice born." Instead, he only reported that had done his best to follow God's teaching. There was no answer for the questions about personal salvation.[27]

Largely for Bush's benefit, Wead composed a more-than-fifty-page primer, offering a step-by-step plan for winning the confidence of the Christian conservative voting bloc. It was a kind of manual detailing the size and numbers of its adherents, where they lived, and what they believed, dividing and subdividing them by denominations. "Over the next three years, Wead helped Bush meet or speak to more than a thousand evangelical leaders, put the vice president's name before millions of churchgoers, and set the standard for evangelical politicking by Republican presidential candidates for the next two decades."[28] Wead's analysis distinguished fundamentalists from charismatics, Pentecostals from Southern Baptists. There were thumbnail sketches of leaders, along with advice to Bush that he stay in communication with evangelical leaders by phone or card. Most of all, Wead advised Bush to send "an early signal" about the depth of his Christian faith. Eventually, the vice president was featured on tape at *Robert Schuller's Hour of Power,* giving his testimony. Wead also suggested that Vice President Bush read C.S. Lewis's *Mere Christianity* and quote passages from it in his speeches, as Reagan had done.[29]

Things progressed more positively when Billy Graham took on the role of family pastor. As friendships grew, Graham would become more ensconced with the Bush family than with any other presidential clan. Actually, Graham had known Bush I's mother, Dorothy Walker Bush, since the mid 1950s, played golf with his father, and become a frequent summer vacationer at the family compound in Kennebunkport. She loved to read scripture and pray with the evangelist. A believing Christian, she had told her children to wear bright colors to their father's funeral to celebrate his arrival in heaven. Craig Fuller judged that "the only person he [Bush I] really trusted was Billy Graham. He would tell people that he knew Graham and that he had discussed a lot of these things with Graham. And when he talked to us, everyone he met in this area he compared to Graham. It made me think that Billy Graham was the one person he was communicating with, and talking to, about his faith. My own guess—and it's only a guess—is that Graham was one of the few people who could get George Bush to confront his spiritual feelings or beliefs." What Bush prized most about Graham was that he had no agenda: "He came to us as a pastor and friend. He gave us comfort."

WILLIAM JEFFERSON CLINTON

Obama is personally much better organized than Bill Clinton as well as more morally disciplined. There is no Monicagate on the horizon for the forty-fourth president! Clinton's critics have charged that he carried on in the White House from the outset on the pattern of a college bull session. Both Clinton and Obama come from low-church Protestant backgrounds. Both of them entered the White House with high ambition—Obama in a more urgent time of crisis and with greater realism. What the leader from the Land of Lincoln could accomplish, of course, still remained to be seen. He probably had the most comprehensive plan for reform and change, probably faced more difficulties from the legacy of his immediate predecessor than did the former Arkansas governor. It was no mean achievement that with great skill, Obama enlisted Hillary Clinton as his secretary of state.

PRO AND CON

Robert E. Reich, secretary of labor in Clinton's first cabinet, subsequently a professor at Brandeis University, offered his evaluation of the administration of which he was a part: "Bill Clinton will be known as the president who presided over the best American economy of the century, who beat back a right-wing Republican tidal wave, and who disgraced his office by reckless personal behavior—probably in that order."[1]

Reich summed up his judgments about the president: "It depends on what day you ask me [about Clinton's service to the nation]. On Monday, Wednesday, and Friday I say, 'Thank God Clinton was there.' He was a bulwark against the right-wing Republican charge that began early on. He ended, for all intents and purposes, Newt Gingrich's career; he stuck it out in the showdown over the government shut down and weathered the storm. And he repositioned the Democrats for a much more successful future and presided over a much more successful economy. So my overall sense is buoyant."

Reich added that on Tuesdays, Thursdays, and Saturdays, he was often more wistful. Had Bill Clinton been more disciplined, not attempting to do so many things all at once—had he handled health care more carefully and avoided the Lewinsky affair, much more could have been accomplished under his leadership.

The forty-second president himself asserted to the end of his time in office that his policy of centrism was principled, not just one of expediency or only a quest for power: "A lot of people criticized me at the time. They said, 'Well he doesn't have a foot in either camp. Therefore, he must not have any convictions.' But that's not how I saw it at all. For example, I didn't think we could have an economic policy that would work unless we both got rid of the deficit and invested more in education and science and technology. I didn't think we could have a welfare reform policy that worked unless we both required people to work, and then rewarded work."[2]

It has been widely argued that Clinton scuttled party loyalties after the 1994 congressional election, but all Democrats did not see it that way. The Democratic Congressional leader in the House, Richard A. Gerhardt, commented: "Just winning two times in a row for the first time in a long time was a huge achievement. We hadn't had a president since Roosevelt who had done it, and a lot of us had begun to wonder whether it would ever happen."[3] Gerhardt urged: "Don't forget where we were. Measure the distance traveled."[4]

Of course, everyone did not agree and Clinton was attacked from both left and right all through his time in office. There was a perennial question: Where did Clinton really stand, personally and on principle?

As early as the end of his first year as president, reporters from *Rolling Stone* asked him, "Are you having fun?" "You bet," he responded, "I like it very much. Not every hour of the day is fun. The country is going through an hour of change." In many respects, he was much more of a hedonist than most other occupants of the White House. "But are you having fun in this job?" the reporter continued. "I genuinely enjoy it," the new president replied. Then the reporter cited the question asked by a young man who requested that his query be passed on to the new chief executive: "What was Clinton willing to stand up for and die for?" The president's face turned red and his voice rose as he responded: "But that's the press's fault too, damn it. I have fought more damn battles here for more things than any president in the last twenty years." Clinton protested vehemently that he had not gotten "one damn bit of credit for it from the knee-jerk liberal press, and I am sick and tired of it and you can put that in the damn article." The leader avowed that he got up every day and "I work till late at night on everything from national service to the budget to the crime bill and all this stuff, and you guys take it and you say, 'Fine, go on to something else, what else I can hit him about.' So if you convince them I don't have any convictions, that's fine, but it's a damn lie. It's a lie."[5] What were Clinton's basic beliefs and how were they reflected in his ethics?

James MacGregor Burns and Georgia J. Sorenson, in their book, *Dead Center: Clinton-Gore Leadership and the Perils of Moderation*, conclude further that the perverse doctrine responsible for many of Clinton's problems was pragmatism.[6] Pragmatism, they judged, lay behind FDR's dealings with the city bosses as well as George Bush Senior's with the new Religious Right.[7] Not abstract, this philosophy lacks both idealism and vision. Although today's pragmatism is anti-ideology, its "true believers" have actually made an ideology of this stance. Its view of the world encourages compartmentalization; that is, the separation of self-serving acts from their ethical implications. How this worked out specifically in the case of Clinton was that the president dealt with different issues by separating them into separate boxes—a personal relations box, a budget box, an election box, a Southern Baptist box, a civil rights box.

The authors attempt a political-science evaluation of Clinton, not primarily a moral much less a religious one. He raised the art of a deal to world-class levels. His legacy is not one of principle but only of only transactional leadership, they conclude. Their thesis is simple: If Bill Clinton aspired to presidential greatness, his strategy of centrism by its very nature assured that he would never achieve it. In fact, he was as committed to it as other politicians earlier had been to liberalism and progressivism. This became clear when Clinton chose as his Rasputin, Dick Morris, an amoral spin doctor who began advising him in 1995 after having worked earlier for Jesse Helms. David Gergen, who served briefly in the Clinton White House, expressed his own set of objections when he suggested that Morris had a relation with the president similar to that of Colonel House with Wilson, Lewis Howe with FDR, or Sherman Adams with Ike. William Safire had his set of objections: "Centrism is fine when it is the result of competing interests. Thesis; antithesis; synthesis. But centrism is vapid when it is the suffocator of interests, seeking to please rather than trying to move. Clinton's approach more often than not was to follow the primrose path of polling down the middle: his motto has become a firm—there must be no compromise without compromise."[8]

Burns and Sorenson report of their first early meeting with the new president: "What struck us most about Bill Clinton was his calm, almost blasé confidence that he could take leadership among the continuing disasters and turmoils of the twentieth century to bring about transforming change."[9] He seemed to have no cynicism, instead, self-confidence and even cockiness. The historical presidential scholars, for their part, are convinced that conviction and strong beliefs, anchored in a set of explicit values and held over time, have been the supreme test of great presidential leadership. They point out that the White House itself does not provide the foundation for leadership; a ruling politician needs an ideology rooted in a set of values that are really his own. It was change not constancy that Clinton championed in his first inaugural address, referencing the third president: "Thomas Jefferson believed that to preserve the very foundations of our nation, we would need dramatic change from time to time. Well, my fellow citizens, this is our time. Let us embrace it."[9] What happened in the end was that, following Morris's advice, Clinton remained in office—by being pragmatic. But he was an extraordinary pragmatist—apparently even a post-modern one. Of course, he recognized the revolutionary change in cultural and moral narratives and models that was taking place in his lifetime and shared in it.

BILL AND HILLARY

The following is a biographer's recent description of "goings on" in the White House: "(His) adultery also demeaned the presidency. Many people in Washington, Hollywood, and elsewhere made the man the butt of jokes and gossip that surely lowered their, and other's respect for the nation's highest office ... Any number of women ... intelligence agents, and journalists might have used their knowledge ... to force concessions ... damaging the presidency, debilitating his administration, and severely disillusioning a populace that, no matter how jaded it seems, looks to a president with hope for reassurance and leadership."[10]

These words were not written in description of Bill Clinton, but of John F. Kennedy—whom Clinton, while a youth, felt honored to meet and shake hands with personally on a trip to Washington, D.C. For a considerable part of the public, they continued to suggest what was going on in the Clinton era as well. Of course, presidential morality is much wider in scope than family ethics. Kennedy in his lifetime had achieved an image of Camelot, one that is now scarred. Clinton never began to reach this level. "Bill Clinton [was] the greatest seducer who ever lived—extremely talented, intellectually facile, an unparalleled campaigner, organizer, and silver-tongued orator, but also a wayward child, requiring continual emotional support and moral supervision." Such was the allegation of the right-wing journalist, David Brock.[11]

Clinton, in fact, managed a unique accomplishment. No other president from George Washington to George Bush has so stimulated the sexual-erotic imagination of the American people. The number of vivid, licentious stories told about him everywhere from bars to homes and civic meetings is probably not exceeded by any of his predecessors. No doubt, part of the phenomenon is due to modern worldwide communications, press, radio, and television. Earlier presidents had been protected by the media (as well as by common decency). Clinton was not—nor was his audience. Even children watching television were exposed to descriptions of sexual practices not always known in detail to their parents.

As a boy, young Bill Clinton had grown up in the gambling and prostitution center of Hot Springs; actually, he has claimed that he comes from Hope, Arkansas. An instantly recognizable student leader type, he was elected president of his junior class in high school. It was while he was also a senator in Boy's Nation that he went to Washington, D.C. and saw Kennedy. Entering Georgetown University, he was chosen as president of the freshman class. After an internship in the Washington office of the Arkansas senator and chairman of the Senate Foreign Relations Committee, J. William Fulbright, he applied for a Rhodes Scholarship with the senator's recommendation. With this sponsorship, he spent two years at Oxford University in England. Returning to the United States in a time of unrest and crisis, Clinton enrolled at Yale Law School. It is reported that he was appraised by his fellow classmates not as a future president, but as a glad-handing hillbilly in floodwater pants.

At Yale, he met Hillary, his future wife. Clinton's relations with a variety of women has brought him notoriety, which perhaps—in an ironical way—even advanced his career. The gossip was that the couple eyed one another for several awkward minutes in the law school library before she came over, introduced herself, and asked his name. Then there was love and romance.[12]

Michael Medved reports: "It struck me that these two had real physical chemistry. These two people unequivocally had the hots for each other. She was so in love. It was so painfully obvious and he looked like he had just swallowed the canary. He was so pleased with himself. And I remember him leaning back and Hillary taking me aside and talking to me and the whole point of the conversation was, 'Look at this. I'm in love. I am happy and I have got this great guy who is going to change the whole world.'"[13]

There was also an implicit foretaste of the future: Guido Calabresi, then a professor at the law school, reflects: "One can describe it [the difference between them] a little bit like taking a cold shower and a hot bath. Bill is much more a kind of all-encompassing intelligence, with a great deal of originality, and I associate it with a hot bath. And Hillary is more of a cold shower, just directly to the point, stimulating, and so on. So that in a way, while he is very smart, hers is the kind of intelligence that one sees more in a law school."[14]

Eventually, Bill brought Hillary to meet his mother in Hot Springs, Arkansas, and the two women in his life were clearly antithetical; it all showed how much Clinton had advanced already. "By most measures, Virginia Kelley and Hillary Rodham were opposites. Virginia spent hours every morning plying her face with heavy makeup; Hillary wore none. Virginia smoked, drank, gambled, and slept around; Hillary didn't. Virginia geared her life toward pleasing her men and making a home."[15]

To move his career forward, Bill Clinton returned to Arkansas, and in time, won the governorship. For the inaugural celebration, the Clintons chose the theme, Diamonds and Denim. It was Camelot in Arkansas! Their election victory confirmed—in their own mind—their virtue and merit, and the couple entered into a unique partnership. "Because Bill was apparently driven more by a need for self-gratification than by any fixed set of beliefs, he relied heavily on Hillary's judgment, principles, and sense of higher purpose in making his decisions ... Hillary became Bill's watchdog, policy adviser, and problem-solver, in addition to playing the roles of wife, mother, and family breadwinner." Brock, who is otherwise a bitterly outspoken critic, is clear that Hillary was principled; pragmatism for her was a tactic, not a philosophy. Over the long haul, she had no intention of conceding the substantive issues or bedrock principles to the other side.[16] What Brock does criticize is Hillary's belief that traditional moral values should be strengthened—with the assistance of the state. Probably it was only because she stood by Clinton publicly that he was able to be elected president or retain the office the full eight years.

Hillary early on proved a loyal and effective governor's wife. When he ran for the state's highest office the last time, Clinton was opposed by a liberal, Tom McRae, head of the Winthrop Rockefeller Foundation. A Harvard-educated patrician-looking man, he seemed to remind people of Lincoln. McRae knew when Clinton would be out of the state, and he planned a mock debate with him to attack his record. In fact, he unveiled a cartoon depicting Clinton nude with his hands over his crotch. On it was the title, "The Emperor Has No Clothes." Hillary anticipated what McRae was going to do and was waiting in the audience. She shouted to him: "Get off it, Tom! I went through all your reports because I've really been disappointed in you as a candidate and I've been really disappointed in you as a person, Tom." The reports of the Rockefeller Foundation had praised some of the very parts of Clinton's policies and actions that McRae was criticizing.[17]

Time magazine summed up well the national mood that enabled Clinton to stay in the White House after his philandering with a young White House intern became public scandal. There was no groundswell calling for the president's impeachment comparable with that in Watergate against Nixon. "In district after district where Clinton is running plenty strong atop a buoyant economy, the president is a wizard, a witch doctor, the guy with spooky powerful voodoo; he can outlive, outlast, outmaneuver anything, even multiple, degrading, humiliating sex scandals."[18] The economy supported him as it had not Nixon. In the White House, Clinton had not been a philanderer on the scale of John F. Kennedy, and Monica was no Marilyn Monroe. "Clinton's life trails him like a peculiarly single-minded mugger, popping out from the shadows every time it seems the president is for a moment safe, to whack the staggering victim," a *New York Times* commentator observed.[19]

THE SOUL—RELIGION

James Carville, Clinton's campaign consultant during his initial run for the presidency, reflected on the candidate's religion: "I also have known very few people who have a better understanding of religion and God than Bill Clinton. Anybody who has talked to him for more than fifteen minutes would draw the same conclusion. He knows more about Catholicism than I do [Carville himself is a Roman Catholic], [and] more about Judaism than a lot of Jews. He knows a hell of a lot about the Bible. I have absolutely no doubt that he is a person who has thought more about God in his lifetime than 99.5 percent of the people in this country. No doubt he understands what faith is, he understands the contours of it, the power of it, the contradictions and limitations. He'd be a year's study away from being a theology professor."[20]

Church attendance is one way for a candidate to affirm good character. While he was governor in Little Rock, Clinton attended

Immanuel Baptist Church. Its plant and sanctuary took up two full city blocks. Its gold-and-tan building stands on a hill looming above the Capitol; it is the largest church in Arkansas. The church had a statewide televised service, and Clinton could be seen singing second tenor in the choir. It was a conservative (if not fundamentalist) congregation and ministry. The Clintons were themselves modernists and not fundamentalists, especially Mrs. Clinton. She had grown up in the North with different traditions than in Arkansas Bible Belt religion. While her husband was at Immanuel Baptist, she attended First Methodist Church, a congregation that included some seventy-six lawyers in its membership and had long traditions of community service, including a child development center and telephone crisis hotline. All this was going on while Clinton, on his own admission, was not fully faithful in his marriage.

It is not fair to say unqualifiedly that Bill Clinton worshiped at Immanuel Baptist Church just to campaign for office. The Baptist Church represented the tradition he had grown up in. What did he still find in it? "Clinton did not go to church for social activism, not for fire and brimstone judgment and guilt-ridden repentance; he went, largely, to search for the better part of himself in a place where he could be accepted at face value."[21] A more psychologically oriented explanation was that Clinton turned to religion in search of something he had never really had in a normal way: a father. He found it in part in his pastor, Dr. Worley Oscar Vaught, a short, bald, bespectacled, stern-voiced conservative preacher. Clinton included Brother Vaught in his list of daily calls and occasionally would remark, Dr. Vaught told me this or that.

Vaught was the one who assured Clinton that capital punishment was not contrary to Christian teaching; the governor "must never worry about whether it's forbidden by the Bible, because it isn't." The biblical teaching is, "thou shalt not murder," not "thou shalt not kill." Execution by the state is not the equivalent of murder.[22]

Vaught also eased Clinton's conscience on the abortion issue. In biblical teaching, the meaning of *personhood, life,* and *death,* come from words that literally mean "to breathe life into." The Baptist pastor's conclusion was that life begins at birth with the first breath of life. He argued that abortion was not right but it was not murder. At the celebration of his fiftieth wedding anniversary, Vaught turned to Clinton in prediction of things to come: "Bill, one of these days, I want to sleep in the Lincoln bedroom." Little did he know how much that room would be used for political purposes!

THE MORAL QUESTION AND
CHARGES AGAINST THE PRESIDENT

The moral question is whether a practicing politician of this sort has the character and tenacity to achieve his goals in spite of the pressures brought to bear on him. The following description faces some of the issues: "A faltering superpower gets a new leader who calls for change, promising an end to political stagnation and economic decline. He is younger by decades than his recent predecessors…His wife, a stylish dresser and savvy political force in her own right, is a source of controversy. Critical of traditional politics and yet very much its product, the nation's new leader wants to focus attention on domestic renewal … Hard liners warn that he promises too much, trying to be all things to all people."[23]

These words were written not about Bill Clinton but in description of the former Soviet president, Mikhail Gorbachev. But Gorbachev never won a popular election. Clinton did, although by a plurality and not a clear majority when he first ran for the White House; there were other significant differences between the two leaders. In the United States, entrance to the presidency is through the grueling ordeal of a protracted election campaign. After he entered the White House, the press and the public continued to ask about Bill Clinton, who he was, and what goals and values he championed after he became president. White House reporter Elizabeth Drew, describing the Clinton administration as "on the edge," evaluated its leader: a complex mixture of the Southern boy who grew up poor white, the young man who matriculated at Georgetown University, Oxford, and Yale Law School, and the adult who traveled in sophisticated intellectual and moneyed and international circles, but had not lost his good old boy, down home, Southern core."[24] The reporter added: "One or another of these aspects of his nature might come to the fore from time to time, but all of them remained within him." Whether intellectuals called it the lack of a vital meta-narrative or post-modern did not matter very much to ordinary citizens.

As in the case of other presidents, Clinton's own personal biography came up for evaluation. "His family background is a thick stew of personal indecency and salacious rumor," David Brock observed in derogation.

Another critic, David Maraniss, argued that Clinton exhibited the classic traits of a child reared by an abusive, alcoholic parent: a strong desire to smooth things over and to please; near-crippling dependence on others; a volatile temper; low self-esteem; and addictive behavior in the form of compulsive politicking and sexual activity. Maraniss notes that in a dysfunctional household, such children learn to thrive in chaos, constantly changing their own behavior to keep things in balance and trying to please everybody through their manipulation and lying. Commitments are made and broken at random. In extreme cases, truth and reality mean little. Outsiders are kept at bay and deceived in a family culture of concealment.[25] But all this did not block Bill Clinton from achieving the presidency.

Like Ronald Reagan, Clinton the campaigner talked values. He even sounded like Reagan as he deplored their loss and absence. "We can't renew our country until we realize that governments don't raise children, parents do."[26] But Reagan had the support of the New Religious Right to legitimate his program; Clinton did not. Politically, he failed to achieve the moral reputation of the Democrat, Franklin Roosevelt, or of the Republicans, Eisenhower and Reagan, all of whom were rumored to be philanderers. Instead, his Arkansas past followed him to the White House. "When are we ever forgiven? When do we leave [it] … behind us?" the president exclaimed to a reporter in the spring of 1994.

Of course, Washington was no place for innocence or naiveté. George Mitchell, Democratic leader in the Senate, who retired at the end of 1994, observed: "The ways of Washington were the ways of Rome in the time of Julius Caesar, were the ways of Paris in the time of Napoleon, or the ways of London in the time of Disraeli. There isn't much under the sun new in these things."[27]

"I made mistakes from ignorance, inexperience, and overwork. I was not meant for the job or the spotlight of public life in Washington.

Here, ruining people is considered sport." These are the words not of Clinton but of his White House attorney, Vincent Foster, who penned them just before he committed suicide. Foster's death "rang the bell" and awakened deep suspicions about the Clintons' land investment project in the Whitewater real estate development. It led eventually to appointment of a special prosecutor. A friend reflected: "Bill and Hillary Rodham Clinton, who promised a centrist course, are ridiculed by the right, abandoned by the left, distrusted by moderates, and challenged by fellow Democrats."[28] The Clintons resented it deeply and felt it unfair; in part, it was the price of power. "One night in the White House," Clinton remarked to his longtime staff member, George Stephanopoulos, son of a Greek Orthodox priest, "I feel like I'm in a Kafkaesque novel."

Was Clinton as much alone and unique as both his friends and critics at times implied? Or was he only an "everyman," like all other presidents simply confronting the perennial risks of the office? Wilson, Hoover, and Johnson all had lost legitimacy before leaving office. Besides, Nixon and Reagan, Carter, and George H. W. Bush (neither of the latter pair of whom won second terms) all concluded their terms significantly discredited. The Arkansas governor won election and continuing tenure in the White House for one primary reason— because he "hung in" when others did not.

As Bill Clinton was about to exit the White House, the *New York Times* ran a final and generally positive evaluation: Todd S. Purdum, wrote on the day before Christmas, December 24, 2000: "For eight years, Bill Clinton has been the bright sun and bleak moon of American politics, embodying much of the best and the worst of his times ..." Purdum summed up his own judgment: "In countless ways, Mr. Clinton has been the unavoidable man. He exploited the daily rhythms of popular culture to redefine his office; he nudged the political culture to the center to reshape the Democratic Party; he rode the unbroken growth of the national economy to high approval ratings; and he helped foster the flowering of the information age, even as it amplified his flaws ... He kept his office relevant, and carried the country along on a wild ride ... Mr. Clinton managed to shape a new kind of limited executive activism that kept the presidency in the thick of things."[29]

Ken Burns, a documentary maker, described the forty-second

president as someone who has moved us from one kind of world to another—from a world in which the Internet was barely a force in American life when he first ran for president to one in which the instantaneous reality of cyberspace affects every aspect of daily life. He has also moved the presidency from card files to e-mail messages."[30]

"Any president in large measure is evaluated on the state of the economy during his administration," Leon E. Panetta, budget director and then chief of staff argued. "If that's the test with Clinton, it will clearly show the economy to be his greatest triumph."[31]

Jason DeParle and Steven A. Holmes, writing in a *New York Times* series, praised Clinton for his understanding that the war on poverty was subtly linked to race in the minds of many Americans. They pointed to the crisis moment when in 1996, under Gingrich's Republican pressure, Clinton had to decide whether or not to sign a popular welfare bill shaped largely by the opposition party.[32] His strategy to do so caused a variety of old images to fade, they believe. Accepting the Republican thesis that welfare recipients need to be forced to work, even those who have very young children, the Democrat in the White House forged a new social bargain with those at the bottom of the economic and social ladder.

The *New York Times* commentators argue that an unprecedented expansion of aid for the poor followed. Billions of dollars were appropriated in wage supplements and subsidies for everything from child care to children's health insurance. The Republican thesis that there was a moral obligation to make work pay was accepted—but Clinton's was a subtle effort to reshape racial perceptions. Theda Skocpol, a political scientist at Harvard who researched programs for the poor, observed: "He ended the most controversial aspects of welfare, but at the same time, he built up supports for working families. And he certainly did see this as an effort to quiet racial disputes about social supports for the vulnerable."[33] The upside was that Clinton proved that progress could be made on problems that many Republicans (as well as members of his own party) had thought impossible.

One of the *New York Times* reporters reflects how much the president's strategy led to the reduction of crime and the increase of wages for unskilled workers—and urban renewal followed. A larger number of Americans escaped poverty under Clinton than under any other president since Lyndon Johnson.

There remain important issues for self-examination as to how Americans would like to have it—in the presidency. Do they want an overly moralistic type leader like Woodrow Wilson who led the nation into world war in the name of utopia, and then could not negotiate a successful peace? Or do they prefer an isolationist style presidency like those of Harding, Coolidge, and Hoover, men who did not have enough economic control to prevent a great depression or to prescribe a way out of it? After the Second World War, a generation of power realists—Kennedy, Johnson, and Nixon—all played a part in the Vietnam quagmire. Carter, changing direction, championed human rights courageously, but blundered in admitting the Shah to the United States and provoked students in Iran. The Southern Baptist seems to have had little understanding of what Shi'ite Muslims were thinking ideologically. Reagan threatened the world with Star Wars, frightening the Soviet leadership into a change that they may well have been on the way to making anyhow, in view of their collapsing economy. So who are the heroes? It is too early to say how historians will view Clinton in the long run; there is not enough distance and perspective. Lesson: A president's character is no guarantee of success or failure, but it is not all unreality—smoke and mirrors!

David Gergen, who earlier worked for Republican presidents before doing a stint in the Clinton White House, reflected: "After the Republicans won the Congressional election of 1994, the president put down the sword he had raised on behalf of causes that he believed in and lost courage completely." Nonetheless, positively, Gergen judges that Clinton combined a natural optimism with ability to stand outside himself. A superb tactician, he also was able to bring a mass of information into a new synthesis. Finding him to be prodigiously bright, Gergen labels Clinton the most talented politician of his generation. Indeed, Gergen judges that he had the most subtle grasp of political issues of any president he had known. But said Gergen, "If I have to choose between intelligence and high integrity, I would choose the latter."[34] Still, Gergen observes that "Clinton remains a sunny figure in spite of his philandering and lying. He never showed the inner darkness of Nixon. But he had no true inner compass, no true north, and let his sexual energy get the better of him." Gergen looks for accompanying reasons: "It may be because his career was too rushed—was he elected too young? Walking on the edge, he signaled that borderline ethics would be tolerated ... Clinton had one hand filled with dust, the other with stars." Yet in his final judgment, Gergen reflects that Clinton's ad hoc strategy left the nation in superb shape.[35]

THE SECOND BUSH PRESIDENCY: GEORGE W. BUSH

The second member of the Bush dynasty was not as successful as his father in the White House even though initially he hoped to accomplish more. The reason why was very soon clear: Whereas Bush I refused to fight on to Baghdad, Bush II invaded the whole country of the enemy. He took his nation into a prolonged and unnecessary war in Iraq. His deference to Wall Street and a policy of weak financial regulation led to economic crisis at the end of his rule. When Bush II's popularity ratings fell to rock bottom, John McCain, the Republican candidate for president, distanced himself as much as possible from the incumbent in the White House. Bush's weakness gave Obama his opportunity. The latter, more of an intellectual, was much more reflective than the Texan. He had opposed the invasion of Iraq from the outset. The first African-American president probably was not mistaken in supposing that much of his time in office would be spent in rectifying his predecessor's failed policies.

THE PARADOX OF THE OFFICE

When the Bush dynasty returned to rule in Washington, D.C. in 2001, it was the second father-and-son succession in the history of the presidency. The first had been that of John Adams and John Quincy Adams two centuries earlier. The paradox underlying the presidential office was doubly evident almost as soon as the younger Bush entered the White House; although the success of a particular occupant depends in a major way on his ability to address the ethos of his time, his skill and character reciprocally determine that ethos in large measure. In short, there was a Bush II ethos; unfortunately, too much determined by the advice of the vice president, Richard Cheney. In the end, Bush II ranks as a loser with a very low rating (thirty-sixth among forty-two predecessors) by professional historians.

The differences in ideology and administration between the new Republican, George W. Bush, and his predecessor, Democrat Bill Clinton, were outstanding. Professor Bert A. Rockman, director of the School of Public Policy and Management at Ohio State University, wrote: "Bush II and Clinton are virtual mirror images of another as presidential personalities. Clinton liked to bury himself in detail, discussing it endlessly, pondering over its implications ... Clinton liked to think about decisions; Bush II likes to make them."[1] Rockman pointed out that the younger Bush had great personal confidence in his judgments and liked to get to bottom lines quickly. Rather than fussing over details or consequences, he wanted action, not contemplation.

Rockman concluded that as president, Bush had been temperamentally too activistic to be classified simply as just a traditional conservative. He has run a "tight ship" administratively. His "aggressive intervention in the executive branch affairs and his responsiveness to core conservative constituencies ... surpasses in some respects even that of Ronald Reagan." The academic finds "a striking similarity to the disputed incumbency of another former president's son—John Quincy Adams."

Early on, Thomas Friedman had described the new president's campaign for office as "Clinton-minus," by which the *New York Times* columnist meant a compassionate conservative who would provide Clinton-like policies on key issues minus Mr. Clinton's personal baggage.[2] This was not the whole story, however. Once in power, Mr. Bush seemed not so much Clinton-minus, but Reagan squared—not a compassionate conservative but a radical conservative. In sum, Bush II is Reagan's—and not his father's—political son, especially with regard to personal ideological proclivities.[3]

The Harvard political scientist, Richard Neustadt, in his classic, *Presidential Power*, develops a suggestive paradigm: "The first president has strong leadership capabilities … but is basically a rule-abiding leader. He does his best to overcome obstacles, but he knows that there are bounds to what he can do. The second president is also a strong leader and a hard bargainer, but the demons of maximization and the strong expectations that he feels he must satisfy force him to do whatever is necessary to overcome his adversaries."[4] The second president's aim is to remove obstacles; he seeks to command his subordinates to his wishes. He takes on the bureaucracy and seeks to bend it to his will. For him, maintaining the status quo is not enough. A number of historians have noted that Bush II initially was aggressive in both foreign and domestic policy. A majority probably are of the opinion that the younger turned out to be less bright than either of his predecessors, Carter or Clinton. Admirers replied that this was deceptively "part of his act," intended to mislead his opponents. He was "street smart," they suggested. This much, at least, soon was clear: Bush II intended to be more innovative and revolutionary than his father. Like Clinton before him, he sounded centrist themes as he campaigned—but with a crucial difference: ideologically, he was further to the right on the political spectrum than his immediate predecessor ever had been. George W. cast himself as a compassionate conservative—advocating personal initiative rather than government intervention. Clinton, by comparison, stood on the left, moving reluctantly toward the center!

Not surprisingly, from the beginning, W. had his derogators. James MacGregor Burns asked: "How could it happen that this long-unfocused man, no longer young but still in his father's shadow, the scion of Eastern moderate Republicans, the half-educated product of Andover and Yale, embarked on a course that would carry him within a few years to the White House as a committed conservative? Bush governed Texas from the Reagan playbook. He admired the former president's ability to blend personal amiability, undiluted conservatism, and political ruthlessness into a winning strategy." Burns appraised Bush II as, like Reagan, a relative late bloomer in electoral politics. As with Reagan, his genial, down-home persona softened the hard edges of his conservatism. And like Reagan, he concentrated on a handful of signature issues from his campaign—pro-business, economic policies, law and order, welfare reform, education … To the state's growing flock of religious conservatives, the governor could offer a compelling personal story of redemption."[5]

As a Bush family member sought to regain to the Oval Office, "A strange thing happened on the way to the White House"—a pattern of events that had seldom if ever occurred before. When W. ran for his first term against the vice president, Al Gore, virtually no one, Republican or Democrat, anticipated the future train of happenings. *Time* magazine described the election contest in the fall of 2000 as the wildest one in the nation's entire history. Although delegates to the Electoral College were scheduled to be chosen in the several states on Tuesday, November 7, no one on that day (or for weeks to come) would know for sure who the next chief executive was to be. What transpired for more than a month and a half subsequently raised continuing constitutional questions.

Retrospectively, it should not be overlooked that no major crisis in international relations was in view; such had not been the main theme of the election campaign. The Republican candidate attacked big government (as well as President Clinton's personal morality) and championed less state interference in public life. As early as July 22, 1999, speaking in Indianapolis, Indiana, W. had electioneered: "We will carry a message of hope and renewal to every community in this country. We will tell every American, 'The dream is for you.' Tell men and women in our decaying cities, 'The dream is for you.' Tell confused young people, starved of ideals, 'The dream is for you.'"[6] Campaigning, candidate Bush at the same time disavowed nation building abroad. Actually, this policy was the reverse of what took place later under his administration.

In the election of 2000, questions of personal morality (Clinton's behavior) played a larger part, albeit in the background of the campaign than they had had in the Nixon-Kennedy race; this may well have cost Gore the election. Justice O'Connor cast the deciding vote in the Supreme Court. Although Gore, the Democratic candidate, had won the popular vote by more than half a million votes, she and her colleagues intervened and gave the election to Bush. In this situation, the incumbent vice president was urged to follow the example of Richard Nixon, a predecessor in the office. Nixon conceded to John F. Kennedy after his first run for the presidency in 1960, in spite of the fact that there were contested ballots outstanding and he might have held out longer. General Dwight Eisenhower advised his vice president not to prolong the race by making demands for a recount or litigation. Republican Nixon was running against a Roman Catholic, and continuation of the contest could have bred lasting inter-religious hostility.

LIFE PHILOSOPHY AND RELIGION

Bush II's life history, as well as his deliberate image as a Texan rather than a New Englander, has been widely examined ever since he entered politics as a young man in an unsuccessful race for Congress. He was not a war hero or a ranking diplomat at the United Nations, as was Bush I. In the family tradition, Bush II had been an undergraduate at Yale. During the Vietnam War, he remained in the United States, served in the Texas Air National Guard, and subsequently studied at Harvard Business School. To his credit, as the son of a president, he made use of the observation and practical knowledge available from his father's experience in the presidency. He had seen the forty-first president at work in the midst of crises and knew first-hand how Cabinet and congressional pressures impose themselves on the White House. Specifically, he had lived through the elder Bush's problems and responsibilities during the first war in Iraq that liberated Kuwait, as well as the loss of the presidency to Bill Clinton.

George W. was born in New Haven, Connecticut, while his father was studying at Yale in the immediate post-World War II era. He was taken to Texas while he was still very young. Thus, the New England-Texas antithesis was engrained in his personality, and when he later ran for president, it was as a Southwesterner, not as a Yankee. Both the older and the younger in the Bush dynasty had chosen to move west and make a new beginning in the oil industry rather than accept a position in the family's stock business in New York. It was George W. who was the most ideologically Western. Certainly, for both father and son, funds and friends were available from the East whenever they needed them.

George W., like his father, attended prep school at Andover in Massachusetts, but did not do nearly as well academically. Rather than excelling scholastically, he was a leader in sports, widely recognized and liked on campus. At home, his childhood had been a happy one—in contrast with that of Bill Clinton, for example. There was an exception: Important in his earlier experience while still very young in Texas was the sorrow over the death of a younger sister from leukemia. Although his family had attempted to shield him from it, the frailty and irrationality of human existence became tragically evident. Bush Junior's exposure to Yale was during the era of the Vietnam War; as a political conservative, he did not participate in the campus anti-war protests led by university chaplain William Sloane Coffin. Put bluntly, he did not learn or accept liberal Christianity in college.

What did the younger Bush believe and want out of life? No doubt, he had times of indolence and confusion while at Yale and afterward. At the conclusion of his enlistment in the Texas National Guard during the war in Vietnam, he was refused admission to the University of Texas at Austin and instead attended Harvard Business School. Then he returned to begin his career in Midland, Texas, where he had lived as a small child; there he married his wife, Laura. He even interrupted their honeymoon with a campaign for Congress—one that he lost. The image of an Eastern university man was invoked against him and proved politically fatal; it was a lesson he never forgot, and he deliberately sought to erase all Ivy League school identity when he entered politics for the second time.

Following his father's example, George W. started out in the oil business. After many dry holes and some successes, his firm merged into a larger company, Harkin Oil. Critics claim that all the time, he was trading on the family name and influence. The younger Bush eventually sold his assets in this corporation at a considerable profit and then successfully became part owner and manager of a Major League Baseball team based near Dallas at Arlington, Texas. Out of an initial investment in the team of somewhat over a half million dollars, held over a period of years as he worked with it, he raised his stakes to 12 million when he sold out—enough to give him financial security for the rest of his life.

When he decided to run for governor in Texas, W's program was a simple, straightforward conservative—one of lower taxes, tort reform, and school improvement. Emphasizing a few well-identified issues and carefully refraining from polemics and anger, he campaigned and won against the incumbent liberal governor, Ann Richards. Bush had the support of the New Religious Right as well as the so-called "country club Republicans." Once in office, he found himself confronting a Democratic legislature led by Lieutenant Governor Bullock—but he reacted positively. Rather than retreating defensively, he established a close friendship and cooperation with Bullock across party lines. Together, they succeeded in securing legislation that would not even have been thought possible in a more partisan situation. When he ran for the presidency, Bush at first attempted to project a similar image as a uniting compassionate conservative (but not for long).

As president, the second Bush (even more than his father) played the role of controlling manager, the man in charge, well-defined morally and ideologically. A Bush advisor explained: "The feeling is that the country deserves governance and if you don't assert the sovereignty and legitimacy of your administration from the outset, you undermine your ability to achieve your goals later."[7] Aligned even more decisively than his father with the new religious right, he was seen by critical opponents as seeking to restore righteousness from a position of power. Key to the younger Bush's piety was his contact with evangelist Billy Graham. It was out of conversations with Graham that the president-to-be eventually underwent a personal religious conversion and change of lifestyle. The outward sign was that he gave up the use of alcohol—which, in his case, had become excessive.

Howard Fineman writes: "Bush, who cares little for the abstract and a great deal for people, responded to the conversion story [of St. Paul]. He liked the idea of knowing Jesus as a friend ... The CBS [Community Bible Study] program gave him, for the first time, an intellectual focus. Here was the product of elite secular education—Andover, Yale, and Harvard—who, for the first time, was reading a book line by line with rapt attention. And it was ... the Bible." Fineman judges that Bush was a more unalloyed product of the Bible Belt than many of his Eastern friends, who may have deeply studied something else in earlier days. In Bible study, he gained the mental and spiritual discipline that he needed to steel himself for his main challenge in life to that point to quit drinking."[8]

The Bush family had been Episcopal on his father's side and Presbyterian on his mother's. George W. Bush, who had been an Episcopal altar boy in his youth, became a Methodist, joining the denomination of his wife, Laura, at the time that their twin daughters were confirmed in Midland, Texas. To his credit, there was no touch of marital infidelity or sexual scandal, as in the case of Kennedy or Clinton. Entering politics, Bush's stance was clear from the title of his campaign autobiography, *A Charge I Have to Keep,* the title of a traditional Methodist Wesleyan hymn.

In a prayer service before W. took the oath of office as governor of Texas, Pastor Mark Craig preached that people "are starved for leaders who have ethical and moral courage ... leaders who have the moral courage to do what is right for the right reason." The new state chief executive reflected that "these words spoke to my heart and life. It was one of those moments that forever change you ... that set you on a different course."[9] His mother told him that they applied to him. W. called leading pastors to the Texas governor's mansion and gave them the word that he had been called to seek a higher office. After September 11, he told his campaign advisor, Karl Rove, the same.

PRIORITY OF FOREIGN AFFAIRS

In fact, the most determining issues for the second Bush administration turned out to be centered more in foreign affairs than on the domestic issues for which the born-again Christian had campaigned. Aaron Wildavsky's paradigm of two contrasting presidencies also helps to explain Bush II's approach.[10] On Wildavsky's model, a foreign policy president often can preside over the vast defense and national security apparatus and yet remain relatively unfettered. Paradoxically, by comparison, a domestically oriented leader more easily feels blocked and frustrated by having his high-priority initiatives rejected by a quarreling Congress. In short, he is constrained by an array of special interests and local considerations that stymie administration initiatives.

Bush's former White House speech writer, David Frum, has expressed his personal opinion that the forty-third president is "a politician of conservative instincts rather than conservative principles. He knew in a general way what he believed and what he did not. But on any specific issue, nobody could ever be sure where the line was beyond which he could not be pushed." When interviewed by Bob Woodward, the second Bush proclaimed: "I'm not a textbook player; I'm a gut player." Woodward judged it to be a visceral reaction, noting that the head of state mentioned *instincts* a dozen times. Woodward's conclusion: "Bush's role as politician, president, and commander-in-chief is driven by secular faith in his instincts—his natural and spontaneous conclusions and judgments. His instincts are almost his second religion."[11] Eventually, Woodward would conclude that Bush was in psychological denial about what was going on in Iraq.

Singer insists that at issue is more than good intentions. He cites a story from a nineteenth-century English mathematician and philosopher, William Clifford. "A shipowner [was] about to send off to sea a ship full of immigrants. He knew that his ship was old and needed repair, so he had doubts about whether it was seaworthy, and wondered if he should go to the expense of having it thoroughly overhauled and refitted. But he decided instead to put his trust in providence ..." After all, God could hardly fail to protect the immigrant families seeking a better life abroad. Assuring himself that all would be well, the ship owner saw off the ship without any qualms. When the vessel went down and there was great loss of life, his own losses were covered by the insurance company.

Clifford's point is that the sincerity of the shipowner's belief does not absolve him of guilt for the lives lost, because on the evidence he had before him, he had no right to believe that the ship was fit to make the voyage. "He had acquired his belief not by honestly earning it in patient investigation, but by stifling his doubt. Even if the ship had proved to be sound and had made the journey safely, that would not mean that the owner was justified in believing it seaworthy. He would still have been wrong to allow the lives of the passengers to hang on his faith, rather than on sound evidence that the ship was seaworthy."[12]

George H.W. Bush (the senior) had raised an international army to fight against the Iraqi dictator, Saddam Hussein, as the Iraqi ruler overran Kuwait, hoping to control the major sources of oil in the Middle East. After success in expelling the invader from his conquest of the oil-rich kingdom of Kuwait, Bush Senior decided not to carry the fight to Baghdad. One reason was that the president and his advisors feared chaos in the area. George W. Bush, asserting that the Iraqi dictator had plotted to assassinate his father when the latter visited Kuwait, had decided to attack the still-defiant head of state and remove him from power—claiming that Saddam held weapons of mass destruction. Colin Powell, Bush's secretary of state, earlier had counseled that if the Middle Eastern country were overrun and captured, a long task of control and reconstruction would lay ahead. Still, he mistakenly claimed before the United Nations Assembly that there were weapons of mass destruction in Iraq.

There was a dramatic incident after Saddam Hussein's country was overrun militarily. Landing on an aircraft carrier in California, Bush II declared victory—but control of the Iraqi capital and the country soon defied his grasp. Terrorist suicide attacks continued to be widespread and the occupation became in many ways unmanageable. In spite of a continuing (and what proved to be an unsuccessful) war on his hands, George W. Bush campaigned for re-election in 2004 on the claim that he had done the right and righteous thing. As in the cases of presidents Woodrow Wilson, Franklin Roosevelt, and Lyndon Johnson, the course of future events would significantly determine judgments about his legacy. Americans were not interested only in who was right or wrong—but in winning.

What would former presidents have done in such circumstances? Lincoln, for example, had spoken out against pre-emptive invasion of counties with which the United States was not officially at war. Certainly, George W. Bush was not mistaken about one long-term aspect of the crisis: President Bill Clinton already had recognized Osama bin Laden, the wealthy Saudi Arabian, as a threat, and had ordered air strikes with the intent of destroying him physically. Unfortunately, the terrorist leader's capture or killing eluded both the Clinton and Bush administrations. Should nuclear materials fall into hands such as his, or to those of rogue regimes similarly murderous, a major threat would be posed to civilization.

In the early period, Jefferson and Madison were not as successful in their leadership in the White House as when they had been Founding Fathers. In spite of his brilliant achievement when he engineered the Louisiana Purchase, which added major territory to the country even as it violated his own state's rights premises, Jefferson's second term was particularly miserable for him. Madison did not avoid war with the British in 1812. A half century later, Lincoln won re-election, it is probable, only because Atlanta was taken by Union armies. If this had not been the case, he might have lost the election to General McClellan.

Woodrow Wilson won re-election on the campaign slogan, "He kept us out of war," and then carried the nation into hostilities in Europe, seeking to make the world safe for democracy in the name of God. In the end, he could not convince his own countrymen about the need for internationalism and the League of Nations. Lyndon Johnson failed to bring peace to Vietnam, and left office with his social programs in retreat. Like Lyndon Johnson, George W. Bush had initiated military action against the enemy rather than holding back and seeking international cooperation. Franklin Roosevelt won election to four terms in office. His goal of the unconditional surrender of Germany (no negotiated peace) was realized at the end of World War II. Still, because Roosevelt trusted Joseph Stalin too readily, Eastern Europe (many of its citizens believe) remained under communist rule for decades. Eisenhower showed restraint in the cold war. Reagan was more aggressive against communist enemies.

For Bush II, the situation was simple but at the same time complex. Major powers were dangerously armed with atomic weapons remaining from the cold war; these had been manufactured and were ready for use against each other. China, India, and Pakistan all had joined the atomic club. One misstep could end in catastrophe. Still, these weapons were of little use in a war against martyr-inspired suicide bombers. Terrorist groups were multiple; the defeat of one would not necessarily lead to the demise of another. If any of them found access to atomic weapons, genocide could follow. Throughout the Arab world, issues were psychological, ideological, and theological, not just political and military. Evidently, victory could not be won by arms alone.

Unlike his father, whose Cabinet was dominated by the doves—James Baker, Snowcroft, and Colin Powell—the second Bush's Cabinet was led by hawks—Rumsfeld, Cheney, and Ashcroft. In the background of his moral claim was Bush's own intuition and religious belief that he knew what was right for the nation and the world; he was seeking to do God's will. Of course, intellectually, he had not attempted to sort out what are commonly identified as second causes or natural law—both belonging to human agency rather than to deity. At the political level, the distinction between his religious consciousness and the president's secular responsibility (as required by the constitutional separation of church and state) had not been thought through. Judged internationally and in interfaith terms, Bush's sense of religious justification was widely challenged.

George Perkovich of the Carnegie Endowment for International Peace argues that "Bush's emphasis on freedom slights its counterpart, justice, and thus, weakens the appeal of the United States in the Middle East and elsewhere. Justice—within and between states, and in the global economy—is or should be the litmus test of any country's foreign policy. In the long run, justice will determine whether or not freedom really reigns."

THEOLOGY

Professor Bruce Lincoln, who teaches at the University of Chicago, analyzes George W. Bush's theology of history as resting on five propositions:

1. God desires freedom for all humanity.

2. This desire manifests itself in history.

3. America is called by history (and thus, implicitly by God) to take action on behalf of this cause.

4. Insofar as America responds with courage and determination, God's purpose is served and freedom's advance is inevitable.

5. With the triumph of freedom, God's will is accomplished and history comes to an end.

Bruce Lincoln's conclusion is that not one but several ideological systems are drawn on by the younger Bush, each one of which has its own force, rationale, and movement. These include an evangelical theology of born-again conversion, a theology of American exceptionalism allegedly grounded in the virtue of compassion, a Calvinistic theology of vocation, and a Manichaean dualism of good and evil. Quite certainly, they all do not say the same thing; multiple theology systems pile up.

Lincoln's criticism is that consistency and coherence are lacking. There is an evident outstanding tension between the history of salvation—one of an impersonal and inevitable process of gradual world perfection—and personal faith. A chosen nation is involved, and in this process, the Creator's goals are achieved though collective actions. By contrast, evangelical faith views salvation individually—and by no means, as inevitable. Lincoln judges that the early Bush synthesis is Pauline, the later one Hegelian—but without Hegel's dialectic or nationalistic reference to Prussia.

Lincoln charges that in the end, Bush's approach is pragmatic. The claim is that Bush the politician uses theology to justify convictions and conclusions he has already decided upon. Lincoln finds his references to history, freedom, and compassion to be vague and rhetorical, designed as a means to activate a broad religious base. Bush's sincerity is impressive and even convincing. Nonetheless, in practice, the details of his rhetoric are largely left for tough neo-conservatives to work out.

In Bush's defense, it must be said that he faced a radically new and different problem: fundamentalist violence that was religiously inspired. Muslims had not figured much on the national horizon since Jefferson sent American warships against Barbary Coast pirates from North Africa. When militant terrorists from the Middle East attacked America, George W. Bush, to his credit, was clear in distinguishing moderate Muslims from extremists. As he did so, a whole world religion dialogue came into view, one centered significantly in Palestine. The conflict in the Middle East was strongly determined (in background) by the founding of Israel, a new state that President Truman recognized against the recommendation of his secretary of state, George Marshall. Already, violence had grown up in the area under the British mandate. Actually, Jewish-Muslim-Christian tensions dated from long centuries of anti-Semitism, and more recently, the Holocaust. The stakes in the region were raised by the Middle East oil riches that Saddam had attempted to control.

PART ONE:
LOOK WHO'S COMING TO THE WHITE HOUSE:
BARACK OBAMA'S INAUGURATION AS PRESIDENT

The premise of this chapter is a simple one: take away Barack Obama's religious commitment and he would be a very different person, not the acclaimed moral leader that he was when he came to office. Put in terms of theology—God is, for him, the "ultimate meaning of meaning," what the philosopher of religion Paul Tillich called the Ground of Being.[1] Of course, Obama is first of all an activist whose morality is reinforced by faith claims about hope. At the same time, the new leader's response to religious questions is not just emotional but reflective and probing. This chapter is not an attempt to systematize his pattern of belief critically as much as to narrate the ins and outs of its development. Speaking as a Christian he professes to conform to the standards of the nation's faith in God, what is commonly known as *civil religion*. The question is how, and with what nuances?

Most of all, the new president was expected to avoid the mistakes of Nixon in Watergate or Clinton in Monicagate. But this negative barrier is not the end of the matter for a leader who acknowledges that in the end God is sovereign over the world and human life. Although the new president moved slowly in choosing a home church in the capital city—where his attendance could bring large crowds and create security problems—he already had chosen his inner circle with whom he was sharing in conversation and prayer. It included Jim Wallis of the Sojourners movement, Bishop T.D. Jakes of the Potter's House (megachurch) Church in Dallas, Kirbyjon Caldwell of the Windsor Village United Methodist Church in Houston, Texas (and also the father of the present pastor of Trinity Church in Chicago, Rev. Otis Moss, Jr.), and Joel C. Hunter, pastor of Northland (megachurch) Church in Logwood, Florida.[2] Obama's ecclesiastical heritage was reflected in the fact that three of the five were African Americans.

In a prayer service before the public ceremony at the inauguration, Dr. Hunter had prayed: "Barack Hussein Obama ... by faith, we call forth the personal qualities of the Holy Spirit that your family and country will need in you: 'love, joy, peace, patience, kindness, goodness, faithfulness, gentleness, and self-control' [Galatians 5:22–23] ... Through your leadership, Mr. President-elect, may God bless the United States of America in a way that makes us a blessing to the whole world. Amen."[3]

In this chapter, we will consider Obama's faith experience before he ran for president, his view of the relationship between church and state as he campaigned for the highest office in the land (in particular, as expressed in the Jeremiah Wright controversy), and the hope and optimism that he sought to renew in the country during financial recession. Running for the highest office in the land he offered different faces to various constituencies as his audience projected their own best images on his piety. Obama has written no systematic text on religion or theology that one can consult. At the same time he is more knowledgeable about world religions than most of his predecessors in the White House. To deal with current issues, he has renamed the White House Agency for Religion the Office for Faith-Based and Neighborhood Partnership. To lead it, he chose Joshua DuBois, a twenty-six-year-old Pentecostal minister who was part of Obama's staff during his election campaign. Kirbyjon Caldwell remarked of the president: "While he may not put 'Honk if You Love Jesus' stickers on the back of his car ... He has a desire to keep in touch with folk outside the Beltway, and to stay in touch with God. He seems to see these as necessary conditions for maintaining his internal compass."

The inauguration of the forty-fourth president of the United States was a glorious victory celebration for the supporters whose votes had brought the new leader to Washington, D.C. His coming to power dramatically fulfilled Martin Luther King's dream—even though much remained to be done in race relations. Now an African American occupied the highest office in the land for the first time in the nation's history. It was high symbolism when the new head of state invited one of the assassinated leader's associates from the Southern Leadership Council, Reverend Joseph Lowrey, a Methodist African American, to give the benediction at the close of the inauguration ritual. Reverend Lowrey opened his prayer by reminding his hearers of the crusade that his earlier generation had waged successfully in the name of God.

"God of our weary years, God of our silent tears, thou, who has brought us thus far along the way, thou, who has by thy might led us into the light, keep us forever in the path we pray ... And while we have sown the seeds of greed—the wind of greed and corruption, and even as we reap the whirlwind of social and economic disruption, we seek forgiveness and we come in a spirit of unity and solidarity in the complex arena of human relations; help us to make choices on the side of love, not hate; on the side of inclusion, not exclusion; tolerance, not intolerance. With your hands of power and your heart of love, help us then, now, Lord, to work for that day when nations shall not lift up sword against nation, when tanks will be beaten into tractors ... when black will not be asked to get in back, when brown can stick around ... when yellow will be mellow ... when the red man can get ahead, man; and when white will embrace what is right. That all those who do justice and love mercy, say amen."[4]

The benediction faithfully summed up the new president's hopes and faith. Pastor Lowrey was expressing the message that Martin Luther King, Jr. would have delivered to the nation if he had still been alive.

A JEWISH VOICE

Rabbi Michael Lerner, the editor of *Tikkun* magazine, was in the nation's capital on Inauguration Day. He especially had come to Washington, D.C. to celebrate the swearing-in of the nation's new leader. The clergyman described his state of mind as follows: "I wish my father and mother had been alive to experience the joy and incredible relief that went through our country as Barack Obama took the oath of office." Lerner wanted to say to them that things will be all right now. They will never be as bad again in the country as they have been during forty years of imperialist war, the undermining of civil liberties, me-firstism, and materialism.[5]

Lerner reflected that there was much to be appreciated in Obama's inaugural speech. Eight years of the systematic undermining of human rights of citizens would come to an end. There would be renewed transparency in government. Important for the liberal rabbi was the new chief executive's acknowledgement that the United States is a country of Christians and Muslims, Jews and Hindus, and non-believers. Finally, there was an affirmation of the common good—a reaffirmation of judging outcomes in terms of results.

"I don't know who Barack Obama will turn out to be as president," Lerner wrote. "The new president is not a savior." The rabbi does not see him as a leader possessed of the vision and courage of Martin Luther King, Jr., or Gandhi. Rather, Lerner views the new head of state as a politician, and a good one who can do a lot of good, much more good if citizens can find the right ways to support what is good in him. The rabbi concluded that "the joy and hope of these [inaugural] moments remains with me to this moment."

In his writings, Rabbi Michael Lerner—who earlier had been consulted and publicly praised by Hillary Clinton while her husband was president—makes a crucial distinction. He contrasts what he calls the "Left Hand" and the "Right Hand of God" as follows: "That very yearning for a world based more on love than on domination over others, for a world in which people respond with awe and wonder rather than with a purely utilitarian attitude toward other human beings and toward nature, is the core of a religious and spiritual tradition that I call the Left Hand of God. Those who belong to this tradition see God as the Force in the universe that makes possible transformation from a world based on pain and cruelty to a world based on love and generosity ... the Force that makes possible a world of nonviolence, peace, and social justice."[6]

In Rabbi Lerner's analysis, the Left Hand of God stands in marked contrast to a view of God as a powerful avenger, the Right Hand of God—"the Force that will overthrow evil through superior power, the Force that seeks to exterminate enemies and suppress dissent."

This vision, often expressed in apocalyptic terms, sometimes conveys the mistaken idea that evil can be wiped out by one more war or by imposing rigid commandments about how to live; citizens are to be forced into goodness by a word from above. Ethics and religion are to be imposed from above.

Rabbi Lerner observes: "Religious triumphalism—'Our God will emerge as the real God at the end of history, and all the rest of you will get your deserved punishment'—is not confined to right-wing Christianity. It is as prevalent in some parts of Judaism, Islam, and many other religions ... The task of building an alternative to tough-guy thinking, muscular religion, and domination-as-the path-to-security is going to be challenging for just this reason: embracing the Left Hand of God will require us to get over our fear of the cynical realism that surrounds us and resonates with the fear inside us ... [We need to] build a society based on the loving and compassionate teachings in Torah, the Prophets, Jesus, Mohammed, the Buddha, and many other religious traditions."[7] The perennial danger is hubris!

The rabbi's description of the right hand could apply even in more secular analysis. Ted Sorenson, one of John Kennedy's closest confidants, reflected on the threat of right-hand forces: "This is an unprecedented mess. By many measures, no incoming president will have inherited quite such a sack of trouble in decades. You have to have not only a sense of confidence but apparently big ego—you have to be almost a fanatic. An aspiring politician not only has to look at everybody else running for the office against him and believe that he is as good as they are. He needs to think not only he is as good as they are but that his ideas are better. And that he can fix what nobody else can fix."[8] In fact, the challenge of the time was not simply a secular one—economic and political. World view and ethics were at stake in the decisions that the new incumbent in the White House sought to bring about.

There were other more positive (left-hand) views: "President-elect Obama has power of his own ... I will not exaggerate the importance of a single personality, but Obama has become a global symbol like none I can recall in my lifetime ... This is a rare moment in history." So the *Newsweek* commentator, Fareed Zakaria, had observed while the president-elect was choosing his Cabinet.[9] "At this time and for this man, there is a unique opportunity to use American power to reshape the world. This is his moment. He should seize it."[10] As the new leader battled for passage of emergency recovery measures in Congress, it was clear that the fight for the programs for which he had campaigned would be no "pushover." The old Clinton-vs.-Gingrich battle lines seemed to emerge as congressmen voted almost entirely along party lines.[11]

The thesis of this chapter is that the new president has a carefully thought-out view of the relation between church and state as well as between religion and politics. This was clear in his choice of the clergy who participated in his instillation in office. Like his mother, the forty-fourth president is willing to learn from a variety of religious traditions; unlike her, he is anchored in one particular faith. The biblical monotheism he espouses remains a radical and revolutionary outlook and has been so from the time that it was accepted in the Jewish community and polytheism was denied: "Thou shalt have no other gods." The Ten Commandments were given by God to Moses. There is only one deity, all wise and all powerful, the Lord of history and the judge of all men's deeds. Biblical monotheism puts the history of human life on earth, evil, and eternal destiny in a particular context. Truth is affirmed not just on the grounds of reason but of revelation in the biblical writings.

What did the change of leaders in the United States of America signify in deed and not just in rhetoric? The name of God had been invoked at all earlier presidential inaugurations in the past. It had also been employed for millennia by kings and emperors at their coronations! Would the nation's power be exercised without hubris and vainglory in the new Obama administration? What were the differences and similarities between a democratic republic like the United States and a monarchy or dictatorship? The answer may not be as simple as it first appears to be!

Obama has understood that from the outset, the United States presidency has carried heavy symbolic religious significance; this continues to the present.[12]

If the forty-fourth president succeeds in the face of the daunting challenges that confront him, his admirers will project a whole series of positive symbols and stories on his person.

How are we to evaluate Obama's chances in the face of enormous obstacles and dangers?[13] His rhetoric amid the solemnities of inauguration had turned austere. His hearers no longer cried out in masses, "Yes we can!" There would be great difficulties ahead, he told them, but in the end the economy would be righted and foreign relations improve.[14]

Obama has acknowledged the reality of religious pluralism: "Given the increasing diversity of America's population, the dangers of sectarianism have never been greater. Whatever we once were, we are no longer just a Christian nation; we are also a Jewish nation, a Muslim nation, a Buddhist nation, a Hindu nation, and a nation of nonbelievers."[15] But he has also argued in defense of civil religion's place in the national traditions of office (as distinguished from institutional religion): "Imagine Lincoln's Second Inaugural Address without reference to 'the judgments of the Lord.' Or King's 'I Have a Dream' speech without references to 'all of God's children.' Their summoning of a higher truth helped inspire what had seemed impossible, and move the nation to embrace a common destiny."

OBAMA'S INAUGURATION AS A KEY TO HIS FAITH

Obama's choice of clergy to lead at his inauguration exemplified his beliefs and helped observers to identify his position and program more clearly: "Pastors, friends of mine like Rick Warren and T.D. Jakes, are wielding their enormous influences to confront AIDS, Third World debt relief, and the genocide in Darfur. Religious thinkers and activists, like our good friend Jim Wallis and Tony Campolo are lifting up the biblical injunction to help the poor as a means of mobilizing Christians against budget cuts to social programs and growing inequality ... Across the country, individual churches like my own and your own are sponsoring day care programs, building senior centers, helping ex-offenders reclaim their lives, and rebuilding our Gulf Coast in the aftermath of Hurricane Katrina."[16]

All of these spiritual leaders are seen as embodying a significant measure of ethical wisdom and religious maturity—the Left Hand of God—in a new generation of clergy. Moreover, they have highlighted aspirations that have been present in Obama's life. One thing that was really significant about the forty-fourth president was that he was explicit about his own understanding of the positive role of religion in public life, one that he knows first hand from his experience in the black community. Explicitly he clearly affirmed the separation of church and state. Faith ought not to be (and in the end, cannot be) imposed by the government from above. For his inauguration ceremony on January 20, 2009, the new president chose Reverend Rick Warren, pastor of the Saddleback Southern Baptist Church in California, to give the opening invocation. Warren had never endorsed Obama's candidacy. Nonetheless, the new president honored him as a leader in a new generation of churchmen who have come on the national scene. Their contribution can be classified under three rubrics: the cultivation and empowerment of personal life, establishment of community ties and worldwide social activism, and a sense of ultimate destiny—what in religious language is often called "eschatology." They have common interests with the new president and employ the resources of the communications revolution on which his campaign was based.

Rick Warren was introduced by *Time* magazine to its readers as a leader whose goal is to change the world. It portrayed him as a jovially super-active preacher, insatiably curious, and one who was riding the newest wave of change in the evangelical community. The magazine's writer was not mistaken when he credited Warren with loosening the hold of an older generation of clergy among Christians, enabling believers to graduate from a domestic political force into global benefactor. His leading book, *The Purpose-Driven Life*, rivaled in sales those that Obama has authored, and he led an entourage of thousands of pastors whom he was helping to revive their congregations. Most outstanding, even at a time of economic crisis, he directed Christians into vast new projects of social action in the struggle against AIDS and poverty internationally.[17]

Warren prayed: "Almighty God, our Father ... today, we rejoice not only in America's peaceful transfer of power for the forty-fourth time, we celebrate a hinge-point of history with the inauguration of our first African-American president of the United States. We are so grateful to live in this land, a land of unequaled possibility, where the son of an African immigrant can rise to the highest level of our leadership ... Give to our new president, Barack Obama, the wisdom to lead us with humility, the courage to lead us with integrity, the compassion to lead us with generosity ... When we fail to treat our fellow human beings and all the earth with the respect that they deserve, forgive us. And as we face these difficult days ahead … Help us to share, to serve, and to seek the common good of all. May all people of good will today join together to work for a more just, a more healthy, and a more prosperous nation and a peaceful planet."[18]

Following Warren's opening prayer, the first African American in the succession of presidents placed his hand on the same bible that Abraham Lincoln had used nearly a century and a half earlier—and made his sacred pledge. The chief justice who administered the oath stumbled over the prescribed words; Barack Obama did not.

Earlier in the day, before the swearing-in ceremony at the Capitol, and at Obama's request, Bishop B. T. Jakes from the Potter's Wheel (a black Pentecostal megachurch in Dallas, Texas) had led in a private prayer service at St. James Episcopal Church, the traditional "church of the presidents" located across from the White House. Jakes's sermon focused on the book of Daniel. He sought God's blessing for the new president, who would be entering into a place comparable with the fiery furnace described in the book of Daniel, one that had been heated seven times hotter than usual because of the Babylonian king's hatred for the Hebrew captives who had defied him. Like Warren, Jakes had not endorsed Obama during the campaign for office; he had been a personal friend of both Bill Clinton and George W. Bush while they were in office.

Obama chose to emphasize his own theme of unity. On the day following his inauguration, a special service of worship that included Jews, Muslims, and Hindus was held at the National Cathedral in Washington, D.C. The new president had selected the head of the Disciples of Christ churches, Reverend Sharon Watson, a female exponent of interfaith cooperation, to preach.

One may ask—why should the new president's tenure be framed with prayers and other civil religious ceremony? A philosophical (not just a historical) explanation can be given. The French existentialist philosopher, Gabriel Marcel, identified a religious view as one that holds that "God and the world are not problems to be solved but mysteries to be lived with." *Mystery*, in this case, does not imply meaninglessness but a reality too full and wonderful to be encompassed simply in argument or concepts alone.[19] Finally, the question about the ultimate meaning of human life is not just a partisan but an existential issue. The wisdom of God is greater than human folly, St. Paul argued. Human answers remain incomplete and are often articulated in symbol and story.

The German refugee theologian, Paul Tillich, claimed that God is not just a being among other beings, but Being Itself. This may be a relevant distinction in explaining the theism of the larger part of American religious life under the Jeffersonian polity of separation of church and state.[20] Buddhism, by contrast, centers on an ultimate emptiness, beyond all distinctions. (It has a "church" but no ultimately determining personal deity.) There have been prophets, reformers, mystics, saints, and martyrs, in a variety of traditions whose witness to hope, faith, and goodness has significantly moralized public life in their time. In the United States, Lincoln believed that he was in the grip of forces greater than himself, and Washington believed that his military victories were providential. The prayer that God bless America on the inauguration of a new president was more than an empty call in a time of crisis. How the relation between mystery and knowledge is interpreted in a change of leaders in the White House is a crucial issue.

APPLICATION: A NEW PRACTICAL POLITICS

Of course, the pressing issues did not center just about religious symbolism; instead, ethics was joined with faith—what Tillich called "ultimate concern"—in the nation's history. Brian Urquhart, former undersecretary-general of the United Nations, reflected at the beginning of the new administration: "A fog of know-nothing ideology, anti-intellectualism, cronyism, incompetence, and cynicism, has, for eight years, enveloped the executive branch of the United States government. America's role in the world and the policies that should shape and maintain it have been distorted by misguided decisions and by willful misinterpretations both of history and of current events. That fog is now being dispersed, and the vast intellectual and managerial resources of the United States are being once again mobilized."[21]

Wishing to be reassured that the fog of misguided decisions and misinterpretation was really being dispersed, Americans liked to know what their new president was doing as they sought to evaluate his achievements and character. Writing of the first thirty days, as she had for a succession of earlier presidents, Washington reporter Elizabeth

Drew pointed out that Obama —unlike Bill Clinton—did not begin his tenure in the White House by holding endless meetings; he refused to clutter up his days in this way.[22] He is not a micromanager on the pattern attributed to Jimmy Carter. His chief of staff, Rahm Emmanuel, deputy chief of staff Jim Messina, and his former campaign manager David Axelrod share responsibility for managing the day-to-day details of his administration. An aide told Drew, "There's a somberness and an intensity on his day that's extraordinary. I saw it occasionally in the campaign, but there were always light moments and banter; there's a funny side to him. Now he's focused and determined in a very serious way; it's a little sad." Drew is sure that from the outset, one of the new president's first intentions was to show the country that George W. Bush does not live in the White House anymore.

As the drama of inauguration gave place to day-by-day sober responsibilities, Obama's career was at a new stage. Aspiration for office was replaced by the exercise of power and rule. Unfortunately, fate had not been kind to him, and events did not follow in the pattern that he had expected when he had campaigned for office. The world economy was collapsing, and a recession was fast turning into depression internationally, not just in the United States. Certainly, Obama's fundamental values remained and he showed determination on the course that he had set. He had promised enactment of universal health care; now he began discussion of how it could be delivered, taking pains not to repeat the mistakes of the Clinton administration. His intention to support international efforts to control global warming (by reversing the Bush policy) drew a positive response from religious leaders. An effort to change the sources of energy over a period time would affect the auto industry (already in crisis), and the new administration would subsidize scientific research and education and tackle immigration problems. A new president, who as a boy had lived in a Muslim-majority country, would need to deal with Islamic fundamentalists in Iraq, Pakistan, and Afghanistan.

What was going on in the large could be summed up by saying that there was a shift away from Reaganomics to Obamanomics. Ronald Reagan had preached national renewal on the premise that "government is the problem," as it limits personal freedom and initiative. He looked for religious support from the Moral Majority-led by Jerry Falwell.

Obama, thinking in more communitarian terms, rejected the radical individualism of this point of view on both political and religious grounds. Practically, as the new president, he had little choice but to initiate major government intervention as he faced reality and sought to solve problems.

What was clear was that morality and not just economics was at the root of the subprime mortgage collapse. In religious terms, it could be called "sinful." The financial crisis had gotten out of hand because federal regulation was ineffective and impotent. It would prove to be no easy matter for the new administration to restore confidence. Nobody seemed to trust anybody else. Franklin Roosevelt's dictum in an earlier era, "We have nothing to fear but fear itself," was relevant. Confidence would have to be restored before the flow of money would begin again throughout the financial system. The second Bush administration had lived in denial throughout much of its time in office. Obama would substitute a much-needed realism.

OBAMA'S CHARACTER

In evaluating Obama's course of action, it is important to hold in mind that only on January 20, 2009 did the forty-fourth president enter the White House. Although his ethical convictions and doctrine of hope were on the record from his books and campaign statements, his economic and foreign policy directives were still being developed. Obama's daily foreign policy briefings informed him that without recovery at home, the crisis abroad could skyrocket out of control. Whenever he approached pressing problems in international relations, age-old religious conflicts seemed to turn up to haunt his efforts.

The question of Barack Obama's persona had been widely probed and debated in the national press as he campaigned for the presidency. Writing just before the opening of the Democratic National Convention in the last part of August 2008, David von Drehle described the five faces of Barack Obama: black man, healer, radical, novice, [and] the future." He has been called a "window into American psyche," the commentator wrote. "Pieces of Obama are open to interpretation because so few of them are stamped from any familiar presidential mold." Von Drehle concluded that four of the faces of Obama posed threats to his victory ... his race, his irenicism, his faroutness, and his newness. At the same time, the commentator argued that what he was calling "the fifth face" expressed positive promise: "Obama's banners tout CHANGE WE CAN BELIEVE IN, and this slogan cuts to the heart of the task before him. The key word isn't change ... Will they [Americans] come to believe that this new doctor, this charismatic mystery, this puzzle, is the one they can trust to prescribe it?"[23] Von Drehle concluded that the key is to believe. Which face would Obama wear as president?

Along with the idealism expressed in *The Audacity of Hope*, there was also an accompanying pragmatism about the strategies of the new head of state. "Vices: Craps and Poker!" which appeared in *Time* magazine while he was running for office was intended as a spoof—albeit a serious one. Both Obama and John McCain, the Republican presidential candidate were known to gamble. In order to make friends and gain political influence, Obama, for example, while a member of the Illinois state legislature, played a watchful, careful game of poker in back rooms; the stakes were generally low. McCain—more sensationally and dramatically at times—won big in craps at the public gambling table. He is the greater risk-taker, *Time* reported, and seeks to impress colleagues.[24]

The writer further noted that in the political arena, as in poker, Obama has held his cards close to the chest, calculating game strategy carefully. It is a stance that has carried over into national politics. McCain, by contrast, had more dramatically moved in and out of the spotlight, rising and falling and then rising again in popularity on his "straight talk express." Was this a legitimate comparison? A range of political observers judged that it was.

At an earlier point in Obama's activist career, it was Saul Alinsky's analysis of power relationships that provided the ideology for his reformist undertakings. Alinsky's legacy lingers on. In particular, he had advised his readers: "When we talk about a person's lifting himself up by his own bootstraps, we are talking about power. Power must be understood for what it is, for the part it plays in every area of our life, if we are to understand it and thereby grasp the essentials of relationships and functions between groups and organizations, particularly in a pluralistic society. To know power and not fear it is essential to its constructive use and control." Alinsky advocated a strategy of working behind the scenes, not just frontal assault, a lesson still reflected in Obama's approach.[25]

While at Harvard, the president-to-be had been elected editor of the prestigious *Law School Review,* the first African American to be so honored. At the time, there were widely recognized tensions between left and right in the school, and Obama moderated between the sides. Throughout his career, his political philosophy has carried a semi-religious reflection and probing of the American dream. Acknowledging its insights as distinctive and unique, he has campaigned for political reform with a post-partisan approach that seeks to uplift the tone of national debate.[26] From the outset of discussion, he accepts the tradition that the United States has proved to be a land of opportunity where success depends on hard work and not on a citizen's place in a class system—in spite of slavery.

Obama points out that much of the country's civil legal code has its roots in its religious heritage: "As a biracial product of a multiracial family, I've never had the option of restricting my loyalties on the basis of race, or measuring my worth on the basis of tribe."[27] At the same time, the president to be has explicitly disavowed being a champion or symbol of post-racial politics. Instead, he proposes that Americans view their nation on something like a split screen. On the one hand, they need to hold in view the just, multiracial society that they seek, and on the other, the reality of an America that is not yet just. While at Occidental College, it was Roger Boesche (who taught political thought) who had a powerful positive influence, guiding the young Obama out of a self-absorbed teenage period. After college, when he worked in Chicago as a community organizer, it was his supervisor, Jerry Kellman, a Jewish convert to Roman Catholicism, who was most influential. Obama was seeking to motivate lower-class occupants of the Roseland and West Pullman areas on the far south side of the city, the largest concentration of black neighborhoods in the country.

STAGES ON LIFE'S WAY

Where was Obama in his own life journey and faith as he entered the White House? A diversity of answers have been given by admirers and critics. The crucial question is whether the new president was in control of his own deepest instincts, what is often called "inner demons." What were the moral and religious qualities of his character? What criteria were applicable? Character measurement is, to say the least, difficult! One path of appraisal is to attempt to relate presidents' "inner history" to the stages on the life's way scheme developed by the psychologist of religion, James Fowler, teaching at Duke University. Fowler based his structural analysis on more than five thousand personal interviews that he had conducted. He set out his judgment following the stage-theories of fellow psychologists, Erik Erikson, Lawrence Kohlberg, and in particular Jean Piaget's theory of cognitive development. The premise was that persons proceed from stage to stage at their own pace.

Fowler defined faith as "an integral, centering process underlying the formation of beliefs, values and meanings that (1) gives coherence and direction to persons' lives, (2) links them in shared trusts and loyalties with others, (3) grounds their personal stances and communal loyalties in the sense of relatedness to a larger frame of reference, and (4) enables them to face and deal with the limit conditions of human life, relying upon that which has the quality of ultimacy in their lives."[28] Our question is how his theoretical framework might illumine Obama's career and actions.

The analysis begins with Primal Faith. Primal Faith forms before there is language, and it enables young children to undergo separation from their parents without undue anxiety or fear of loss of self. Fowler's description then moves on to a second step, Intuitive-Projective Faith. This stage emerges with the acquisition of language. Imagination is stimulated by stories, gestures, and symbols. Representations of God take conscious form in this period.

Mythic-Literal Faith, according to Fowler, involves "concrete operational thinking"—a "developing ability to think logically emerges to help us order the world with categories of causality, space, time and number, sort out the real from the make-believe, the actual from fantasy."

Synthetic-Conventional Faith, the fourth stage, "characteristically in early adolescence brings the ability to think abstractly and make sense of one's world." Some persons never reach it, through no fault of their own.

Fifth level: Individuative-Reflective Faith leads to such questions as *who am I when I'm not defined by being my parents' son or daughter, so-and-so's spouse or the work I do?* Persons question, examine, and reclaim the values and beliefs that have been previously formed in their lives. Eventually, a sixth level emerges: Conjunctive Faith. Often beginning in midlife, individuals embrace and integrate opposites and polarities in their lives, recognizing themselves as both constructive people and inadvertently destructive people.

Fowler's final and highest stage is one of Universalizing Faith. "Beyond paradox and polarities, persons in the Universalizing Faith stage are grounded in a oneness with the power of being or God. Such persons are devoted to overcoming division, oppression, and violence, and live in effective anticipatory response to an inbreaking commonwealth of love and justice, the reality of an inbreaking kingdom of God." In Fowler's analysis, this stage includes an unswerving commitment and devotion ("calling" or "lifestyle") that cannot be hindered or quenched.

Of course, psychological typologies are generalizations and must be treated with great caution. At what level can one place Barack Obama—the faith of the sixth stage or even the seventh? Negatively, it is clear that Richard Nixon's life as well as the careers of Lyndon Johnson and Bill Clinton, in spite of the latter's professions of faith, did not advance all the way up on the scale. Certainly, none of these stages applies only to Christianity. Gandhi and King are candidates for the highest level. How much can a ruling president follow their example in a post-modern world?

A LAW STUDENT'S EVALUATION OF HIS PROFESSOR

Seeking clues about the new president's conviction, the evaluation of John K. Wilson, who studied at the University of Chicago Law School under Obama's direction, remains important; it is based on personal contact: "Obama wears his religion on his sleeve, but he doesn't shove it in your face. He embraces a government that doesn't wear religion of any sort."

"I am a big believer in the separation of church and state," Obama has explained, but not in the separation of religion and politics. Personally, he denies an ideology of secularism that views religion as a purely private activity. If religion is not kept separate from politics, it would poison the common well of government. At the same time, Obama finds public discussion of faith issues of positive value, in particular, as positively it can be a way to close the gap between believers and non-believers.[29]

Wilson concludes that Obama walks a delicate line while speaking honestly and openly about his religion, without trying to be a religious politician. "As someone brought up as a rational secularist, exposed to many religions but never indoctrinated into any one of them, Obama could have chosen a path rejecting religion. He could have rebelled against his upbringing and become a fundamentalist of the Christian or Muslim variety."

Wilson judges that Obama's perspective on God is a thoughtful, decent approach to religion. He rejects an either/or between hardcore devotion that will never hear the other side or a watered-down wishy-washy centrism that ultimately believes in nothing. Instead, he has found a third way that embraces an open mind with committed values.[30]

Wilson has his own special take on Obama's religious views: God is the great questioner who forces him to align his activity with his values. Viewing prayer as "an ongoing conversation with God," he engages in it in order to take stock of himself and maintain his moral compass. In short, it is a way to check his own ego. "Am I doing this because I think its advantageous to me politically or because I think it's the right thing to do?"[31]

Jason Byassee has reflected: "One of the brightest points in Barack Obama's rising political star has been his ability to talk about Jesus without faking."[32] In the midst of the political swirl of his campaigns for office, it remains a fair observation that Obama does not exploit his religion for personal gain.

In her research as a social scientist, Obama's mother was interested in the history of religions. In this field, she found Joseph Campbell's writings about myth and symbol an illuminating guide. Described sociologically, in terms that Obama's mother would have understood, religion is cult, community, creed, and conduct. The University of Chicago, where Obama taught, has had its own distinguished specialists in the history of religions, including one of the greatest, Mircea Eliade.

Of crucial importance in the long story of the sacred and holy is the so-called Axial Period of the eighth to fifth centuries BCE. It was the era of the birth of the world's great religions, Buddhism in India, Confucianism in China, possibly Zoroastrianism in Persia (its prophet is the hardest of all to date), the Hebrew prophets in Israel, and the classical philosophical thinkers in Greece. Piety was internalized and morality spiritualized in vast regions across the known world in this period.

There can be little doubt that the legacy of the new president's mother remains with him. It was she who gave him "a working knowledge of the world's great religions." He reports that Ann taught him "the values that many Americans learn in Sunday school: honesty, empathy, discipline, delayed gratification, and hard work. She raged at poverty and injustice, and scorned those who were indifferent to both." He has never abandoned what he calls "my mother's fundamental faith—in the goodness of people and in the ultimate value of this brief life we've each been given."

Still Obama went his own way, accepting Christianity as it was practiced in the black community where he worked as an organizer in Chicago. "I became much more familiar with the ongoing tradition of the historic black church and its importance in the community. And the power of that culture to give people strength in very difficult circumstances, and the power of that church to give people courage against great odds, and it moved me deeply." Obama was seeking "a vessel for my beliefs ... I was drawn to the power of the African-American religious tradition to spur social change." The black church also showed him that "faith doesn't mean that you don't have doubts, or that you relinquish your hold on this world ... I had no community or shared traditions in which to ground my most deeply held beliefs ... Without an unequivocal commitment to a particular community of faith, I would be consigned so some level to always remain apart, free in the way that my mother was free, but also alone in the same way she was ultimately alone."

TOLERANCE: FAITH AND DOUBT

Wilson reflects: "It was not because he believed ... religion necessary for morality, or because he had some personal problems that he needed to cure ... For him, Jesus is not a magical creature to be worshiped blindly; he's a real person to be imitated for his moral example ... faith doesn't mean that you don't have doubts, or that you relinquish your hold on this world."[33]

The president has warned: "I think there is an enormous danger on the part of public figures to rationalize or justify their actions by claiming God's mandate ... I think that religion at its best comes with a big dose of doubt." Echoing his mother, he affirms: "I believe that there are many paths to the same place, and belief that there is a higher power, a belief that we are connected as a people, that there are values that transcend race or culture, that move us forward, and that there's an obligation for all of us individually as well as collectively to take responsibility to make these values lived."[34]

Obama continues to express the belief that underlying world religions is a common set of beliefs about how you treat other people and how you aspire to act, not just for yourself but for the common good. In short, he is skeptical toward all assertions of absolute and full knowledge of reality. "I retain from my childhood and my experiences growing up a suspicion of dogma, and I'm not somebody who is always comfortable with language that implies I've got a monopoly on the truth, or that my faith is automatically transferable to others."

Wilson concludes: "Obama is a rationalist who genuinely respects religion, giving him enormous power to sway a vast number of Americans ... Of course, Obama has never wavered from his principled stand for individual freedoms."[35]

PART TWO:
OBAMA IN THE WHITE HOUSE: CHARITABLE CHOICE
A CLUE ABOUT HOW CONVICTION INFLUENCES ACTION

As soon a he came to the White House, Obama took measures to expand the program known as "Charitable Choice." It was a project that had been a favorite of George W. Bush who, after much ballyhoo about establishing it with a special office in the White House, failed to carry through on major funding. Was Obama shifting ground, going over to the side of a failed president in church-state relations? On the contrary, he had favored it while campaigning. Bill Clinton had endorsed Charitable Choice while he was in office. Similarly, Al Gore had called for its enactment.

The justification for the project was that religious groups (like the black churches) in particular in impoverished areas, were especially well prepared to give needed aid as social agencies. They ought not to be hampered from doing so because of non- proselytizing restrictions premised on the separation of church and state. Already for years, Roman Catholic and Lutheran agencies had been receiving large grants for non-sectarian charity projects. Charitable Choice would give funding for church service agencies, going around what otherwise would be needless restrictions and government red tape. Believers should not be restricted from social service activities in the public realm simply because of their faith commitment. To protect the separation of church and state, they should be expected to hire staff on a non-sectarian basis, Obama argued. Jews and Roman Catholics could mix together with Protestants in a variety of positions. This is the way it had been in his own social service programs in Chicago. It was all well and good in theory. But sectarian political considerations intervened. Projected nationally, Obama's requirement at this point evoked immediate controversy, as ecclesiastical organizations sought to preserve their own turf. Eventually he adopted the policy that his staff would rule on disputed hiring issues on a case-by-case basis, rather than issuing a general edict.[36]

Obama's former home congregation in Chicago, for example, would benefit from such a program. It had long had wide social service outreach with multiple community activities. The largest United Church of Christ (Congregationalist in affiliation) in the nation, it is located on Chicago's South Side. Here the president-to-be made his confession of faith, married his wife, and baptized his children. The local congregation was identified in its faith statement as deliberately Afri-centrist, unashamedly black, and unapologetically Christian. The institutional intention was to avoid being a white church in blackface. This polity is evident during worship. During church services, the Trinity choir and clergy wear brightly colored robes. The huge choir sways and sings in African dress, leading with hand-waving and amens. Drums and tambourines and even a washboard at times accompany congregational singing.

Why has the tradition of emotion-laden folk religion in the black church not centered as much on prophecies of doom and the approaching end of the age, as in some white communities (Reagan style)? There has been too much practical work to do, too many problems to face, to envisage apocalypticism on the pattern of Hal Lindsay's book, *The Late Great Planet Earth*. For a long period of time, this volume was a leading bestseller along with the Bible. Reflecting the black church ethos, Obama is realistically this-worldly and not escapist. "Conservatives find the African church too political, and liberals may squirm over its revivalist emotion … But the black church continues to make converts in unlikely places, reflecting a God who makes a way where there is no way."[37]

Obama speaks of his position being "anchored" in his faith but not rigid or dogmatic. He devotes several pages of his second major book to explaining "the difference between being religiously faithful in an open-ended way and claiming religious certainty in a publicly problematic way." He makes the difficult judgment calls of abortion and gay marriage illustrations of his approach. His judgment is that abortion should be legal and gay marriage should not be legal. However, he accepts some restrictions on late-term abortion, supports civil unions for gays and lesbians, and does not claim absolute certainty for the positions he takes.

A SECOND CLUE:
THE SOJOURNERS PROGRAM OF SOCIAL ACTION

Rev. Jim Wallis, who now directs the Sojourners movement nationally, is in a number of respects the leading Christian counterpart to Rabbi Lerner. How much was the new president signifying confidence and agreement when he invited Wallis into his own intimate prayer circle? We should not presume too much. But the two men share a common pool of social problems and religious conviction about what to do about them. Obama, before he became president, frequently spoke and dialogued on the Sojourners platform. Wallis earlier identified what he called a post-religious right situation in his bestselling book, *God's Politics, Why the Right Gets It Wrong and the Left Doesn't Get It.* In a later 2008 volume, he describes what he calls *The Great Awakening, Reviving Faith and Politics in a Post-Religious Right America.* Wallis is positive, especially in view of the Obama phenomenon. "We've gone from a narrow religious agenda which was used as a wedge to divide people, to a wider and deeper vision of faith and values, which could be the bridge that brings diverse people and groups together on some of the most significant issues of our time. For too long, ideological religion was a big part of our problems, but now an engaged spirituality could be a big part of our solutions."[38]

To refuse ideology—as Obama does in both politics and religion— is not to deny faith, Wallis emphasizes. Tolerance and freedom do not require that citizens remain silent about their faith in God. Wallis argues: "The answer to bad religion isn't secularism or withdrawal, but better religion—both personal and public. True faith wants public engagement, but not political co-optation." [39] For Wallis the question is whether it can become involved in politics without being usurped by it.

Wallis is a Christian theologian, communicating to the world from a historical tradition. He argues that a new president cannot be expected to leave his faith fully behind, especially if he affirms, as does Obama: "I strongly believe that faith matters and that it can make a difference, not only in personal lives but also in our world."[40]

Wallis identifies the dilemma that "post-religious right" Christian leaders seek to overcome, citing N.T. Wright, the evangelical bishop of Durham, England. "For generations the church has been polarized between those who see the main task being the saving of souls for heaven and the nurturing of those souls through the valley of this dark world, on the one hand, and on the other hand those who see the task of improving the lot of human beings and the world, rescuing the poor from their misery." Bishop Wright protests that modern Westerners bring their own prejudices to the text of the Bible. "When I lecture about this people will pop up and say, 'Surely Jesus said my kingdom is not of this world.' And the answer is no, what Jesus said in John 18 is, 'my kingdom is not from this world.' ... It's quite clear in the text that Jesus' kingdom does not start with this world. It isn't a worldly kingdom, but it is for this world. It's from somewhere else, but it's for this world."[41]

So the crucial question is about the meaning of the kingdom of God—a biblical phrase. In looking for an answer, Wallis turns to John Howard Yoder, a Protestant who taught at Notre Dame University in Indiana. "The ministry and the claims of Jesus are best understood as presenting to [people] not the avoidance of political options, but one particular social political ethical option ... If God is the kind of God active in history of whom the Bible speaks, then concern for the course of history is not itself illegitimate or an irrelevant concern."[42] In short, the kingdom of God brings not just peace of soul but requires action; no mystical or existentialistic or spiritualistic depreciation of the course of events is justified for the Christian.

ACTIVIST RULES OF ENGAGEMENT

In an attempt to understand the will of God in the Obama era, Wallis proposes contemporary rules of constructive political and religious engagement for a pluralistic democratic society. His list is as follows:[43]

1. God hates injustice.

2. The kingdom of God is a new order. Defining this second rule, Wallis cites *The Presence of the Kingdom* by Jacques Ellul, the French sociologist and theologian who was a resistance leader during the Second World War.[44] "The Christian's share in the preservation of the world is to be an inexhaustible revolutionary force ... the Christian finds himself by that very fact, involved in a state of permanent revolution ... the prophets of Israel always had a political part to play which, in connection with their civilization ... [required them] to judge the world ... in the name of a truth which does not yet exist, that which is coming—and it is to do so, because we believe this truth to be more genuine and more real than the reality which surrounds us."[45]

3. The church is an alternative community. [The kingdom of God is a new order.] Martin Luther King, Jr. made this point: "But there are some things in our social system to which I am proud to be maladjusted and to which I suggest that you too ought to be maladjusted. I never intend to adjust myself to the viciousness of mob rule. I never intend to adjust myself to the viciousness of segregation and the crippling effects of discrimination ... Through such maladjustment we will be able to emerge from the bleak and desolate midnight of man's inhumanity to man into the glittering daybreak of freedom and justice."[46] Wallis cites Yoder: "A minority can do for a society what the conscience does for an individual."[47]

4. The kingdom of God transforms the world by addressing the specifics ... Yoder: "The kingdom of God is not a description of how to create the ideal society, but of how the state can best fulfill its responsibilities in a fallen world. The Christian witness will therefore always express itself in terms of specific

criticisms, addressed to given injustices in a particular time and place, and specific suggestions for improvements to remedy the identified abuse ..."[48]

5. The church is the conscience of the state, holding it accountable for upholding justice and restraining its violence.

6. Take a global perspective.

7. Seek the common good.

How much would Obama accept this list? How much was it echoed in his call for change? It can be argued that Obama espoused most of Wallis's positions when he campaigned for office. To the extent that Wallis's ideas were accepted into the new president's outlook, they were translated into more universal secular terms, a strategy the candidate specifically endorsed for religious believers. The perennial question is what is the relation of the Kingdom of God, which Jesus preached to the kingdoms of this world? What is relevant and possible?

A NEGATIVE CLUE

Politically, religion can be socially constructive or destructive, an asset or liability. Rabbi Michael Lerner's symbolism of the Left Hand and the Right Hand of God turned out to be relevant in Obama's home church. The most difficult religious problem for the senator from Illinois when he campaigned for the presidency was the crisis precipitated by the preaching of his former pastor, Jeremiah A. Wright. While Obama was campaigning for the presidency, a major dramatic incident developed and the candidate felt forced to leave and resign from his home Trinity Church in Chicago. It came to a crisis in mid-March of 2008, as remarks by the retired former pastor of Trinity Church were widely circulated on national television. (As part of the tape record, they were bound to surface sooner or later.)

About patriotism and race, Pastor Wright had said most notoriously in 2003: "The government ... wants us to sing 'God Bless America.' No, no, no. God damn America; that's in the Bible, for killing innocent people. God damn America for treating our citizens as less than human." He commented that the 9/11 attack was "America's chickens ... coming home to roost." As late as July 22, 2007, he continued to speak out against "The United States of white America." For over a year, while running for the highest office in the land, Obama had not given dominant attention to the relation between religion and race, publicly at length. Now he had a major crisis on his hands, loaded with explosive issues.[49]

In a number of respects, Wright had been influenced by James Cone, the academic father of black theology in the United States, and author of *A Black Theology of Liberation*.[50] (Obama would not agree!) "Because white theology has consistently preserved the integrity of the community of oppressors," Cone argued, "white theology is not Christian theology at all ... Insofar as this country is seeking to make whiteness the dominating power throughout the world, whiteness is the symbol of antichrist. There will be no peace in America until whites begin to hate their whiteness, asking from the depths of their being: 'How can we become black?'"[51]

One of Wright's sermons, replayed on YouTube, exemplified much of his style and message: Jesus was a poor black man who lived in a country—and in a culture—that was controlled by rich white people. The Romans were rich, the Romans were Italian, which means they were European, which means they were white, and the Romans ran everything in Jesus's country.

What remains most important is that Obama responded to the potential lethal threat to his presidential campaign from his former pastor by making one of his most impressive and historic speeches. He scheduled a televised appearance at the National Constitutional Center in Philadelphia and was at his historical best as an orator. In short, controversy in his then home church gave him the occasion for the most memorable commentary about religion and politics delivered by any candidate in the 2008 campaign. It has been compared by admirers to earlier addresses by Lincoln, Kennedy, and Martin Luther King, Jr. Addressing the larger historical issues, Obama asked his hearers to grapple with racial divisions and then to transcend them—a bold, risky request politically.

Obama has identified Abraham Lincoln as his ideal ever since he officially announced his candidacy on the steps of the Illinois Capitol, the location where the Emancipator had spoken earlier: "The life of a tall, gangly, self-made Springfield lawyer tells us that a different future is possible ... He tells us that there is power in hope," Obama said, invoking the ethics of Gandhi and Martin Luther King, Jr. as well.[52]

The candidate's attack was directed in particular against the Bush II-Cheney regime—most of all its blundering into a "stupid" war in Iraq. Soon after winning election to national office in the United States Senate, he had enunciated his own reformist rationale, translating religious convictions into universal and non-confessional terms. His hearers recognized it as something else besides politics as usual:

"There are those who believe that there isn't much we can do about this as a nation. That the best idea is to give everyone a big refund on their government—divvy it up into individual portions, hand it out, and encourage everyone to use their share to go buy their own health care, their own retirement plan, their own child care, education, and so forth. In Washington, they call this the Ownership Society. But in our past there has been another term for it—Social Darwinism—every man or woman for him- or herself. It's a tempting idea, because it doesn't require much thought or ingenuity. It allows us to say that those whose health care or tuition may rise faster than they can afford—tough luck. It allows us to say to the Maytag workers who have lost their job—life isn't fair. It lets us say to the child who was born into poverty—pull yourself up by your bootstraps.

But there is a problem. It won't work. It ignores our history. It ignores the fact that it's been government research and investment that made the railways possible and the Internet possible. It has been the creation of a massive middle class, through decent wages and benefits and public schools—that has allowed all of us to prosper. Our economic dominance has depended on individual initiative and belief in the free market; but it has also depended on our sense of mutual regard for each other, the idea that everybody has a stake in the country, that we're all in it together and everybody's got a shot at opportunity—that has produced our unrivaled political stability."[53] The audacity of hope had ethical and religious bases.

SOCIAL GOSPEL

Obama's inclusivism was evident; how radical was it and how much could he turn it into action in the White House? In articulating his own view of democracy, Obama has given priority to community and equality, advocating an overview that transcends individualism and economic success. Campaigning, he was specific about the present: "Americans must build a community where, at the very least, everyone has the chance to work hard, get ahead, and reach their dreams." Speaking prophetically to the contemporary situation, he rejected George W. Bush's notion of an ownership society as exclusively individualistic, and called instead for a sense of mutual responsibility and guarantees of equal opportunity. In a speech at Knox College, Obama was explicit that the forty-third president had overemphasized the roles of individual initiative and personal freedom. The candidate's own alternative joined instead ideas of community, equality, and individualism, relating them to the American dream and seeking to balance rights and responsibilities. He rejected "the idea of people as atomistic individuals, viewing us instead as social beings who need a sense of belonging and a shared moral framework that we find in political activity."

Appealing ethically to history and emphasizing education, the senator from Illinois cited Jefferson, the author of religious freedom in the United States: talent and virtue needed in a free society should be educated regardless of wealth, birth, or other accidental conditions, the third president had said. Obama at the same time commended empathy and mentioned, in particular, faith-based initiatives.

"Because of its past, the black church understands in an intimate way the biblical call to feed the hungry and clothe the naked and challenge powers and principalities." Obama sees not just Jefferson alone as being his ally among the Founding Father as he appeals for education of the spirit as well as new science and technology. He cites Abraham Lincoln as the president who nurtured government-sponsored scientific research, infrastructure spending, and government support for higher education. Obama's models are as diverse as Jacksonian democracy, the New Deal as well as the civil rights movement.

Seeking to follow Lincoln's example, the president has not become not lost in theory or in idealistic religious rhetoric. Today, because the global economy challenges the American dream, he has argued, citizens must work harder. "To compete, America needs to invest in itself." Negatively, the candidate labeled fundraising as the corrupting original sin of everyone running for public office. Most of all, he disavowed ideological warfare. He finds that the common unhappy political choice to be avoided is either trivialization of issues in grays or a course of "cut and run." Seeking to circumvent this dilemma, on principle he rejects the very concept of ideology. In his judgment, such an approach too often leads people to ignore facts that contradict their long-cherished assumptions. Looking for "a better way," he invokes as models the recent figures Theodore Roosevelt, along with Robert Kennedy and Martin Luther King, Jr. Kennedy, in particular, he believes, was able to combine the "hard headed and big-hearted."[54]

It is on this pattern that Obama's religious conviction has been transferred into political action. In an interview with *American Prospect* magazine, the presidential candidate was asked a question as to whether he was a liberal, progressive, or centrist. Obama answered, " Only in the sense that I don't like how the categories are set up." Later he added," I share all the aims of Paul Wellstone or Robert Kennedy when it comes to the end result. But I'm much more agnostic, much more flexible on how we achieve those ends."[55] At the same time, Obama has warned against a centrism that simply seeks a middle-of-the-road approach or compromise for its own sake. Judging that voters are tired of partisanship, his stress is on competence, integrity, and empathy. At times quite complex in his rhetoric, he points out that he has been influenced by the black church, experience as a law professor, and a smattering of Hawaii, Indonesia, and maybe Kansas.

A SOCIAL SCIENCE EVALUATION

Political scientists Martin Dupius and Keith Boeckelman commend Obama for his high aptitude for public communication, organizational capacity, political vision, and intellectual ability, as well as his emotional intelligence.[56] Concentrating on the wider majority of voters, not just simply on a narrower, passionate base of enthusiasts left or right as he ran for president, and utilizing the Internet, he developed a coalition of highly skilled professionals, minorities, women, and white members of the working class. As the national election campaign climaxed, the candidates were forced to move to a new stage. At least this is the opinion of *Time* magazine commentator Joe Klein. "We are witnessing something remarkable here: Obama's race [as an African American] is receding as he becomes more familiar. His steadfastness has trumped his skin color; he is being judged on the content of his character ... in many ways ... the national desire for substance, the unwillingness to be diverted by 'lipstick on a pig' trivialities, has been so striking" in his campaign.[57]

So how much did religious conviction influence politics? Where did Obama really stand "existentially" and not just in terms of causes? The latter is the issue that von Drehl —portraying the candidate as having five different faces—had attempted to speak to. Obama replied to a question from Klein about his own orientation in explicitly ethical terms: "There's a core decency to the American people that doesn't get enough attention. Figures like Oprah, Tiger, Michael Jordan give people a shortcut to express their better instincts. You can be cynical about this. You can say, 'It's easy to love Oprah. Its harder to embrace the idea of putting more resources into opportunities for young black men—some of whom aren't so lovable.' But I don't feel that way. I think it's healthy, a good instinct. I just don't want to stop with Oprah [who belonged to the same church congregation as Obama]. I'd rather say, 'If you feel good about me, there's a whole lot of young men out there who could be me if given the chance.'"[58]

Obama's moral conviction was explicit in dealing with the crisis in which he found the nation when he entered the White House. Selfishness and greed had finally reaped their consequences in the world of high finance. Moving out from the United States, a threat of depression was spreading throughout the globe. Mortgages had been sold and resold in places where they did not originate; collateral often turned out to be lacking in so-called leveraged deals. Credit card debts throughout the land reached into the billions of dollars. The pattern of finance does not respect national borders in the international banking system. Economist Robert Samuelson observed: "Greed and fear, which routinely govern financial markets, have seeded this global crisis ... short-term rewards blinded them to the long-term dangers."[59]

The new president's response was one of deliberative restraint, a *New York Times* writer noted. He characteristically requires time to mull, and instead resists responding hastily in quick judgments to day-to-day fluctuations. Rather he goes through a series of steps. He does copious research, solicits expertise, projects all likely scenarios, devises a plan, anticipate objections, adjusts his plan—and then sticks to it.

A CLUE FROM THE BLACK COMMUNITY
ENTER REV. KIRBYJON CALDWELL

It needs to be emphasized that there were a number of rising and nationally politically active clergy, some of them African Americans (apart from Wright) to whom Obama looked for support. Some of them, like Rick Warren, declined to support the candidate publicly. Others, like Rev. Kirbyjon Caldwell, minister of the Windsor Village United Methodist Church in Houston, switched to the Democratic Party. He had introduced George W. Bush at both Republican National Conventions; in 2008, he changed sides and endorsed Obama. *Newsweek* magazine even went so far (rightly or wrongly) as to fete him as Barack Obama's second pastor.[60] Caldwell's endorsement of the Democratic candidate turned out to be part of a protracted procession. Earlier he had presided at the marriage of Bush's daughter at the ranch. Now he telephoned the forty-third president and signed off from the Republican Party candidate.

In a many respects, the Texas preacher was more typical than Wright of the new progressive post-religious right generation of progressive African-American clergy. Like Warren, he had built a megachurch from small beginnings. Both preachers' rise to prominence somewhat paralleled that of Obama; in its own way, it reflected widespread popular interest. Warren began developing his congregation simply, for months, by asking in his neighborhood what the religious interests and needs of the people really were.

Pastor Caldwell had memories of the past from his own experience of discrimination in the '60s. Although he remembered how racists backed their truck into his father's clothing shop in the 1960s, destroying and looting, he nonetheless was part of the post-religious right revival of religion that favored cooperation. A Houston native, Caldwell attended Carleton College in Minnesota as an undergraduate and finished graduate work at the University of Pennsylvania's Wharton School of Business as well as Southern Methodist University's Perkins School of Theology. His life has not been without personal tragedy.

His first wife was killed in the crash of Congressman Mickey Leland's airplane on a mission to Africa.

Visitors to the Windsor Village church service on Sunday are given a brochure with the large letters KB on its cover. The church's main building, a former Kmart store now skillfully remodeled, bears the words "Kingdom Builders Center" across its main entrance. "Thanks for coming," Caldwell writes in the brochure. "The Lord is doing a new thing in our lives and in the life of our communities ... We are a Caring, Cutting-edge Christian Community. The Windsor Village Church Family is a dynamic Christian ministry that places a strong emphasis on equipping and empowering people to be faithful and fruitful disciples of Jesus Christ in every area of their lives. Our holistic ministry is carried out through relevant biblical preaching and teaching, multiple ministries, growth groups, and outreach projects that offer healing and hope to persons and institutions throughout the Greater Houston Community."

Working for Obama's election, Caldwell even developed his own website in support of the challenger to the status quo. As the book of James teaches, he reflected "faith without works is dead!" When Hurricane Katrina struck New Orleans, the minister was in the vanguard of organizing relief in and from Texas. In short, like Obama, he is an activist. In his home community, he led in development of a new subdivision, which he helped to organize. A wide web of service agencies and church members' sub-meetings offer a coming-together place for young and old—thousands of them. But Windsor Village is not an independent megachurch. Rather, it reflects the strength and wisdom of one of the largest Protestant denominations in the land, the United Methodist Church. In short, Caldwell is not a loner but a responsible ecclesiastical participant.

Caldwell describes his congregation's activities under the rubric of "Kingdom Building." The reference is to the New Testament. Jesus came preaching the gospel of the Kingdom and calling for repentance; the theme was developed in his own way by Wallis in the Sojourners movement. Jesus himself did not use the phrase, "building the Kingdom" in his lifetime. But he did teach about what its reign would mean in his Sermon on the Mount. His parables were parables about the Kingdom. The poor of spirit and meek would be blessed, entering first. Jesus's kingdom was not of this world, he said. Still it was visible, and if one chose to enter into it, taking up one's cross brought practical life consequences. His disciples were to seek to lay up treasure in heaven, not on earth. The unrepentant and proud would not understand this message, but sinners would be redeemed. In short, Jesus's ministry held the promise of the coming of a new kingdom, unlike that of the Roman Empire, by God's special initiative. His disciples, living between the old and the new ages, were called to prepare. Of course, the skeptical and unbelievers did not heed the call any more than today.

Explicitly, the intention of the Windsor Village Church's ministry is to follow Jesus in the present era. Certainly, there are parallels with Obama's former connection, Trinity United Church of Christ in Chicago. There are also significant differences that distinguish Obama's first and (so-called) second pastor. The milieu in which they worked was not the same. It would be a mistake to suppose that the Texas African-American congregation is less politicized than the Chicago one. Neither pastor has been a quietist. Why did Caldwell accede when Bush eight years ago called and asked the pastor to introduce him at the Republican National Convention? He genuinely liked the candidate and was sincere in his endorsement. Bush was a fellow Methodist, and they seemed to share common versions of Christian ethics and American idealism. By 2008, the minister recognized that Bush had failed!

Caldwell reluctantly understood that Bush's Charitable Choice had not amounted to anything; in the end it was not among the forty-third president's priorities and remained largely unfunded. At the same time, his own congregation undertook heroic work in caring for the needy, even as it converted a former Kmart building into a megachurch sanctuary. His congregation includes a large body of professionally successful believers, well off and supporting Obama. The Texas pastor was not naïve about what was taking place in the black community—and believed that change was really underway.

A DECISIVE CLUE
OBAMA'S THEOLOGIAN: REINHOLD NIEBUHR

How does Obama unite the diverse religious ideas and themes that come before him from leaders like Wallis and Caldwell? One answer could be that he welcomes diversity over intellectual synthesis. *New York Times* columnist David Brooks recounts talking with him on the telephone late one afternoon during the national election campaign. Their conversation was lagging; the candidate was tired and somewhat cranky, Brooks reports. To liven up their exchange of opinion, he asked Obama what he thought about Reinhold Niebuhr, the Christian ethicist and theologian of the last generation.

Niebuhr (1892–1971) was a professor at Union Theological Seminary in New York City from 1930 to 1960. When Brooks mentioned Niebuhr in the telephone conversation, suddenly everything came alive, he reports. The junior senator from Illinois talked nonstop for twenty minutes in an exemplary organized discussion of Niebuhr's book, *The Irony of American History*.[61] No other member of the Senate could have given such an informed, critical response, Brooks concluded. Niebuhr's ideas about power, democracy, tragedy, and evil, as well as democracy, engaged the candidate. They did so because they offered a challenge to the naïve nationalistic pieties commonly mouthed in American politics. In fact, they did not conform simply to Obama's slogan, "Yes we can!"

Niebuhr is credited as the author of the Serenity Prayer, which in the version he is said to have preferred, reads: "God, give us grace to accept with serenity the things that cannot be changed, courage to change the things that should be changed, and the wisdom to distinguish the one from the other." Seeking support at home as well as abroad, a new chief executive will encounter the phenomenon that Reinhold Niebuhr identified in his *Moral Man and Immoral Society*.[62] Niebuhr's compelling insight was that social psychology is different than individual psychology—less personal, more symbolic and ideological in the large. Dealing with individuals, a leader may establish personal contact and rapport in friendship. Adjustment can be made to different viewpoints and power demands. Larger groups are more omnibus and less ethically sensitive. Collectively, as in mass warfare, they often threaten to use violent power strategies that would not be accepted by more ethically conscious individuals in their own career—including atomic weapons. Conscience becomes more general and less compelling.

The philosopher-theologian, who was a social activist in New York City for more than thirty years, has been classified as a Christian realist and credited with a perceptive critique of nationalistic ideology. Is he now Obama's house theologian, more than the preachers with whom he now associates? Indeed, Niebuhr is currently more appropriately so designated than Jeremiah Wright or any of the clergy who prayed at the inauguration. Niebuhr was a telling and effectual social analyst who served a German Reformed Church congregation as their pastor in Detroit during the period immediately after the First World War. It was an era of labor unrest and of the activity of the Ku Klux Klan in the city. He summarized his experience in the years there retrospectively in an autobiographical record, *The Diary of a Tamed Cynic*. In part because of his concern for politics and ethics, the pastor and social critic was invited to teach ethics in New York City. Eventually before World War II, Dietrich Bonhoeffer would be among his students. In the civil rights struggle, he contributed to Martin Luther King, Jr. insights.

Niebuhr was a former liberal, a pacifist who turned interventionist in the period of the Second World War. Our thesis is not that Obama agrees with him on every issue; as a politician, Obama in a number of respects is more professedly optimistic ("Yes we can!") But because the professor spoke to continuing similar problems in an earlier era, he engages the president's reflection. The fact is that Obama's admiration for Niebuhr tells more about the new president's orientation than most other religious references. Obama has explained: "[Niebuhr] is one of my favorite philosophers. I take away [from his works] the compelling idea that there's serious evil in the world, and hardship and pain. And we should be humble and modest in our belief we can eliminate these things. But we shouldn't use that as an excuse for cynicism and inaction. I take away the sense we have to make these efforts knowing they are hard."[63]

Andrew J. Bacevich, who wrote an introduction to the republished volume of Niebuhr's *The Irony of American History*, argues that in this book, Niebuhr provided "the master key to understanding the myths and delusions that underpin American statecraft." Why is it that a theologian and ethicist wrote the most important book ever written on United States foreign policy, Bacevich asks?[64] Kevin Mattson, author of *The Good Society*, explains: "Niebuhr is important ... today precisely because he warned about America's tendency—including the left's tendency—to do bad things in the understanding of where the Bush administration went wrong in Iraq."[65]

There is convincing evidence that Obama has assimilated major insights from Niebuhr's critique of the use of power. Obama's problem as president is not just one of good will but how to rule and effect change. Niebuhr remains an appropriate reference in a time of economic recession and war in the Middle East. In the course of his career, the Union seminary professor abandoned the perfectionist ethic often espoused by liberal as well as pietistic Christians for a more pragmatic and realistic view of politics—without becoming cynical. The outstanding problems of his era were the depression totalitarianism, fascism and communism in World War II, and then the cold war. It would have been immoral not to resist and fight on the side of democracy, Niebuhr argued. Human freedom makes democracy possible, he noted. Human sin makes it necessary!

The American historian Arthur Schlesinger, Jr. labeled Niebuhr "the supreme American theologian of the twentieth century."[66] Niebuhr's realism contributed significantly to the generation of political thinkers who during the period of cold war plotted a strategy to avoid an atomic holocaust—while still resisting communism. Its principles are still relevant in the Middle East to the present, Obama understands. The theologian's critique of Americans' sometimes naive adherence to what Rabbi Lerner identifies as the Right Hand of God was sometimes biting. Lincoln, Niebuhr pointed out, by contrast for his part countered nationalist fanaticism by speaking of Americans as an "almost chosen" people. Obama's understanding that good intentions do not necessarily lead to successful results and consequences is evident. Power and force are necessary in civil government. They were necessary in the civil rights struggle for racial equality; they are still necessary for democratic freedoms around the world.

In sum, as a Christian activist as well as a public theologian, Niebuhr championed a tough-minded, realistic approach to domestic and international issues—war and peace, race, economics in a situation not too different from that faced by the new president. Religionists should not deceive themselves that absolute solutions of historical problems are easily in human control, he warned. Utopian attempts to make the world safe for democracy inevitably fail because they ignore problems of political power. It is not immoral to exercise power; the outstanding question is how and what is done with it. Christianity, Niebuhr argued, does not prescribe naive optimism about human nature. His own approach—like that of Obama—was in many respects pragmatic rather than ideological. How to use power: What you do often matters more than what you say.

In *The Irony of American History,* Niebuhr asked:

> *"Could there be a clearer tragic dilemma than that which faces our civilization? [He wrote during the cold war.] Though confident of its virtue, it must yet hold atomic bombs ready for use, so as to prevent a possible world conflagration. It may actually make the conflict more inevitable by this threat, but yet it cannot abandon this threat ... no one can be sure that a war won by the use of modern means of mass destruction would leave enough physical and social substance to rebuild a civilization among either victors or the vanquished ...*
>
> *Pure tragedy elicits tears of admiration and pity for the hero who is willing to brave death or incur guilt for the sake of some great good. Irony, however, prompts some laughter and a nod of comprehension beyond the laughter; for irony involves comic absurdities which cease to be altogether absurd when fully understood."*

Obama assuredly understands that Niebuhr's analysis is relevant in the new millennium as he confronts terrorist forces in a variety of settings. Niebuhr observed: "We were not only innocent a half century ago with the innocency of irresponsibility ... Now we are immersed in world-wide responsibilities."[67]

WAR AND PEACE: THE TERRORIST THREAT

Mark Juergensmeyer, in a recent research study he entitled "Terror in the Mind of God," identified the alternatives faced currently by the United States and its allies.[68] The options open to Obama as he came to office included:

First: *Destroying Violence by Violence.*

This is the strategy world leaders accepted after President Bush's call for warfare against the Taliban. Realistically, what is possible? The American Armed Forces initially were more successful in Afghanistan than Russian troops had been earlier in that country. At first, the Taliban was defeated with American bombings, using highly technological modern weapons. But Iraq was not pacified. Still, finding individual terrorists like Mullah Omar or bin Laden in their hiding places turned out to be a much more difficult kind of task. Iraq erupted into chaos and sectarian civil war under United States occupation. As Obama came to office, terrorist attacks in Afghanistan were on the rise. During his first month in office, he gave orders to increase American troop strength in the country by fifteen thousand.

A second alternative identified by the same author is *Terrifying the Terrorists.* Perhaps this is what happened in the case of Libya, which earlier had sponsored the attack on Pan Am flight 103 that exploded over Lockerbie, Scotland in December 1988, killing 259 passengers. The Libyan dictator, Muammar el-Ghadafi, eventually sought to rejoin the civilized world. But terrifying terrorists is no sure thing. They may resume belligerency—as they have in Afghanistan.

A third alternative, *Terrorism Wins,* at times has seemed to be the case in Palestine. Both Jews and Arabs engaged in a cycle of violence at the expense of civilians. Of course, the problems faced by leaders of governments willing to compromise for peace were not simple. Sadat in Egypt and Rabin in Israel were assassinated. But countering violence with violence led to an unending cycle; Israel faced off in nearly perennial warfare with the Palestinians. There were thousands of civilian casualties in Gaza. The new president appointed former senator George Mitchell to be his envoy, seeking peace in the area.

Juergensmeyer's fourth suggested alternative is *Separation of Religion from Politics.* He describes it as a long-term strategy. The Enlightenment way, he notes, sought to privatize religion. Of course, fundamentalist terrorists view such privatization as leading to the secularism, which they attack. Separation of church and state means that the tolerance and demythologizing of warring ideologies required for the survival of peace and civilized life in the post-modern world is supported in state documents. Of course, it is opposed by theocrats to the present.

A fifth alternative is *Healing with Religion*. Secular authorities themselves embrace tolerant moral values, including those associated with religion. Granted that religious fanaticism needs to be removed from public life, the outstanding question becomes how faith resources may be appropriated to achieve this goal. Can dialogue between different parties in religions and also between diverse faiths be successful? Radical re-evaluation of religious loyalties and attitude would be required.

Practically, violence and political dialogue are not fully discontinuous. The new president will probably employ a variety of strategies. Propaganda and ideology belong to the struggle for position and dominance. As against "hard power" (the military use of force, death, and destruction) "soft power" (belief, conviction, and argument) has at times proved effective. Such is the situation in the Middle East, as historic faiths and contemporary ideologies now compete in contest for the loyalties of nations and peoples.

"No peace in the world without peace between religions," the Roman Catholic theologian, Hans Kung, long has warned.[69] The lack of interfaith dialogue and understanding has had tragic results worldwide: the scene has been left for dominance by terrorists and gangsters. For a new president, the question remained as to how established religions can reinforce the moral and responsible use of power in support of universal human rights—or how much they worked against it.

PUTTING OBAMA'S ETHICS AND WORLD VIEW ALL TOGETHER: APPRAISAL AND PROSPECTS

Obama's outlook, like that of Niebuhr, can be appropriately described as critical realism. For such an outlook, the good is not invented; it is discovered and has universal outreach ethically. This premise was evident in the Enlightenment outlook of the Founding Fathers, which Obama shares (even though on their part it was limited by slavery). The American Enlightenment premised intrinsic natural laws of morality given at the outset of human life on earth. No doubt, historically, religionists have too often denied this premise by their actions, notably by practicing slavery. What Martin Luther King, Jr. and his associates asked, as Lowrey's inaugural prayer affirmed, was nothing less than their God-given rights.

Of course, it is crucial as to who holds political power, as well as how that power is dispensed. No doubt modern life is enhanced by remarkable technological progress in transportation and communication—electric lights, automobiles, radio and television and computers, to name only a small part of what moderns take for granted. New medical discoveries make possible a longer lifespan. The entire world longs for the benefits of such discoveries but also for justice—the fair and righteous use of power. At the same time, modern technology—from cell phones to atomic bombs—continues to supply a range of new possibilities, both terrible and promising. Efforts to control the atomic arms race as well as global warming are not simply an "animal struggle" for the survival of the fittest, although that is often visible. Democracy premises a second, more human level, as it seeks fairness and justice.

To be sure, there are a variety of limitations on how much a new president can influence the ethos of his time. In the end, many of them will apply to Obama's administration. An American president may supply much of the music for the political dance, but he is not the sole player. He must work along with other leaders of nations of diverse religious heritages, some of whom believe in religious liberty and others of whom do not. At the very least, he must dialogue internationally, not refuse to speak to those with whom he disagrees. The clash of religions opinions—the Left Hand and the Right Hand of God—intensifies ideological conflict. This, assuredly, has been one of the lessons of the Middle East crisis.

There is no absolute certainty that the United States will continue to be the sole world's great power. What will take place with the new developing great world powers in Asia, China, and India? Political symbols of good and evil are championed in war and peace amid propaganda. Nationalistic leaders justify their strategies in denial of what is really going on; for example, George W. Bush in the invasion of Iraq, demonizing the opposition. American presidents are required to address national and international problems in the large. In practice, their level of social conscience has at times been less sensitive than in personal life; for example, in Harry Truman's atomic bombing of Japan or in American intervention in Vietnam. The whole range of psychology is different—more mass and indiscriminate. It is easier to have as an enemy a nation's people rather than individuals that one knows personally.

The strategies and forces that a leader employs to succeed are complex. In the case of national leaders who hold power, financial or military, results matter. It is important to tell the truth prophetically, but it is also necessary to get something accomplished. "The road to hell is paved with good intentions." Presidents learn the hard way that it is not sufficient to advocate peace or economic prosperity; a successful leader must bring about change—Lincoln against slavery, for example. A ruling president can be compared to the director of an orchestra (not just a player), as he reaches out to a variety of instruments, using a range of strategies ranging from conversation to coercion. A statesman need not always to tip his hand. In good faith, he may seek freedom of action, to change his approach and promises. It is an illusion to suppose that it is morally wrong to use power. Presidents, by virtue of their office, traffic in power, military and psychological, not just one type or the other but both. How to secure peace and prosperity is not a simple matter; there is no sure road to Utopia. Obama's dream is nothing less than to remake the structure and goals of United States politics from below with the help of providence. The open question is whether he will turn out to be a transformative or a transactional president, a great president or a failed one.

In an address on foreign policy in Washington, D.C., Obama reflected:

> *"Imagine, for a moment, what we could have done in those days and months and years after 9/11.*
>
> *We could have deployed the full force of American power to hunt down and destroy Obama bin Laden, al Qaeda, the Taliban, and all of the terrorists responsible for 9/11, while supporting real security in Afghanistan.*
>
> *We could have secured loose nuclear materials around the world, and updated a twentieth century non-proliferation framework to meet the challenges of the twenty-first.*

We could have invested hundreds of billions of dollars in alternative sources of energy to grow our economy, save our planet, and end the tyranny of oil.

We could have strengthened old alliances, formed new partnerships, and renewed international institutions to advance peace and prosperity ... We could have rebuilt our roads and bridges ... and made college affordable for every American, to strengthen our ability to compete. Instead, we have lost thousands of American lives, spent nearly a trillion American dollars, alienated allies, and neglected emerging threats—all in the cause of fighting a war for well over five years in a country that had absolutely nothing to do with the 9/11 attack. [70]

If the United States seeks to lead internationally and maintain its immense power, it must face up to world social problems of disease and poverty, Obama recognizes. What will be the status of global warming and climate change, even in decades, not just in centuries to come? Obama's support for international control began to make a difference, even early in his tenure. There is no certainty that the forty-fourth president will not wake up some morning to hear news that an atomic or hydrogen weapon has been released somewhere in the world. Such a possibility is an international, not just a national problem. Obama probably hears discussion of such a threat often at his morning security briefings. A secular eschatology is possible—an end of the age even more terrible than two world wars.

Now that he is in control of United States policy from the White House, the forty-fourth president has made clear that the responsibility of his presidency reaches out beyond external history—time, space, things—to the internal history of the soul and spirit, intention and vision. (In street parlance, the war on terrorism cannot be won by force alone but is significantly spiritual.) Law and order are necessary against the barbarians, but so also are faith and hope, if human existence is to remain meaningful for individuals, cultures, and civilizations. Progress is not inevitable. Presidents succeed or fail. Time alone does not heal. What matters crucially is how a national leader answers—under momentous pressure—life's great questions; in short, whether he or she really trusts in a power beyond his or her control, ordering and redeeming in history.

At the opening inaugural event, the day before Barack Obama took office, on Sunday evening, January 19, 2009, the Right Reverend V. Gene Robinson, Episcopal bishop of New Hampshire, offered a thoughtful and challenging prayer—recognizing the plurality of religious life in the United States as well as the needs of the hour, when he invoked God's presence at the Lincoln Memorial in Washington, D.C.[71]

> *O God of our many understandings, we pray that you will … bless us with tears—for a world in which over a billion people exist on less than a dollar a day, where young women from many lands are beaten and raped for wanting an education, and thousands die daily from malnutrition, malaria, and AIDS ….*
>
> *Bless us with discomfort—at the easy, simplistic "answers" we've preferred to hear from our politicians, instead of the truth—about ourselves and the world, which we need to face if we are going to rise to the challenges of the future ….*
>
> *And God, we give you thanks for your child Barack, as he assumes the office of president of the United States.*
>
> *Give him wisdom beyond his years, and inspire him with Lincoln's reconciling leadership style, President Kennedy's ability to enlist our best efforts, and Dr. King's dream of a nation for ALL the people. Give him a quiet heart, for our Ship of State needs a steady, calm captain in these times. Give him stirring words, for we will need to be inspired and motivated to make the personal and common sacrifices necessary to facing the challenges ahead. Give him … strength … that he might do the work we have called him to do, that he might find joy in this impossible calling, and that in the end, he might lead us as a nation to a place of integrity, prosperity and peace. AMEN.*

NOTES

PRESIDENTS' RELIGION

1. Bono, *Sojourners*, January 2009.

2. John J. Dululio, Jr., "Keep Rigor and Vigor" *Sojourners*, January 2009.

3. Francis Fukuyama, *Newsweek*, October 13, 2008, 29.

4. Cf., Thurston Clarke, *Robert Kennedy and the 82 Days that Inspired America* (New York: Holt, 2008).

5. George Will, "Like Lemmings Toward a Cliff," September 24, 2008, *Townhall.com*.

6. Andy Server and Allan Sloan, "The Price of Greed," *Time*, September 29, 2008.

7. Ibid.

8. Cf., Marshall G. S. Hodgson, *The Venture of Islam, Conscience and History in a World Civilization* (Chicago: University of Chicago Press), 1974.

9. Ibid.

10. Lisa Miller and Richard Wolffe, "Finding His Faith," *Newsweek*, July 21, 2008.

11. Ibid.

12. Max Lerner, *Wounded Titans, American Presidents and the Perils of Power* (New York: Arcade, 1996).

13. Cf., *The Toqueville Reader* (Malden: Oxford, 2002)

14. Anthony D. Smith, *Myths and Memories of Nations* (New York: Oxford, 1999).

15. Michael Novak, *Choosing Presidents: Symbols of Political Leadership* (New Brunswick, N.J.: Transaction Publishers, 1992), 44 et seq .

16. Ibid.

17. Cf., Martin Marty, *Religion and republic, the American circumstance*, (Boston: Beacon, 1987)

18. Robert Bellah, "Civil Religion," Daedalus, Winter 1967.

19. David McCullough, *John Adams* (New York: Simon and Schuster, 2001).

20. Eboo Patel, *Sojourners,* January 2009.

21. Soon-Chan Rah, *Sojourners,* January 2009.

PRESIDENTS' ETHICS

1. Barack Obama, Call to Renewal address.

2. Stephen L. Carter, *God's Name in Vain, The Wrongs and Rights of Religion in Politics* (New York: Basic Books, 2000).

3. Ibid.

4. C. S. Lewis, *Christian Behaviour* (London: G. Bles, 1945). Cf., also, Clyde S. Kilby, *A Mind Awake, An Anthology of C. S. Lewis* (New York: Harcourt Brace Jovanovich, 1980).

5. Ibid.

6. Robert Bellah, *Habits of the Heart, Idealism and Commitment in American Life* (Berkeley: University of California Press, 1985).

7. Claes G. Ryn, *Democracy and the Ethics of Life* (Washington, D.C., Catholic University of America Press, 1990).

8. Robert McNamara, *In Retrospect, The Tragedy and Lessons of Vietnam* (New York: Times Books, 1995), 323.

9. Theodore H. White, *Breach of Faith: The Fall of Richard Nixon* (New York: Athenium, 1975).

10. Ibid.

11. Cf., Radoslav A. Tsanoff, *The Great Philosophers* (New York: Harper, 1953), 433 et seq.

12. Alasdair McIntrye, *Virtue, a Study in Moral Theory* (Notre Dame, Indiana: University of Notre Dame Press, 1981).

13. Barber, op. cit.

WASHINGTON

1. Cf., Lawrence Roger Thompson, *Emerson and Frost, Critics of Their Times* (Folcroft, Pennsylvania: Folcroft Editions, 1973).

2. Michael Novak, *Washington's God* (New York: Basic Books, 2006), 19.

3. Forrest McDonald, *The American Presidency, An Intellectual History* (Lawrence, Kansas: University Press of Kansas, 1994).

4. Ibid.

5. Barry Schwartz, *George Washington: The Making of an American Symbol* (New York: The Free Press, 1987), 202.

6. Ibid., 113.

7. Ibid., 179.

8. Ibid., 113.

9. Ibid., 114.

10. Ibid, 119.

11. Ibid., 179.

12. Ibid.

13. Ibid., 180.

14. Gary Scott Smith, *Faith and the Presidency* (New York: Oxford, 2006), vii.

15. Ibid.

16. Ibid.

17. McDonald, op. cit., xi.

18. David L. Holmes, *Faiths of the Founding Fathers* (New York: Oxford, 2006).

19. Smith, op. cit.

20. Schwartz, op. cit.

21. Paul F. Boller, *George Washington and Religion* (Dallas: Southern Methodist Press, 1963), 141–143. Boller comments on the Valley Forge prayer story on page 10.

22. Ibid.

23. Novak, op. cit.

24. Ibid.

25. Joseph J. Ellis, *His Excellency: George Washington* (New York: Knopf, 2004), 188 et seq.

26. Ibid.

27. Ibid.

28. Ibid.

29. Ibid.

30. Ibid.

31. Ibid.

32. Ibid.

JEFFERSON

1. Charles B. Sanford, *The Religious Life of Thomas Jefferson* (Charlottesville, University of Virginia Press, 1987), 172.

2. Ibid.

3. Ibid.

4. Michael P. Riccards, *The Ferocious Engine of Democracy, A History of the American Presidency*, (Lanham, Maryland: Madison Books, 1995), vol. 1, 51 et seq.

5. Edwin S. Gaustad, *Sworn on the Altar of God, a religious biography of Thomas Jefferson* (Grand Rapids, Michigan: Eerdmans, 1996), 27.

6. Paul Johnson, *A History of the American People*, Johnson (New York: Harper Collins, 1997). 143 et seq.

7. Ibid.

8. Ibid.

9. Joseph E. Ellis, *American Sphinx, The Character of Thomas Jefferson* (New York: Knopf, 1997).

10. Ibid.

11. Sanford, op. cit.

12. Gaustad, op. cit.

13. Gary Scott Smith, *Faith and the Presidents* (New York: Oxford, 2006).

14. Ibid.

15. Ibid.

16. Ibid.

17. Paul K. Conkin, "The Religious Pilgrimage of Thomas Jefferson," in Peter S. Onuf, *Jeffersonian Legacies* (Charlottesville: University of Virginia Press, 1993), 19–49.

18. Ibid.

19. Ibid.

20. Peter S. Onuf, *The Mind of Thomas Jefferson* (Charlottesville: University of Virginia Press, 2007), 139 et seq.

21. Ibid., 146.

22. Ibid., 148.

23. Ibid., 155.

24. Ibid. Cf., also Charles F. Irons, "The Spiritual Fruits of Revolution: Disestablishment and the Rise of Virginia Baptists," *Virginia Magazine of History and Biography*, 109 (2002), 159–186.

25. Onuf, op. cit., 157.

26. Ibid.

27. Ibid., 159

28. Ibid.

29. Ibid.

LINCOLN

1. Smith, op. cit.

2. Ibid.

3. Cf., Elton Trueblood, *Abraham Lincoln, Theologian of American Anguish* (New York: Harper and Row, 1973).

4. Ibid., 107.

5. Paul Johnson, *A History of the American People* (New York: HarperCollins, 1997), 486.

6. Ibid.

7. Ibid., 438–440.

8. Cf., Olivier Fraysse, *Lincoln, Land, and Labor*, tr. Sylvia Neely (Urbana: University of Illinois Press, 1994), 153–155.

9. Johnson, op. cit., 438.

10. Ibid.

11. Cf., Smith, op. cit., 85–87.

12. Alan Brinkley, *The Unfinished Union, A Concise History of the American People* (New York: McGraw Hill, 1995), 305 et seq.

13. Johnson, op. cit.

14. Ibid.

15. Ibid., 441 et seq.

16. Ibid.

17. Riccards, op. cit., vol. 1, 260.

18. Ethan Fishman, "Under the Circumstances: Abraham Lincoln and Classical Prudence," in Williams and Peders, *Abraham Lincoln, Sources and Style of Leadership,* ed., Frank J. Williams, Williams D. Pederson, and Vincent Marsala (Westport, Connecticut: Greenwood Press, 1994), 3–15.

19. Cf., John Patrick Diggins, *Max Weber, Politics and the Spirit of Tragedy* (New York: Basic Books, 1996).

20. Smith, op. cit.

21. Joshua Wolf Shenk, *Lincoln's Melancholy, How Depression Challenged a President and Fueled His Greatness* (Boston: Houghton Mifflin, 2005), 81–83.

22. Allen C. Guezlo, *Abraham Lincoln, Redeemer President* (Grand Rapids, Michigan: Eerdmans,) 38.

23. Fraysee, op. cit., 29 et seq.

24. Stewart Winger, *Lincoln, Religion, and Romantic Cultural Politics* (DeKalb: Southern Illinois University Press, 2003), 91.

25. Smith, op. cit., 95.

26. Winger, op. cit., 82.

27. Ibid., 84.

28. Ibid., 87.

29. Ibid., 55 et seq.

30. Ibid.

31. Ibid., 46–47.

32. Ibid., 97–98.

33. Ibid., 99–103.

34. Ibid., 51.

35. Ibid., 59.

36. Ibid., 72.

37. Ibid., 93.

38. Ibid., 84.

39. Ibid., 97.

40. Ibid., 208–209.

41. Ibid., 179.

42. Guezlo, op. cit., 155.

43. Ibid., 155–156.

44. Trueblood, op. cit.

45. Ibid., 8 et seq.

WILSON

1. Smith, op. cit., 159.

2. Ibid.

3. Cf., John A. Thompson, *Woodrow Wilson* (London: Longman, 2002).

4. David James Barber, *The Pulse of Politics, Electing Presidents in the Media Age* (New York: W.W. Norton, 1980), 111.

5. G. R. Coyne, *Woodrow Wilson, British Perspectives, 1912–1921* (London: Macmillan, 1992), 158.

6. Ibid. 164.

7. Paul Johnson, *A History of the American People* (New York: Harper Collins, 1997), 627 et seq.

8. Coyne, op. cit., 193.

9. Johnson, op. cit.

10. Samuel and Dorothy Rosenman, *Presidential Style, Some Giants and a Pygmy in the White House* (New York: Harper and Row, 1976), 551–555.

11. Sigmund Freud and William C. Bullitt, *Thomas Woodrow Wilson, A Psychological Study* (Boston: Houghton Mifflin, 1924).

12. Jack Mitchell, *Executive Privilege, Two Centuries of White House Scandals* (New York: Hippocrene Books, 1992), 145.

13. Ibid.

14. William Allen White, *Woodrow Wilson, The Man, his Times, and his Task* (New York: Houghton Mifflin, 1924), 377.

15. Cf., Cary T. Grayson, *Woodrow Wilson, An Intimate Memoir* (New York: Holt, Rinehart and Winston, 1960).

16. Cf., Arthur Link, *Woodrow Wilson's Revolution, War and Peace* (Arlington Heights, Illinois: AHN, 1971).

17. John A. Thompson, *Woodrow Wilson* (New York: Longman, 2002).

18. Ibid.

19. Ibid.

20. Smith, op. cit.

21. Ibid.

22. Ibid.

23. Johnson, op. cit.

24. Ibid

25. Coyne, op. cit.

26. Johnson, op. cit.

27. Lloyd George, *The Truth About Peace Treaties* (London: Gollancz, 1938).

28. Johnson, op. cit.

29. Freud and Bullitt, op. cit.

30. John Mark Mulder, "The Gospel of Order, Woodrow Wilson and the Development of His Religious, Political, and Educational Thought, 1856–1910," unpublished dissertation in modern history, Princeton University, 1974, 218 et. seq.

31. Mitchell, op. cit., 145.

32. Ibid., 146.

33. Barber, *The Pulse of Politics,* 111, 133.

34. Ibid.

35. Freud and Bullitt, op. cit., 209–210.

36. Smith, op. cit.

37. Richard V. Pierard and Robert G. Lindner, *Civil Religion and the Presidency* (Grand Rapids, Michigan: Academic Books, 1988).

HARDING

1. Rosenman, op. cit., 514.

2. Ibid., 515.

3. Ibid., 522.

4. Hofstadter, op. cit.

5. Andrew Sinclair, *The Available Man, The Life Behind the Masks of Warren Gamaliel Harding* (Chicago: Quadrangle Books, 1965), 84.

6. Ibid., 136.

7. Rosenman op. cit., 538.

8. Ibid., 241.

9. Ibid, 198.

10. Eugene P. Trani and David L. Wilson, *The Presidency of Warren G. Harding* (Lawrence, Kansas: University Press of Kansas), 183–185.

11. Roseman, op. cit., 549. Gaston B. Means, *The Strange Death of President Harding* (New York: Gould, 1930).

12. Sinclair, op. cit., 297.

13. Ibid., 295.

14. Rosenman, op. cit., 549.

15. Sinclair op. cit., 295.

16. Barber, *Presidential Character,* 214–216.

17. Charles Williams Thompson, *Presidents I've Known,* 1. Ayer, 1970.

18. Rosenman, op. cit., 517.

COOLIDGE

1. Cf., William Allen White, *A Puritan in Babylon* (New York: Macmillan, 1938).

2. Barber, *Presidential Character,* 171.

3. Ibid.

4. Ibid.

5. Ibid., 170.

6. Ibid.

7. Ibid.

8. Ibid., 175.

9. Quoted in Donald R. McCoy, *Calvin Coolidge, The Quiet President* (New York: Macmillan, 1967), 54–55.

10. Cf., Charles M. Fuess, *Calvin Coolidge, The Man from Vermont* (Hamden, Connecticut: Archon Books, 1984).

11. Cf., John Almon Waterhouse, *Calvin Coolidge Meets Charles Edward Gorman* (Rutland, Vermont: Academy Books, 1984).

12. Barber, *Presidential Character,* 177.

13. McCoy, op. cit., 251.

14. Ibid., 171.

15. Ibid., 417–422.

<u>HOOVER</u>

1. John Edward Keynes, *Economic Consequences of the Peace,* cited in Hofstadter, op. cit., 283.

2. Barber, *Presidential Character,* 65.

3. Martin L. Fausold, *The Presidency of Herbert C. Hoover* (Lawrence, Kansas: University Press of Kansas, 1985, 1.

4. Ibid.

5. Hofstadter, op. cit., 283.

6. Fausold, op. cit., 12–13.

7. Herbert C. Hoover, *American Individualism* (Doubleday, 1922).

8. Hofstadter, op. cit., 288.

9. David Burner, *Herbert Hoover: The Public Life* (New York: Knopf, 1979).

10. Barber, *Presidential Character,* 54 et. seq.

11. Ibid.

12. Ibid., 62 et seq.

13. Ibid, 58.

14. Hofstadter, op. cit., 284.

15. Ibid.

16. Fausold, op. cit., 201.

17. Ibid.

18. Ibid. 203.

19. Ibid, 241–243.

20. Ibid, 245.

ROOSEVELT

1. Smith, op. cit., 191.

2. Ibid.

3. William E. Leuchtenburg, "Franklin D. Roosevelt: The First Modern President," in Fred I. Greenstein, *Leadership in the Modern Presidency* (Cambridge: Harvard University Press, 1988), 11.

4. Cf., Myron C. Taylor, "President Franklin D. Roosevelt's Ambassador Extraordinary," *cornell.law.edu.*

5. Richard Hofstadter, *The American Political Tradition and the Men Who Made It* (New York: Vintage Books, 1948).

6. Leuchtenburg, op. cit., 16.

7. Forrest McDonald, *The American Presidency, An Intellectual History* (Lawrence, Kansas: Kansas University Press, 1994).

8. Barber, *Politics by Humans,* 157.

9. Leuchtenburg, op. cit., 19.

10. Paul Johnson, op. cit., 747.

11. Alley, op. cit., 58 et seq.

12. Ibid.

13. Hofstadter, op. cit., 315.

14. Ibid., 331.

15. Leuchtenberg, op. cit., 8. Cf. also Barber, *Politics by Humans,* 158.

16. Cf., Smith, op. cit., 193 et seq.

17. Lerner, op. cit., 171.

18. Ibid., 157.

19. Barber, *Politics by Humans,* 173 et seq.

20. Leuchtenberg, op. cit., 31.

21. McDonald, op. cit., 443.

22. Johnson, op. cit., 752.

23. Ibid., 754..

24. Ibid., 755.

25. Skowronek, op. cit., 299.

26. Leuchtenberg, op. cit., 28–29.

27. Hofstadter, op. cit., 315.

28. Leuchtenberg, op. cit., 25–26.

29. Ibid., 28–30.

30. Doris Kearns Goodwin, *No Ordinary Time, Franklin & Eleanor Roosevelt: The Home Front in World War II* (New York: Simon and Schuster, 1995), 121.

31. Ibid., 377–378.

32. McDonald, op. cit.

33. Hofstadter, op. cit., 351–352.

34. Alley, op. cit.

35. Smith, op. cit.

36. Leuchtenberg, op. cit., 38.

TRUMAN

1. Alley, op. cit., 60 et seq.

2. Ibid.

3. Robert H. Ferrell, Harry S. Truman, A Life (Columbia: University of Missouri Press, 1994) 91.

4. Ibid.

5. Robert Shogun, The Riddle of Presidential Power from Truman to Bush (New York: Dutton, 1991) 53.

6. Alonso L. Hamby, "Harry S. Truman: Insecurity and Responsibility," in Greenstein, op. cit., 313.

7. Ibid.

8. Ferrell, op. cit., 153.

9. Lerner, op. cit.

10. Hamby, op. cit., 45.

11. Barber, Presidential Character, 307.

12. Ibid.

13. Ferrell, op. cit., 295.

14. Barber, Presidential Character, 316 et seq.

15. Ibid.

16. Ferrell, op. cit., 91.

17. Ibid., 230.

18. Hamby, op. cit., 158-159, 306.

19. Cf., Time, June 14, 1999.

20. Barber, Politics by Humans, 102.

21. Hamby, op. cit., 54.

22. Ibid.

23. Cf., ibid., 326 et seq.

24. Barber, Politics by Humans, 105.

25. Ibid.

26. Ibid.

27. Ibid.

28. Lerner, op. cit.

29. Ibid

30. Patrick Anderson, The Presidents' Men, Garden City, New York: Doubleday, 1968. Cf., Barber, Politics by Humans, 107.

31. Cf., Hamby, op. cit., 73.

32. Cf., Dean Atcheson, Sketches from the Life of Men I Have Known, New York: Knopf, 1963.

33. Cf., William E. Pemberton, Harry S. Truman, Fair Dealer and Cold Warrior, Boston, Twayne Publishers, 1989.

34. Ferrell, op. cit., 297.

35. Shogan, op. cit., 46.

36. Ibid., 299.

37. Hamby, op. cit., 572.

38. Ferrell, op. cit., 279.

39. Ibid.

40. Ibid., 300.

41. Shogan, op. cit., 38.

42. Ferrell, op. cit., 284

43. Ibid.

EISENHOWER

1. *New York Times*, May 4, 1948. Smith, op. cit., 221.

2. *Life* magazine, Eisenhower's papers have been edited by Stephen E. Ambrose and Alfred D. Chandler.

3. Barber, *Politics by Humans*, 109.

4. Chester J. Patch, Jr. and Elmo Richardson, *The Presidency of Dwight D. Eisenhower* (Lawrence, Kansas: University Press of Kansas, 1991), 2. Cf., also, Peter G. Boyle, *Eisenhower* (London: Longman), 20 et seq.

5. Barber, *Presidential Character*, 172.

6. Fred I. Greenstein, "Dwight D. Eisenhower, Leadership Theorist in the White House," in Greenstein, op. cit., 81.

7. Barber, *Politics by Humans*, 77.

8. Ibid., 83.

9. Ibid.

10. Ibid., 112.

11. Greenstein, op. cit., 98.

12. Barber, *Politics by Humans*, 108 et seq.

13. Greenstein, op. cit., 77.

14. Barber, *Politics by Humans*, 108 et seq.

15. Ibid.

16. Ibid.

17. Ibid., 110.

18. Ibid., 111.

19. Ibid.

20. Ibid.

21. Greenstein, op. cit., 103.

22. Barber, *Presidential Character*, 185.

23. Patch and Richardson, op. cit., 71.

24. Greenstein, op. cit., 102–103.

25. Patch and Richardson, 239.

26. Ibid., 237 et seq.

27. Ibid.

28. Ibid.

29. Patch and Richardson, op. cit.

30. Patrick Anderson, *The Presidents'Men* (New York: Doubleday, 1968)

31. William Appleman Williams, *Some Presidents: Wilson to Nixon* (New York: Vintage Books, 1972), 72 et seq.

32. Thomas Bailey, *Presidential Greatness* (New York: Appleton Century, 1966).

33. Ibid.

34. Ibid.

35. Cf., Robert S. Alley, *The Supreme Court on Church and State* (New York: Oxford, 1988). Ibid., 227.

36. Ibid., 244–245.

37. Ibid., 231 et seq.

38. Ibid.

39. Will Herberg, *Catholic, Protestant, Jew, An Essay in American Sociology* (Garden City, New York: Anchor Books, 1960), 258.

40. Smith, op. cit., 258.

KENNEDY

1. Thomas C. Reeves, *A Question of Character, A Life of John F. Kennedy* (New York: Free Press, 1991), 2.

2. Ibid.

3. Arthur Schlesinger, Jr., *A Thousand Days: John F. Kennedy in the White House* (Boston: Houghton Mifflin, 1968). Garry Wills, *The Kennedy Imprisonment A Meditation on Power* (New York: Little, Brown, 1981), 140.

4. Cf., Carl M. Brauer, *John F. Kennedy and the Second Reconstruction* (New York: Columbia University Press, 1977).

5. Cf., Theodore C. Sorenson, *Kennedy* (New York: Harper and Row, 1965), 245–248.

6. Gary Wills, *The Kennedy Imprisonment, a meditation on power* (New York, Pocket Books, 1984) 61.

7. Brauer, op. cit.

8. Ibid., 110.

9. Shogan, op. cit., 77.

10. Thomas C. Reeves, op. cit., 27.

11. Barbara Gibson and Ted Schwartz, *Rose Kennedy and Her Family, The Best and Worst of Their Lives and Times* (New York: Birch Lane Press, 1995), 93.

12. Wills, op. cit., 130.

13. Thomas C. Reeves, op. cit.

14. Wills, op. cit., 152.

15. Thomas C. Reeves, op. cit., 82–83.

16. Wills, op. cit.

17. Thomas C. Reeves, op. cit., 111.

18. Ibid., 163.

19. Richard Reeves, *President Kennedy, Profile of Power* (New York: Simon and Schuster, 1993), 19.

20. Ibid.

21. James MacGregor Burns, *Running Alone, Presidential Leadership, JFK to Bush II, Why It Has Failed and How We Can Fix It* (New York: Basic Books, 2000), 33.

22. Ibid., 36.

23. Ibid., 41.

24. Victor Lasky, *JFK: The Man and the Myth* (New York: Macmillan, 1977).

25. Schlesinger, op. cit.

26. Michael Novak, *A New Generation, American and Catholic*, (New York: Herder, 1964), and *A Theology for Radical Politics*, (New York: Herder, 1969).

27. Brauer, "John F. Kennedy, The Entrance of Inspirational Leadership," 117.

28. Novak, op. cit.

29. Brauer, *John F. Kennedy and the Second Reconstruction* op. cit., 130.

30. Ibid., 132.

31. Ibid., 203.

32. Ibid.

33. Ibid., 212.

34. Ibid.

35. Ibid., 245.

36. Ibid., 415.

37. Wills, op. cit.

38. Ibid.

39. Ibid.

40. Ibid.

41. Richard Reeves, op. cit.

42. Wills, op. cit., 237.

43. Ibid., 277.

44. Ibid.

45. Ibid.

46. James Snow White, "The Kennedy Myth, American Civil Religion in the Sixties," unpublished doctoral dissertation at Graduate Theological Union, Berkeley, 1975.

47. Smith, op. cit., 290 et seq.

48. Cf., Andrew Greeley, *The Catholic Experience, an Interpretation of the History of American Catholicism* (Garden City, New York: Image Books, 1969).

49. Ibid.

50. Cf., Colleen Carroll Campbell, "The Enduring Costs of John F. Kennedy's Compromise, *Ignatius Insight*, March 30, 2007

51. Burns, op. cit. 3 et seq.

52. Smith op. cit.

53. Cf., Theodore White, *America in Search of Itself: The Making of the President, 1956–1980* (New York: Harper and Row, 1982).

54. Burns, op. cit.

JOHNSON

1. Alley, op. cit., 108 et seq.

2. Barber, *Politics by Humans,* 116–117.

3. Ibid., p. 117.

4. Ibid., p. 114.

5. Ibid., p. 115.

6. Ibid., p. 116.

7. Alley, op. cit., 111.

8. Ibid.

9. Barber, *Presidential Character,* 76.

10. Barber, *Politics by Humans,* 116.

11. Barber, *Presidential Character,* 77.

12. Vaughn Davis Bornet, *The Presidency of Lyndon B. Johnson* (Lawrence, Kansas: University Press of Kansas, 1983), 66.

13. Ibid., 73.

14. Ibid.

15. Ibid., 75.

16. Ibid., 85.

17. Barber, *Presidential Character,* 65 et seq.

18. Ibid.

19. Ibid.

20. Ibid.

21. Eric F. Goldman, *The Tragedy of Lyndon Johnson* (New York: Knopf, 1969).

22. Ibid.

23. Ibid.

24. Barber, *Presidential Character,* 80.

25. Robert Caro, *The Years of Lyndon Johnson* (New York: Knopf, 1982).

26. Cf., Doris Kearns Goodwin, *Lyndon Johnson and the American Dream* (New York: Harper, 1976).

27. Ibid.

28. Ibid.

29. Ibid.

30. Ibid.

31. Ibid.

32. Ibid.

33. Ibid.

34. Ibid.

35. Bornet, op. cit., 102–103.

36. Ibid, 159.

37. Ibid.

38. Barber, *Presidential Character*, 65 et seq.

39. Cf., Fred I. Greenstein, *Leadership in the Modern Presidency* (Cambridge: Harvard, 1988).

40. Lerner, op. cit., 101 et seq.

41. Cf., Doris Kearns Goodwin, op.cit.

42. Barber, op. cit.

43. Goldman, op. cit.

44. Ibid.

45. Barber, op. cit.

46. Cf., Caro, op. cit.

47. Ibid.

48. Ibid.

NIXON

1. Cf., Lerner, op. cit., 84–85.

2. Ibid., p. 77.

3. Tom Wicker, *One of Us, Richard Nixon and the American Dream* (New York: Random House, 1991), 387.

4. Lerner, op. cit., 60.

5. Barber, *Politics by Humans,* 123.

6. Wicker, op. cit., 22–24.

7. Ibid., 26.

8. Lerner, op. cit., 81.

9. Garry Wills, *Nixon Agonistes, The Crisis of the Self-Made Man* (Boston: Houghton Mifflin, 1970).

10. Wicker, op. cit., 24.

11. Ibid, 29.

12. Wills, op. cit.

13. Wicker, op. cit., 24.

14. Joan Hoff, *Nixon Reconsidered* (New York: Basic Books, 1994).

15. Ibid.

16. Ibid..

17. Ibid. Cf., also, Charles P. Henderson, *The Nixon Theology,* (New York: Harper and Row, 1972) 177, 195.

18. Richard Nixon, *Six Crises,* (Garden City, New York: Doubleday, 1962)

19. Novak, op. cit.

20. Stephen E. Ambrose, *Nixon, Ruin and Recovery* (New York: Simon and Schuster, 1987).

21. Robert Shogun, *The Riddle of Power, Presidential Leadership from Truman to Bush* (New York: Dutton, 1991), 279.

22. Ibid., 165.

23. Ibid., 7.

24. Lerner, op. cit., 40.

25. Shogun, op. cit.

26. Ibid., 160.

27. Ibid.

28. Ibid., 162.

29. Theodore H. White, *Breach of Faith, the Fall of Richard Nixon* (New York: Athenium, 1975).

30. Ibid.

31. Novak, op. cit.

32. Ibid.

33. Gibbs and Duffy, 157–158.

34. Ibid., 217.

35. Ibid.

36. Ibid., 218.

37. Ibid., 231.

38. Lerner, op. cit., 33.

39. Ambrose, op. cit.

FORD

1. Roger Porter, "Gerald R. Ford, A Healing Presidency," in Fred I. Greenstein, *Leadership in the Modern Presidency,* (Cambridge, Massachusetts: Harvard, 1988), 215.

1. Ibid., 202.

2. Edward L. and Frederick H. Schapsmeier, *Gerald R. Ford's Date with Destiny, A Political Biography* (New York: Peter Land, 1989), xix.

3. Ibid., xx.

4. Robert Shogan, *The Riddle of Power, Presidential Leadership from Truman to Bush* (New York: Dutton, 1991), 181.

5. Schapsmeier, op. cit., 8–9.

6. James Cannon, *Time and Chance, Gerald Ford's Appointment with History* (New York: Harper Collins, 1994), 21.

7. Ibid., 39.

8. Ibid., 44.

9. Ibid.

10. Shogan, op. cit., 177.

11. Ibid., 180.

12. Ibid.

13. Schapsmeier, op. cit., 165

14. Nancy Gibbs, *Time*, "The Other Born-Again President, January 4, 2007.

15. Cannon, op. cit. 100.

16. Ibid., 93.

17. Schapsmeier, op. cit., 145.

18. Cannon, op. cit., 57.

19. Ibid., 235.

20. Ibid., 249.

21. Shogan, 186.

22. *Commonweal,* September 27, 1974, 515–516. *The Christian Century,* October 2, 1974, 900–902. Cf., also, B. Doyle and J. C. Hefley, "Prayer and a Quiet Faith," *Christianity Today,* August 30, 1974, 900–902.

23. Cf., *Time,* September 16, 1974, 13, and *Time,* September 23, 1974, 35 et seq.

24. Ibid.

25. Ibid.

26. Shogan, op. cit., 192.

27. Barber, Presidential Character, 128.

28. Ibid.

29. Schapsmeier, op. cit., 259.

30. Ibid., 197.

31. Ibid., 205.

32. Ibid., 213.

33. Ibid., 220.

34. Ibid.

35. Ibid., 221.

36. Ibid., 250.

CARTER

1. Smith, op. cit., 293.

2. Ibid.

3. Shogan, op. cit., 198.

4. Barber, *Politics by Humans,* 435.

5. Cf., Edwin C. Hargrove, "Jimmy Carter and the Politics of Public Goods," in Fred I. Greenstein, *Leadership in the Modern Presidency,* (Cambridge, Massachusetts: Harvard, 1988), 229–233.

6. Michael J. Adee, "American Civil Religion and the Presidential Rhetoric of Jimmy Carter," in *The Domestic Presidency and Domestic Policies of Jimmy Carter,* ed. Herbert D. Rosenbaum and Alexej Ugrinsky, (Westport, Connecticut: Greenwood Press, 1993).

7. Ibid.

8. John Dumbrell, *The Carter Presidency, A Re-evaluation* (Manchester, England: Manchester University Press, 1993), 2.

9. Ibid.

10. Peter James Meyer, *James Earl Carter, the Man and the Myth* (Kansas City: Sheed, Andrews and McMeel, 1978).

11. Lewis Lapham, *Harper's* editor wrote "Easy Chair."

12. *Encyclopedia Britannica,* IV, 908.

13. Dumbrell, op. cit., 19–20.

14. Ibid., 141.

15. Cf., Colin Campbell, *Managing the Presidency, Carter, Reagan and the Search for Executive Harmony,* (University of Pittsburgh Press, 1986.

16. Dumbrell, op. cit., 118.

17. Ibid.

18. Cf., Michael E. Genovese, "Jimmy Carter and the Age of Limits: Presidential Power in a Time of Decline and Diffusion," Rosenbaum and Ugrinsky, op. cit., 200 et seq.

19. James A. Speer, "Jimmy Carter Was a Baptist President," Rosenbaum and Ugrinsky, op. cit.

20. Cf., Genovese, op. cit., 205.

21. Speer, op. cit., 84–86

22. Ibid.

23. Ibid.

24. Ibid., 93.

25. Ibid.

26. Ibid.

27. Barber, *Presidential Character*, 435.

28. Ibid.

29. Dumbrell, op. cit., 21 et seq.

30. Ibid.

31. Ibid.

32. Smith, op. cit., 306 et seq.

33. Ibid.

REAGAN

1. Garry Wills, *Reagan's America* (New York: Penguin, 1988).

2. Wilber Edel, *The Reagan Presidency, An Actor's Finest Performance* (New York: Hippocrene Books, 1992), 215.

3. Ibid., 139.

4. Dinesh D'Souza, Ronald Reagan, How an Ordinary Man Became an Extraordinary Leader (New York: Free Press, 1997).

5. Bob Slosser, *Reagan Inside Out* (Waco, Texas: Word, 1984), 2.

6. This is Wills's suggestion.

7. Wills, op. cit., 6

8. Robert Shogan, *The Riddle of Political Power from Truman to Bush*, (New York: Dutton, 1991).

9. Skowronek, op. cit., 411.

10. Quoted by Wills, op. cit., 451.

11. Shogan, op. cit.

12. Ibid.

13. Edel, op. cit., 6.

14. Shogan, op. cit.

15. Ronald Reagan, An American Life, (New York: Simon and Schuster, 1990). Cited in Thomas W. Evans, The Education of Ronald Reagan, The General Electric Years and the Untold Story of His Conversion to Conservativism (New York: Columbia University Press, 2006), ix.

16. Ibid.

17. Wills, op. cit., 301.

18. Martin Anderson, *Revolution, The Reagan Legacy* (Stanford, California: Hoover Institution Press, 1990), xxi.

19. Ibid., xixx.

20. Ibid., xix.

21. Williams K. Muir, *The Bully Pulpit, The Presidential Leadership of Ronald Reagan*, (Richmond, California: ICS Press, 1992).

22. Edel, op. cit.

23. Cf., *New York Times*, August 24, 1984, section 1, 1.

24. Ibid.

25. Ibid.

26. Ibid.

27. Smith, op. cit., 354 et seq.

28. Edel, op. cit., 159.

29. Donald Regan, *From Wall Street to Washington*, (New York: Harcourt Brace Jovanovich, 1988).

30. Richard G. Hutcheson, Jr., *God in the White House*, 164–165.

31. Eugene D. Genovese, *Commentary*, op. cit., 48–50.

32. Ibid.

33. Wills, op. cit., 468.

34. Cf., Barber, *Presidential Character*, 255 et. seq.

35. Neustadt, op. cit. 317.

36. Cf., Wills, op. cit. 309.

37. Ibid.

38. Edel, op. cit., 306–307.

39. Cf., Lou Cannon, *Reagan* (New York: Putnam, 1982).

40. Michael Beschloss, *Presidential Courage, Brave Leaders and How They Changed America 1789–1989* (Simon and Schuster, 2007), 285.

41. Wills, op. cit., 121.

42. Ibid.

BUSH I

1. Cf., Colin Campbell, S. J., and Bert A. Rockman, *The Bush Presidency, First Appraisals* (Chatham, New Jersey: Chatham House, 1991), 54.

2. Barber, *Politics by Humans,* 473.

3. Barber, *Presidential Character,* 465.

4. Barber, *Politics by Humans,* 472.

5. Ibid.

6. Shogan, op. cit., 269.

7. Cf., Campbell and Rockman, op. cit., 188.

8. Ibid., 285.

9. Barber, *Presidential Character,* 481.

10. David Mervin, *George Bush and the Guardianship Presidency* (Basingstoke: Macmillan, 1996).

11. Ibid.

12. Ibid.

13. Ibid.

14. Ibid.

15. Ibid.

16. Ibid.

17. Doug Wead, *George Bush, Man of Integrity* (Eugene, Oregon: Harvest House, 1988), appendix 7.

18. Ibid.

19. Ibid.

20. Ibid.

21. Martin J. Medhurst, ed., *The Rhetorical Presidency of George H. W. Bush* (College Station, Texas: A&N University Press, 2006), 13.

22. Mervin, op. cit.

23. Medhurst, op. cit., 14.

24. Ibid., 5.

25. Ibid., 10. Barber, op. cit., 474.

26. Wead, op. cit.

27. Ibid.

28. Ibid.

29. Ryan J. Barilleaux, "George Bush and the Changing Context of Presidential Leadership," in Ryan J. Barilleaux and Mary C. Stuckey, *Leadership and the Bush Presidency* (Westport, Connecticut: Praeger, 1992), 17.

CLINTON

1. *New York Times,* December 25, 27, 2000.

2. Cf., Bill Clinton, *My Life* (New York: Knopf, 2004).

3. *New York Times,* December 27, 2000, A12.

4. Ibid.

5. Clinton, op. cit.

6. James MacGregor Burns and Georgia J. Sorenson, *Dead Center, Clinton-Gore Leadership and the Perils of Moderation* (New York: Scribner, 1999), 355.

7. Ibid., 328.

8. Ibid., 15.

9. Bill Clinton, First Inaugural Address, January 20, 1993. Cf., *Great Books on Line.*

10. David Brock, *The Seduction of Hillary Rodham* (New York: Free Press, 1996), 416.

11. Ibid., 37.

12. Ibid., 40.

13. Ibid.

14. Ibid., 42.

15. Ibid., 45.

16. Ibid., 147.

17. Ibid., 235.

18. *Time*, Vol. 151, No. 14, April 15, 1998, 51.

19. Ibid.

20. Cf., Carville and Matalin, *All's Fair,* 322.

21. David Maraniss, *First in His Class, A Biography of Bill Clinton* (New York: Simon and Schuster), 1995, 432.

22. Ibid., 433.

23. Greg Guna, cited in Sam Smith, *Shadows of Hope, A Freethinker's Guide to Politics in the Time of Clinton* (Bloomington: Indiana University Press, 1994), 115–116.

24. Elizabeth Drew, *The Clinton Presidency* (New York: Simon and Schuster, 1994) 70.

25. Brock, op. cit.

26. Ibid.

27. Ibid.

28. Bob Woodward, *The Agenda, Inside the Clinton White House* (New York: Simon and Schuster, 1994), 327.

29. *New York Times*, December 24, 2000.

30. Ibid.

31. "Former White House Chief of Staff, Leo Panetta: Clinton's Legacy," *CNN.com*, January 17, 2001.

32. *New York Times*, December 26, 2000.

33. Ibid.

34. David Gergen, *Eyewitness to Power, The Essence of Leadership, Nixon to Clinton*.

35. Ibid.

BUSH II

1. Colin Campbell and Bert A. Rockman, eds., *The George W. Bush Presidency: Appraisals and Prospects,* (Washington, D.C.: CQ Press, 2004).

2. For a later opinion by Friedman cf., *Deseret News*, November 25, 2005.

3. Campbell and Rockman, op. cit.

4. Richard Neustadt, *Presidential Power, Modern Presidents and the Politics of Leadership from Roosevelt to Reagan* (New York: Free Press, 1990).

5. James MacGregor Burns, *Running Alone, Presidential Leadership, JFK to Bush II, Why It Has Failed and How We Can Fix It* (New York: Basic Books, 2006), 158 et seq.

6. Cf. Campbell, op. cit., 12–13.

7. Burns, op. cit., 158 et seq. Cf., also, Petra Pinzzler and Gunther Wessel, *George W. Bush—Wende in Amerika* (Hamburg: Rohrwalt Taschenbuch, 2001). Neustadt, op. cit.

8. Cf., *Newsweek*, March 10, 2003.

9. Cf., John Kenneth White and John J. Zogby, "Likeable Partisan, George W. Bush and the Transformation of the American Presidency," in Steven E. Schier, *High Risk and Big Ambition, The Presidency of George W. Bush* (Pittsburgh: University of Pittsburgh Press, 2004), 83.

10. Nelson W. Polsby and Aaron Wildavsky, *Presidential Elections, Strategies and Structures* (New York: Chatham House, 2000).

11. Bob Woodward, *State of Denial* (New York: Simon and Schuster, 2006).

12. Peter Singer, *The President of Good and Evil, Taking George W. Bush Seriously* (London: Granta, 2004), 1.

13. Bruce Lincoln, 'The Theology of George W. Bush," *The Religion and Culture Web Forum,* Martin Center, The University of Chicago, October 2004.

OBAMA

1. Cf., F. Forrester Church, ed., *The Essential Tillich* (New York: Macmillan, 1987).

2. *New York Times,* March 15, 2009.

3. Ibid.

4. Posted by Jim Naughton on January 18, 2009.

5. *Huffington Post,* January 27, 2008.

6. Michael Lerner, *The Left Hand of God, Taking Back our Country from the Religious Right* (San Francisco: Harper, 2006), 2 et. seq.

7. Ibid.

8. Peter Baker, "The Mindset in the Middle of the Storm," *Newsweek*, November 29, 2008.

9. Fareed Zakaria, "Wanted a Grand New Strategy," *Newsweek*, November 29, 2008.

10. Ibid.

11. Baker, op. cit.

12. Michael Novak, *Chosing Presidents: Symbols and Presidential Leadership,* (New Brunswick, N.J.: Transaction Publishers, 1992), 44 et seq.

13. Ibid.

14. Ibid.

15. Cf., Barack Obama, Call for Renewal Keynote Speech.

16. "Obama points to Rick Warren, T. D. Jakes as models for faith-driven action," *The Christian Post*, June 25, 2007.

17. Rick Warren, *The Purpose-Driven Life* (Grand Rapids, Michigan: Zondervan, 2002.)

18. Naughton, op. cit.

19. Gabriel Marcel, *The Mystery of Being* (South Bend, Indiana: St. Augustine's Press, 2001).

20. Paul Tillich, *Christianity and the Encounter of World Religions* (Minneapolis: Fortress, 1994).

21. Elizabeth Drew, *New York Review of Books,* March 26, 2009, 10.

22. Ibid.

23. *Time*, August 21, 2008.

24. *Time*, July 14, 2008, "Candidates' Vices."

25. Saul Alinsky, *Rules for Radicals, a practical primer for realistic radicals* (New York: Random House, 1971).

26. Cf., *The Economist*, July 26–August 1, 2008, 15.

27. Martin Dupius and Keith Boeckelman, *Barack Obama, the New Face of American Politics* (Westport, Connecticut: Praeger, 2008), 126.

28. James Fowler, *Faithful Change* (Nashville, Tennessee: Abingdon, 1996).

29. John K. Wilson, *This Improbable Quest* (Boulder: Paradigm, 2008), 140.

30. Ibid., 141

31. Ibid., 138.

32. Jason Byassee, "A Visit to Chicago's Trinity UCC," *Christian Century*, May 29, 2007, vol. 124, no. 11, 28–23.27. Wilson, op. cit., 135.

33. Wilson, op. cit.

34. Ibid., 137.

35. Ibid., 132.

36. Cf., David A. Sherwood, *Charitable Choice, the challenge and opportunity of faith-based community services* (Botsford, Connecticut: North American Association of Christians in Social Work, 2000).

37. Cf., Dwight N. Hopkins, *Race, Culture and Religion* (Minneapolis: Fortress, 2005).

38. Jim Wallis, *The Great Awakening, Reviving Faith and Politics in a Post-Religious Right America* (New York: HarperCollins, 2008).

39. Ibid.

40. Ibid.

41. Ibid., 54, 57.

42. Ibid.

43. Ibid., 59 et seq.

44. Ibid., 62.

45. Ibid., 63–64.

46. Ibid., 66.

47. Ibid.

48. Ibid., 67.

49. Cf., Hopkins, op. cit.

50. James Cone, *A Black Theology of Liberation* (Maryknoll, New York: Orbis, 1986).

51. Cf., Evin A. Carruthers, Frederick G. Haynes, Jr., Jeremiah A. Wright, Jr., *Blow the Trumpet in Zion* (Minneapolis, Minnesota: Fortress, 2005).

52. Barack Obama, "Our Past, Future and Vision for America," Springfield, Illinois, February 10, 2007. Obama's speech announcing his candidacy for president, cf., Dupius and Boeckelman, 133 et seq.

53. Ibid., 104. Obama's statement on Hurricane Katrina Relief at the National Law Center.

54. Ibid., 112. "21st Century Schools for a 21st Century Economy."

55. Dupius and Boeckelman, op. cit

56. Ibid..

57. Joe Klein, "The Obama Surge, Will it Last?" *Time,* October 9, 2008.

58. Ibid.

59. Jim Wallis, "Nightmare on Wall Street," *Sojourners,* November 2008.

60. Cf., Nancy Gibbs, "The Temperament Factor, Who's Best Suited to the Job?" *Time,* October 15, 2008.

61. Lisa Miller, "Obama's Other Pastor," *Newsweek,* October 4, 2008.

62. Reinhold Niebuhr, *Moral Man and Immoral Society* (New York: Scribner, 1932).

63. Reinhold Niebuhr, *The Irony of American History* (New York: Scribner, 1952).

64. Andrew J. Bacevich. Cf., also, David Brooks and E. J. Dionne, "Reinhold Niebuhr and the American Present," *Speaking of Faith,* February 12, 2009.

65. Cf., Kevin Mattson, "Why Obama Matters," *Guardian UK,* December 19, 2007.

66. Cf., Arthur Schlesinger, Jr., "The Long Shadow of Reinhold Niebuhr," *New York Times,* June 22, 1993.

67. Niebuhr, *The Irony of American History.*

68. Mark Juergensmeyer, *Terror in the Mind of God, the global rise of religious violence* (Berkeley: University of California Press, 2002).

69. Hans Kung, Global Responsibility, In Search of a New World Ethic (New York: Crossroad, 1991)

70. Barack Obama, "A New Strategy for a New World," Washington, D.C., July 15, 2008.

71. Naughton, op. cit.

BUY A SHARE OF THE FUTURE IN YOUR COMMUNITY

These certificates make great holiday, graduation and birthday gifts that can be personalized with the recipient's name. The cost of one S.H.A.R.E. or one square foot is $54.17. The personalized certificate is suitable for framing and will state the number of shares purchased and the amount of each share, as well as the recipient's name. The home that you participate in "building" will last for many years and will continue to grow in value.

Here is a sample SHARE certificate:

YES, I WOULD LIKE TO HELP!

I support the work that Habitat for Humanity does and I want to be part of the excitement! As a donor, I will receive periodic updates on your construction activities but, more importantly, I know my gift will help a family in our community realize the dream of homeownership. **I would like to SHARE in your efforts against substandard housing in my community!** *(Please print below)*

PLEASE SEND ME _____ SHARES at $54.17 EACH = $ $_____

In Honor Of: _____

Occasion: (Circle One)   HOLIDAY   BIRTHDAY   ANNIVERSARY

      OTHER: _____

Address of Recipient: _____

Gift From: _____ *Donor Address:* _____

Donor Email: _____

I AM ENCLOSING A CHECK FOR $ $_____ PAYABLE TO HABITAT FOR HUMANITY <u>OR</u> PLEASE CHARGE MY VISA OR MASTERCARD *(CIRCLE ONE)*

Card Number _____ Expiration Date: _____

Name as it appears on Credit Card _____ Charge Amount $ _____

Signature _____

Billing Address _____

Telephone # Day _____ Eve _____

PLEASE NOTE: Your contribution is tax-deductible to the fullest extent allowed by law.
Habitat for Humanity • P.O. Box 1443 • Newport News, VA 23601 • 757-596-5553
www.HelpHabitatforHumanity.org